The Minimalist Program

Current Studies in Linguistics
Samuel Jay Keyser, general editor

The Minimalist Program

Noam Chomsky

The MIT Press
Cambridge, Massachusetts
London, England

Second printing, 1996

© 1995 Massachusetts Institute of Technology

All rights reserved. No part of this book may be reproduced in any form by any electronic or mechanical means (including photocopying, recording, or information storage and retrieval) without permission in writing from the publisher.

This book was set in Times Roman by Asco Trade Typesetting Ltd., Hong Kong and was printed and bound in the United States of America.

Library of Congress Cataloging-in-Publication Data

Chomsky, Noam.
  The minimalist program / Noam Chomsky.
    p.   cm. — (Current studies in linguistics; 28)
  Includes bibliographical references and index.
  ISBN 0-262-03229-5 (alk. paper). — ISBN 0-262-53128-3
  (pbk.: alk. paper)
  1. Minimalist theory (Linguistics). I. Title. II. Series:
Current studies in linguistics series; 28.
P158.28.C48   1995
410′.1—dc20   95-4654
                                                      CIP

Contents

Introduction

The chapters that follow are based in large part on regular lecture-seminars at MIT from 1986 through 1994. These have been continuing now for over 30 years, with broad participation by students, faculty, and others, from various institutions and disciplines. In these introductory remarks I will outline some of the background for the material that follows.

This work is motivated by two related questions: (1) what are the general conditions that the human language faculty should be expected to satisfy? and (2) to what extent is the language faculty determined by these conditions, without special structure that lies beyond them? The first question in turn has two aspects: what conditions are imposed on the language faculty by virtue of (A) its place within the array of cognitive systems of the mind/brain, and (B) general considerations of conceptual naturalness that have some independent plausibility, namely, simplicity, economy, symmetry, nonredundancy, and the like?

Question (B) is not precise, but not without content; attention to these matters can provide guidelines here, as in rational inquiry generally. Insofar as such considerations can be clarified and rendered plausible, we can ask whether a particular system satisfies them in one or another form. Question (A), in contrast, has an exact answer, though only parts of it can be surmised in the light of current understanding about language and related cognitive systems.

To the extent that the answer to question (2) is positive, language is something like a "perfect system," meeting external constraints as well as can be done, in one of the reasonable ways. The Minimalist Program for linguistic theory seeks to explore these possibilities.

Any progress toward this goal will deepen a problem for the biological sciences that is already far from trivial: how can a system such as human language arise in the mind/brain, or for that matter, in the organic world, in which one seems not to find anything like the basic properties of human language? That problem has sometimes been posed as a crisis for the cognitive sciences. The concerns are appropriate, but their locus is misplaced; they are primarily a problem for biology and the brain sciences, which, as currently understood, do not provide any basis for what appear to be fairly well established conclusions about language.[1] Much of the broader interest of the detailed and technical study of language lies right here, in my opinion.

The Minimalist Program shares several underlying factual assumptions with its predecessors back to the early 1950s, though these have taken somewhat different forms as inquiry has proceeded. One is that there is a component of the human mind/brain dedicated to language—the language faculty—interacting with other systems. Though not obviously correct, this assumption seems reasonably well-established, and I will continue to take it for granted here, along with the further empirical thesis that the language faculty has at least two components: a cognitive system that stores information, and performance systems that access that information and use it in various ways. It is the cognitive system that primarily concerns us here.

Performance systems are presumably at least in part language-specific, hence components of the language faculty. But they are generally assumed not to be specific to particular languages: they do not vary in the manner of the cognitive system, as linguistic environments vary. This is the simplest assumption, and is not known to be false, though it may well be. Knowing of no better ideas, I will keep to it, assuming language variation to be restricted to the cognitive system.

I also borrow from earlier work the assumption that the cognitive system interacts with the performance systems by means of levels of linguistic representation, in the technical sense of this notion.[2] A more specific assumption is that the cognitive system interacts with just two such "external" systems: the articulatory-perceptual system A-P and the conceptual-intentional system C-I. Accordingly, there are two *interface levels*, Phonetic Form (PF) at the A-P interface and Logical Form (LF) at the C-I interface. This "double interface" property is one way to express the traditional description of language as sound with a meaning, traceable at least back to Aristotle.

Though commonly adopted, at least tacitly, these assumptions about the internal architecture of the language faculty and its place among other systems of the mind/brain are not at all obvious. Even within the general framework, the idea that articulation and perception involve the same interface representation is controversial, and arguably incorrect in some fundamental way.[3] Problems relating to the C-I interface are still more obscure and poorly understood. I will keep to these fairly conventional assumptions, only noting here that if they turn out to be correct, even in part, that would be a surprising and hence interesting discovery.

The leading questions that guide the Minimalist Program came into focus as the principles-and-parameters (P&P) model took shape about fifteen years ago. A look at recent history may be helpful in placing these questions in context. Needless to say, these remarks are schematic and selective, and benefit from hindsight.

Early generative grammar faced two immediate problems: to find a way to account for the phenomena of particular languages ("descriptive adequacy"), and to explain how knowledge of these facts arises in the mind of the speaker-hearer ("explanatory adequacy"). Though it was scarcely recognized at the time, this research program revived the concerns of a rich tradition, of which perhaps the last major representative was Otto Jespersen.[4] Jespersen recognized that the structures of language "come into existence in the mind of a speaker" by abstraction from experience with utterances, yielding a "notion of their structure" that is "definite enough to guide him in framing sentences of his own," crucially "free expressions" that are typically new to speaker and hearer.

We can take these properties of language to set the primary goals of linguistic theory: to spell out clearly this "notion of structure" and the procedure by which it yields "free expressions," and to explain how it arises in the mind of the speaker—the problems of descriptive and explanatory adequacy, respectively. To attain descriptive adequacy for a particular language L, the theory of L (its grammar) must characterize the state attained by the language faculty, or at least some of its aspects. To attain explanatory adequacy, a theory of language must characterize the initial state of the language faculty and show how it maps experience to the state attained. Jespersen held further that it is only "with regard to syntax" that we expect "that there must be something in common to all human speech"; there can be a "universal (or general) grammar," hence a perhaps far-reaching account of the initial state of the language faculty in this domain, though "no one ever dreamed of a universal morphology." That idea too has a certain resonance in recent work.

In the modern period these traditional concerns were displaced, in part by behaviorist currents, in part by various structuralist approaches, which radically narrowed the domain of inquiry while greatly expanding the database for some future inquiry that might return to the traditional —and surely valid—concerns. To address them required a better understanding of the fact that language involves "infinite use of finite means," in one classic formulation. Advances in the formal sciences provided that understanding, making it feasible to deal with the problems constructively. Generative grammar can be regarded as a kind of confluence of long-forgotten concerns of the study of language and mind, and new understanding provided by the formal sciences.

The first efforts to approach these problems quickly revealed that traditional grammatical and lexical studies do not begin to describe, let alone explain, the most elementary facts about even the best-studied languages. Rather, they provide hints that can be used by the reader who already has tacit knowledge of language, and of particular languages; the central topic of inquiry was, in substantial measure, simply ignored. Since the requisite tacit knowledge is so easily accessed without reflection, traditional grammars and dictionaries appear to have very broad coverage of linguistic data. That is an illusion, however, as we quickly discover when we try to spell out what is taken for granted: the nature of the language faculty, and its state in particular cases.

This is hardly a situation unique to the study of language. Typically, when questions are more sharply formulated, it is learned that even elementary phenomena had escaped notice, and that intuitive accounts that seemed simple and persuasive are entirely inadequate. If we are satisfied that an apple falls to the ground because that is its natural place, there will be no serious science of mechanics. The same is true if one is satisfied with traditional rules for forming questions, or with the lexical entries in the most elaborate dictionaries, none of which come close to describing simple properties of these linguistic objects.

Recognition of the unsuspected richness and complexity of the phenomena of language created a tension between the goals of descriptive and explanatory adequacy. It was clear that to achieve explanatory adequacy, a theory of the initial state must allow only limited variation: particular languages must be largely known in advance of experience. The options permitted in Universal Grammar (UG) must be highly restricted. Experience must suffice to fix them one way or another, yielding a state of the language faculty that determines the varied and complex array of expressions, their sound and meaning; and even the most superficial look reveals the chasm that separates the knowledge of the language user from the data of experience. But the goal of explanatory adequacy receded still further into the distance as generative systems were enriched in pursuit of descriptive adequacy, in radically different ways for different languages. The problem was exacerbated by the huge range of phenomena discovered when attempts were made to formulate actual rule systems for various languages.

This tension defined the research program of early generative grammar —at least, the tendency within it that concerns me here. From the early 1960s, its central objective was to abstract general principles from the complex rule systems devised for particular languages, leaving rules that are simple, constrained in their operation by these UG principles. Steps in this direction reduce the variety of language-specific properties, thus contributing to explanatory adequacy. They also tend to yield simpler and more natural theories, laying the groundwork for an eventual minimalist approach. There is no necessity that this be the case: it could turn out that an "uglier," richer, and more complex version of UG reduces permissible variety, thus contributing to the primary empirical goal of explanatory adequacy. In practice, however, the two enterprises have proven to be mutually reinforcing and have proceeded side by side. One illustration concerns redundant principles, with overlapping empirical coverage. Repeatedly, it has been found that these are wrongly formulated and must be replaced by nonredundant ones. The discovery has been so regular that the need to eliminate redundancy has become a working principle in inquiry. Again, this is a surprising property of a biological system.

These efforts culminated in the P&P model (see Chomsky 1981a, for one formulation). This constituted a radical break from the rich tradition of thousands of years of linguistic inquiry, far more so than early generative grammar, which could be seen as a revival of traditional concerns and approaches to them (perhaps the reason why it was often more congenial to traditional grammarians than to modern structural linguists). In contrast, the P&P approach maintains that the basic ideas of the tradition, incorporated without great change in early generative grammar, are misguided in principle—in particular, the idea that a language consists of rules for forming grammatical constructions (relative clauses, passives, etc.). The P&P approach held that languages have no rules in anything like the familiar sense, and no theoretically significant grammatical constructions except as taxonomic artifacts. There are universal principles and a finite array of options as to how they apply (parameters), but no language-particular rules and no grammatical constructions of the traditional sort within or across languages.

For each particular language, the cognitive system, we assume, consists of a computational system CS and a lexicon. The lexicon specifies the elements that CS selects and integrates to form linguistic expressions —(PF, LF) pairings, we assume. The lexicon should provide just the information that is required for CS, without redundancy and in some optimal form, excluding whatever is predictable by principles of UG or properties of the language in question. Virtually all items of the lexicon belong to the *substantive categories*, which we will take to be noun, verb, adjective, and particle, putting aside many serious questions about their nature and interrelations. The other categories we will call *functional* (tense, complementizer, etc.), a term that need not be made more precise at the outset, and that we will refine as we proceed.

Within the P&P approach the problems of typology and language variation arise in somewhat different form than before. Language differences and typology should be reducible to choice of values of parameters. A major research problem is to determine just what these options are, and in what components of language they are to be found. One proposal is that parameters are restricted to *formal features* with no interpretation at the interface.[5] A still stronger one is that they are restricted to formal features of functional categories (see Borer 1984, Fukui 1986, 1988). Such theses could be regarded as a partial expression of Jespersen's intuition about the syntax-morphology divide. I will assume that something of the sort is correct, but without trying to be very clear about the matter, since too little is understood to venture any strong hypotheses, as far as I can see.

In this context, language acquisition is interpreted as the process of fixing the parameters of the initial state in one of the permissible ways. A specific choice of parameter settings determines a *language* in the technical sense that concerns us here: an I-language in the sense of Chomsky 1986b, where I is understood to suggest "internal," "individual," and "intensional."

This way of formulating the issues, within the P&P model, brings out clearly a crucial inadequacy in the characterization of language as a state of the language faculty. The latter can hardly be expected to be an instantiation of the initial state with parameter values fixed. Rather, a state of the language faculty is some accidental product of varied experience, of no particular interest in itself, no more so than other collections of phenomena in the natural world (which is why scientists do experiments instead of recording what happens in natural circumstances). My personal feeling is that much more substantial idealization is required if we hope to understand the properties of the language faculty,[6] but misunderstandings and confusion engendered even by limited idealization are so pervasive that it may not be useful to pursue the matter today. *Idealization*, it should be noted, is a misleading term for the only reasonable way to approach a grasp of reality.

The P&P model is in part a bold speculation rather than a specific hypothesis. Nevertheless, its basic assumptions seem reasonable in the light of what is currently at all well understood, and they do suggest a natural way to resolve the tension between descriptive and explanatory adequacy. In fact, this departure from the tradition offered the first hope of addressing the crucial problem of explanatory adequacy, which had been put aside as too difficult. Earlier work in generative grammar sought only an evaluation measure that would select among alternative theories of a language (grammars) that fit the format prescribed by UG and are consistent with the relevant data. Beyond that, nothing seemed conceivable apart from some notion of "feasibility," left imprecise (Chomsky 1965). But if something like the P&P concept of I-language proves to be accurate–capturing the essential nature of the concept of language that is presupposed in the study of performance, acquisition, social interaction, and so on—then the question of explanatory adequacy can be seriously raised. It becomes the question of determining how values are set by experience for finitely many universal parameters, not a trivial problem by any means, but at least one that can be constructively pursued.

If these ideas prove to be on the right track, there is a single computational system C_{HL} for human language and only limited lexical variety. Variation of language is essentially morphological in character, including the critical question of which parts of a computation are overtly realized, a topic brought to the fore by Jean-Roger Vergnaud's theory of abstract Case and James Huang's work on typologically varied interrogative and related constructions.

This account of the P&P approach overstates the case. Further variation among languages would be expected insofar as data are readily available to determine particular choices. There are several such domains.

One is peripheral parts of the phonology. Another is "Saussurean arbitrariness," that is, the sound-meaning pairing for the substantive part of the lexicon. I put these matters aside, along with many others that appear to be of limited relevance to the computational properties of language that are the focus here, that is, that do not seem to enter into C_{HL}: among them, variability of semantic fields, selection from the lexical repertoire made available in UG, and nontrivial questions about the relation of lexical items to other cognitive systems.

Like the earliest proposals in generative grammar, formulation of the P&P model led to discovery and at least partial understanding of a vast range of new empirical materials, by now from a wide variety of typologically different languages. The questions that could be clearly posed and the empirical facts with which they deal are novel in depth and variety, a promising and encouraging development in itself.

With the tension between descriptive and explanatory adequacy reduced and the latter problem at least on the agenda, the tasks at hand become far harder and more interesting. The primary one is to show that the apparent richness and diversity of linguistic phenomena is illusory and epiphenomenal, the result of interaction of fixed principles under slightly varying conditions. The shift of perspective provided by the P&P approach also gives a different cast to the question of how simplicity considerations enter into the theory of grammar. As discussed in the earliest work in generative grammar, these considerations have two distinct forms: an imprecise but not vacuous notion of simplicity that enters into rational inquiry generally must be clearly distinguished from a theory-internal measure of simplicity that selects among I-languages (see Chomsky 1975a, chapter 4). The former notion of simplicity has nothing special to do with the study of language, but the theory-internal notion is a component of UG, part of the procedure for determining the relation between experience and I-language; its status is something like that of a physical constant. In early work, the internal notion took the form of an evaluation procedure to select among proposed grammars (in present terms, I-languages) consistent with the permitted format for rule systems. The P&P approach suggests a way to move beyond that limited though nontrivial goal and to address the problem of explanatory adequacy. With no evaluation procedure, there is no internal notion of simplicity in the earlier sense.

Nevertheless, rather similar ideas have resurfaced, this time in the form of economy considerations that select among derivations, barring those that are not optimal in a theory-internal sense. The external notion of simplicity remains unchanged: operative as always, even if only imprecisely.

At this point still further questions arise, namely, those of the Minimalist Program. How "perfect" is language? One expects "imperfections" in morphological-formal features of the lexicon and aspects of language induced by conditions at the A-P interface, at least. The essential question is whether, or to what extent, these components of the language faculty are the repository of departures from virtual conceptual necessity, so that the computational system C_{HL} is otherwise not only unique but in some interesting sense optimal. Looking at the same problem from a different perspective, we seek to determine just how far the evidence really carries us toward attributing specific structure to the language faculty, requiring that every departure from "perfection" be closely analyzed and well motivated.

Progress toward this further goal places a huge descriptive burden on the answers to the questions (A) and (B): the effect of the interface conditions, and the specific formulation of general considerations of internal coherence, conceptual naturalness, and the like—"simplicity," in the external sense. The empirical burden, already substantial in any P&P theory, now becomes far more severe.

The problems that arise are therefore extremely interesting. It is, I think, of considerable importance that we can at least formulate such questions today, and even approach them in some areas with a degree of success. If recent thinking along these lines is anywhere near accurate, a rich and exciting future lies ahead for the study of language and related disciplines.

The chapters that follow are almost but not quite in chronological order. The first, written jointly with Howard Lasnik for a general Handbook on syntax (Chomsky and Lasnik 1993), is a general introduction to the P&P approach, as we understood it in 1991. It is included here for general background. Chapter 2 (Chomsky 1991c), written in 1988, is largely based on lectures in Tokyo and Kyoto in 1987 and MIT lecture-seminars from fall 1986. Chapter 3 (Chomsky 1993), written in 1992, is based on the fall 1991 lecture-seminars. These chapters explore the possibility of a minimalist approach, sketch some of its natural contours, and pursue it in some central areas. Chomsky 1994b, based on the fall 1993 lecture-seminars, revises this picture and extends it to different aspects of language. It provides much of the basis for chapter 4, which, however, is

a more far-reaching departure, taking much more seriously the conceptual framework of a minimalist approach and attempting to keep to its
leading ideas in a more principled way; and in the course of so doing,
revises substantially the approach developed in Chomsky 1994b and the
first three chapters here.

The field is changing rapidly under the impact of new empirical materials and theoretical ideas. What looks reasonable today is likely to take
a different form tomorrow. That process is reflected in the material that
follows. Chapters 1 and 2 are written from much the same perspective.
The approach is changed in chapter 3, considerably more so in chapter
4. Though the general framework remains, the modifications at each
point are substantial. Concepts and principles regarded as fundamental
in one chapter are challenged and eliminated in those that follow. These
include the basic ideas of the Extended Standard Theory that were
adopted in the P&P approaches: D-Structure; S-Structure; government;
the Projection Principle and the θ-Criterion; other conditions held to apply at D- and S-Structure; the Empty Category Principle; X-bar theory
generally; the operation Move α; the split-I hypothesis; and others. All
are eliminated or substantially revised in successive chapters, particularly
the last.

The end result is a picture of language that differs considerably from
even its immediate precursors. Whether these steps are on the right track
or not, of course, only time will tell.

Notes

1. For some discussion of this issue, see Chomsky 1994a,c, referring to Edelman
1992. Edelman takes the crisis to be serious if not lethal for cognitive science
generally, whether computational, connectionist, or whatever.

2. Adapted, essentially, from Chomsky 1975a.

3. The term *articulatory* is too narrow in that it suggests that the language faculty is modality-specific, with a special relation to vocal organs. Work of the past
years in sign language undermines this traditional assumption. I will continue to
use the term, but without any implications about specificity of output system,
while keeping to the case of spoken language.

4. For some discussion, see Chomsky 1977, chapter 1.

5. *Interpret* here is of course to be understood in a theory-internal sense. In a
looser informal sense, interpretations are assigned by the language faculty (in
a particular state) to all sorts of objects, including fragments, nonsense expressions, expressions of other languages, and possibly nonlinguistic noises as well.

6. Thus, what we call "English," "French," "Spanish," and so on, even under idealizations to idiolects in homogeneous speech communities, reflect the Norman Conquest, proximity to Germanic areas, a Basque substratum, and other factors that cannot seriously be regarded as properties of the language faculty. Pursuing the obvious reasoning, it is hard to imagine that the properties of the language faculty—a real object of the natural world—are instantiated in any observed system. Similar assumptions are taken for granted in the study of organisms generally.

Chapter 1

The Theory of Principles and Parameters
with Howard Lasnik

1.1 Introduction

Principles-and-parameters (P&P) theory is not a precisely articulated theoretical system, but rather a particular approach to classical problems of the study of language, guided by certain leading ideas that had been taking shape since the origins of modern generative grammar some 40 years ago. These ideas crystallized into a distinctive approach to the topic by about 1980. In the years since, many specific variants have been developed and explored. The empirical base of these inquiries has also greatly expanded as they have extended to languages of widely varying types and have engaged a much broader range of evidence concerning language and its use, also penetrating to far greater depth. In this survey we will not attempt to delineate the variety of proposals that have been investigated or to assess their empirical successes and inadequacies. Rather, we will pursue a particular path through the array of ideas and principles that have been developed, sometimes noting other directions that have been pursued, but without any attempt to be comprehensive; similarly, bibliographic references are far from comprehensive, usually indicating only a few studies of particular questions. The choice of a particular path should be regarded only as an expository device, an effort to indicate the kinds of questions that are being addressed, some of the thinking that guides much research, and its empirical motivation. We

This chapter, coauthored with Howard Lasnik, was originally published in *Syntax: An International Handbook of Contemporary Research*, edited by Joachim Jacobs, Arnim von Stechow, Wolfgang Sternefeld, and Theo Vennemann (Berlin and New York: Walter de Gruyter, 1993). It appears here, with minor revisions, by permission of the publisher.

do not mean to imply that these particular choices have been well established in contrast to others, only some of which we will be able even to mention.

The study of generative grammar has been guided by several fundamental problems, each with a traditional flavor. The basic concern is to determine and characterize the linguistic capacities of particular individuals. We are concerned, then, with states of the language faculty, which we understand to be some array of cognitive traits and capacities, a particular component of the human mind/brain. The language faculty has an initial state, genetically determined; in the normal course of development it passes through a series of states in early childhood, reaching a relatively stable steady state that undergoes little subsequent change, apart from the lexicon. To a good first approximation, the initial state appears to be uniform for the species. Adapting traditional terms to a special usage, we call the theory of the state attained its *grammar* and the theory of the initial state *Universal Grammar* (UG).

There is also reason to believe that the initial state is in crucial respects a special characteristic of humans, with properties that appear to be unusual in the biological world. If true, that is a matter of broader interest, but one of no direct relevance to determining the properties and nature of this faculty of the mind/brain.

Two fundamental problems, then, are to determine, for each individual (say, Jones) the properties of the steady state that Jones's language faculty attains, and the properties of the initial state that is a common human endowment. We distinguish between Jones's *competence* (knowledge and understanding) and his *performance* (what he does with that knowledge and understanding). The steady state constitutes Jones's mature linguistic competence.

A salient property of the steady state is that it permits infinite use of finite means, to borrow Wilhelm von Humboldt's aphorism. A particular choice of these finite means is a particular language, taking a language to be a way to speak and understand, in a traditional formulation. Jones's competence is constituted by the particular system of finite means he has acquired.

The notion of "infinite use" requires further analysis. In the light of insights of the formal sciences in the 20th century, we distinguish two senses of this notion, the first relating to competence, the second to performance. In the first sense, a language specifies an infinite range of symbolic objects, which we call *structural descriptions* (SDs). We may think of the language, then, as a finitely specified generative procedure (function) that enumerates an infinite set of SDs. Each SD, in turn, specifies the full array of phonetic, semantic, and syntactic properties of a particular linguistic expression. This sense of "infinite use" relates to Jones's linguistic competence: the generative procedure with its infinite scope.

The second sense of "infinite use" has to do with Jones's performance as he makes use of his competence to express his thoughts, to refer, to produce signals, to interpret what he hears, and so on. The language faculty is embedded in performance systems, which access the generative procedure. It is in this broader context that questions of realization and use of SDs arise, questions of articulation, intentionality, interpretation, and the like: How does Jones say X? What is Jones talking about? What does Jones take Smith to be saying or intending to convey? And so on. We might think of the SD as providing instructions to the performance systems that enable Jones to carry out these actions.

When we say that Jones has the language L, we now mean that Jones's language faculty is in the state L, which we identify with a generative procedure embedded in performance systems. To distinguish this concept of language from others, let us refer to it as *I-language*, where I is to suggest "internal," "individual," and "intensional." The concept of language is internal, in that it deals with an inner state of Jones's mind/ brain, independent of other elements in the world. It is individual in that it deals with Jones, and with language communities only derivatively, as groups of people with similar I-languages. It is intensional in the technical sense that the I-language is a function specified in intension, not extension: its extension is the set of SDs (what we might call the *structure* of the I-language). Two distinct I-languages might, in principle, have the same structure, though as a matter of empirical fact, human language may happen not to permit this option. That is, it might turn out that the range of I-languages permitted by UG is so narrow that the theoretical option is simply not realized, that there are no distinct I-languages generating the same set of SDs. This seems, in fact, not unlikely, but it is not a logical necessity. When we use the term *language* below, we mean I-language.

In the earliest work in generative grammar, it was assumed that Jones's language generates an SD for each of the permissible phonetic forms for human language, a set to be specified by UG. Thus, Jones's language assigns a particular status to such expressions as (1), where t (trace) indicates the position in which the question word is construed.

(1) a. John is sleeping
    b. John seems sleeping
    c. what do you think that Mary fixed *t*   (answer: the car)
    d. what do you wonder whether Mary fixed *t*   (answer: the car)
    e. how do you wonder whether Mary fixed the car *t*   (answer: with a wrench)
    f. expressions of Swahili, Hungarian, etc.

In fact, some of the most instructive recent work has been concerned with the differences illustrated by (1d–e), both in some sense "deviant," but assigned a different status by Jones's language (sections 1.3.3, 1.4.1); and one might well learn about the languages of Jones and Wang by studying their reactions to utterances of Swahili.

Another notion that appears commonly in the literature is "formal language" in the technical sense: set of well-formed formulas; in a familiar variety of formal arithmetic, "$(2 + 2) = 5$" but not "$2 + = 2)5($". Call such a set an *E-language*, where *E* is to suggest "external" and "extensional." In the theory of formal languages, the E-language is defined by stipulation, hence is unproblematic. But it is a question of empirical fact whether natural language has any counterpart to this notion, that is, whether Jones's I-language generates not only a set of SDs but also a distinguished E-language: some subset of the phonetic forms of UG, including some but not all of those of (1). Apart from expository passages, the concept of E-language scarcely appears in the tradition of generative grammar that we are considering here. As distinct from the notions discussed earlier, it has no known status in the study of language. One might define E-language in one or another way, but it does not seem to matter how this is done; there is no known gap in linguistic theory, no explanatory function, that would be filled were such a concept presented. Hence, it will play no role in our discussion.

In the study of formal languages, we may distinguish *weak generation* of E-language from *strong generation* of the structure of the language (the set of SDs). The *weak generative capacity* of a theory of I-languages is the set of E-languages weakly generated, and its *strong generative capacity* is the set of structures strongly generated. In the study of natural language, the concepts of structure and strong generation are central; the concepts of E-language and weak generation at best marginal, and perhaps not empirically meaningful at all. Note that if E-languages do exist, they are at a considerably further remove from mechanisms and behavior than I-language. Thus, the child is presented with specimens of behavior in particular circumstances and acquires an I-language in some manner to be determined. The I-language is a state of the mind/brain. It has a certain structure (i.e., strongly generates a set of SDs). It may or may not also weakly generate an E-language, a highly abstract object remote from mechanisms and behavior.

In the terms just outlined, we can consider some of the classical problems of the study of language.

(2) a. What does Jones know when he has a particular language?
    b. How did Jones acquire this knowledge?
    c. How does Jones put this knowledge to use?
    d. How did these properties of the mind/brain evolve in the species?
    e. How are these properties realized in mechanisms of the brain?

Under (2a), we want to account for a wide variety of facts, for example, that Jones knows that

(3) a. *Pin* rhymes with *bin.*
    b. Each expression of (1) has its specific status.
    c. If Mary is too clever to expect anyone to catch, then we don't expect anyone to catch Mary (but nothing is said about whether Mary expects anyone to catch us).
    d. If Mary is too angry to run the meeting, then either Mary is so angry that *she* can't run the meeting, or she is so angry that *we* can't run the meeting (compare: *the crowd is too angry to run the meeting*); in contrast, *which meeting is Mary too angry to run* has only the former (nondeviant) interpretation.
    e. If Mary painted the house brown, then its exterior (not necessarily its interior) is brown.
    f. If Mary persuaded Bill to go to college, then Bill came to intend to go to college (while Mary may or may not have).

The proposed answer to problem (2a) would be that Jones has language L generating SDs that express such facts as (3). Note that Jones has this knowledge whether or not he is aware of these facts about himself; it may take some effort to elicit such awareness, and it might even be beyond Jones's capacities. This is a question that falls within the broader context of performance systems.

The answer to problem (2b) lies in substantial part in UG. The correct theory of the initial state will be rich enough to account for the attainment of a specific language on the basis of the evidence available to the child, but not so rich as to exclude attainable languages. We may proceed to ask as well how environmental factors and maturational processes interact with the initial state described by UG.

Problem (2c) calls for the development of performance theories, among them, theories of production and interpretation. Put generally, the problems are beyond reach: it would be unreasonable to pose the problem of how Jones decides to say what he does, or how he interprets what he hears in particular circumstances. But highly idealized aspects of the problem are amenable to study. A standard empirical hypothesis is that one component of the mind/brain is a *parser*, which assigns a percept to a signal (abstracting from other circumstances relevant to interpretation). The parser presumably incorporates the language and much else, and the hypothesis is that interpretation involves such a system, embedded in others.

It has sometimes been argued that linguistic theory must meet the empirical condition that it account for the ease and rapidity of parsing. But parsing does not, in fact, have these properties. Parsing may be slow and difficult, or even impossible, and it may be "in error" in the sense that the percept assigned (if any) fails to match the SD associated with the signal; many familiar cases have been studied. In general, it is not the case that language is readily usable or "designed for use." The subparts that are used are usable, trivially; biological considerations lead us to expect no more than that. Similarly, returning to problem (2b), there is no a priori reason to expect that the languages permitted by UG be learnable—that is, attainable under normal circumstances. All that we can expect is that some of them may be; the others will not be found in human societies. If proposals within the P&P approach are close to the mark, then it will follow that languages are in fact learnable, but that is an empirical discovery, and a rather surprising one.

Problems (2d–e) appear to be beyond serious inquiry for the time being, along with many similar questions about cognition generally. Here again one must be wary of many pitfalls (Lewontin 1990). We will put these matters aside.

A grammar for Jones is true if (or to the extent that) the language it describes is the one Jones has. In that case the grammar will account for such facts as (3), by providing a language that generates appropriate SDs. A true grammar is said to meet the condition of *descriptive adequacy*. A theory of UG is true if (or to the extent that) it correctly describes the initial state of the language faculty. In that case it will provide a descriptively adequate grammar for each attainable language. A true theory of UG meets the condition of *explanatory adequacy*. The terminology is intended to suggest a certain plausible pattern of explanation. Given an array of facts such as (3), we can give an account of them at one level by providing a grammar for Jones, and we can provide an explanation for them at a deeper level by answering problem (2b), that is, by showing how these facts derive from UG, given the "boundary conditions" set by experience. Note that this pattern of explanation, though standard, makes certain empirical assumptions about the actual process of acquisition that are by no means obviously true, for example, that the process is *as if* it were instantaneous. Such assumptions are indirectly supported to the extent that the explanations succeed.

Any serious approach to complex phenomena involves innumerable idealizations, and the one just sketched is no exception. We do not expect to find "pure instantiations" of the initial state of the language faculty (hence of UG). Rather, Jones will have some jumble of systems, based on the peculiar pattern of his experience. The explanatory model outlined deals specifically with language acquisition under the idealized conditions of a homogeneous speech community. We assume that the system described by UG is a real component of the mind/brain, put to use in the complex circumstances of ordinary life. The validity of this assumption is hardly in question. To reject it would be to assume either (1) that nonhomogeneous (conflicting) data are required for language acquisition, or (2) that the mind/brain does indeed have the system described by UG, but it is not used in language acquisition. Neither assumption is remotely plausible. Rejecting them, we accept the approach just outlined as a reasonable approach to the truth about humans, and a likely prerequisite to any serious inquiry into the complex and chaotic phenomenal world.

Furthermore, even if a homogeneous speech community existed, we would not expect its linguistic system to be a "pure case." Rather, all sorts of accidents of history would have contaminated the system, as in the properties of (roughly) Romance versus Germanic origin in the lexicon of English. The proper topic of inquiry, then, should be a theory of the initial state that abstracts from such accidents, no trivial matter. For working purposes (and nothing more than that), we may make a rough and tentative distinction between the *core* of a language and its *periphery*, where the core consists of what we tentatively assume to be pure instantiations of UG and the periphery consists of marked exceptions (irregular verbs, etc.). Note that the periphery will also exhibit properties of UG (e.g., ablaut phenomena), though less transparently. A reasonable approach would be to focus attention on the core system, putting aside phenomena that result from historical accident, dialect mixture, personal idiosyncrasies, and the like. As in any other empirical inquiry, theory-internal considerations enter into the effort to pursue this course, and we expect further distinctions to be necessary (consider, for example, the phenomenon of *do*-insertion in English as in (1c–e), not on a par with irregular verbs, but not of the generality of fronting of question words).

The preceding remarks are largely conceptual, though not without empirical consequences. We now proceed along a particular path, in the manner indicated earlier, assuming further empirical risk at each point.

We assume that the language (the generative procedure, the I-language) has two components: a computational system and a lexicon. The first generates the form of SDs; the second characterizes the lexical items that appear in them. Many crucial questions arise as to how these systems interact. We will assume that one aspect of an SD is a system of representation, called *D-Structure*, at which lexical items are inserted. D-Structure expresses lexical properties in a form accessible to the computational system.

We assume further a distinction between *inflectional* and *derivational* processes of morphology, the latter internal to the lexicon, the former involving computational operations of a broader syntactic scope. These computational operations might involve *word formation* or *checking*. Consider for example the past tense form *walked*. The lexicon contains the root [walk], with its idiosyncratic properties of sound, meaning, and form specified; and the inflectional feature [tense], one value of which is [past]. One of the computational rules, call it R, associates the two by combining them (either adjoining [walk] to [tense], or conversely). We might interpret this descriptive comment in two ways. One possibility is that [walk] is drawn from the lexicon as such; then R combines it with [past]. A second possibility is that processes internal to the lexicon (*redundancy rules*) form the word *walked* with the properties [walk] and [past] already specified. The rule R then combines the amalgam with [past], checking and licensing its intrinsic feature [past]. In this case the lexicon is more structured. It contains the element [walk], as before, along with rules indicating that any verb may also intrinsically possess such properties as [past], [plural], and the like. Similar questions arise about complex words (causatives, noun incorporation structures, compound nouns, etc.). As these topics are pursued with more precision, within more closely articulated theories, important and often subtle empirical issues arise (Marantz 1984, Fabb 1984, Baker 1988, Di Sciullo and Williams 1988, Grimshaw 1990).

The SD provides information (to be interpreted by performance systems) about the properties of each linguistic expression, including its sound and its meaning. We assume that the design of language provides a variety of symbolic systems (*levels of representation*) fulfilling these tasks, including the level of *Phonetic Form* (PF) and the level of *Logical Form* (LF), specifying aspects of sound and meaning, respectively, insofar as they are linguistically determined. Another is the level of D-Structure, which relates the computational system and the lexicon.

The level PF must satisfy three basic conditions of adequacy. It must be *universal*, in the sense that an expression of any actual or potential human language is representable within it. It must be an *interface*, in that its elements have an interpretation in terms of the sensorimotor systems. And it must be *uniform*, in that this interpretation is uniform for all languages, so as to capture all and only the properties of the system of language as such.

The same three conditions hold for LF. To capture what the language faculty determines about the meaning of an expression, it must be universal, in that any thought expressible in a human language is representable in it; an interface, in that these representations have an interpretation in terms of other systems of the mind/brain involved in thought, referring, planning, and so on; and uniform, in just the sense that the phonetic system is. We will put aside important questions concerning the nature of the LF interface: does it involve a conceptual system (Jackendoff 1983, 1990b), a use theory of meaning, a causal theory of reference, etc.? The conditions are more obscure than in the case of the phonetic analogue, because the systems at the interface are much less well understood, but there is nonetheless a wealth of evidence firm enough to allow substantive inquiry.

According to this conception, then, each SD contains three interface levels: the external interface levels PF and LF, and the internal interface level of D-Structure. The elements at these levels are further analyzed into features: phonological, selectional, categorial, and so on. In general, each symbol of the representations is a feature set, in respects to be further specified.

A further assumption, developed in the *Extended Standard Theory* (EST), is that these levels are not related directly; rather, their relations are mediated by an intermediate level of *S-Structure*. Adopting this view, each SD is a sequence (π, λ, δ, σ), where π and λ are representations at the external interface levels PF and LF, δ is at the internal interface of computational system and lexicon, and σ is derivative. The first three levels meet empirical conditions imposed by the performance systems and the lexicon. The level of S-Structure must relate to these three levels in the manner specified in UG; we might think of it, informally, as the (presumably unique) "solution" to this set of conditions. In the subsequent discussion we restrict ourselves largely to the levels D-Structure, S-Structure, and LF, and the relations among them (syntax in a narrow sense). We are thus concerned primarily with the derivation from D-Structure to LF in (4).

(4)   D-Structure ← − − Lexicon
                  ↓
    PF ← − − S-Structure
                  ↓
              LF

Subtle questions arise as to how the relations among these levels are to be construed: specifically, is there an inherent "directionality," so that the relations should be construed as a mapping of one level to another, or is there simply a nondirectional relation? To formulate this as a real empirical issue is not a simple matter, and empirical evidence to distinguish such possibilities is not easy to come by. But interesting (and conflicting) arguments have been presented. Discrimination among these alternatives becomes particularly difficult if we adopt (as we will) the standard EST assumption, from the early 1970s, that representations may include *empty categories* (ECs): elements (feature sets) that are perfectly substantive from the point of view of the computational system, but that do not happen to be assigned an interpretation by the mapping from S-Structure to PF, though they may have indirect phonetic effects; thus, the contraction rules of English convert *want to* into the phonological word *wanna* when there is no trace intervening (*who do you wanna see* but not *who do you wanna see John* (Chomsky and Lasnik 1977)).

We will tentatively proceed on the assumption that the relations are, in fact, directional: D-Structure is mapped to S-Structure, which is (independently) mapped to PF and LF.

The earliest modern work in generative grammar borrowed standard ideas of traditional grammar, which recognized (I) that a sentence has a hierarchy of phrases (noun phrases, clauses, etc.) and that these (or their heads) enter into certain grammatical relations; and (II) that sentences belong to various grammatical constructions with systematic relations among them, some more "basic" than others (actives more basic than passives, declaratives more basic than interrogatives, etc.). Correspondingly, the earliest versions of UG provided two kinds of rules: (I) phrase structure rules generating SDs that express the hierarchy of phrases; and (II) transformational rules that form grammatical constructions from abstract underlying forms, with more transformations involved in formation of the less basic constructions (thus, only obligatory transformations apply to form active declaratives (*kernel sentences*), but some optional ones are involved in formation of passives, interrogatives, etc.). The phrase structure rules provide a "geometrical" account of grammatical relations, understood relationally; that is, subject is not a syntactic category like noun phrase or verb, but is understood as the relation subject-of holding of the pair (*John, left*) in *John left*, and so on (Chomsky 1951, 1965, 1975a). These notions were defined in such a way that the phrase structure rules (I) generate D-Structures (deep structures), each a *phrase marker* that represents hierarchy and relations. Transformations convert these objects into new phrase markers. In the later EST version, as noted, D-Structures are mapped to S-Structures by such derivations, and the latter are mapped independently to PF and LF.

The resort to phrase structure rules was also suggested by other considerations. The earliest work concentrated on what is now called generative phonology, and in this domain "rewriting rules" of the form $X \rightarrow Y$, where X is an expression "rewritten" as Y in the course of derivation, seems an appropriate device. If these rules are restricted to the form $XAY \rightarrow XZY$, A a single symbol and Z nonnull, then we have a system of rules that can form phrase structure representations in a natural way (*context-free* rules if X, Y are null). Further motivation derived from the theory of formal systems. Grammatical transformations as generative devices were suggested by work of Harris (1952), which used formal relations among expressions as a device to "normalize" texts for the analysis of discourse.

As for UG, the earliest versions assumed that it provided a format for rule systems and an evaluation metric that assigned a "value" to each generative procedure of the proper format. The crucial empirical condition on UG, then, is that the system provide only a few high-valued I-languages consistent with the kinds of data available to the child, perhaps only one. If UG is *feasible* in this sense, the fundamental problem (2b) can be addressed (Chomsky 1965).

This approach recorded many achievements, but faced a fundamental and recurrent problem: the tension between descriptive and explanatory adequacy. To achieve descriptive adequacy, it seemed necessary to enrich the format of permissible systems, but in doing so we lose the property of feasibility, so that problem (2b) is still unresolved. The conflict arises as soon as we move from the intuitive hints and examples of traditional grammar to explicit generative procedures. It was quickly recognized that the problem is inherent in the kinds of rule systems that were being considered. The most plausible approach to it is to try to "factor out" overarching principles that govern rule application generally, assigning them to UG; the actual rules of grammar can then be given in the simplest form, with these principles ensuring that they will operate in such a way as to yield the observed phenomena in their full complexity (Chomsky 1964, Ross 1967). The limit that might be reached is that rules are eliminated entirely, the "apparent rules" being deduced from general principles of UG, in the sense that the interaction of the principles would yield the phenomena that the rules had been constructed to describe. To the extent that this result can be achieved, the rules postulated for particular languages will be shown to be epiphenomena.

Such ideas were pursued with a good deal of success from the early 1960s, leading to the P&P approach, which assumed that the limit can in fact be attained: the hypothesis is that all principles are assigned to UG and that language variation is restricted to certain options as to how the principles apply. If so, then rule systems are eliminable, at least for the core of the language.

To illustrate, consider again (1c–e), repeated here.

(1) c. what do you think that Mary fixed *t*
    d. what do you wonder whether Mary fixed *t*
    e. how do you wonder whether Mary fixed the car *t*

The goal is to show that the question words move from the position of t by a general principle that allows movement quite freely, with the options, interpretations, and varying status determined by the interaction of this principle with others.

What is the status of the rules (I) (phrase structure) and (II) (transformational) under this conception? The transformational rules still exist, but only as principles of UG, freely applicable to arbitrary expressions. Such devices appear to be unavoidable in one or another form, whether taken to be operations forming derivations or relations established on representations. As for phrase structure rules, it appears that they may be completely superfluous. That would not be too surprising. With the advantage of hindsight we can see that, unlike transformational rules, they were a dubious device to begin with, recapitulating information that must be presented, ineliminably, in the lexicon. For example, the fact that *persuade* takes a noun phrase (NP) and clausal phrase (CP) as complements, as a lexical property, requires that there be phrase structure rules yielding V–NP–CP as an instantiation of the phrase XP headed by the verb *persuade*; and completely general properties require further that XP must be VP (verb phrase), not, say, NP. The apparent eliminability of phrase structure rules became clear by the late 1960s, with the separation of the lexicon from the computational system and the development of *X-bar theory* (section 1.3.2).

The issues can be sharpened by considering two properties that descriptive statements about language might have or lack. They may or may not be language-particular; they may or may not be construction-particular. The statements of traditional grammar are typically both language- and construction-particular, and the same is true of the rules of early generative grammar. Consider the rule analyzing VP as V–NP, or the rules fronting the question word in different ways in (ic–e). Spelled out in full detail, these phrase structure and transformational rules are specific to English and to these constructions. There are few exceptions to this pattern.

The P&P approach aims to reduce descriptive statements to two categories: language-invariant, and language-particular. The language-invariant statements are principles (including the parameters, each on a par with a principle of UG); the language-particular ones are specifications of particular values of parameters. The notion of construction, in the traditional sense, effectively disappears; it is perhaps useful for descriptive taxonomy but has no theoretical status. Thus, there are no such constructions as Verb Phrase, or interrogative and relative clause, or passive and raising constructions. Rather, there are just general principles that interact to form these descriptive artifacts.

The parametric options available appear to be quite restricted. An assumption that seems not unrealistic is that there is only one computational system that forms derivations from D-Structure to LF; at some point in the derivation (S-Structure), the process branches to form PF by an independent phonological derivation (as in (4)). Options would then be restricted to two cases: (1) properties of the lexicon, or (2) the point in the derivation (4) from D-Structure to LF at which structures are mapped to PF (S-Structure) (Stowell 1986).

In the category (1), apart from Saussurean arbitrariness and some limited variety in the choice of substantive elements, we have options as to how nonsubstantive (functional) elements are realized (Borer 1984, Fukui 1986, Speas 1986) and variations in global properties of heads (e.g., do verbs precede or follow their complements?) (Travis 1984).

In the category (2) we find, for example, languages with overt movement of question phrase (English, Italian, etc.) and languages without overt movement (Chinese, Japanese, etc.). In these *in-situ* languages, with the question phrase in the position that would be occupied by a trace in languages with overt movement, there is good evidence that similar movement operations take place, but only in the mapping from S-Structure to LF, with no indication in the physical form itself; the branch point at which PF is formed from S-Structure precedes these operations in the derivation (4) from D-Structure to LF (Huang 1982, Lasnik and Saito 1984, 1992). Similarly, we find languages with overt manifestation of grammatical case (Greek, German, Japanese, etc.) and others with virtually no such manifestation (English, Chinese, etc.). But again, there is good reason to believe that the case systems are basically similar cross-linguistically and that the differences lie primarily in their phonetic realization (the mapping to PF).

The general expectation, for all constructions, is that languages will be very similar at the D-Structure and LF levels, as in the examples just discussed. It is unlikely that there are parameters that affect the form of LF representation or the computational process from S-Structure to LF; little evidence is available to the language learner bearing on these matters, and there would be no way for values to be determined with any reliability. Accordingly, any variations at the LF level must be reflexes of D-Structure parameter settings, or of variations in the mapping from

D-Structure to S-Structure to the extent that its properties are determined from inspection of PF forms. D-Structure, in turn, reflects lexical properties; these too appear to be limited in variety insofar as they affect the computational system. At the PF level, properties of the language can be readily observed and variation is possible within the fixed repertoire of phonetic properties and the invariant principles of universal phonetics. S-Structures are not constrained by interface conditions and can vary within the range permitted by the variation of the interface levels, the branch point to the PF mapping, and any independent conditions that may hold of S-Structure.

The principles that have been investigated fall into two general categories: principles that are applied to construct derivations (transformational operations and conditions on the way they operate), and principles that apply to representations (licensing conditions). The transformational operations are movement (adjunction, substitution), deletion, and perhaps insertion; we may think of these as instances of the general operation *Affect* α, α arbitrary (Lasnik and Saito 1984). Conditions of locality and others constrain the application and functioning of these operations. Licensing conditions at the external interface levels PF and LF establish the relation of language to other faculties of the mind/brain. D-Structure conditions specify the manner in which lexical properties are expressed in grammatical structures. That there should be S-Structure conditions is less obvious, but it seems that they may exist (see section 1.3.3).

The principles have further structure. There are natural groupings into *modules* of language (binding theory, θ-theory, Case theory, etc.). Certain unifying concepts enter into many or all modules: conditions of locality, "geometrical" properties defined on phrase markers, and so on. There are also certain general ideas that appear to have wide applicability, among them, principles of economy stating that there can be no superfluous symbols in representations (the principle of Full Interpretation, FI) or superfluous steps in derivations (Chomsky 1986b, chapters 2–4 of this book). As these principles are given an explicit formulation, they become empirical hypotheses with specific import and range.

The principle FI is assumed as a matter of course in phonology; if a symbol in a representation has no sensorimotor interpretations, the representation does not qualify as a PF representation. This is what we called the "interface condition." The same condition applied to LF also entails that every element of the representation have a (language-independent) interpretation. There can, for example, be no true expletives, or vacuous quantifiers, at the LF level. The principle of economy of derivation requires that computational operations must be driven by some condition on representations, as a "last resort" to overcome a failure to meet such a condition. Interacting with other principles of UG, such economy principles have wide-ranging effects and may, when matters are properly understood, subsume much of what appears to be the specific character of particular principles.

The shifts in focus over the years alter the task of inquiry considerably and yield different conceptions of what constitutes a "real result" in the study of language. Suppose we have some collection of phenomena in a particular language. In the early stages of generative grammar, the task was to find a rule system of the permitted form from which these phenomena (and infinitely many others) could be derived. That is a harder task than the ones posed in pregenerative grammar, but not an impossible one: there are many potential rule systems, and it is often possible to devise one that will more or less work—though the problem of explanatory adequacy at once arises, as noted.

But this achievement, however difficult, does not count as a real result if we adopt the P&P approach as a goal. Rather, it merely sets the problem. The task is now to show how the phenomena derived by the rule system can be deduced from the invariant principles of UG with parameters set in one of the permissible ways. This is a far harder and more challenging task. It is an important fact that the problem can now be posed realistically, and solved in interesting ways in some range of cases, with failures that are also interesting insofar as they point the way to better solutions. The departure from the long and rich tradition of linguistic inquiry is much sharper and more radical than in early generative grammar, with problems that are quite new and prospects that appear promising.

Other traditional problems also assume a different form under a P&P approach. Questions of typology and language change will be expressed in terms of parameter choice (Lightfoot 1991). The theory of language acquisition will be concerned with acquisition of lexical items, fixing of parameters, and perhaps maturation of principles (Hyams 1986, Roeper and Williams 1987, Borer and Wexler 1987; Chien and Wexler 1991, Crain 1991, Pierce 1992). It might turn out that parsers are basically uniform for all languages: the parsers for English and Japanese would differ only in that parameters are set differently (Fong 1991). Other issues would also require some rethinking, if this approach turns out to be correct.

Much of the most fruitful inquiry into generative grammar in the past years has pursued the working hypothesis that UG is a simple and elegant theory, with fundamental principles that have an intuitive character and broad generality. By dissolving the notion of construction and moving toward "rule-free" systems, the P&P approach carries this tendency considerably forward. A related assumption is that UG is "nonredundant," in the sense that phenomena are explained by interaction of principles in one particular way. Discovery that phenomena are "overdetermined" has commonly been taken to indicate a theoretical deficiency that should be overcome by new or refined principles. These working hypotheses have proven successful as a guide to inquiry, leading to the discovery of a vast range of empirical phenomena in widely varied languages and to forms of explanation that much exceed what could be contemplated not many years ago. These are rather surprising facts. The guiding ideas resemble those often adopted in the study of inorganic phenomena, where success has often been spectacular since the 17th century. But language is a biological system, and biological systems typically are "messy," intricate, the result of evolutionary "tinkering," and shaped by accidental circumstances and by physical conditions that hold of complex systems with varied functions and elements. Redundancy is not only a typical feature of such systems, but an expected one, in that it helps to compensate for injury and defect, and to accommodate to a diversity of ends and functions. Language use appears to have the expected properties; as noted, it is a familiar fact that large parts of language are "unusable," and the usable parts appear to form a chaotic and "unprincipled" segment of the full language. Nevertheless, it has been a fruitful working hypothesis that in its basic structure, the language faculty has properties of simplicity and elegance that are not characteristic of complex organic systems, just as its infinite digital character seems biologically rather isolated. Possibly these conclusions are artifacts reflecting a particular pattern of inquiry; the range of completely unexplained and apparently chaotic phenomena of language lends credibility to such skepticism. Still, the progress that has been made by the contrary stance cannot be overlooked.

The P&P approach is sometimes termed *Government-Binding (GB) Theory*. The terminology is misleading. True, early efforts to synthesize current thinking in these terms happened to concentrate on the theories of government and of binding (Chomsky 1981a), but these modules of language stand alongside many others: Case theory, θ-theory, and so on. It may turn out that the concept of government has a kind of unifying role, but there is nothing inherent to the approach that requires this. Furthermore, insofar as the theories of government and binding deal with real phenomena, they will appear in some form in every approach to language; this approach has no special claim on them. Determination of the nature of these and other systems is a common project, not specific to this particular conception of the nature of language and its use.

1.2   The Lexicon

A person who has a language has access to detailed information about words of the language. Any theory of language must reflect this fact; thus, any theory of language must include some sort of lexicon, the repository of all (idiosyncratic) properties of particular lexical items. These properties include a representation of the phonological form of each item, a specification of its syntactic category, and its semantic characteristics. Of particular interest in this discussion are the s(-emantic) selection and thematic properties of lexical heads: verbs, nouns, adjectives, and pre- or postpositions. These specify the "argument structure" of a head, indicating how many arguments the head licenses and what semantic role each receives. For example, the verb *give* must be specified as assigning an agent role, a theme role, and a goal/recipient role. In (5) *John*, *a book*, and *Mary* have these respective thematic (θ-)roles.

(5) John gave a book to Mary

The association between assigned θ-roles and argument positions is to a large extent predictable. For example, "agent" is apparently never assigned to a complement. And to the extent that the association is predictable rather than idiosyncratic, it need not (hence, must not) be stated in particular lexical entries.

This conception of the lexicon is based on that developed in the 1960s (Chomsky 1965), but it departs from it in certain respects. There, subcategorization and selectional conditions played a central role. The former conditions state for a lexical head what phrasal categories it takes as complements—for example, that *kick* takes an NP complement. The latter conditions specify intrinsic semantic features of the complement(s) and subject. In this case the NP complement of *kick* is [+concrete]. It was noted in section 1.1 that phrase structure rules are (largely) redundant with subcategorization, hence are (largely) eliminable. But now note that subcategorization follows almost entirely from θ-role specification. A verb with no θ-role to assign to a complement will not be able to take a complement. A verb with (obligatory) θ-roles to assign will have to occur in a configuration with enough arguments (possibly including complements) to receive those θ-roles. Further, at least in part, selectional restrictions will also be determined by thematic properties. To receive a particular θ-role, the inherent semantic features of an argument must be compatible with that θ-role.

These tentative conclusions about the organization of the lexicon raise important questions about the acquisition of lexical knowledge. Suppose that subcategorization (c-selection) is artifactual, its effects derived from semantic properties (s-selection). It is reasonable to ask whether this is a consequence of the acquisition procedure itself (Pesetsky 1982). Pesetsky (developing ideas of Grimshaw (1979)) suggests that this must be so. He compares the primitives of c-selection (syntactic categories such as NP, CP, etc.) with those of θ-theory ("agent," "patient," "goal," etc.) and argues that the latter, but not the former, meet what we may call the condition of *epistemological priority*. That is, they can plausibly be applied by the learner to provide a preliminary, prelinguistic analysis of a reasonable sample of data and thus can provide the basis for development from the initial state to the steady state. This is an attractive line of reasoning, but, given our current understanding of these issues, it is not conclusive. While it does seem correct that the primitives of c-selection do not have epistemological priority, it is not at all clear that those of s-selection do have such a status. Although the notion "agent of an action" is possibly available to the child in advance of any syntactic knowledge, it is less clear that the θ-theoretic notion "agent of a *sentence*" is. That is, before the child knows anything about the syntax of his or her language (beyond what is given by UG), can the child determine what portion of a sentence constitutes the agent? Further, the evidence available to the learner likely consists of sentences rather than simply individual verbs in isolation. But such sentences explicitly display c-selection properties: they exhibit verbs along with their complements. Thus, the child is simultaneously presented with evidence bearing on both s-selection (given that sentences are presented in context, and assuming that the relevant contexts can be determined) and c-selection. It is reasonable to assume that both aspects of the evidence contribute to the development of the knowledge. Alongside the state of affairs outlined by Pesetsky, the converse situation with c-selection evidence in fact providing information about the meanings of verbs (Lasnik 1990, Gleitman 1990) might also obtain. For example, exposure to a sentence containing a clausal complement to an unfamiliar verb would lead the learner to hypothesize that the verb is one of propositional attitude.

This scenario is not necessarily in conflict with Pesetsky's initial point about the organization of lexical entries. The means by which knowledge is arrived at is not invariably reflected in the form that the knowledge ultimately takes. For example, Grimshaw (1981) argues that the acquisition of the syntactic category of a lexical item is based in part on the notion "canonical structural realization" (CSR). The CSR of a physical object is N, that of an action is V, and so on. In the absence of evidence, the child will assume that a word belongs to its CSR—that, say, a word referring to an action is a verb. As Grimshaw indicates, while such "semantic bootstrapping" might constitute part of the acquisition procedure, the resulting steady-state lexicon has no such requirement. Languages commonly have nouns, like *destruction*, referring to actions (as well as verbs, like *be*, that don't refer to actions).

Note that this consideration indicates that lexical entries contain at least some syntactic information, in addition to the phonological and semantic information that surely must be present. Grimshaw argues that further syntactic specification is needed as well, c-selection in addition to s-selection. To consider one example, Grimshaw observes that the semantic category "question" can be structurally realized as either a clause, as in (6), or an NP, as in (7).

(6) Mary asked [what time it was]

(7) Mary asked [the time]

The verb *ask* semantically selects a question. Grimshaw argues that it is also necessary to specify that it c-selects clause or NP in order to distinguish it from *wonder*, which only takes a clause (where * indicates deviance).

(8) Mary wondered [what time it was]

(9) *Mary wondered [the time]

Since, as suggested above, it is possible to reduce most of c-selection to s-selection, the question arises whether such reduction might somehow be available in this instance as well. Pesetsky argues that it is. As we will see in section 1.4.3, NPs must receive abstract Case from a Case assigner while clauses need not. (Henceforth, we will capitalize the word *Case* in its technical usage.) Given this, Pesetsky proposes that the difference between *ask* and *wonder* need not be stated in terms of c-selection, but rather follows from a Case difference: *ask* assigns objective Case but *wonder* does not. In this regard, *wonder* patterns with adjectives, which also do not assign objective Case.

(10)   Mary is uncertain [what time it is]

(11)   *Mary is uncertain [the time]

Pesetsky presents further evidence for this Case-assigning distinction between verbs like *ask* and those like *wonder*. In English, generally only objective Case-assigning verbs can occur in the passive. Given this, (6) and (8) contrast in precisely the predicted fashion.

(12)   it was asked what time it was

(13)   *it was wondered what time it was

As Pesetsky notes, a descriptive generalization pointed out by Grimshaw now follows: among the verbs that s-select questions, some c-select clause or NP while others c-select only clause; none c-select only NP. There are Case-assigning differences among verbs, and these are relevant to c-selection of NP (because of the Case requirement of NPs), but not of clauses.

This reduction seems quite successful for a wide range of cases, but it is important to note that formal syntactic specifications in lexical entries have not been entirely eliminated in favor of semantic ones. Whether or not a verb assigns objective Case is, as far as is known at present, a purely formal property not deducible from semantics. While much of c-selection follows from s-selection, there is a syntactic residue, statable, if Pesetsky is correct, in terms of lexically idiosyncratic Case properties.

We will introduce further properties of the lexicon as required by the exposition.

1.3   Computational System

1.3.1   General Properties of Derivations and Representations

The generative procedure that constitutes the (I-)language consists of a lexicon and a computational system. In section 1.2 we outlined some properties of the lexicon. We now turn to the computational system. Under the general assumptions of section 1.1, we consider the four levels of representation of the EST system and the relations that hold among them, focusing attention on "narrow syntax," that is, the derivation relating D-Structure, S-Structure, and LF.

D-Structure, LF, and PF are interface levels, which satisfy the general condition FI in a manner to be made precise. Each level is a symbolic system, consisting of atomic elements (primes) and objects constructed from them by concatenation and other operations. We take these objects to be phrase markers in the familiar sense (represented conventionally by trees or labeled bracketing). Each prime is a feature complex, though for orthographic convenience we will generally use conventional symbols. For concreteness, take categories to be as in (14), for nouns, verbs, adjectives, and pre- and postpositions, respectively.

(14) a. $N = [+N, -V]$
     b. $V = [-N, +V]$
     c. $A = [+N, +V]$
     d. $P = [-N, -V]$

The feature $[+N]$ is the traditional substantive; the feature $[+V]$, predicate.

The primes constituting the terminal string of a phrase marker are drawn from the lexicon; others are *projected* from these *heads* by operations of the computational system. Elements that project no further are *maximal projections*. In informal notation, XP is the maximal projection from the terminal category X; thus, NP is the maximal projection of its head N, and so on. See section 1.3.2.

The two basic relations of a phrase marker are *domination* and *linearity*. In the phrase marker (15) we say that B dominates D and E, C dominates F and G, and A dominates all other categories (nodes). Furthermore, B precedes C, F, and G; D precedes E, C, F, and G; and so on.

(15)

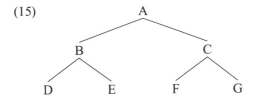

If X is a head, its "sister" is its *complement*; thus, if D and F are heads, then E and G are their complements in (15). We assume that ordering relations are determined by a few parameter settings. Thus, in English, a *right-branching* language, all heads precede their complements, while in Japanese, a *left-branching* language, all heads follow their complements; the order is determined by one setting of the *head parameter*. Examples below that abstract from particular languages are usually to be interpreted independently of the order given. Domination relations are determined by general principles (section 1.3.2).

One fundamental concept that applies throughout the modules of grammar is *command* (Klima 1964, Langacker 1969, Lasnik 1976, Reinhart 1976, Stowell 1981, Aoun and Sportiche 1981). We say that α *c-commands* β if α does not dominate β and every γ that dominates α dominates β. Thus, in (15) B c-commands C, F, G; C c-commands B, D, E; D c-commands E and conversely; F c-commands G and conversely. Where γ is restricted to maximal projections, we say that α *m-commands* β.

A second fundamental concept is *government* (Chomsky 1981a, 1986a, Rizzi 1990), a more "local" variety of command to which we return in section 1.4.1.

Given the language L, each SD is a sequence $(\pi, \lambda, \delta, \sigma)$, these being phrase markers drawn from the levels PF, LF, D-Structure, and S-Structure, respectively. The element δ reflects properties of the items selected from the lexicon as these are interpreted by the principles of UG, with the parameters fixed for L. The elements σ and λ are formed by successive application of operations of the computational system to δ; they will have the properties of δ, as modified by these operations. The PF representation π is a string of phonetic primes with syllabic and intonational structure indicated, derived by a computation from σ. We assume that the primes themselves are not modified in the course of the derivation from δ to λ.

A typical lexical entry consists of a phonological matrix and other features, among them the categorial features N, V, and so on; and in the case of Ns, Case and agreement features (person, number, gender), henceforth ϕ-*features*. In principle, any of these features may be lacking. In one case of particular interest, the entire phonological matrix is lacking. In this case the element is an EC (empty category). Among these ECs we have the elements *e* of (16), (17); we use * to indicate severe deviance, ? a weaker variety.

(16) a. John expected [*e* to hurt himself]
     b. it is common [*e* to hurt oneself]

(17) *e arrived yesterday   ("he arrived yesterday")

We refer to the EC of (16) as *PRO*, an element that can be *controlled* by its *antecedent* (*John*, in (16a)) or can be arbitrary in interpretation, as in (16b). Possibly the latter is also a case of control by an EC occupying the same position as *for us* in (18) (Epstein 1984).

(18) it is convenient for us [for others to do the hard work]

If so, PRO is always controlled. See section 1.4.2.

The EC of (17) is a pronominal element, henceforth *pro*. It is not permitted in this position in English; the counterpart would be grammatical in Italian, a *null subject language*. On factors relevant to fixing the parameters, see Rizzi 1982, 1986a, Huang 1984, Borer 1984, Jaeggli and Safir 1989. This EC acts much in the manner of an ordinary pronoun, having reference fixed by context or by some antecedent in an appropriate position. The structural relations of (antecedent, *pro*) pairs are, furthermore, generally like those of (antecedent, pronoun) and unlike those of control. For example, in a null subject language we find the equivalents of (19a–b), analogous to the pair (19c–d) (*John* taken to be the antecedent of *pro*, *he*).

(19) a.   the people that *pro* taught admired John
     b.   *pro admired John
     c.   the people that he taught admired John
     d.   *he admired John

The behavior of *pro* and *he* is similar, while PRO can never appear in these positions.

A third type of EC, not drawn from the lexicon but created in the course of a derivation, is illustrated in (20).

(20) a. I wonder [who John expected [*e* to hurt himself]]
     b. John was expected [*e* to hurt himself]

We refer to this EC as *trace* (*t*), a relational notion *trace-of* X, where X is the moved element serving as the antecedent *binding* the trace. Thus, *John* binds *e* in (20b) much as *e* binds the reflexive or as *they* binds the reciprocal in (21), in turn binding the reflexive.

(21) they expected [each other to hurt themselves]

In (20a) *e* is the trace of the NP *who*. The trace functions as a variable bound by *who*, understood as a restricted quantifier: 'for which *e*, *e* a person'. Here, *e* in turn binds *himself*, just as *each other* binds *themselves* in (21) and *Bill* binds *himself* in (22), with *Bill* substituting for the variable of (20a).

(22) John expected [Bill to hurt himself]

In (20a) both *e* and *himself* function as variables bound by the restricted quantifier, so that the LF form would be interpreted 'I wonder [for which *e*, *e* a person, John expected *e* to hurt *e*]'. Note that we are using the term *bind* here to cover the association of an antecedent with its trace quite generally, including the case of the (syntactic) binding of a variable by a quantifier-like element; and we also use the term, at LF, in the sense of quantifier-variable binding.

In (20b) the verb *was* is composed of the lexical element *be* and the inflectional elements [past, 3 person, singular]. Assume now that the process of composition adjoins the copula to the inflectional elements (raising). Recall that there are two interpretations of this process: (1) raising of *be* to the inflection position of the sentence to construct the combined form [*be* + inflections], or (2) raising of [*be* + inflections] (= *was*, drawn from the lexicon with its features already assigned) to the inflection position, where the features are checked. Either way, we have a second trace in (20b) = (23).

(23) John was e_2 expected [e_1 to hurt himself]

The EC e_2 is the trace of *be* or *was*; e_1 is the trace of *John*, binding *himself*. In each case the trace occupies the position from which its antecedent was moved. For concreteness, we adopt the checking theory (2), so that we have *was* raising in (23).

Raising of *was* to the inflection position is necessary to check inflectional properties. The same is true of the other inflected verbs, for example, *wonder* in (20a), which is [present, 1 person, singular]. Thus, a fuller (though still only partial) representation would be (24), where e_1 is the trace of *wonder*.

(24) I wonder e_1 [who John expected [e_2 to hurt himself]]

There is reason to believe that in English (24) is an LF representation, while the counterpart in other similar languages (e.g., French) is an S-Structure representation; (23) and its counterparts are S-Structure representations in both kinds of language (Emonds 1978, Pollock 1989).

Thus, English auxiliaries raise at S-Structure but main verbs raise only at LF, while the corresponding French elements all raise at S-Structure. English and French would then be identical in relevant respects at D-Structure and LF, while differing at S-Structure, with English (25a) (corresponding to the basically shared D-Structure) versus French (25b) (corresponding to the basically shared LF form).

(25) a. John often [kisses Mary]
     b. Jean embrasse souvent [t Marie]
        Jean kisses   often   Marie

Informally, the trace functions throughout as if the antecedent were in that position, receiving and assigning syntactic and semantic properties. Thus, e is in the normal position of the antecedent of a reflexive in both (20a) and (20b). And in (25b), the trace is the verbal head of VP, assigning a particular semantic role and grammatical Case to its nominal object.

Note that PRO and trace are quite different in their properties. Thus, an element that controls PRO is an independent argument in the sense of section 1.2, assigned an independent semantic role; but an element that binds a trace is not. Compare (16a) and (20b), repeated here:

(26) a. John expected [e to hurt himself]
     b. John was expected [e to hurt himself]

In (26a) *John* is the subject argument of *expected*, exactly as in (22); the EC controlled by *John* has its independent function as subject of *hurt*. In (26b), in contrast, *John* has no semantic role other than what it "inherits" from its trace, as subject of *hurt*. Since the subject of *is expected* is assigned no independent argument role, it can be a nonargument (an *expletive*), as in (27).

(27) there is expected [to be an eclipse tomorrow]

Other differences of interpretation follow. Compare, for example, (28a) and (28b).

(28) a. your friends hoped [e to finish the meeting happy]
     b. your friends seemed [e to finish the meeting happy]

In (28a) *your friends* and *e* are independent arguments, assigned their semantic roles as subjects of *hope* and *finish*, respectively; therefore, the EC must be PRO, controlled by *your friends*. But *seem* assigns no semantic role to its subject, which can again be an expletive, as in (29).

(29) a. it seems [your friends finished the meeting happy]
     b. there seems [*e* to be a mistake in your argument]

Accordingly, the EC in (28b) must be trace, with its antecedent *your friends* receiving its semantic role as an argument as if it were in that position. We know further that the adjective *happy* modifies the subject of its own clause, not that of a higher clause. Thus, in (30) *happy* modifies *meeting*, not *your friends*; the sentence means that your friends hoped that the atmosphere would be happy when the meeting ends.

(30) your friends hoped [the meeting would finish happy]

In (28), then, *happy* modifies PRO in (a) and trace in (b). Example (28a) thus means that your friends had a certain wish: that they would be happy as the meeting ends. But (28b) has roughly the meaning of (29a), with *happy* modifying *your friends*.

Other differences of meaning also appear, as in (31a) and (31b) (Burzio 1986).

(31) a. one translator each was expected t' to be assigned t to the
        visiting diplomats
     b. one translator each hoped PRO to be assigned t to the visiting
        diplomats

In (31a) neither *one translator each* nor its trace t' is in a position with independent argument status. Therefore, the argument phrase *one translator each* is interpreted as if it were in the position of the trace t, with the argument status of object of *assigned*; the meaning is that it was expected that one translator each would be assigned to the visiting diplomats (i.e., each diplomat would be assigned one translator). In (31b), in contrast, *one translator each* and PRO are independent arguments; it is PRO, not *one translator each*, that binds t and is interpreted as if it were in that position. The subject *one translator each* is thus left without an interpretation, very much as it is in the similar construction (32).

(32) one translator each hoped that he would be assigned to the visiting
     diplomats

Although the argument status of the antecedent of a trace is determined in the position of the trace, the antecedent may still have an independent semantic role in other respects. Compare the examples of (33).

(33) a. *it seems to each other [that your friends are happy]
     b. your friends seem to each other [*t* to be happy]
     c. it seems [that all your friends have not yet arrived]
     d. all your friends seem [to have not yet arrived]

In (33a) *your friends* cannot bind the reciprocal *each other*, but it can in (33b), thus functioning in its overt position, not that of its trace. In (33c) and (33d) the overt positions are relevant for determining scopal properties: thus, only (33c) can mean that it seems that not all your friends have arrived, with *not* taking scope over *all*. We see, then, that scopal properties and argument status are determined in different ways for antecedent-trace constructions. Such facts as these ought to fall out as consequences of the theory of ECs and semantic interpretation. See section 1.4.2.

PRO and trace also differ in their syntactic distribution. Thus, in (34) we see the properties of control, with the antecedent and PRO functioning as independent arguments; but the properties of trace, with only one argument, cannot be exhibited in the analogous structures, as (35) illustrates.

(34) a. John asked whether [PRO to leave]
     b. John expected that it would be fun [PRO to visit London]

(35) a. *John was asked whether [*t* to leave]
     b. *John was expected that it would be fun [*t* to visit London]

In fact, trace and PRO do not overlap in their distribution; the facts should, again, fall out of the theory of ECs.

We also allow a fourth type of EC, one that has only the categorial features $[\pm N, \pm V]$, projecting in the usual way. They serve only as targets for movement, to be filled in the course of derivation. Since these elements have no semantic role, they will not satisfy the condition FI at D-Structure (as we will sharpen this below), and we may tentatively assume that they and the structures projected from them are inserted in the course of derivation, in a manner permitted by the theory of phrase structure. See section 1.4.3 for further comment.

If these kinds of EC are indeed distinct, then we expect them to differ in feature composition (Chomsky 1982, Lasnik 1989). Optimally, the features should be just those that distinguish overt elements. As a first approximation, suppose that overt NPs fall into the categories *anaphor* (reflexives, reciprocals), *pronoun*, and *r-expression* (*John, the rational square root of 2*, and other expressions that are "quasi-referential" in the internalist sense of section 1.1). We might assume, then, that we have two two-valued features, [anaphor] and [pronominal], with potentially four categories.

(36) a. [+anaphor, −pronominal]
    b. [−anaphor, +pronominal]
    c. [−anaphor, −pronominal]
    d. [+anaphor, +pronominal]

An expression that is [+anaphor] functions referentially only in interaction with its antecedent; the reference of an expression that is [+pronominal] may be determined by an antecedent (but it does refer). Reflexives and reciprocals thus fall into category (36a) and pronouns into category (36b). The third category contains elements that refer but are not referentially dependent: r-expressions. The four ECs discussed above would have the typology of (37).

(37) a. Trace of NP is [+anaphor, −pronominal].
    b. *Pro* is [−anaphor, +pronominal].
    c. Trace of operator (variable) is [−anaphor, −pronominal].
    d. PRO is [+anaphor, +pronominal].

Thus, trace of NP is nonreferential, *pro* has the properties of pronouns, and variables are "referential" in that they are placeholders for r-expressions. Controlled PRO falls into category (37d), hence all PRO if apparent uncontrolled PRO actually has a hidden controller (see (18)). We would expect, then, that trace of NP, *pro*, and variable would share relevant properties of overt anaphors, pronouns, and r-expressions, respectively. Such elements as English *one*, French *on*, German *man* might be partial overt counterparts to PRO, sharing the modal interpretation of arbitrary PRO and its restriction to subject position (Chomsky 1986b).

These expectations are largely satisfied, when we abstract away from other factors. Thus, the structural relation of a trace to its antecedent is basically that of an anaphor to its antecedent; in both cases the antecedent must c-command the trace, and other structural conditions must be met, as illustrated in (38), with the examples kept slightly different to avoid factors that bar the unwanted structures.

(38) a. i.   John hurt himself
         ii. John was hurt *t*
     b. i.   *himself thought [John seems to be intelligent]
        ii. *t* thought [John seems that it is raining]
     c. i.   *John decided [himself left early]
        ii. *John was decided [*t* to leave early]

These properties sharply restrict the options for movement of NPs: raising not lowering, object-to-subject but not conversely, and so on (Fiengo 1977).

Similar but not quite identical conditions hold of PRO. Thus, the C-Command Condition is illustrated by (39).

(39) a.   John expects [PRO to hurt himself]
     b. *[John's mother] expects [PRO to hurt himself]
     c. *John expects [PRO to tell [Mary's brother] about herself]

In (39c) PRO is in a position to bind *herself* but the C-Command Condition requires that its antecedent be *John*, not *Mary*.

Similarly, variables share relevant properties of r-expressions, as expected.

(40) a. i.   They think [John will leave tomorrow]
         ii. I wonder who they think [*t* will leave tomorrow]
     b. i.   *it seems [John to be intelligent]
        ii. *I wonder who it seems [*t* to be intelligent]
     c. i.   he thinks [John is intelligent]
        ii. I wonder who [he thinks [*t* is intelligent]]
        iii. John thinks [he is intelligent]
        iv. I wonder who [*t* thinks [he is intelligent]]

In (40a) the name and the variable appear as Case-marked subjects of finite clauses, and the expressions are well formed, satisfying the Case-marking condition on r-expressions, to which we return directly. In (40b) the name and the variable appear as subjects of infinitives lacking Case, and the expressions are severely deviant. In (40ci) *he* is not referentially bound by *John* (we cannot take *he* to refer to John, as we may in (40ciii)); and in the parallel structure (40cii) *he* and the variable *t* are unrelated referentially (we cannot take *he* to be a variable bound by the operator *who*, which binds *t*, as we may in (40civ)). Again, many conditions on movement fall out as special cases.

These ECs also have other features of overt expressions, specifically, φ-features. Thus, the trace in (20a) has the features [masculine, singular]; hence the choice of overt anaphor.

An EC lacking the typological features of (37) or φ-features is uninterpretable, hence impermissible at LF by the principle FI. Such an element, identified only by its categorial features (NP, V, etc.), may appear in the course of a derivation, but only as a position to be filled or otherwise eliminated.

It is an open question whether movement always leaves a trace, and whether, when it does, there are independent reasons for this. For the purposes of exposition, we tentatively assume that movement of an element α always leaves a trace and, in the simplest case, forms a *chain* (α, *t*), where α, the *head* of the chain, is the moved element and *t* is its trace. The chain is an *X-chain* if its head has the property X; we return to relevant choices of X. The elements subject to interpretation at the interface level LF are chains (sometimes one-membered), each an abstract representation of the head of the chain.

The movement operation (henceforth Move α) is an invariant principle of computation, stating that a category can be moved to a target position. We take the moved category and the target to be primes (lexical items, EC targets for movement, or projections from these minimal elements), with two options: either the moved category α replaces the target β (substitution), or it adjoins to it (adjunction), as in (41) (order irrelevant, *t* the trace of α, β_1 and β_2 two occurrences of β).

(41)

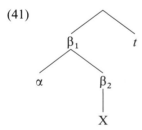

Any further constraints on movement will be derivative from other principles, including conditions on representations.

There are two natural interpretations of the elements formed by adjunction: we might assume that each occurrence of β in (41) is a category in its own right (Lasnik and Saito 1992) or that together they form a single category $[\beta_1, \beta_2]$ with the two occurrences of β as its *segments*

(May 1985, Chomsky 1986a). Empirical differences follow, as usual, as further theoretical structure is articulated.

The segment-category distinction requires a sharpening of the concepts of dominance and those derived from it (command, etc.). Let us say that the category $[\beta_1, \beta_2]$ in (41) *includes* X, *excludes* t, and *contains* α (and whatever is dominated by these elements). We restrict domination to inclusion. Thus, $[\beta_1, \beta_2]$ dominates only X. We say that a segment or category α *covers* β if it contains β, includes β, or $= \beta$. Defining the command relations as before, α c-commands t in (41), since it is not dominated (only contained) by β; but Y included in α does not. We carry over the properties of head and command to the postadjunction structure. Thus, if γ was the head of the preadjunction category β and c-commanded δ, then in the postadjunction structure $[\beta_1, \beta_2]$, γ remains the head and c-commands δ. Where no confusion arises, we will refer to the postadjunction category $[\beta_1, \beta_2]$ simply as β.

Substitution is constrained by a UG principle of *recoverability of deletion*, which requires that no information be lost by the operation; thus, α may substitute for β only if there is no feature conflict between them. The target of substitution will therefore always be an EC with the same categorial features as the moved category (the structure-preserving hypothesis of Emonds 1976). A similar property holds for adjunction, it appears (see section 1.3.3).

Move α permits multiple (*successive-cyclic*) movement, as in (42), derived from the D-Structures (43), with the targets of movement inserted.

(42) a. John seems [t' to have been expected [t to leave]]
     b. I wonder [who John thought [t' Bill expected [t to leave]]]

(43) a. *e* seems [*e* to have been expected [John to leave]]
     b. I wonder [*e* John thought [*e* Bill expected [*who* to leave]]]

In (42a) we have the chain (*John*, t', t) with the *links* (*John*, t') and (t', t); in (42b) the chain (*who*, t', t), also with two links. The *heads* of the chains are *John*, *who*, respectively.

We have so far assumed that the operation Move α forms a single link of a chain. Alternatively, we might assume that the operation is not Move α but rather Form Chain, an operation that forms the full chains of (42) from the D-Structures (43) in a single step. Within a richer theoretical context, the distinction may be more than merely notational (see chapter 3). We tentatively assume the more conventional Move α interpretation. The operation Move α satisfies narrow locality conditions.

Suppose that the position of the intermediate trace *t* in (42) is filled, as in (44), so that the chain must be formed with a single link, skipping the blocked position (occupied by *it*, *whether*, *whether*, respectively).

(44) a.   *John seems that [*it* was expected [*t* to leave]]
     b.   ?what did John remember [*whether* Bill fixed *t*]]
     c.   *how did John remember [*whether* Bill fixed the car *t*]]

The chains (*John*, *t*), (*what*, *t*), (*how*, *t*) violate the locality conditions, and the expressions are deviant, though in strikingly different ways, facts that demand explanation in terms of properties of UG. Note that in case (44c) it is the PF form with *this interpretation*—that is, with *how* construed in the position of the trace—that is deviant; if *how* is construed with *remember*, there is no deviance. The single PF form has two distinct SDs, one sharply deviant, the other not.

Recall that each element must have a uniform, language-independent interpretation at the interface level LF (the principle FI). Some elements are arguments assigned specific semantic roles (θ-roles), such as agent and goal (see section 1.2); overt anaphors, PRO, and r-expressions (including variables) are all arguments. Expletives (e.g., English *there*, Italian *ci*) are assigned no θ-roles. Some elements (e.g., English *it*, French *il*, Italian *pro*) may ambiguously serve as arguments or expletives. By FI, expletives must be somehow removed at LF (section 1.3.3).

An argument must receive a θ-role from a head (θ-marking). An argument may also receive a semantic role (whether to be considered a θ-role or not is a theory-internal question that we put aside) by predication by an XP (see Williams 1980), possibly an open sentence (e.g., the relative clause of (45), with a variable position *t*).

(45)   the job was offered to Mary, [who everyone agreed *t* had the best qualifications]

Other XPs (*adjuncts*, such as adverbial phrases) assign a semantic role to a predicate, a head, or another adjunct. As illustrated in (44b–c), movement of adjuncts and arguments has quite different properties (Huang 1982, Kayne 1984, Lasnik and Saito 1984, 1992, Aoun 1986, Rizzi 1990, Cinque 1990). A *θ-position* is a position to which a θ-role is assigned. The elements receiving interpretation at LF are chains. Hence, each argument chain (46) must contain at least one θ-position.

(46) $(\alpha_1, \ldots, \alpha_n)$

Furthermore, α_n, the position occupied by α_1 at D-Structure, must be a θ-position. The reason lies in the interpretation of D-Structure as a grammatical realization of lexical properties. Accordingly, θ-marking must take place at D-Structure: an element, moved or not, will have at LF exactly the θ-marking properties (assigning and receiving θ-roles) that it has at D-Structure. From the same consideration, it follows that nothing can move into a θ-position, gaining a θ-role that was not assigned to it at D-Structure. Thus, a chain can have no more than one θ-position, though any number of semantic roles may be assigned in this position. In (47), for example, *the wall* receives a semantic role from both *paint* and *red*.

(47) we painted the wall red

The theory of Case (section 1.4.3) requires that every argument have abstract Case (possibly realized overtly in one or another way, depending on specific morphological properties of the language). Hence, an argument chain (46) must have one and only one θ-position (namely, α_n) and at least one position in which Case is assigned (a *Case position*). Following Joseph Aoun, we might think of the function of Case as to make an argument chain *visible* for θ-marking. The Last Resort condition on movement (see section 1.1) requires that movement is permitted only to satisfy some condition, in particular, to satisfy visibility (hence, FI). Once an element has moved to a Case position, it can move no further, all relevant conditions now being satisfied. It follows, then, that every argument chain must be headed by a Case position and must terminate in a θ-position (the *Chain Condition*).

Note that these conclusions hold only for arguments other than PRO, an anomaly to which we return in section 1.4.3. On the status of chains headed by expletives with regard to the Chain Condition, see section 1.3.3.

We have so far considered chains that originate from an NP argument position of D-Structure. These fall into the two types illustrated in (42), repeated here.

(48) a. John seems [t' to have been expected [t to leave]]
       b. I wonder [who John thought [t' Bill expected [t to leave]]]

In (48a) we have, among others, the argument chain (*John*, t', t) and in (48b) the operator-variable chain (*who*, t', t).

Chains may also originate from non-NP positions. One case, already mentioned, is the movement of a lexical category (*head movement*), as in

(23), (24), repeated here, illustrating the raising of V to the inflectional positions.

(49) a. John was *t* expected to hurt himself

   b. I wonder *t* who John expected to hurt himself

Here we have the chains (*was*, *t*) and (*wonder*, *t*), the latter an LF chain for English.

Head movement is also involved in formation of compound words in many languages. Suppose we were to form a causative verb meaning 'cause-to-fall' from the underlying D-Structure (50) by adjoining *fall* to *cause*.

(50)

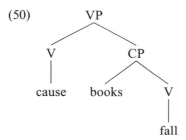

This operation yields the structure (51), *t* the trace of *fall*.

(51)

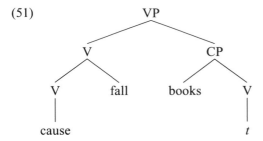

See Baker 1988. Here *cause* is the head of a two-segment verbal category, if we assume a segment theory of adjunction.

A second kind of chain originating from a non-NP position arises from movement of nonarguments (adjuncts, predicates), as in (52).

(52) a. [to whose benefit] would that proposal be *t*

   b. [how carefully] does he expect to fix the car *t*

   c. [visit England], he never will *t*

   d. [as successful as Mary], I don't think that John will ever be *t*

In each case the bracketed nonargument is the antecedent of the trace; the chains, then, are ([*to whose benefit*], *t*), ([*how carefully*], *t*), ([*visit England*], *t*), ([*as successful as Mary*], *t*), respectively. The questioned element in (52a) is really *who*; the rest is "carried along" because *who* cannot be extracted from the D-Structure position (53) ("pied-piping"; Ross 1967).

(53) that proposal would be [to who + POSSESSIVE benefit]

The natural interpretation reflects the D-Structure form; the meaning is 'for which person x, that proposal would be to x's benefit'. There is evidence that the LF form should indeed be construed in something like this manner (see section 1.3.3). Case (52b) might be interpreted similarly; thus, the interpretation would be 'for what degree x, he expects to fix the car [x carefully]'. We might, then, argue that these are not really cases of movement of adjunct phrases as such, but rather of the question elements *who, how*, with the adjunct phrase carried along. We might conclude further that operator movement is the only kind of movement to which adjunct phrases are subject, unlike arguments, which can form argument chains. The conclusion is supported by the observation that although adjuncts can typically appear in many sentence positions, they are not interpreted as if they had moved from some more deeply embedded position (Saito 1985). Thus, (54a) is not given the interpretation of (54b), as it would be if *carefully* in (54a) had been moved from the D-Structure position of *carefully* in (54b).

(54) a. carefully, John told me to fix the car
      b. John told me to [fix the car carefully]

This suggests that (52b) might also be regarded as a kind of pied-piping, with the moved element *how* carrying along the larger phrase *how carefully*. See chapters 3 and 4.

   Within the theory of empty categories and chains, we can return to the question of directionality of interlevel relations raised in section 1.1. As noted there, such questions are obscure at best, and become even more subtle under the assumptions of trace theory. Consider again the S-Structure representations (42) derived from the D-Structure representations (43) (repeated here).

(55) a. John seems [t' to have been expected [t to leave]]
      b. I wonder [who John thought [t' Bill expected [t to leave]]]

(56) a. *e* seems [*e* to have been expected [John to leave]]
     b. I wonder [*e* John thought [*e* Bill expected [*who* to leave]]]

We now ask whether (55a–b) are derived from (56a–b), respectively, by movement of *John*, *who*; or whether D-Structure is derived from S-Structure by algorithm (Sportiche 1983, Rizzi 1986b), so that D-Structure is, in effect, a derived property of S-Structure; or whether there is simply a nondirectional relation between the paired expressions. These are alternative expressions of the relation between S-Structure and the lexicon. All three approaches are "transformational" in the abstract sense that they consider a relation between a "displaced element" and the position in which such an element is standardly interpreted; and in the case of (55b), the position in which it would be overt at S-Structure in languages of the Chinese-Japanese variety (see section 1.1). Such displacement relations are a fundamental feature of human language, which must be captured somehow. Apparent differences among alternative formulations often dissolve, on inquiry, to notational questions about how this property is expressed; similar questions arise with regard to apparent differences between "multilevel" approaches and "unilevel" alternatives that code global properties of phrase markers in complex symbols (Chomsky 1951, Harman 1963, Gazdar 1981). In the present case the empirical distinguishability of the approaches turns on highly theory-internal considerations. We will continue to adopt the derivational approach of section 1.1. We assume that this is, at root, a question of truth and falsity, though a subtle one.

To see some of the problems that arise, consider the locality conditions on Move α. A general condition, illustrated in (44), is that the target of movement must be the closest possible position, with varying effects depending on the kind of movement involved. The condition is very strict for head movement, which cannot pass over the closest c-commanding head (the *Head Movement Constraint* (HMC), a special case of more general principles; see section 1.4.1). Thus, in (57) formation of (b) from the D-Structure (a), raising *will* to the clause-initial position, satisfies the HMC; but raising of *read* to this position, crossing the possible target position occupied by *will*, violates the HMC, yielding the sharply deviant interrogative expression (57c).

(57) a.   John will read the book
     b.   will John *t* read the book
     c.   *read John will *t* the book

But the locality relations expressed in the step-by-step computation might not be directly expressed at the output levels. That is, a derivation may satisfy the HMC in each step, but the output may appear to indicate that the condition is violated. Consider again the formation of a causative verb meaning 'cause-to-fall' by adjoining *fall* to *cause*, as in (51). Recall that a verb must also be raised to the inflection position. Hence, the newly formed category *cause-fall* must now raise to this position, forming the structure (58) (where TP is tense-headed phrase, t_f is the trace of *fall*, and t_c is the trace of *cause-fall*).

(58)

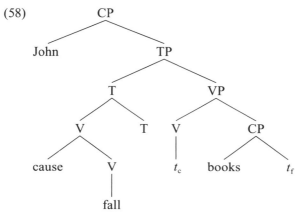

Here we have two chains: (*cause-fall*, t_c) and (*fall*, t_f). Each step of chain formation satisfies the strict locality condition. But the resulting chain headed by *fall* does not. In the S-Structure, the chain (*fall*, t_f) violates the HMC, because of the intervening head t_c, a possible target of movement that is "skipped" by the chain. The form should thus be as deviant as (57c), but it is well formed. The locality conditions are satisfied stepwise in the derivation, but are not satisfied by the output chain. Modifications required under nonderivational approaches are not entirely straightforward.

1.3.2 D-Structure
The computational system forms SDs that express the basic structural facts (syntactic, phonological, and semantic) of the language in the form of phrase markers with terminal strings drawn from the lexicon. We are assuming that such properties of natural language as "displaced elements" are expressed by multiple representational levels, each simple in form

and with simple operations such as Move α relating them. Each level captures certain systematic aspects of the full complexity. The relation of the computational system to the lexicon is expressed at the internal interface level of D-Structure. D-Structure is mapped to LF, the interface with conceptual and performance systems; at some point (S-Structure), perhaps varying somewhat from language to language, the derivation "branches" and an independent mapping (phonology) forms the PF representation that provides the interface with the sensorimotor systems. See (4).

The earliest attempts to develop generative grammar in the modern sense postulated a single level of syntactic representation, formed by rules of the form (59), where A is a single symbol and X, Y, Z are strings (X and Y possibly null), S is the designated initial symbol, and there is a set of designated terminal symbols that are then mapped by other rules to phonetic forms.

(59) XAY → XZY

The symbols were assumed to be *complex*, consisting of two kinds of elements: categorial and structural. Categorial elements were NP, V, and so on. Structural elements were features that coded global properties of phrase markers; for example, NP-VP agreement in *the men are here* is coded by the [+plural] feature assigned to S and "inherited" by NP and VP through application of the rule [S, +plural] → [NP, +plural] [VP, +plural] (Chomsky 1951). Subsequent work "factored" the complexity into two components, restricting the symbols to just their categorial part (phrase structure rules forming phrase markers) and adding transformational rules to express global properties of expressions (Chomsky 1975a, Lees 1963, Matthews 1964, Klima 1964). A later step restricted the recursive part of the generative procedure to rules of the form (59) and separated the lexicon from the computational system (Chomsky 1965). This provided a two-level system: phrase structure rules and lexical insertion form D-Structure and transformations form the derived phrase markers of *surface structure*, then subjected to phonetic interpretation. The *Standard Theory* assumed further that only D-Structures are subjected to semantic interpretation, a position elaborated in *Generative Semantics* (Lakoff 1971). The *Extended Standard Theory* (EST) proposed that surface structure determines crucial elements of semantic interpretation (Jackendoff 1972, Chomsky 1972). Later work led to the four-level conception of EST outlined earlier, and the P&P

approach, which dispenses entirely with rule systems for particular languages and particular constructions.

Separation of the lexicon from the computational system permits simplification of the rules (59) to context-free, with X, Y null. Thus, instead of (59), we have the context-free rules (60).

(60) a. $A \rightarrow Z$
      b. $B \rightarrow l$

Here A, B are nonterminal symbols, Z is a nonnull string of nonterminal symbols or grammatical formatives, and l is a position of lexical insertion. B is a nonbranching *lexical* category, and Z contains at most one lexical category. Z of (60a) is therefore as in either (61a) or (61b), where C_i is a nonlexical category, X and Y are strings of nonlexical categories, and L is a lexical category.

(61) a. $A \rightarrow C_1 \ldots C_n$
      b. $A \rightarrow XLY$

These moves exposed the crucial redundancy in phrase structure rules already discussed (sections 1.1, 1.2): the form of Z in (60a) depends on inherent properties of lexical items. Further redundancies are also immediately apparent. In (60b) the properties of the lexical category B are completely determined by the lexical element inserted in l. Considering the possible forms in (61), we observe further that in (61b) the properties of A are determined by L: thus, if L is N, A is NP; if L is V, A is VP; and so on. The rule is *endocentric*, with the *head* L of the construction *projecting* the dominating category A. Suppose we assume that the rules (61a) are also endocentric, taking A to be a projection of one of the C_is (an expression of ideas developed in structural linguistics in terms of discovery procedures of constituent analysis (Harris 1951)). We now have rules of the form (62).

(62) a. $X^n \rightarrow ZX^mW$
      b. $X^0 \rightarrow l$

Here n is typically $m + 1$ and X^i is some set of categorial features (see (14)); and X^0 is a lexical category. The element inserted in position l determines the features of X^i and, to a substantial extent, the choices of Z and W. At this point phrase structure rules are largely eliminated from particular languages; they are expressed as general properties of UG, within the framework of *X-bar theory*.

A further proposal restricts the rules (62a) to the forms (63).

(63) a. $X^n \to ZX^{n-1}$
   b. $X^m \to X^m Y$
   c. $X^1 \to X^0 W$

For n maximal, we use the conventional symbol XP for X^n; $n = 0$ is often dropped, where no confusion arises. To form a full phrase marker, each X^0 is replaced by a lexical element with the categorial features of X.

Suppose that $n = 2$ and $m = 1$ or 2 in (63), so that the possible rule forms are (64).

(64) a. $X^2 \to X^2 Y$
   b. $X^2 \to ZX^1$
   c. $X^1 \to X^1 Y$
   d. $X^1 \to X^0 W$

The nonterminal elements are X^1, X^2 (conventionally, X', X'', or $\overline{X}$, $\overline{\overline{X}}$), $X^2 = XP$. Assume further that Z, Y are single symbols. We call Z the *specifier* (Spec) of X^2, the elements of W the *complements* of X^0, and Y in (64a) an *adjunct* of X^2. The status of Y in (64c) is ambiguous, depending on further articulation of the theory; let us tentatively classify it as an adjunct. Note that the notions specifier, complement, and adjunct are functional (relational), not categorial; thus, there is no categorial symbol *Spec*, but rather a relation specifier-of, and so on.

This is essentially the system of Chomsky 1981a, and the basis for further concepts defined there. We continue with these assumptions, turning later to modifications required under alternatives.

Muysken (1982) proposes that the bar levels are determined by the feature system [projected, maximal]. Thus, $X^0 = [X, -\text{projected}, -\text{maximal}]$, $X^1 = [X, +\text{projected}, -\text{maximal}]$; $X^2 = [X, +\text{projected}, +\text{maximal}]$. Note that this approach permits a distinction between adjunction structures formed at D-Structure and by adjunction operations. See also Jackendoff 1977, Stowell 1981, Speas 1986, Fukui 1986, Baltin and Kroch 1989.

With the move to X-bar theory, the phrase structure system for a particular language is largely restricted to specification of the parameters that determine the ordering of head-complement, head-adjunct, and specifier-head. Choices above are typical for a *head-initial* language. The rules (62)–(64) themselves belong to UG (order aside), not to particular grammars. As discussed in sections 1.1 and 1.2, the elimination of phrase structure rules has always been a plausible goal for linguistic theory, because of their redundancy with ineliminable lexical properties. If X-bar theory can be sustained in its most general form, choice of items from the lexicon will determine the D-Structure phrase markers for a language with parameters fixed.

Items of the lexicon are of two general types: with or without substantive content. We restrict the term *lexical* to the former category; the latter are *functional*. Each item is a feature set. Lexical elements head NP, VP, AP, and PP, and their subcategories (adverbial phrases, etc.). At D-Structure and LF, each such XP must play its appropriate semantic role, satisfying FI, as discussed earlier. The heads of these categories have (1) categorial features; (2) grammatical features such as ϕ-features and others checked in the course of derivations, continuing to assume one of the interpretations of morphological structure discussed in section 1.1; (3) a phonological matrix, further articulated by the mapping to PF; (4) inherent semantic and syntactic features that determine *s(emantic)-selection* and *c(ategorial)-selection*, respectively. Thus, *persuade* has features determining that it has an NP and a propositional complement, with their specific θ-roles. As discussed in section 1.2, c-selection is at least in part determined by s-selection; if the determination is complete, we can restrict attention to s-selection. We may now assume that a complement appears at D-Structure only in a θ-position, θ-marked by its head. Since the computational rules can add no further complements, it follows that at every level, complements are θ-positions, in fact, θ-marked the same way at each level (the *Projection Principle*). The Projection Principle and the related conditions on θ-marking provide a particular interpretation for the general condition FI at D-Structure and LF.

Functional items also have feature structure, but do not enter into θ-marking. Their presence or absence is determined by principles of UG, with some parameterization. Each functional element has certain selectional properties: it will take certain kinds of complements, and may or may not take a specifier. The specifiers typically (though perhaps not always) are targets for movement, in the sense discussed earlier. Hence, they have no independent semantic role at all. As suggested in section 1.3.1, we may assume them to be inserted in the course of derivation, unless some general condition on D-Structure requires their presence.

We assume that a full clause is headed by a complementizer C, hence is a CP, satisfying X-bar theory. C may have a specifier and must have a complement, a propositional phrase that we assume to be headed by another functional category I (inflection), which has the obligatory complement VP. Hence, a clause will typically have the form (65) (Bresnan 1972, Fassi Fehri 1980, Stowell 1981, Chomsky 1986a).

(65) [$_{CP}$ Spec [$_{C'}$ C [$_{IP}$ Spec [$_{I'}$ I VP]]]]

Specifiers are typically optional; we assume this is true of [Spec, CP]. The *Extended Projection Principle* (EPP) states that [Spec, IP] is obligatory, perhaps as a morphological property of I or by virtue of the predicational character of VP (Williams 1980, Rothstein 1983). The specifier of IP is the *subject of* IP; the nominal complement of VP is the *object of* VP. We take these to be functional rather than categorial notions; for different views, see Bresnan 1982, Perlmutter 1983. By the Projection Principle, the object is a θ-position. The subject may or may not be; it may be filled by an expletive or an argument at D-Structure. [Spec, IP] is therefore a potential θ-position. An actual or potential θ-position is an *A-position*; others are $\overline{A}$-*positions* (A-bar positions). As matters stand at this point, complement and subject ([Spec, IP]) are A-positions, and [Spec, CP] and adjunct positions are $\overline{A}$-positions. A chain headed by an element in an A-position is an *A-chain*; a chain headed by an element in an $\overline{A}$-position is an $\overline{A}$-*chain*. The distinction between A- and $\overline{A}$-positions, and between A- and $\overline{A}$-chains, plays a central role in the theory of movement and other modules of grammar. We return to some problems concerning these notions.

Recall the two interpretations of the syntactic rule *R* that associates lexical items with their inflectional features: word formation by adjunction, or checking (see section 1.1). If we adopt the former approach, it follows that the operation *R* must apply in the D- to S-structure derivation, because it "feeds" the rules of the phonological (PF) component. The checking alternative does not strictly imply that morphological properties must be determined by S-Structure, but we will assume that this is nevertheless true. It follows that the inflected head of VP must have its features assigned or checked by I at S-Structure, either through lowering of I to V or through raising of V to I (see sections 1.3.1, 1.3.3). In the lowering case the S-Structure chain is deficient. There must therefore be an LF operation that raises the adjunction structure [V–I] to replace the trace of the lowered I, voiding the potential violation and providing an LF similar to what we find in a language with raising at S-Structure (on some empirical consequences, see chapter 2). At LF, then, V will always be at least as high as I in (65).

The [V–I] complex may also raise further to C. In *V-second* languages such as Germanic generally, V raises to C and some other phrase raises to [Spec, CP] in the main clause (Den Besten 1989, Vikner 1990). The same phenomenon appears more marginally in English questions and some other constructions. We assume these to have the form illustrated in (66), *who* being in [Spec, CP], *has* raising to C and leaving the trace *t*, t_w being the trace of *who*.

(66) [$_{CP}$ who has [$_{IP}$ John t [$_{VP}$ met t_w]]]

By virtue of the general properties of X-bar theory, the only options in the pre-IP position, introducing a clause, are YP–X^0 or X^0; X^0 may be null and commonly must be in embedded clauses if [Spec, CP] is nonnull (the *Doubly Filled Comp Filter*; see Keyser 1975). We assume that in general, overt movement of the question words is to the [Spec, CP] position, and the same is true of other constructions.

Structures of the form (65) may also appear in embedded position, as in the indirect question (67a) or the declarative clauses (67b).

(67) a. (I wonder) [$_{CP}$ who C [$_{IP}$ John has met t_w]]
     b. i.   (I believe) [$_{CP}$ that [$_{IP}$ John has met Bill]]
        ii. (I prefer) [$_{CP}$ for [$_{IP}$ John to meet Bill]]
        iii. (it was decided) [$_{CP}$ C [$_{IP}$ PRO to meet Bill]]

In (67a) and (67biii) the C head of CP is null; in (67bi) it is *that*; and in (67bii) it is *for*. The head of IP is [+tense] in (67a), (67bi); it is [−tense] in (67bii–iii). [Spec, CP] is unfilled in (67b), but it can be realized in other embedded constructions, for example, (67a), the relative clause (68a), or the complex adjectival clause (68b), where there is good reason to believe that Op is an empty operator in [Spec, CP]. C is empty in both cases and *t* is the trace of Op.

(68) a. the man [$_{CP}$ Op C [$_{IP}$ John met t]]
     b. Mary is too clever [$_{CP}$ Op C [$_{IP}$ PRO to catch t]]

The embedded clauses of (68) are predicates, open sentences with a variable position. In (68a) Op could be *who*, also semantically vacuous in this case. As a matter of (nontrivial) empirical fact, FI at LF includes the property of *strong binding*: every variable must have its range fixed by a restricted quantifier, or have its value determined by an antecedent. Since the operators in (68) are vacuous, the value of the variable must be fixed by the antecedents *man*, *Mary*, the choice being determined by locality conditions on predication.

These properties suffice to explain such examples as (3c), repeated here as (69a), the *if*-clause having the form (69b).

(69) a. if Mary is too clever to expect anyone to catch, then we don't expect anyone to catch Mary
  b. Mary is too clever [$_{CP}$ Op C [$_{IP}$ PRO to expect [anyone to catch *t*]]]

The embedded CP is a typical case of long (successive-cyclic) movement, analogous to (70) with *who* in place of Op.

(70) (I wonder) [who he expected [them to catch *t*]]

The variable must not be bound by *anyone* or PRO in (69b), just as it must not be bound by the elements *them* or *he* in (70); we return to the operative principle of binding theory in sections 1.3.3, 1.4.2. By the strong binding condition, the variable must therefore have *Mary* as its antecedent. Furthermore, PRO must be arbitrary, for if it is bound by *Mary* (as in *Mary is too clever* [*PRO to catch Bill*]), then the variable will be bound by PRO, violating the principle just illustrated. We therefore have the interpretation (69a). Note that the account assumes crucially that binding is based upon an equivalence relation; see section 1.4.2.

On the same assumptions, we can reduce the problem of explaining the deviance of (71) to that of the deviance of overt operator movement, as in the analogous example of (72).

(71) a. *the man [you met people that caught *t*]
  b. *Mary is too clever [to meet [people that caught *t*]]

(72) *who did John meet people that caught *t*

In all cases the locality conditions on movement are violated. See section 1.4.1.

We have assumed so far that embedded infinitivals are CPs, as in (67bii–iii) or (73).

(73) I wonder who he decided [$_{CP}$ C [PRO to catch *t*]]

In such cases the embedded subject must be PRO if the C head is empty and must be an overt NP if it is the Case-assigning element *for*, with dialectal variation. But there are other propositional phrases in which neither PRO nor the Case-assigning complementizer *for* can appear, for instance, (74).

(74) a. John believes [Bill to be intelligent]
     b. John considers [Bill intelligent]
     c. that gift made [Bill my friend for life]

Thus, in (74a) we cannot have *for Bill* or PRO instead of *Bill*. Similarly, in such constructions as these, the embedded subject can be trace, unlike the infinitival CPs. Compare:

(75) a. Bill is believed [t to be intelligent]
     b. *Bill was decided [$_{CP}$ [t to be intelligent]]

In general, the embedded subject of (74) behaves very much as if it were an object of the verb of the main clause (the *matrix* verb), though it is not a θ-marked complement of the verb, but rather the subject of an embedded clause. Constructions of the form (74a) are rather idiosyncratic to English; in similar languages (e.g., German), the corresponding expressions have the properties of (67bii–iii), (73), and so on.

The embedded clause of (74a) contains I, hence IP; there is no evidence for any further structure. To account for the differences from the embedded CP infinitivals, we must assume either that the embedded clause is just IP, or that there is an EC complementizer that assigns Case, like *for* (Kayne 1984). On the former assumption, which we will pursue here, the embedded subject is governed by the matrix verb, a relation that suffices to assign Case, license trace, and bar PRO, as in verb-object constructions. Note that the question whether (75a) is a raising construction (like *John seems* [t *to be intelligent*]) or a passive construction (like *his claims were believed t*) does not arise, these concepts having been discarded as taxonomic artifacts (section 1.1). The construction is formed by Move α as a "last resort," the Case-assigning property of the verb having been "absorbed" by the passive morphology. In the examples of (74b–c) there is no overt functional head. Assuming the phrase boundaries indicated, either there is an EC I, or the embedded phrases are projections of their predicates, so-called *small clauses* (Stowell 1978, 1981). Either way, *Bill* is the subject of the embedded clause, behaving as in (74a) and unlike the subject of an embedded CP.

We have so far considered two functional categories: I and C. A natural extension is that just as propositions are projections of functional categories, so are the traditional noun phrases. The functional head in this case is D, a position filled by a determiner, a possessive agreement element, or a pronoun (Postal 1966a, Brame 1981, 1982, Abney 1987).

The phrases *that picture of Bill* and *John's picture of Bill* would therefore have the forms (76).

(76) a. [$_{DP}$ that [$_{NP}$ picture of Bill]]

　　 b. [$_{DP}$ John Poss [$_{NP}$ picture of Bill]]

In (76a) [Spec, DP] is missing; in (76b) it is filled by the "subject" of the DP, *John*, to which the affix Poss is adjoined by a phonological operation. The D head is *that* in (76a) and Poss in (76b) (in some languages—for instance, Turkish—manifesting visible agreement with the subject; see Kornfilt 1985). Noun phrases in the informal sense are thus similar in internal structure to clauses (possibly even containing a "complementizer" position; Szabolcsi 1987). We might expect, then, to find N-raising to D, analogous to V-raising to I; see Longobardi 1994. There are numerous other consequences, which we cannot pursue here. We will use the informal notation Noun Phrase for DP or NP, unless confusion would arise.

We might ask whether these considerations generalize to other major categories, so that AP and VP are also complements of a functional element, even in V–VP or Modal–VP constructions. If so, a natural choice would be an element involved in Case assignment and agreement (call it *Agr*, a collection of φ-features). Such possibilities suggest a reconsideration of the functional element I, which has the strange property of being "double-headed" in the version of X-bar theory we are considering, assuming that T(ense) and Agr are independent heads. Following Pollock (1989), let us assume that T and Agr head separate maximal projections. Assuming that VP (and AP) is a complement of Agr, we now have the structure [Spec–T–Agr–VP] for the phrase we have called IP (now a term of convenience only), with T having AgrP as its complement, and VP, AP being complements of the Agr head of AgrP. Pollock argues on different grounds for the same structure: [Spec–T–Agr–VP]. In this structure the specifier of IP is not commanded (c- or m-commanded) by Agr, hence not governed by it. Hence, if (as we assume throughout) the operative relations among elements are based on such local relations, there would be no natural expression of subject-verb agreement. There is other evidence to suggest that the order should be Agr–T (Belletti 1990), where Agr is involved in subject agreement and nominative Case assignment. The proper reconciliation of these conflicting proposals may be that there are two Agr elements in IP, each a collection of φ-features, one involved in subject agreement and subject Case, the other in object agreement and object Case. Thus, the full structure will be (77), where

Agr_s and *Agr_O* are informal notations to distinguish the two functional roles of Agr, *Spec* indicates a functional role as before, and IP = AgrP.

(77)

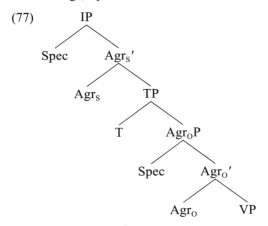

Here we omit a possible [Spec, TP]. Embedded in this structure there might also be a phrase headed by the functional element *Negation*, or perhaps more broadly, a category that includes an affirmation marker and others as well (Pollock 1989, Laka 1990). We might proceed to assume that Case and agreement generally are manifestations of the Spec-head relation (Koopman 1987, Mahajan 1990; also see section 1.4.3 and chapters 2, 3).

The status of [Spec, IP] is anomalous in several respects. One is that it may or may not be a θ-position, depending on lexical choices. Thus, in (78) the subject of *hurt* is a θ-position occupied by the trace of the argument *John*, taken to be the agent of *hurt*; but the subject of *seems* is a non-θ-position, which can also be occupied by the expletive *it*.

(78) a. John seems [*t* to have hurt himself]
     b. it seems [that John has hurt himself]

[Spec, IP] is also the only position in which θ-role is not assigned within the m-command domain of a lexical head.

Such idiosyncratic properties would be eliminated if we were to assume that a thematic subject originates from a position internal to VP, then raising to [Spec, IP]. Collapsing the inflectional nodes to I for convenience, the D-Structure underlying *John met Bill* would then be (79) (Kitagawa 1986, Kuroda 1988, Sportiche 1988, Koopman and Sportiche 1991).

(79)

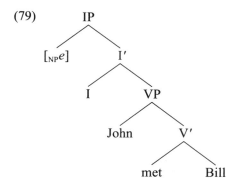

The subject and object are now θ-marked within the m-command domain of the verb *met*, within VP. On the present assumptions, *John* is [Spec, VP] and raises to [Spec, IP] to receive Case and produce a visible chain. By LF, *met* will have raised to I. If V raises to I at S-Structure and its subject raises to [Spec, IP] only at LF, we have a VSO language (at S-Structure). If the θ-role assigned to subject (the *external* θ-role, in the sense of Williams 1980) is in part compositionally determined (Marantz 1984), then these properties might be expressed internal to VP, as properties of the paired elements (subject, V').

The assumptions sketched out here provide a certain version of a "universal base hypothesis," a notion that has been explored from various points of view. If they are on the right track, typological variation should reduce to the ordering parameters and properties of functional elements. As discussed earlier, we expect that D-Structure and LF vary little in essential properties, D-Structure reflecting lexical properties through the mechanisms of X-bar theory and the parametric options for functional elements, and LF being the outcome of an invariant computational process that maps D-Structure to S-Structure and then to LF. A further proposal is that there is a uniform structural representation of θ-roles: thus, agent is typically associated with [Spec, VP], theme or patient with complement to V, and so on. This appears more plausible as evidence mounts questioning the existence of ergative languages at the level of θ-theory (Baker 1988, Johns 1987). See section 1.2.

We have so far kept to the assumption of Chomsky 1981a that all internal θ-roles (all θ-roles apart from the role of subject) are assigned to sisters of the head. This assumption has repeatedly been questioned and has largely been abandoned. To mention a few cases, Kayne (1984) proposes that all branching is binary (yielding "unambiguous paths"). If so, some internal θ-roles will be assigned to nonsisters. Kayne suggests, for example, that double-object verbs have the structure in (80), in which case *give* will θ-mark NPs properly contained within its complement.

(80) give [Mary books]

Similar ideas have been pursued in other studies as well. Belletti and Rizzi (1988) argue that the underlying structure of "psych-verb" constructions such as *the problem disturbed John* is (81), where the sister of *disturb* is assigned the θ-role theme (as usual), then raising to [Spec, IP], while the sister of V′ receives the θ-role experiencer (see also Pesetsky 1995, Bouchard 1991).

(81)

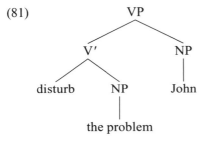

Larson proposes that double-object verbs such as *give* enter into D-Structures of the form (82) (Larson 1988, 1990; for an opposing view, see Jackendoff 1990a).

(82)

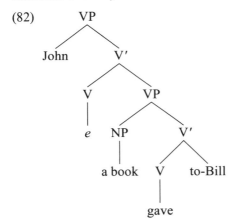

V raises to the empty main verb position of the higher *VP shell*, yielding *John gave a book to Bill*. Alternatively, operations similar to those yielding the passive construction could "absorb" the Case of *Bill*, forcing it to raise to the subjectlike position of *a book*, which in turn becomes an adjunct, yielding *John gave Bill a book*. In (82) the direct object *a book*, though θ-marked as theme by the verb, is not its sister. Larson also indicates that adverbs are the innermost complements of V. Thus, the structure underlying *John read the book carefully* would be (83).

(83)

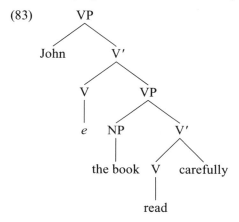

In this case the sister of the verb is an adverb that is not θ-marked at all, and the sole internal θ-role is assigned to a nonsister (*the book*).

With such modifications, the notion "θ-position" is still well defined, but "A-" and "Ā-position" are not. These notions are formally quite different in character. A particular occurrence of a category in a phrase marker is, or is not, a θ-position, depending on whether it is θ-marked in that phrase marker. The notion "A-position," however, depends upon "potential θ-marking," which is to say that it presupposes an equivalence relation among phrase markers: an A-position is one that is θ-marked in the equivalent position of some member of the equivalence class. This is not an entirely straightforward notion, and with modifications of the sort just outlined, it becomes unspecifiable in any way that will bear the considerable theoretical burden that has been laid on the A versus Ā distinction, which enters crucially into large areas of current work.

The intuitive content of the distinction to be captured is reasonably clear. θ-positions and specifiers of inflectional elements share a range of structural properties; other non-θ-marked positions ([Spec, CP], elements adjoined to XP, non-θ-marked positions governed by a head) share a different range of structural properties. These are the former

A- and $\overline{\text{A}}$-positions, respectively. There are various proposals as to how to capture this distinction in terms of natural classes, and how to extend and sharpen it (e.g., for [Spec, DP]).

One approach (see chapter 3) is based on the observation that certain functional elements are, in effect, features of a head, in that they must be adjoined to this head to check its inherent features (alternatively, to assign these inherent features to it). Tense and the Agr elements are features of V in this sense, but C is not. Given a lexical head L, we say that a position is *L-related* if it is the specifier or complement of a feature of L. The L-related positions are the former A-positions, with the exception of non-θ-marked elements such as *carefully* in (83). But this exception will not be problematic if independent considerations block movement of such elements to any L-related position (raising). If economy considerations permit raising only when it is required (i.e., only Last Resort movement), then the issue will not arise; see sections 1.1, 1.3.1.

Along these lines, one might reconstruct something like the A versus $\overline{\text{A}}$ distinction. The account now relies on properties of occurrences of a category in a phrase marker, without reference to equivalence classes of phrase markers. Other uses of these notions, as in binding theory, appear to fall into place without too much difficulty. We leave the matter with these informal indications of a direction to explore, merely noting here that certain concepts that serve as foundations for much current work were originally defined on the basis of assumptions that have been widely abandoned and therefore must be reconstructed in some different way. With these qualifications, we will continue to use the notions with their intuitive content, as is standard in current technical work.

1.3.3 Derived Syntactic Representations

We have adopted the EST assumption that the derivations from D-Structure to PF and LF have a common part: D-Structure is mapped to S-Structure by Affect α, and the derivation then branches into two independent paths, one forming PF, the other forming LF (the *PF component* and the *LF component*, respectively). These are the two external interface levels. Since our concern here is syntax in the narrow sense, we restrict ourselves to the computation from D-Structure to LF.

The part of this derivation that maps S-Structure to LF is sometimes trivial, but whenever structural properties relevant to meaning are not already expressed at S-Structure, this mapping is substantive. Following Chomsky (1977), May (1977), we assume that scope of operators is structurally represented at LF in terms of c-command. For interrogative operators, as will be discussed below, movement to an appropriate scope position takes place sometimes between D-Structure and S-Structure and sometimes between S-Structure and LF. Movement of quantifiers (May's "quantifier raising," QR) is generally an S-Structure to LF operation. The examples of "inversely linked" quantification discussed by May, as in (84), clearly indicate that S-Structure configuration does not suffice.

(84) everybody in some Italian city likes it.

Here *some Italian city* has wide scope, even though at S-Structure it is contained within the universally quantified NP. The correct interpretation is structurally represented in (85), with the entire subject NP having undergone QR, and the existential expression having raised still further.

(85) $[_{IP}[\text{some Italian city}]_i \ [_{IP}[\text{everybody in } t_i]_j \ [_{IP} \ t_j \text{ likes it}]]]$

See May 1977, 1985, for further motivation for QR.

Since it is an interface level, there are further requirements on LF. Given FI, every element of the LF representation of an expression must be subject to interpretation at the interface. As noted in section 1.1, this entails that there should be no true expletives in an LF representation. In such expressions as (86), then, the expletive element *there* must somehow be eliminated in the mapping from S-Structure to LF.

(86) there is a man in the room

One possibility that can be readily dismissed is that the expletive is simply deleted. The EPP demands that a clause have a subject at every syntactic level. Deletion of *there* would violate this requirement at LF. The expletive also appears to have φ-features that enter into agreement with the inflected verb. In (86) those features are [3 person, singular]; in (87) they are [3 person, plural].

(87) There are men in the room

A strong form of recoverability of deletion would presumably prevent the deletion of an element with φ-features. Given that *there* must be eliminated and cannot be deleted, the remaining possibility is that it is the target of a movement operation, with the *associate* of the expletive (*a man* in (86) and *men* in (87)) moving to the position of the expletive. Whether it is construed as substitution or adjunction, we may assume that this operation produces a new element combining the relevant features of the expletive and its associate: [*there, a man*] in (86), [*there, men*] in (87). Let us call this an *amalgamated expletive*, leaving open its exact form.

We now have an account for the apparently anomalous rightward agreement in these cases, that is, the fact that the inflected verb agrees with the NP that follows it: *is* and *are* cannot be interchanged in (86), (87). The LF movement analysis directly predicts this paradigm. *There* must be replaced, but the phrase amalgamating with it must be nondistinct from it in features. If the operation is substitution, this requirement will follow from the recoverability condition. If the operation is adjunction, it will follow from a feature-matching requirement. Alternatively, we might assume that *there* lacks ɸ-features and that the overt agreement is an S-Structure reflex of agreement at the LF level between the inflected verb and the amalgamated expletive, its agreement features provided by the associate. Note further that one of the central properties of these constructions—that there *is* an argument associated with the expletive—also follows, since FI demands that the expletive be replaced.

From an S-Structure corresponding to (86), then, we derive the LF representation (88), *t* the trace of *a man*.

(88) [there, a man] is *t* in the room

Since the expletive occupies an A-position at S-Structure ([Spec, IP]), the LF movement forming the amalgamated expletive is A-movement. It follows that the relation between the associate and its trace meets the narrow conditions on A-movement. We now have an account for the fact that in the overt expression, the expletive and its associate conform to the locality requirements of A-chains. This follows from the fact that at LF, they are amalgamated to form an A-chain. We therefore have expletive-associate relations of the kind illustrated, but not those of (89), analogous to (90).

(89) a. **there* seems that *a man* is in the room
     b. **there* seems that John saw *a man*
     c. **there* was thought that [pictures of *a man* were on sale]

(90) a. **a man* seems that *t* is in the room
     b. **a man* seems that John saw *t*
     c. **a man* was thought that [pictures of *t* were on sale]

Note that the locality condition on the expletive-associate pair is that of A-movement, not binding, which is permissible in the analogue to (90c).

(91) *we* thought that [pictures of *each other* were on sale]

We return in section 1.4.3 to some problematic features of this analysis.

In section 1.3.1 we alluded to an approach to Case in terms of visibility for θ-marking. Expletives appear to contradict the principle, since they are not θ-marked but appear only in positions to which Case is assignable—in fact, only in a subset of such positions (subjects), but this follows from the fact that D-Structure complements are present only if they have a semantic role (typically, a θ-role). Thus, we find (92a) with nominative *there* and (92b) with accusative *there*, but (92c) is impossible.

(92) a. I believe [there is a man here]
     b. I believe [there to be a man here]
     c. *I tried [there to be a man here]

But now these facts fall neatly under the visibility approach. At LF we will have (93), where *t* is the trace of *a man* and EA is the amalgamated expletive.

(93) a. I believe [[$_{EA}$ *there, a man*] is *t* here]
     b. I believe [[$_{EA}$ *there, a man*] to be *t* here]
     c. *I tried [[$_{EA}$ *there, a man*] to be *t* here]

When an expletive is in a Caseless position at S-Structure, its associated argument will necessarily be in that position at LF and will, as a consequence, be invisible for θ-marking.

The analysis just sketched suggests that Case is checked at LF even though manifest at S-Structure; that is, it suggests that conditions requiring checking or assignment of Case are LF conditions, not S-Structure conditions, despite appearances. The same conclusion is suggested by the general approach to Case in terms of visibility, which links Case assignment to θ-theory. As discussed earlier, there is a preference on general conceptual grounds for interface conditions rather than S-Structure conditions. The various considerations so far adduced point in the same direction, but serious problems arise in trying to pursue this course. We return to the topic in section 1.4.3.

Turning to the S-Structure representation, with parameters fixed this is determined (presumably uniquely) by the choice of D-Structure and LF representations. S-Structure is unlike the three basic levels (D-Structure, PF, LF) in that it satisfies no constraints external to the computational system. It would therefore be reasonable to expect that conditions involving the interface (in particular, conditions bearing on the semantic

interpretation of SDs) should be restricted to the interface levels themselves, not applying at S-Structure. Nevertheless, there may be conditions of UG that must be satisfied at the S-Structure level.

There is some cross-linguistic variation in the character of S-Structure;
in particular, functional elements vary in the ways they are articulated at
S-Structure and hence are realized overtly. Languages may also differ, as
noted, with regard to the placement of S-Structure in the derivation of
LF from D-Structure, that is, the point of branching to PF. One well-
studied case concerns the application of Move α that determines the
scope of a question phrase (commonly called the "*wh*-phrase," by historical accident), moving it to the periphery of the proposition.

In English-type languages the effects of the movement operation are
visible, yielding the S-Structure form (94), where t is the trace of *what*.

(94) a. what do you want [John to give t to Bill]
     b. what do you want [John to give t to whom]

In a *multiple* question such as (94b), only one of the question phrases
moves by S-Structure.

In the counterpart to (94a) in a Chinese-type language, the analogue
to *what* is "in situ" at S-Structure, occupying the position of the trace
in (94). We assume, following Huang 1982 and much subsequent work,
that the phrase is moved to clause-peripheral position at LF, yielding an
LF form resembling (94). More generally, in both types of language all
question phrases will have moved to scopal position under this operation
in the course of the derivation, within the LF component if not before
(Higginbotham and May 1981, Aoun, Hornstein, and Sportiche 1981).

The D-Structure forms are therefore alike in relevant respects in En-
glish- and Chinese-type languages, as are the LF forms, the standard
expectation (see section 1.1). But the S-Structure forms differ, depending
on whether the operation that places the question phrase in the position
that determines scope applies before or after the branching to the PF
component at S Structure. One type of language (English, French, etc.)
employs *overt movement* of a question phrase in the course of derivation
of S-Structure from D-Structure, feeding the phonological component;
another type (Chinese, Japanese, etc.) leaves all question phrases in situ
at S-Structure. Both types of language employ *covert movement* within
the LF component for any in-situ question phrase. A third type of
language (e.g., Polish) has overt movement of all question phrases.

D-Structure and LF representations are again similar to the other two language types, but the S-Structures differ (Lasnik and Saito 1984).

Given a narrow theory of parametric variation of the sort discussed, these three language types should differ in properties of functional features. Cheng (1991) argues that mood (interrogative, declarative, etc.) must be indicated at S-Structure in the pre-IP position, hence by choice of either C or [Spec, CP]; the head of CP and its specifier thus serve as "force indicators" in something like the Fregean sense. If the lexicon contains an element Q (marking *yes-no* questions), then this element will suffice to identify an expression as an interrogative whether or not it contains an in-situ question phrase. There is no need, then, for the question phrase to raise to [Spec, CP] at S-Structure. Lacking the element Q, a language must employ overt movement of a question phrase to [Spec, CP] to be identified as an interrogative at S-Structure.

Suppose further that economy principles favor operations that do not feed the PF component over others that do; hence, if operations need not be overt to satisfy some condition, they will be assigned to the LF component, applying as "late" in the derivation as possible, at the point where they are forced by LF conditions (in the case under discussion, conditions of scope). These assumptions lead us to expect two basic categories of language in the simplest case: (1) languages with a Q element and the question phrase in situ (Chinese, Japanese); and (2) languages lacking a Q element and with a single question word in [Spec, CP] (English, German). At LF all question phrases will have moved, so that the quasi quantifier can be interpreted with its scope determined and a bound variable heading an argument chain. Other typological differences should then be reducible to internal morphology of the question phrase —for instance, languages of the Polish-Hungarian type with multiple fronting of question phrases at S-Structure (though perhaps not to [Spec, CP]; see Cheng 1991). On assumptions such as these, there are conditions that must be satisfied by S-Structure representations.

Overt and covert movement might have different properties. Huang (1982) proposed that the bounding conditions on overt movement are relaxed in the LF component so that we have such pairs as (95a) in English and (95b) in Chinese.

(95) a. *who do you like [books that criticize *t*]
     b. ni   xihuan [piping shei de shu]
         you like   [criticize who REL book]

Both expressions have the interpretation 'for which person x, you like books that criticize x', but only (95b) is well formed. The English example (95a) violates a locality condition on movement (*Subjacency*); its Chinese counterpart is free from this constraint (for varying approaches, see, among others, Huang 1982, Lasnik and Saito 1984, Nishigauchi 1986, Fiengo et al. 1988, Watanabe 1991).

A similar phenomenon is found in multiple questions in English-type languages. Thus, English (96a) is well formed with the interpretation (96b) expressed in the LF form (96c).

(96) a. who [t likes books that criticize whom]
     b. for which persons y, x, [x likes books that criticize y]
     c. [whom$_j$, who$_i$] [t_i likes books that criticize t_j]

We have assumed that overt movement, as in (94) or (96a), places the question phrase in the position [Spec, CP]. Possibly covert movement, not required for mood specification, may adjoin the question phrase to IP, treating it like a quantifier phrase assigned scope by QR. Typically, such question phrases as *who, whom* share semantic and distributional properties of quantifier phrases, and might be composed of an indefinite quantifier, a *wh*-feature, and the restriction on the quantifier (Chomsky 1964, Kuroda 1965, Nishigauchi 1986, Kim 1990, Watanabe 1991). Accordingly, *who* would be composed of [some x, *wh*-, x a person]; and so on. It would not then be surprising if such question phrases were to share properties of the indefinite quantifier, adjoining to IP in the LF component by QR, though it remains to explain why they move so freely, unlike QR, which is typically clause-bound.

In English-type languages, relative clauses are formed in much the same manner as interrogatives: an operator phrase, which may be either an EC operator Op or morphologically identical to a question phrase, is moved to [Spec, CP], leaving a trace that functions as a variable, as in (97).

(97) a. the people [who John expected to meet t]
     b. the people [Op (that) John expected to meet t]

In either case, the relative clause is an open sentence functioning as a predicate (see (68)). In these constructions, movement is in the overt (pre-S-Structure) syntax, as shown in (97a), and satisfies the bounding conditions on overt movement, as illustrated in (98).

(98) a. *the man [who you like books that criticize *t*]
    b. *the man [Op (that) you like books that criticize *t*]

While Chinese and Japanese have question words in situ, relative clauses show the properties of overt movement (Huang 1982, Watanabe 1991, Ishii 1991). These observations suggest that relative clauses require overt movement. The reason might be that predication must be established at S-Structure (Williams 1980). If so, we have another example of an S-Structure condition. It would remain to extend the analysis to languages that form relatives with in-situ pronouns (resumptive pronouns) and full NP heads in the position of the variable above (Sells 1984, Demirdache 1991).

These considerations extend to other constructions with EC operators, such as the complex adjectivals discussed in section 1.3.2 ((68)–(69)), with the locality properties of overt movement (repeated here).

(99) a. Mary is too clever [$_{CP}$ Op C [$_{IP}$ PRO to expect [anyone to catch *t*]]]
    b. *Mary is too clever [$_{CP}$ Op C [$_{IP}$ PRO to meet [anyone who caught *t*]]]

Given the locality properties, the open sentences functioning as predicates must have been formed by overt movement, pre-S-Structure.

Some semantic properties of linguistic expressions appear to be determined by S-Structure configurations, independently of operations of the LF component. Let P be such a property. Then two accounts are possible.

(100) a. P holds at S-Structure.
    b. P holds at LF under *reconstruction*, that is, with the moved phrase treated "as if" it were in the position of its trace.

If the former is correct, then the property P involves a condition on S-Structure. There are various ways of construing the notion of reconstruction.

A good deal of insight into these questions derives from the principle of binding theory—call it *Command*—stipulating that a pronoun cannot c-command its antecedent (see sections 1.3.2, 1.4.2). We can formulate this as a requirement that an r-expression α must be *A-free*, that is, not c-commanded by a pronoun in an A-position linked to α in the binding-theoretic sense. Thus, in (101a) and (101b) *John* is A-free; the pronoun (*him, his*) does not c-command *John* and can take *John* as its antecedent.

But in (101c) *he* c-commands *John* and must be assigned reference in some other way.

(101) a. John thought Mary took a picture of him
       b. [his mother] thought Mary took a picture of John
       c. he thought Mary took a picture of John

The principle Command applies to r-expressions generally, hence to variables as well as *John*, as we see in (102), analogous to (101), with the trace of *who* in the position of *John* in (101).

(102) a. the man who [*t* thought Mary took a picture of him]
       b. the man who [[his mother] thought Mary took a picture of *t*]
       c. the man who [he thought Mary took a picture of *t*]

In (102a) and (102b) the pronoun does not c-command *t*. Even if the pronoun and variable are referentially linked, the variable is A-free, though $\overline{\text{A}}$-bound by its operator. The variable and the pronoun can now be construed as variables bound ($\overline{\text{A}}$-bound) by *who*. The interpretations are 'the man x such that x thought Mary took a picture of x', 'the man x such that x's mother thought Mary took a picture of x', respectively; the deviance of (102b), if any, is slight (Chomsky 1982, Higginbotham 1983, Lasnik and Stowell 1991).

But in (102c) *he* c-commands *t* and therefore cannot be linked to this variable or it will not be A-free; (102c) therefore cannot have the interpretation 'the man x such that x thought Mary took a picture of x'. There is nothing "wrong" with this interpretation; in fact, it is the interpretation of (102a). But it cannot be assigned to (102c), by virtue of Command (the property of *strong crossover*; Postal 1971, Wasow 1972, Lasnik 1976).

The principle Command also enters into the explanation of the meaning of the complex adjectivals of (99), as discussed earlier (see (68)–(69)).

We now ask at what level Command applies. Consider the examples (103).

(103) a. you said he liked [the pictures that John took]
       b. [how many pictures that John took] did you say he liked *t*
       c. who [*t* said he liked [how many pictures that John took]]

In (103a) *he* c-commands *John* and cannot take *John* as antecedent; in (103b) there is no c-command relation and *John* can be the antecedent of *he*. In the multiple-question-phrase construction (103c) *John* in fact cannot be the antecedent of *he*. It must be, then, that *he* c-commands *John* at the level of representation at which Command applies; the binding properties of (103c) are those of (103a), not (103b).

Returning to the two options of (100), we seem to be led here to adopt the first: that Command applies at S-Structure, before the bracketed question phrase is moved to preclausal position at LF, at which point (103c) would be formally similar to (103b), not (103a). Alternatively, we could assume, in the face of examples such as these, that the second option, reconstruction, holds for LF raising but not overt movement. More simply, we could dispense with both options, rejecting the tacit assumption that LF movement formed (104) from (103c), *t'* the trace of the LF-moved phrase.

(104) [[how many pictures that John took] who] [*t* said he liked *t'*]

Recalling that LF movement does not meet the strict locality conditions of S-Structure movement, we might reject the assumption that the entire NP is pied-piped when *how many* is raised to the scopal position, assuming rather that *how many* is extracted from the NP, yielding an LF form along the lines of (105), *t'* the trace of *how many*.

(105) [[how many] who] [*t* said he liked [*t'* pictures that John took]]

The answer, then, could be the pair (*12, Bill*), meaning that Bill said he liked 12 pictures that John took. But in the LF form (105), *he* c-commands *John* so that Command applies as in (103a). Pursuing such lines as these, we would not be led to adopt the assumption that Command applies at S-Structure, leaving us with the preferable option that conditions involving interpretation apply only at the interface levels. A further consequence would be that (103b–c) have somewhat different forms at LF; the empirical effect is unclear (Hornstein and Weinberg 1990).

Other constructions illustrate the process of reconstruction and are thus consistent with the restriction of the conditions on interpretation to the LF level. Consider (106).

(106) a. they said he admires John's father
      b. who [*t* said he admires John's father]
      c. (guess) whose father [they said he admires *t*]

In (106a) and (106b) *he* c-commands *John* and cannot take *John* as its antecedent, given Command. In (106b) *he* does not c-command *t*, so both can be taken as variables bound by *who*, yielding the interpretation 'for which person x, x said x admires John's father'. In (106c) *he* does not c-command *who*, but it cannot be taken as a variable bound by *who*, even though this interpretation would leave t A-free. The complement of *guess* is interpreted as (107) with *he* unbound, analogous to (106a).

(107) for which person x [they said he admires x's father]

Thus, we have reconstruction: treatment of [*whose father*] as if the phrase were in the position of its trace t in (106c) (Chomsky 1977, Freidin and Lasnik 1981).

Questions proliferate quickly with further inquiry. Consider, for example, such constructions as (108), formed by successive-cyclic movement of the question phrase from the position of t, to the position of t', to [Spec, CP] of the matrix clause.

(108) a. [which picture of himself] did *John* say [t' that *Bill* liked t best]
       b. [which pictures of each other] did *they* say [t' that *we* liked best]

Barss (1986) observes that the anaphor can take either of the italicized NPs as its antecedent. But an anaphor can only be bound by the closest c-commanding subject, as we see in the corresponding expressions (109), without *wh*-movement.

(109) a. John said [that Bill liked [that picture of himself] best]
       b. they said [that we liked [those pictures of each other] best]

Here the antecedents must be *Bill*, *we*. In (108) the same binding condition requires that each of the traces be "visible," the question phrase being interpreted for binding as if it were in one or the other of these positions (*chain binding*).

Another problematic example is (110a), with the interpretation (110b) and, on our current assumptions, the LF representation (110c) (Higginbotham 1980, 1983).

(110) a. guess which picture of which boy [they said he admires t]
       b. for which boy x, which picture y of x, [they said he admires y]
       c. [[which boy]$_i$ [which picture of t_i]]$_j$ [they said he admires t_j]

Reconstruction in the manner of (106c) and (107) does not yield a structure barred by Command. Nevertheless, *he* cannot be construed as an occurrence of the bound variable x.

The formal property entering into reconstruction here seems to be that the pair (r-expression α, pronoun β) are referentially disconnected at LF if there is a γ such that γ contains α and β c-commands γ or its trace. But that principle, applying at S-Structure, yields incorrect results for (103), barring binding of the pronoun in (103b). The discrepancy suggests that the problem with (110) lies elsewhere.

The problems are more general. Consider (111).

(111) a. the claim that John was asleep, he won't discuss t
      b. the claim that John made, he won't discuss t

Case (111a) is analogous to (110); case (111b) to (103b). On our current assumptions, the pronoun must not take *John* as antecedent in (111a) or (111b); the conclusion is correct for (111a) but not for (111b). Still further complications arise when we consider differences between these examples of A̅-movement and "scrambling" constructions in which the normal subject-object order is inverted.

We leave the topic in this unsettled state. For further discussion of these and related matters, from various points of view, see Lakoff 1968, Reinhart 1976, 1983, Van Riemsdijk and Williams 1981, Higginbotham 1980, 1983, Langendoen and Battistella 1982, Barss 1986, Freidin 1986, Lebeaux 1988, Saito 1989, and chapter 3.

Consideration of LF A̅-movement also suggests that there is an S-Structure condition licensing *parasitic gap* (PG) constructions such as (112a), interpreted as (112b).

(112) a. which book did you file t [without my reading e first]
      b. for which x, x a book, you filed x without my reading x first

Licensing of PGs by A̅-chains is quite general, but those formed by LF movement do not license PGs, as illustrated in (113), with the S-Structure (113a) and the LF form (113b).

(113) a. *who [t filed which book [without my reading e]]
      b. *[[which book]$_j$ who$_i$] [t_i filed t_j [without my reading e]]

The interpretation cannot be 'for which book x, who filed x without my reading x'. PG constructions, then, provide some evidence for the existence of S-Structure conditions.

The condition that licenses PGs must also account for the fact that these constructions are licensed by A̅-chains but not A-chains. Thus, the A-chain (*the book*, t) of (114) does not license the PG e, unlike the A̅-chain (*which book*, t) of (112a), with the same t-e relation.

(114) *the book was filed t [without my reading e first]

For further discussion, see Taraldsen 1981, Engdahl 1983, 1985, Chomsky 1982, 1986a, Kayne 1984, Longobardi 1985, Browning 1987, Cinque 1990.

Note that even the acceptable PGs are somewhat awkward; as in earlier cases discussed, we are interested in the relative deviance of various constructions, which is quite clear and demands explanation. The general literature on PGs regularly uses for illustration such pairs as (115), where the first is completely grammatical and the second sharply deviant, but these cases do not suffice to show that $\overline{\text{A}}$-chains license PGs while A-chains do not, because (115b) is ruled out for independent reasons of control theory, as illustrated in (116) (Lasnik and Uriagereka 1988).

(115) a. the book that you filed [without PRO reading e]
       b. *the book that was filed [without PRO reading e]

(116) a. the book that you filed [without PRO thinking]
       b. *the book that was filed [without PRO thinking]

The question of S-Structure conditions also arises in connection with elements lexically identified as affixes (e.g., pronominal clitics, verbal inflections, Case features). Since these properties are commonly overt at PF, they must be manifested at S-Structure (Lasnik 1981; we omit here the possibility that rules of the PF component might be rich enough to handle the phenomenon). As indicated earlier, the question becomes rather subtle if we assume the checking interpretation of inflectional features. Suppose again that English *walked* is inserted into D-Structure with the properties [walk], [past], the latter being checked and licensed by a syntactic rule R that joins [past] and *walked*. Suppose further that such functional elements as [tense] lack phonological matrices and are thus invisible at PF. We need not then assume that R is a lowering rule adjoining [past] to *walked*, to be reversed at LF; an alternative possibility is that the D- and S-Structures are alike, with R raising the verb to the inflectional position at LF, mirroring the process that is overt with auxiliaries and in French-type languages (for theory-internal arguments bearing on the matter, see chapters 2 and 3). The same question arises with regard to Case marking. Even if it is overt, the conceptual possibility remains that elements enter the computational system with their Case features already indicated, these being checked only at the LF level. Any apparent S-Structure requirement for Case would have to be satisfied in some other way. See section 1.4.3 and chapter 3.

Other theory-internal considerations suggest that empty categories must be licensed at S-Structure, in particular, traces in argument chains (Lasnik and Saito 1984, 1992; see section 1.4.1). If the relation of predication holding between an XP and its (syntactic) subject must satisfy S-Structure conditions, as suggested earlier, it is also natural (though not necessary) to suppose that licensing of an EC subject of predication should also take place at this level. Thus, according to Rizzi's theory, the null subject parameter reduces to properties of the system of the verbal inflection: in Italian, "strong" agreement (Agr) licenses *pro* subject; in French or English, the "weaker" Agr does not. We might expect, then, that this condition must be satisfied by the S-Structure configuration.

The plausibility of this assumption is enhanced by consideration of properties of expletive *pro*. Consider the D-Structures (117).

(117) a. *e* was stolen a book
      b. *e* seems [*e'* to be a book missing]

In a null subject language, the expressions can surface in this form, with *e* being expletive *pro* and *e'* its trace; here *pro* is licensed by strong Agr. But in a non–null subject language, *e* must be replaced by S-Structure, either by an overt expletive or by raising of *a book* to fill this position, as in (118).

(118) a. i. ?there was stolen a book
         ii. a book was stolen *t*
      b. i. there seems [*t* to be a book missing]
         ii. a book seems [*t* to be *t'* missing]

Some S-Structure property, it appears, must ensure that the options of (118) have been taken by the S-Structure level, not in the LF component. The problem becomes more severe if we adopt the strong version of FI that requires that expletives be replaced at LF (sections 1.3.1, 1.3.3). Then the S-Structure forms of (117) will appear at LF essentially as the (ii) forms of (118). It would follow, then, that the relevant distinctions must be established at S-Structure: *pro* is licensed at S-Structure, permitting (117) in Italian but not English. For alternative analyses, see chapters 3, 4.

It has also been proposed that some of the conditions that have been assumed to apply at LF actually apply within derivations from S-Structure to PF (Jaeggli 1980, Aoun et al. 1987). It cannot be that the conditions apply at the level of PF representation itself, because at the interface level PF we have only phonetic features with no further relevant structure. The assumption would be, then, that these conditions apply either at S-Structure or at some level intermediate between S-Structure and PF.

We have assumed so far that X-bar theory applies at D-Structure, its properties being "carried over" to S-Structure and LF by the computational processes. Suppose that X-bar theory applies at S-Structure as well. Van Riemsdijk (1989) argues that on this assumption, movement need not be restricted to minimal and maximal phrases (X^0 and XP), as so far tacitly assumed. Movement of X' ($=X^1$) could be allowed, to be followed by a process of "regeneration" that forms a proper X-bar structure at the S-Structure level in a minimal way. On this analysis, (119) would be derived by movement of the N' category *Lösung*, followed by generation of *eine* to satisfy X-bar theory at S-Structure, *eine* being a "spelling out" of the ϕ-features of *Lösung*.

(119) [eine Lösung] hat er [eine bessere   *t*] als   ich
        a   solution has he a   better (one)   than I

If X-bar theory applies at S-Structure, Emonds's structure-preserving hypothesis for substitution (section 1.3.1) follows in essentials, since conflict of categorial features will violate X-bar-theoretic principles. A similar conclusion will also hold for adjunction. Suppose, for example, that an X^0 element is adjoined to the YP Z, forming (120).

(120) $[_{YP} X^0 YP]]$

This structure violates X-bar theory, which requires that X^0 head an X' structure. Adjunction of XP to YP, however, would yield a structure consistent with X-bar theory. Adjunction of X^0 to Y^0 yields a two-segment category $[Y^0, Y^0]$, with an internal structure "invisible" to X-bar theory. Pursuing this line of thinking, it may be possible to derive a version of the structure-preserving hypothesis for adjunction: essentially, the condition that a category can be adjoined only to a category of the same bar level.

1.4 Modules of Language

1.4.1 Government Theory
We have referred several times to the notion of *government*, a more "local" variety of command (section 1.3.1). We assume tentatively that

the relevant notion of command is c-command. The concept of government has entered extensively into the study of the various modules of grammar. Hence, slight modifications in formulation have wide-ranging empirical consequences (see, among others, Aoun and Sportiche 1981, Chomsky 1981a, 1986a, Kayne 1984, Lasnik and Saito 1984, 1992, Rizzi 1990).

We say that α governs β if α c-commands β and there is no category γ that "protects" β from government by α. γ protects β in this sense if it is c-commanded by α and either (121a) or (121b) holds.

(121) a. γ is a *barrier* dominating β.

   b. γ *intervenes* between α and β.

Government is *canonical* if the linear order of (α, β) accords with the value of the head parameter (Kayne 1984). We speak of "X-government" when the governor has the property X. There are two main categories of government to be considered: *antecedent government* of α by an antecedent of α, and *head government* of α by a head. We refer to these categories as *proper government*.

To make the concept of locality precise, we have to spell out the notions "barrier" and "intervene" in (121). Consider the two in turn.

We take a barrier to be an XP that is not a complement, putting aside now the ambiguous status of noncomplements to V under the various ramifications of Kayne's unambiguous path theory (section 1.3.2). Thus, in (122) the bracketed expressions are all XPs, but only those subscripted *B* are barriers for the elements they contain.

(122) a.   I wonder which book [John told the students [that [they
           should read *t*]]]

   b.   ??I wonder which book [John met [someone [$_B$ who read *t*]]]

   c.   *I wonder how [John met [someone [$_B$ who [fixed the car *t*]]]]

   d.   ??I wonder which book [John left New York [$_B$ before
        he read *t*]]

   e.   *I wonder how [John left New York [$_B$ before he fixed
        the car *t*]]

In each case the trace indicates the position of extraction, under the intended interpretation: thus, (122e) asks how John fixed the car, not how he left New York. If we extract from within a barrier, the trace left behind will not be antecedent-governed; otherwise, it will be. When extraction crosses a barrier, the expression is deviant, indicating that antecedent government is a condition on properly formed chains. In (122a) no barriers are crossed and the sentence is fully grammatical. In the other cases a barrier is crossed and the sentences are deviant. The violations are more severe in cases (122c) and (122e), illustrating a characteristic difference between argument and adjunct extraction.

It appears that not only a complement but also its specifier is exempt from barrierhood. Belletti and Rizzi (1981) observe that the process of *ne*-cliticization in Italian extracts *ne* from the object of the verb but not from its subject. The object, the complement of the verb, is not a barrier to government; the clitic *ne* thus governs the trace left by *ne*-extraction from the object, as required. But the trace of *ne*-extraction from the subject will not be antecedent-governed: the subject is not a complement, hence is a barrier, whether government is based on c-command or m-command. Hence, we have (123a) but not (123b).

(123) a. *pro* ne-ho   visto [molti *t*]
          I   of.them-have seen   many
          'I have seen many of them'
      b. *[molti *t*] ne-sono   intelligenti]
          many   of.them-are intelligent

But now consider (124b), derived from the D-Structure (124a).

(124) a. *pro* ritengo [$_\alpha$[molti ne]   intelligenti]
          I   believe   many of.them intelligent
      b. ne-ritengo   [[molti *t*] intelligenti]
          of.them-I.believe   many   intelligent
          'I believe many of them (to be) intelligent'

Here the complement α of *ritengo* is a small clause. The phrase [*molti ne*] is the specifier of the small clause, hence is not a complement. But extraction is nevertheless permitted. We return to other illustrations of the same point.

We conclude, then, that XP is not a barrier if it is the complement of a head H or the specifier of the complement of H. The configuration of properties is not surprising, given that the head typically shares the features of its maximal projection and agrees with its specifier, so there is an indirect agreement relation between a maximal projection and its specifier. The same observation suggests that we generalize the property further: if α is the complement of H, then the daughters of α (its specifier and its head) are not barriers. When the head is an X^0, the question of extraction from it does not arise, but it could arise in other configurations. Suppose that in a small clause (125), YP = XP, with XP being the head of YP and NP its specifier (the subject of the predicate XP).

(125) V [$_{YP}$ NP XP]

In (124a), then, α = YP = AP, and its head is the AP *intelligenti*. We have already seen that the specifier is not a barrier. Example (126) illustrates the fact that the same is true of the head.

(126) whom does he consider [$_{AP}$ Bill [$_{AP}$ angry at *t*]]

The status of (126) is no different from that of *whom is he angry at*. Thus, neither the complement nor the head of a complement is a barrier. Similarly, in (127) the main verb phrase of the embedded clause is not a barrier, and its VP head is also not a barrier, so that *who* extracts freely.

(127) I wonder [who [John [$_{VP}$[$_{VP}$ met *t*] [last night]]]]

Note that in the case of the small clause (126) as well as (127), we might also appeal to the segment theory of adjunction (section 1.3.1), requiring that a barrier be a category, not a segment, and taking the heads to be segments, hence not possible barriers.

We have dealt in a preliminary way with case (a) of (121); consider now case (b), with the configuration (128), where γ intervenes between α and β.

(128) ... α ... γ ... β ...

Recall that α c-commands the intervening element γ, which we assume further to c-command β; thus, left-to-right order in (128) expresses the c-command relation. Two cases of intervention have been explored; following Rizzi (1990), let us call them *rigid minimality* and *relativized minimality*.

(129) a. Rigid: γ is a head H (α arbitrary).
     b. Relativized: γ is of the same "type" as α.

Rigid minimality can be restated in terms of barriers, taking the category immediately dominating γ to be a barrier. To spell out the concept of relativized minimality, we must characterize the relevant types. These are given in (130).

(130) a. If α is a head, γ is a head.
     b. If α is in an A-position, then γ is a specifier in an A-position.
     c. If α is in an $\overline{\text{A}}$-position, then γ is a specifier in an $\overline{\text{A}}$-position.

Recall that the concepts A- and Ā-position are not properly defined in current theory; we suggested a way to approach the problem at the end of section 1.3.2 and continue to assume it here.

The three basic cases of relativized minimality are illustrated in (131) for heads, A-positions, and Ā-positions, respectively, γ in capitals (see (44), (57)).

(131) a. *how fix [John WILL [t the car]]
      b. *John seems [that [$_{IP}$ IT is certain [t to fix the car]]]
      c. *guess [$_{CP}$ how [John wondered [WHY [we fixed the car t]]]]

In conventional terminology, case (131a) illustrates the *Head Movement Constraint* (HMC); case (131b) *superraising*; and case (131c) the *Wh-Island Constraint*. As the structure indicates, (131c) is to be understood as expressing John's puzzlement as to how we fixed the car, not as a query about how he wondered.

In (131a) *will* intervenes between *fix* and its trace, and both *fix* and *will* are heads. In (131b) *it* intervenes between *John* and its trace, both *it* and *John* are in A-positions, and *it* is the specifier of IP. In (131c), *why* intervenes between *how* and its trace, both *why* and *how* are in Ā-positions, and *why* is the specifier of CP. In all three cases the expression is severely deviant.

We noted earlier that adjuncts and arguments behave somewhat differently with regard to extraction from barriers (see (122)). The same is true in case (130c) of intervention: compare (131c) (adjunct extraction) with (132) (argument extraction).

(132) ??guess [$_{CP}$ what [John wondered [*why* [we fixed t]]]]

While unacceptable, (132) is a much less serious violation than (131c).

These observations have a wide range of descriptive adequacy, but fall short of a satisfactory explanatory principle. We return to the question at the end of this section.

We have discussed some of the properties of the first case of proper government: antecedent government. Let us turn now to the second case: head government. Throughout the modules of grammar, we find relations (H, XP), where H is a head and XP a phrase with some property assigned (or checked) by H. These relations meet locality conditions that are typically narrower than either variety of command and have therefore often been considered to fall under the category of government. We noted earlier that government by a verb suffices to assign Case, bar

PRO, and license trace (section 1.3.2). In all cases the relation is narrower than command.

In Case theory we find that a verb V can assign (or check) the Case of an XP only if the XP is in a local relation to V. The verb *find* assigns accusative Case to *the book* in (133) but not in (134).

(133) a. we found the book
   b. we found [$_{AP}$ the book incomprehensible]

(134) a. we found [$_{CP}$ that [$_{IP}$ the book was incomprehensible]]
   b. we found the answer [$_\alpha$ when the book arrived]

In (133) no barrier protects *the book* from government by *find*. The same is true of (134a), but here the intervening head C^0 ($= that$) bars government of *the book* by *find*. In (134b) α is a barrier. In (134), then, *the book* must receive Case in some other way. If the construction in which it appears is infinitival, it will not receive Case at all, and the construction is ungrammatical, as in (135).

(135) a. *we tried [$_{CP}$ e [$_{IP}$ the book to win a prize]]
   b. *we found John [$_\alpha$ when the book to arrive]

In (135a) the intermediate head C ($= e$) bars government of *the book*, as in (134a). It is natural to suppose, then, that government enters crucially into Case theory.

The positions to which a verb can assign Case are also, typically, those in which a trace can appear, suggesting that government by a verb can license trace. Thus, alongside (133), (134), and (135), we have (136) and (137).

(136) a.   the book was found *t*
   b.   the book was found [$_{AP}$ *t* incomprehensible]
   c.   the book was believed [*t* to be incomprehensible]
   d.   the book seems [*t* to be incomprehensible]

(137) a. *the book was found [$_{CP}$ that [$_{IP}$ *t* was incomprehensible]]
   b. *the book was tried [$_{CP}$ e [$_{IP}$ *t* to win a prize]]

Turning to PRO, we find a similar configuration. PRO cannot appear in governed positions, those in which, with the proper form of the verb, Case can be assigned or trace licensed.

(138) a. *we found PRO
   b. *we found [$_{AP}$ PRO incomprehensible]

PRO is also excluded from positions that are governed but in which Case cannot be assigned, as in (139).

(139) a. *they expressed the belief [$_{IP}$ PRO to be intelligent]
      b. *we expected [there to be found PRO]
      c. *it was believed [PRO to be intelligent]
      d. *it seems [PRO to be intelligent]

As discussed in section 1.3.2, we assume that the verb *believe* in English takes an IP, not a CP, complement. Thus, PRO is governed by *belief* in (139a) and *believed* in (139c), though no Case marking is possible. The constructions are barred. Thus, (139a) does not mean that they expressed the belief that someone or other is intelligent, with arbitrary PRO, or that they expressed the belief that they are intelligent, with PRO bound by *they*. Similarly, (139c) does not mean that it was believed that someone or other is intelligent; the phonetic form can only be interpreted with *it* raised, leaving a trace in the position of PRO. And (139b) does not mean that we expected there to be found someone or other, with arbitrary PRO.

A locality relation between a head and an XP also is found in θ-theory. Thus, a verb θ-marks only XPs within the VP that it heads. On the assumptions of section 1.3.2, the verb θ-marks the specifier of the VP and sisters of V', relations that do not strictly fall under government theory, along with the complement, which does.

A closer look at head government shows that C ($=C^0$), whether overt or null, behaves rather differently from other heads we have considered. Thus, PRO is not barred from positions governed by C, as illustrated in (140).

(140) we decided [$_{CP}$ e [$_{IP}$ PRO to leave at noon]]

Similarly, C does not appear to license trace. Thus, we find that XPs move fairly freely, including VP and CP, but IP does not.

(141) a. [$_{VP}$ admit that he was wrong], John never will t_{VP}
      b. [the claim t_{CP}] was made [$_{CP}$ that John was wrong]
      c. *[$_{IP}$ Bill will visit tomorrow], I think [that t_{IP}]

C also does not license trace of subject. Thus, although C governs the trace in (142), extraction is barred; as is well known, languages have various special devices to overcome the problem (see below).

(142) *who did you say [$_{CP}$ that [$_{IP}$ t left yesterday]]

Properties of C are further illustrated in (143).

(143) a. *John was decided [$_{CP}$ e [$_{IP}$ t to leave at noon]]
    b. *we decided [$_{CP}$ e [$_{IP}$ John to leave at noon]]
    c.   we decided [$_{CP}$ e [$_{IP}$ PRO to leave at noon]]

If the head e of CP were to license the trace in (143a), raising of *John* to the main clause subject position would be permitted. Note that e does not intervene between *John* and its trace if we adopt the notions of relativized minimality (it does under the assumptions of rigid minimality). Examples (143b) and (143c) illustrate the fact that e does intervene between the matrix verb and the embedded subject, blocking a government relation between them. Thus, in (143b) *John* cannot receive Case from a matrix verb, and in (143c) PRO is allowed, neither the matrix verb nor C properly governing it. Thus, C functions as an intervening head, but not a proper governor, licensing trace.

Similarly, while other X^0s typically raise, head-governing and thus licensing the trace left behind, that is not true of C. We find V-raising to V or I, N-raising to V (noun incorporation), I-raising to C (V-second), and so on, but we do not find C-raising to the matrix verb that governs it (e.g., incorporation into a higher verb of a verb that has been raised to V-second position). These facts too would follow from failure of C to properly govern.

C also differs from other heads with respect to barrierhood. Recall that a head typically frees a complement and its daughters (specifier and head) from barrierhood. But the situation is different in the case of C. Consider the following observations of Torrego (1985), who notes the contrast between (144) and (145) in Spanish.

(144) a.   [$_\alpha$ de que autora] [no sabes   [$_{CP}$[$_\beta$ qué traducciones t_α]
              by what author don't you know   what translations
           [t_β han ganado premios internacionales]]]
              have won   international awards
    b. *esta es la autora [$_{CP}$[$_\alpha$ de la que] C [$_{IP}$[$_\beta$ varias
          this is the author [[by whom]   several
          traducciones t_α] han ganado premios internacionales]]
          translations   have won   international awards]

In (144a) CP is the complement of *sabes* and is therefore not a barrier; its specifier β is also not a barrier, and antecedent government is not blocked, so extraction is permitted. In (144b), however, extraction is blocked; even though β is the specifier of the complement of C, it is a barrier blocking antecedent government. A plausible conclusion is that C does not free its complement (or the daughters of the complement) from barrierhood, unlike other X^0s that we have considered, though pursuit of this issue takes us into complexities that we will ignore here.

C is unlike other heads that we have considered in other respects as well. Unlike inflectional elements, it is not a feature of the verb; thus, its specifier is not L-related, and is therefore an $\overline{A}$-position, not an A-position as are other specifiers (section 1.3.2). C also lacks the semantic content of some other heads.

In general, a good first approximation is that the proper governors are restricted to the lexical features (lexical categories, inflectional features of the verb, and perhaps others) and that only proper governors free their complements from barrierhood.

We have seen that C does not suffice as the required head governor of a subject trace. In (143a) the null complementizer *e* failed to license the trace of A-movement. The same failure is observed with an overt C in the similar configuration (145).

(145) *John is important [$_{CP}$ (for) [$_{IP}$ *t* to leave at noon]]

The paradigm with $\overline{A}$-movement (as opposed to A-movement) of the subject is less straightforward. While (142) is unacceptable, it becomes perfectly well formed if the overt complementizer is absent.

(146) who did you say [$_{CP}$[$_{IP}$ *t* left yesterday]]

In the approach outlined above, the question is how the subject trace is head-governed. Suppose there is a null complementizer and the movement of *who* proceeded successive-cyclically via the Spec of the lower CP. Then the representation would be as in (147).

(147) who did you say [$_{CP}$ *t'* *e* [$_{IP}$ *t* left yesterday]]

Spec-head agreement takes place between *t'* and *e* in this configuration. We tentatively suggest that this agreement provides *e* with features allowing it to license the trace *t*. The ungrammaticality of (142) (commonly called the *that-trace effect*), on the other hand, indicates that such feature sharing is not possible with the overt complementizer *that*. Note too that there is no derivation similar to that in (147) available for (143) since, quite generally, movement to an A-position cannot proceed through [Spec, CP]. Such "improper movement" results in an illicit A-bound variable, as in constructions that fall under the principle Command discussed in section 1.3.3 (see also section 1.4.2).

One concern of some of the early literature on proper government (Huang 1982, Lasnik and Saito 1984) was the absence of *that*-trace effects with adjuncts. Thus, (148) is good with or without *that*.

(148) why do you think [(that) John left *t*]

Since adjuncts, like subjects, are not complements, the question arises how their traces are head-governed. When *that* is absent, the same mechanism is available as we posited for (147). But when *that* is present, no such mechanism exists, as demonstrated by (142) (see Rizzi 1990). The framework of Lasnik and Saito was slightly different so that the technical problem was actually apparent lack of *antecedent* government, but their solution can carry over under present assumptions. They suggest that as a consequence of the Projection Principle, argument traces must be licensed (γ-marked, in their terminology) at S-Structure, while adjunct traces are licensed only at LF. (142) will thus be ruled out at S-Structure while (148) will not be. Then in the LF component, *that*, being semantically empty, can be eliminated. The resulting configuration will allow government of the adjunct trace in just the same way that it allowed government of the subject trace in (147), if the head government requirement holds at LF.

In the examples we have been considering, an adjunct trace is possible in a situation in which a subject trace is not. We also find (nearly) the opposite state of affairs. (149), with movement of the adjunct *how*, is completely impossible, whereas (150), with movement of a subject, is much less severely deviant.

(149) *how do you wonder [whether John said [Mary solved the problem *t*]]

(150) ??who do you wonder [whether John said [*t* solved the problem]]

In both examples the initial trace is appropriately governed, in the manner just discussed. The difference between (149) and (150) must lie elsewhere.

Consider the structures of the examples in more detail. We assume that *whether* occupies the Spec of the CP in which it appears.

(151) *how do you wonder [$_{CP}$ whether [$_{IP}$ John said [$_{CP}$ *t'* *e* [$_{IP}$ Mary solved the problem *t*]]]]

(152) ??who do you wonder [$_{CP}$ whether [$_{IP}$ John said [$_{CP}$ t' e [$_{IP}$ t solved
        the problem]]]]

Lasnik and Saito argue that not just initial traces, but also intermediate
traces, must be appropriately governed. But the intermediate trace t' is
not antecedent-governed in either (151) or (152). In the case of (152),
Lasnik and Saito argue, the intermediate trace antecedent-governs the
initial trace t and then is deleted in the LF component. Such a derivation
is not possible for (151) if, as they suggest, all licensing of adjunct traces
is at the level of LF. Thus, if t' is present in the LF representation of
(151), t will be properly governed but t' will not be. And if t' is not
present at the LF level, then t will not be antecedent-governed. Either
way, then, the representation contains a trace that is not properly governed.

We have just seen how (149) and (150) can be distinguished in terms
of proper government. In (149) there will inevitably be an "offending
trace," but there need not be one in (150). However, although (150) is
much better than (149), it is not perfect, and that fact remains to be
explained. Evidently, *wh*-movement is not permitted to bypass an intermediate [Spec, CP], as it did in both (151) and (152). This is one consequence of the subjacency constraint on movement proposed by Chomsky
(1977) as a partial unification of several earlier constraints on movement,
including those of Chomsky (1964) and Ross (1967). Subjacency violations are characteristically less severe than proper government violations,
all else equal. Another property of subjacency that distinguishes it
from proper government was alluded to in section 1.3.3. Subjacency
constrains overt movement, but apparently does not constrain covert
movement between S-Structure and LF. This is seen in the following
near-minimal pair, repeated from (95a), (96a):

(153) *who do you like [books that criticize t]

(154)   who [t likes books that criticize whom]

The S-Structure position of *whom* in (154) is the LF position of the trace
of *whom* after LF raising, which yields a structure that is, in relevant
respects, identical to the S-Structure (and LF) representation of (153).
Yet the two examples contrast sharply in grammaticality. Similarly, as
discussed by Huang (1982), in languages with interrogative expressions
in situ, such as Chinese, the LF movement of those expressions is not
constrained by Subjacency. (155) (=(95b)) is the Chinese analogue of
(153), but it is acceptable, much like (154).

(155) ni xihuan [piping shei de shu]
      you like [criticize who REL book]

While LF movement seems not to conform to Subjacency, it does respect the proper government requirement. The following Chinese example allows LF movement of *sheme* 'what' into the higher clause, but does
not allow such movement for *weisheme* 'why'.

(156) ni xiang-zhidao [Lisi weisheme mai-le sheme]
      you wonder   Lisi why   bought what

(156) can mean (157) but not (158).

(157) what is the thing such that you wonder why Lisi bought that thing

(158) what is the reason such that you wonder what Lisi bought for that
      reason

The trace of the LF movement of *weisheme* to the higher clause will not
be properly governed, under the operation that yields the barred interpretation (158).

Having reviewed some aspects of the theory of movement, let us return to the basic concept of government that enters crucially into this
and apparently other modules of grammar. We noted that government is
a "local" form of command, tentatively taking the operative notion to
be c-command. Two elements of locality were introduced: government is
blocked by certain barriers and by an intervening category (the Minimality Condition). The Minimality Condition has two variants: Rigid
and Relativized Minimality. We kept to the latter, following Rizzi (1990).
For the theory of movement, we took the relevant forms of government,
proper government, to be antecedent government and head government
by a lexical head or its features (the verbal inflections).

As discussed earlier, these ideas have considerable descriptive adequacy but lack the generality and clarity that we would hope to find in an
explanatory theory of language (see section 1.1). In particular, the basic
and appealing intuition that lies behind the principle of Relativized Minimality is not really captured by the mechanisms proposed, which list
three arbitrary cases and add unexplained complexity (the role of
specifier for two of the cases); see (130).

The basic intuition is that the operation Move α should always try
to construct "the shortest link." If some legitimate target of movement
is already occupied, the cost is deviance (see Rizzi 1990, 22–24; also

chapter 3). We may regard this as part of the general principle of economy of derivation. Conditions quite independent of Relativized Minimality require that only heads can move to head positions, and only elements in A-positions to A-positions. Furthermore, again for independent reasons, XPs can move only to specifier positions, and α can move only to a position that c-commands it. Hence, the special properties listed in (130) can be eliminated from the formulation of the condition, which reduces to (159).

(159) Minimize chain links.

If this approach is viable, we can eliminate the intervention condition of (121) in favor of a general condition on economy of derivations, restricting the definition of government to (160).

(160) α governs β if α c-commands β and there is no barrier for β c-commanded by α.

We want government to be constrained by the same locality condition that appears in binding theory and elsewhere. Thus, an antecedent α binds an anaphor β just in case it is the *local* binder; that is, there is no γ bound by α and binding β (see section 1.4.2). Similarly, α governs β only if there is no γ governed by α and governing β. This condition is now satisfied for antecedent government, by the economy condition (159). But an analogue still has to be stipulated for head government. That raises the question of whether the head government condition is, in fact, superfluous (Frampton 1992; also see chapter 3). We will proceed on the assumption that it is required, noting the problematic aspect of this assumption.

To make this intuitive account more precise and descriptively more accurate, we have to explain in what sense a "cost" accrues to failure to make the shortest move, and why violation of the economy condition is more severe for adjuncts than arguments, as noted throughout. Adapting mechanisms just discussed, we might suppose that when a chain link is formed by Move α, the trace created is assigned * if the economy condition (159) is violated as it is created (a version of the γ-marking operation of Lasnik and Saito 1984, 1992).

Note further that only certain entities are legitimate LF objects, just as only certain entities are legitimate PF objects (e.g., a [+high, +low] vowel, or a stressed consonant, is not a legitimate PF object, and a derivation that yields such an output fails to form a proper SD). We therefore need some notion of legitimate LF object. Suppose that the chain C of (161) is a legitimate LF object only if C is *uniform* (see Browning 1987).

(161) $C = (\alpha_1, \ldots, \alpha_n)$

The only other legitimate LF objects are operator-variable constructions (α, β), where α is in an $\overline{A}$-position and β heads a legitimate (uniform) chain.

Uniformity is a relational notion: the chain C is *uniform with respect to* P (UN[P]) if each α_i has property P or each α_i has non-P. One obvious choice for the relevant property P is L-relatedness, which we have suggested to ground the distinction between A- and $\overline{A}$-positions; see section 1.3.2. A chain is UN[L] if it is uniform with respect to L-relatedness. Heads and adjuncts are non-L-related and move only to non-L-related positions; hence, the chains they form are UN[L]. An argument chain consists only of L-related positions, hence is UN[L]. The basic types—heads, arguments, adjuncts—are therefore uniform chains, legitimate objects at LF.

Taking this as a first approximation, we now regard the operation of deletion, like movement, as a "last resort" principle, a special case of the principle of economy of derivation (make derivations as short as possible, with links as short as possible): operations in general are permissible only to form a legitimate LF object. Deletion is impermissible in a uniform chain, since these are already legitimate. Deletion in the chain C of (161) is, however, permissible for α_i in an $\overline{A}$-position, where $n > i > 1$ and α_n is in an A-position—that is, the case of successive-cyclic movement of an argument. In this case a starred trace can be deleted at LF, voiding the violation; in other cases it cannot.

An expression (an SD) is a Subjacency violation if its derivation forms a starred trace. It is an Empty Category Principle (ECP) violation if, furthermore, this starred trace remains at LF; hence, ECP violations are more severe than Subjacency violations, which leave no residue at LF. Note that the concept ECP is now a descriptive cover term for various kinds of violations that are marked at LF, among them, violations of the economy principle (Relativized Minimality).

We continue to assume that traces must be properly governed: both antecedent- and head-governed by a lexical feature (i.e., not C). To unify the account, let us say that a trace is marked * if it fails either of these conditions. Thus, a trace will be marked ** if it fails both, or if it fails one along with the economy condition, and it will be marked *** if it fails all three, with multiple starring indicating increased deviance. We have failure of antecedent government in the case of movement over a barrier, or in the case of lowering in violation of the C-Command Condition; unless the offending trace deletes, the violation remains at LF. We speculated earlier that only proper governors free their complement from barrierhood. It will follow, then, that IP (the complement of C) will be free from barrierhood only if C has a lexical feature: that will happen if V–I raises to C.

Government now is the special case of local c-command when there is no barrier. Subjacency violations fail the economy condition that requires chain links to be minimal. There is generally further deviance if the violation leaves a residue in the LF representation. Traces must be properly governed (head- and antecedent-governed), requiring raising rather than lowering, with deviance if raising crosses a barrier. The special properties of C, manifest in many respects as we have seen, impose further constraints on extraction of subjects. Deletion, like movement, is driven by FI: the requirement that derivations must form legitimate LF objects. The guiding principle is economy of derivations and representations: derivations contain no superfluous steps, just as representations contain no superfluous symbols. See chapters 2 and 3 for further discussion.

1.4.2 Binding Theory
Among the imaginable anaphoric relations among NPs, some are possible, some are necessary, and still others are proscribed, depending on the nature of the NPs involved and the syntactic configurations in which they occur. For example, in (162) *him* can be referentially dependent upon *John* (can take *John* as its antecedent), while in (163) it cannot.

(162) John said Mary criticized him

(163) John criticized him

That is, (163) has no reading in which *him* refers to John, in the way that *himself* in (164) does.

(164) John criticized himself

Apparently, a pronoun cannot have an antecedent that is "too close" to it. Note that in (162), where antecedence is possible, a clause boundary intervenes between pronoun and antecedent. There is no such boundary between pronoun and antecedent in (163).

As we have seen in section 1.3.3, distance in this sense does not always suffice to make antecedence possible. Consider (165), where a clause boundary intervenes between *he* and *John*, yet an anaphoric connection is impossible.

(165) he said Mary criticized John

Importantly, it is not the linear relation between pronoun and name that inhibits anaphora. This is evident from consideration of (166), in which *he* once again precedes *John*, yet anaphora is possible.

(166) after he entered the room, John sat down

Similarly, in (167) *his* can take *John* as its antecedent.

(167) his boss criticized John

The generalization covering (165)–(167) is approximately as in (168).

(168) A pronoun cannot take an element of its (c-command) domain as
       its antecedent.

The *c-command domain* of an element is the minimal phrase containing it. Thus, in (165) the domain of the pronoun is the entire sentence. Since, trivially, the putative antecedent is included in that domain, the anaphoric interpretation is inconsistent with the generalization (168). In (166), on the other hand, the domain of the pronoun is the adverbial clause, which does not include the antecedent *John*. Similarly, in (167) the domain of the pronoun is the subject NP, *his boss*, which does not include *John*.

There are a number of ways that the generalization in (168), which relates aspects of the structure and meaning of an utterance, might be expressed in the theory. One way is in terms of a constraint (171) on *binding*, a structural relation defined in (169), and *freedom* defined in (170).

(169) α *binds* β if α c-commands β and α, β are coindexed.

(170) If β is not bound, then β is free.

(171) An *r-expression* (fully referential expression—not a pronoun or an
       anaphor) must be free.

The fundamental relation in this approach, *coindexation*, is a symmetric one. For an alternative in terms of an asymmetric relation, *linking*, see Higginbotham 1983, 1985. Consider how (171), often called *Condition C* of the binding theory, will treat the examples in (165)–(167). Representation (172), for sentence (165), will be excluded, while representations (173) and (174), for (166) and (167), respectively, will be allowed.

(172) *he$_i$ said Mary criticized John$_i$

(173) after he$_i$ entered the room, John$_i$ sat down

(174) his$_i$ boss criticized John$_i$

Note that according to (171), (175) is permitted if i ≠ j.

(175) he$_i$ said Mary criticized John$_j$

Hence, if (171) is truly to play a role in capturing the generalization in (168), an interpretation must be provided for the indexing in (175) that explicitly precludes the impossible interpretation. (176) suffices in this case.

(176) If the index of α is distinct from the index of β, then neither α nor β is the antecedent of the other.

Shortly we will see reason to strengthen this constraint on interpretation of contraindexation.

    Returning now to the phenomenon in (163), given that there, too, we found a constraint on antecedence, it is reasonable to suppose that (176) should again play a role in the account. Evidently, all that is necessary is that the configuration (177) be allowed and (178) prohibited.

(177) John$_i$ criticized him$_j$

(178) *John$_i$ criticized him$_i$

(171) will not be effective in excluding (178), since that constraint is limited to circumstances where the bindee is an r-expression, while in (178) the bindee is a pronoun. Further, we do not want to generalize (171) to include pronouns as bindees, since that would incorrectly preclude antecedence in (162) by disallowing representation (179).

(179) John$_i$ said Mary criticized him$_i$

As noted earlier, there is a locality effect involved in this paradigm. A pronoun is clearly able to be within the domain of its antecedent, hence, is allowed to have a binder, but must not be "too close" to it. (180) is a rough statement of the necessary constraint (*Condition B* of the binding theory).

(180) A pronoun must be free in a local domain.

The precise nature of the relevant local domain remains to be specified. The examples under consideration suggest that the local domain is approximately the minimal clause containing the pronoun. We will limit our attention here to purely structural approaches. See Williams 1989 for an account in terms of θ-roles, and Reinhart and Reuland 1993 for one based on predication.

Note that, as predicted, a pronoun can have an antecedent in its clause just as long as that antecedent does not c-command it. (181) is a permissible representation.

(181) John's$_i$ boss criticized him$_i$

Anaphors, such as reciprocals and reflexives, require antecedents that bind them. In this, their behavior is quite different from that of pronouns, which *may* have binding antecedents, but *need* not. Additionally, at least in English and a number of other languages, the antecedent of an anaphor must be local to the anaphor. In particular, we have (182), *Condition A* of the binding theory.

(182) An anaphor must be bound in a local domain.

Under the null hypothesis that the "local domain" is the same for Condition A and Condition B, we predict complementarity between pronouns and anaphors. This prediction is confirmed to a substantial degree. The ill-formed (178) becomes grammatical, if its bound pronoun is replaced by an anaphor, as in (183).

(183) John$_i$ criticized himself$_i$

Conversely, the well-formed (179) becomes bad, if its pronoun is replaced by an anaphor.

(184) *John$_i$ said Mary criticized himself$_i$

All that remains for this rough approximation is to specify the interpretation for coindexation. That is, we must guarantee that (183) cannot mean that John criticized Harry. The necessary principle of interpretation is not entirely obvious. For the moment, let us assume (185), temporarily leaving open the precise import of the notion "antecedent."

(185) If the index of α is identical to the index of β, then α is the
       antecedent of β or β is the antecedent of α.

We now have three syntactic constraints, repeated as (186A–C), and
the two principles of interpretation (176) and (185).

(186) A. An anaphor must be bound in a local domain.
       B. A pronoun must be free in a local domain.
       C. An r-expression must be free.

Before considering further the precise nature of the local domain involved in Conditions A and B, we return briefly to the semantic import
of indexing relations. Earlier, we hinted that (176) would need to be
strengthened. Consider, in this regard, representation (187).

(187) after John$_i$ walked in, John$_j$ criticized him$_i$

This representation is fully consistent with the only relevant syntactic
conditions, Conditions B and C. Neither occurrence of *John* is bound,
and *him* is free in its clause. According to (176), *John$_j$* cannot be the
antecedent of *him$_i$*, but *John$_i$* is an appropriate antecedent. It is thus unclear why (187) does not have the interpretation (and status) of (188),
where coreferential interpretation for the two occurrences of *John* con-
tributes only a minor degree of deviance.

(188) after John$_j$ walked in, John$_j$ criticized himself$_j$

Given the sharp contrast between (188) and (187) on the relevant interpretation, the extreme deviance of (187) cannot be attributed to repeti-
tion of the name, but rather must stem from the relation between the
second occurrence of the name and the pronoun. We must rule out (intended) coreference between these two NPs, even when the second does
not take the first as its antecedent. We achieve this result by strengthening (176) to (189).

(189) If the index of α is distinct from the index of β, then α and β are
       noncoreferential.

(185) must now be modified, in corresponding fashion, to (190).

(190) If the index of α is identical to the index of β, then α and β are
       coreferential.

Consider the contrast between the mildly deviant (191) and the severely
degraded (192), both on the relevant interpretation involving only one
individual.

(191) ?after John walked in, John sat down

(192) *John criticized John

Condition C excludes representation (193) for (192), while permitting (194).

(193) *John$_i$ criticized John$_i$

(194) John$_i$ criticized John$_j$

(189) now correctly guarantees noncoreference for the two NPs in (194). But now consider (191). On the desired interpretation, the two occurrences of *John* cannot be contraindexed, since (189) would demand noncoreference for such a representation. Coindexation, too, would be problematic under (185), since (185) demands antecedence in one direction or the other, yet a name, being fully referential in its own right, presumably cannot have an antecedent. This problem does not arise once (190) is substituted for (185).

Thus far we have limited our attention to anaphoric relations among singular NPs. Certain complications arise when we extend the scope of the investigation to plurals. The configurations giving rise to noncoreference effects, by the mechanisms outlined above, seem to give rise to *disjoint reference* effects as well (Postal 1966a). Just as a coreferential interpretation of the two NPs is markedly degraded in (195), so is overlap degraded in (196).

(195) he likes him

(196) they like him

Correspondingly, (197), whose NPs lexically demand coreference, is bad, and (198), whose NPs lexically demand overlap in reference, is substantially degraded also.

(197)   *I like me

(198) ?*we like me

This suggests that (189) should be further strengthened.

(199) If the index of α is distinct from the index of β, then α and β are
       disjoint in reference.

In (195)–(198) Condition B excludes coindexing. (199) then demands disjoint reference of the necessarily contraindexed NPs. But a problem arises for pronouns not in configurations subject to Condition B. Consider (200) and (201).

(200) they think he will be victorious

(201) we think I will be victorious

In contrast with (197) and (198), (200) and (201) allow an interpretation where the reference of the second NP is included in the reference of the first. The result is that (200) is ambiguous and (201) is grammatical. But given the two principles of interpretation (190) and (199), there is now no possible representation available for these examples. Neither (202) nor (203) will yield a consistent interpretation for (201).

(202) we$_i$ think I$_j$ will be victorious

(203) we$_i$ think I$_i$ will be victorious

By (199), in representation (202) *we* and *I* must be disjoint in reference, but this is inconsistent with the lexical meanings of the two pronouns. And by (190), in representation (203) the two pronouns must be coreferential, which is again inconsistent with their lexical meanings. Note further that it will not do to weaken (190) so that it only demands overlap in reference, rather than coreference. This is so since in (204), for example, coreference is clearly demanded between the subject pronoun and the object reflexive, but under the hypothesized weakening, overlap should suffice.

(204) they$_i$ praised themselves$_i$

Evidently, we require a richer set of notational possibilities than we have seen so far. At least three circumstances—coreference, disjoint reference, and overlap in reference—must be accommodated. But the purely binary distinction provided by coindexing versus contraindexing straightforwardly allows for only two. To overcome this limitation, one notational device sometimes used is an index that is not a simple integer, but rather is a set of integers (Sportiche 1985). (It might seem tempting to take cardinality of index to correspond to cardinality of the referent of the NP. But such a move has no formal basis and faces insurmountable difficulties. See Higginbotham 1985, Lasnik 1989.) In accord with this convention, *free* is redefined as follows:

(205) β is free with respect to α if either α does not c-command β or the intersection of the indices of α and β is null.

Correspondingly, we modify interpretive rule (199).

(206) If the intersection of the index of α and the index of β is null, then α and β are disjoint in reference.

The problematic contrast between (198) and (201) is now straightforwardly handled. By Condition B, *me* in (198) must be free, as in (207a) or (207b).

(207) a. we$_{\{i\}}$ like me$_{\{j\}}$
      b. we$_{\{j,k\}}$ like me$_{\{i\}}$

(206) then demands of these representations that the subject and object be disjoint in reference. In (201), on the other hand, Condition B is irrelevant. The indices of subject and object are therefore permitted to overlap (though still not to be identical, given (190), which we maintain).

(208) we$_{\{i,j\}}$ think I$_{\{i\}}$ will be victorious

The phenomenon of split antecedence is similarly accommodated, as displayed in (209a–b).

(209) a. John$_{\{i\}}$ told Mary$_{\{j\}}$ that they$_{\{i,j\}}$ should leave
      b. John$_{\{i\}}$ told Mary$_{\{j\}}$ that they$_{\{i,j,k\}}$ should leave

Several other possibilities might also be considered. Thus, in place of the resort to set indices, we might enrich the interpretation provided for simple indices of the sort considered earlier. Consider the following interpretive procedure:

(210) a. Suppose NP and α are coindexed. Then
         i. if α is an anaphor, it is coreferential with NP;
         ii. if α is a pronoun, it overlaps in reference with NP.
      b. Suppose NP and α are contraindexed. Then they are disjoint.

The standard cases of coreference, distinct reference, and disjoint reference now fall into place. In (195)–(198) contraindexing is required by Condition B, and the pronouns are interpreted as disjoint. In (200)–(204) coindexing is permitted, and (210aii) yields the intended interpretation of overlap in reference. It remains, however, to deal with the phenomenon of split antecedence, and further questions arise in the case of more complex constructions that we have not considered.

Another possibility would be to unify the indexing and interpretive procedures along with the binding conditions themselves, dispensing with indexing and simplifying (210) to (211), where D is the relevant local domain.

(211) a. If α is an anaphor, interpret it as coreferential with a
c-commanding phrase in D.
b. If α is a pronoun, interpret it as disjoint from every
c-commanding phrase in D.

Following Lasnik (1976), we restate the former indexing requirement for r-expressions along the same lines.

(212) If α is an r-expression, interpret it as disjoint from every
c-commanding phrase.

Nothing is said about interpretation in other cases. The standard examples are interpreted straightforwardly. Split antecedence is now understood to be a special case of free reference. Thus, in (209) any interpretation is permitted, including those indicated in (209), and also others, for example, an interpretation in which *they* is taken to refer to John and some third party, but not Mary.

What about more complex cases such as (213) (Wasow 1972)?

(213) the woman who loved him$_i$ told him$_j$ that John$_i$ was intelligent

Here, we have to exclude the interpretation in which the two pronouns and *John* all corefer. The problem is that the binding conditions permit both *John$_i$* and *him$_j$* to corefer with *him$_i$*. It then follows, incorrectly, that *John$_i$* and *him$_j$* can be coreferential. In the theory outlined earlier, this was excluded by the fact that coindexing is an equivalence relation, so that coindexing of both *John$_i$* and *him$_j$* with *him$_i$* entails that *John* is coindexed with *him$_j$*, which is barred by Condition C. But we now have no coindexing, hence no equivalence relation.

However, the same result is achieved simply as a consequence of the interpretation itself (Lasnik 1976). By (212), *John$_i$* is disjoint from *him$_j$*. Free interpretation allows the two pronouns to corefer and allows *John$_i$* to corefer with *him$_i$*. If we adopt these options, *him$_j$* and *John$_i$* corefer, and we have an inconsistent interpretation, with *John$_i$* both coreferential with and disjoint from *him$_j$*. Nothing further need be said. Many other complex cases follow in the same way.

The theory outlined earlier, which is the standard one, involved an indexing procedure that satisfies the binding conditions and (explicitly or implicitly) an interpretive procedure. The approach just sketched unifies all three into an interpretive procedure. Whichever approach is followed, it now remains to consider the "local domain" in which anaphors must be bound and pronouns free.

Thus far the local domain has been the minimal clause containing the anaphor or pronoun. But this characterization is inadequate for a wider range of phenomena. In (214) the anaphor is free in its minimal clause, yet the example is well formed.

(214) John$_i$ believes [himself$_i$ to be clever]

Similarly, (215) is deviant even though the pronoun is free in the complement clause.

(215) *John$_i$ believes [him$_i$ to be clever]

We take the relevant difference between these examples and the embedded clause cases considered earlier to be in terms of government. In (214) and (215) the main verb governs the subject of the infinitival complement, as is evident from the accusative Case that shows up on that subject. In (216), on the other hand, there is clearly no such government relation, and the grammaticality judgments are the reverse of those in (214), (215).

(216) a. *John$_i$ believes [himself$_i$ is clever]
      b. John$_i$ believes [he$_i$ is clever]

The local domain, or *governing category* as it is frequently called, involves reference to government, roughly as in (217), as a first approximation.

(217) The governing category (GC) of α is the minimal clause containing α and a governor of α.

In (214) and (215) the GC for the anaphor or pronoun is the entire sentence, since the governor, *believe*, is in the higher clause. Since both the anaphor and pronoun are bound in that domain, the former example is good, in obedience to Condition A, and the latter bad, in violation of Condition B. In (216) the GC is the lower clause, since the subject is assigned nominative Case by a governor internal to that clause, finite I (assuming that government is defined in terms of m-command). Since within the lower clause, there is no binder for the subject of that clause, (216a) is in violation of Condition A, and (216b) is in conformity with Condition B. Note that (217) correctly predicts that the difference between finite and infinitival complements is limited to subject position. With respect to object position, finite and nonfinite clauses are parallel.

(218) a. *John$_i$ believes [Mary likes himself$_i$]
      b.   him$_i$

(219) a. *John$_i$ believes [Mary to like himself$_i$]
      b.   him$_i$

In all four examples the GC for the anaphor or pronoun is the embedded clause, since the verb of the embedded clause is a governor of its object.

The local domain for Conditions A and B can be NP as well as IP, as seen in (220).

(220) *John$_i$ likes [$_{NP}$ Bill's stories about himself$_i$]

This suggests that (217) should be extended in the obvious way to include NP. The large NP would then be the GC for *himself* since *about* governs that anaphor. However, matters are slightly more complicated than that: unexpectedly, (221) is grammatical.

(221) John$_i$ likes [stories about himself$_i$]

Under the suggested extension, (221) should also be bad.

Note that in (220), in contrast with (221), the large NP contains not just the anaphor, but also a "potential" binder, that is, another NP that c-commands the anaphor. Our final modification incorporates this observation, and also generalizes from NP and IP to *complete functional complex* (CFC), where a CFC is a projection containing all grammatical functions compatible with its head.

(222) The GC for α is the minimal CFC that contains α and a governor of α and in which α's binding condition could, in principle, be satisfied.

This correctly distinguishes (220) from (221). As noted above, there is a potential binder, *Bill's*, for the anaphor in the large NP in (220), but none in (221). In the latter example the GC for the anaphor is thus the entire sentence, and Condition A is satisfied. Under the hypothesis alluded to in section 1.3.2 that subjects are base-generated internal to VP, the VP will be the GC, with the trace of the subject (which has itself moved to the [Spec, IP]) serving as the binder.

Note that the presence or absence of a potential binder (as opposed to an actual one) should play no role for Condition B, since there is no requirement that a pronoun have a binder at all. Hence, the minimal CFC containing α and a governor of α (where α is a pronoun) should always be the minimal such CFC in which α's binding condition could, in principle, be satisfied. This predicts that (223) and (224) should *both* be good, if in fact the NP object of *likes* in (224) qualifies as a CFC.

(223) John$_i$ likes [Bill's stories about him$_i$]

(224) John$_i$ likes [stories about him$_i$]

As expected, (223) is perfect. (224), while perhaps slightly worse, is still reasonably acceptable. This latter example thus provides one context where the usual distinctness in distribution between anaphors and pronouns seems to break down. (221), with *himself* in place of *him*, was also, of course, grammatical. Note that, as predicted, distinct distribution is maintained if there is an actual binder within the large NP, as in (225).

(225) a.   I like [John's$_i$ stories about himself$_i$]
      b. *   him$_i$

The NP *John's stories about* _____ is the smallest potential CFC in which Condition A or B could be satisfied. While in (225a) Condition A is satisfied in that domain, in (225b) Condition B is not.

There is some evidence that the apparent overlap in distribution seen in (221), (224) is only illusory. In (224), where *him* is construed as *John*, the stories are not taken as John's. This becomes even clearer in (226), since in that example the meaning of the verb virtually forces the stories to be John's.

(226) ?*John$_i$ told [stories about him$_i$]

This suggests that (224) actually can have a structure similar to (223), but with the subject of the NP phonetically null. In that case the NP object of *likes* would clearly constitute a CFC. In (226), on the other hand, even if the NP object of *told* has a null subject, him$_i$ will still be illicitly bound in the minimal CFC, since that subject is understood as *John*.

However, there is one other situation where the usual disjoint distribution definitely breaks down. English has, to a limited extent, configurations permitting "long-distance" anaphors. (227) is a representative example.

(227) Mary$_i$ thinks [[pictures of herself$_i$] are on display]

Though *herself* is free within both an NP and a finite clause here, it is bound in its GC, the entire clause. There is no potential binder for the anaphor anywhere in the lower clause, so Condition A could not be satisfied, even in principle, within the lower clause. Thus, *herself* is permitted to seek its binder in the upper clause, where, in fact, it finds it. Now note that a pronoun is possible in place of the anaphor.

(228) Mary$_i$ thinks [[pictures of her$_i$] are on display]

The NP *pictures of her* (if it has a phonetically null subject), or the embedded clause (otherwise), is the smallest CFC that contains *her* and a governor of *her* (*of* or *pictures*, depending on certain assumptions about assignment of genitive Case; see section 1.4.3) and in which *her* could, in principle, be free. And *her* is, in fact, free in that domain. The limited overlap in distribution that exists is thus correctly accounted for by the "relativized" notion of GC in (222).

There is one remaining problem to consider before we leave this topic. Recall example (216a), repeated here as (229).

(229) *John$_i$ believes [himself$_i$ is clever]

Under the earlier absolute notion of GC, this was correctly excluded by Condition A. But under the characterization in (222), it is not. Though *himself* has a governor (finite Infl) in the lower S, there is no potential binder. The GC should therefore be the entire sentence, and *John* should be available as a legal binder. Assuming the basic correctness of the formulation of binding theory we have been developing, something other than Condition A must be responsible for the ill-formedness of (229). We suggest that the relevant condition is one discussed in section 1.4.1, which excludes traces from configurations in which they are not properly governed. On the face of it, this condition might seem irrelevant, because there is no trace evident in (229). However, it is plausible to regard the relation between a reflexive and its antecedent as involving agreement. Since agreement is generally a strictly local phenomenon, the reflexive must move to a position sufficiently near its antecedent. This might happen in the syntax, as in the cliticization processes of the Romance languages. If not, then it must happen in the LF component. In (229) this movement will leave a trace that is not properly governed. This approach directly accounts for the familiar observation that binding relations and movement processes fall under abstractly very similar constraints. Further, if it is, indeed, the requirement of agreement that is forcing the (LF) movement of the reflexive, (230), which otherwise could have been problematic, is ruled out.

(230) *himself left

Notice that there is no potential binder for the reflexive, so Condition A does not exclude the example, given the formulation of GC in (222). However, in the absence of an antecedent, the agreement require- ment cannot be satisfied. These speculations suggest that for reflexives without agreement, there will be no locality requirement (Yang 1983, Pica 1987).

Given that the Condition A requirement on reflexives is thus partially subsumed under the proper government requirement on traces, the ques- tion arises of whether these two constraints fall together even more gen- erally. Heim, Lasnik, and May (1991), expanding upon a proposal of Lebeaux (1983), suggest that the locality requirement between reciprocal expressions and their antecedents is attributable to conditions on move- ment. To the S-Structure of sentence (231), an LF operation of *each*- movement, adjoining the distributor *each* to its "antecedent," will be applicable, giving (232).

(231) The men saw each other

(232) $[_{IP}[_{NP}[_{NP}$ the men$]_i$ each$_j]$ $[_{VP}$ saw $[_{NP}$ t_j other$]]]$

In (233) this LF movement can be long distance. One reading (the non- contradictory one) of this sentence is representable as (234).

(233) they said that they are taller than each other

(234) $[_{IP}[_{NP}[_{NP}$ they$]_i$ each$_j]$ $[_{VP}$ said $[_{CP}$ that they$_j$ are taller than $[t_j$ other$]]]]]$

When the verb of the main clause is a "nonbridge" verb, however, move- ment is characteristically blocked. Compare (235) with (236).

(235)   who did they say that they are taller than t

(236) ?*who did they mutter that they are taller than t

Correspondingly, the "wide scope" reading for *each* is unavailable with the nonbridge verb, leaving only the contradictory reading.

(237) they muttered that they are taller than each other

Thus, both major classes of lexical anaphors, reflexives and reciprocals, display constraints suggestive of movement.

We turn finally to the question of the level(s) of representation rele- vant to the binding conditions. (238), whose derivation involves raising of the antecedent to the appropriate position to bind the reflexive, suggests that D-Structure need not meet Condition A.

(238) John$_i$ seems to himself$_i$ [t_i to be clever]

The issue is not entirely clear-cut, given the considerations of the preceding discussion, but we will tentatively assume that this is correct. Now observe that (239), from a D-Structure like that of (240), indicates that Condition C likewise need not be satisfied at D-Structure.

(239) [who that John$_i$ knows] does he$_i$ admire

(240) he$_i$ admires [who that John$_i$ knows]

Compare sentence (241), a standard Condition C violation.

(241) *he$_i$ admires everyone that John$_i$ knows

Further, (242) indicates that LF satisfaction of Condition C would not suffice. The LF representation of (241), following QR, shown in (242), is structurally very similar to the S-Structure (and LF, presumably) of (239).

(242) [everyone that John$_i$ knows]$_j$ [$_{IP}$ he$_i$ admires t_j]

The relevant difference between (239) and (242) seems to show up neither at LF nor at D-Structure, but rather, only at S-Structure. Alternatively, as discussed in section 1.3.3, reconstruction could be at issue here. Under the null hypothesis that the binding conditions apply in a block, the level of representation at which they apply is S-Structure, or, assuming reconstruction, LF.

With respect to Condition A, we have considered the distribution and interpretation of reflexives. The empty category PRO, which was briefly discussed in section 1.3.1, is very similar in its interpretation and in some aspects of its distribution. Controlled PRO generally has just the interpretation that a reflexive would have. This, in fact, was the motivation for the *self*-deletion analysis of these constructions offered in Chomsky and Lasnik 1977. Further, the principles relevant to the control of PRO appear, on first inspection, to be similar to those involved in the assignment of antecedents to anaphors. For example, as already discussed, an anaphor as subject of an infinitival clause can successfully be bound by the next subject up, as in (243), just as a PRO can be bound in the parallel configuration in (244).

(243) John$_i$ believes [himself$_i$ to be clever]

(244) John$_i$ tries [PRO$_i$ to be clever]

And as subject of a finite clause, neither is permitted.

(245) *John$_i$ believes [himself$_i$ is clever]

(246) *John$_i$ promises [PRO$_i$ will attend class]
        cf. John$_i$ promises [PRO$_i$ to attend class]

Further, while both are allowed as the subject of a nonfinite clause, in most circumstances the antecedent must be the next subject up for both.

(247) *John$_i$ expects [Mary to believe [himself$_i$ to be clever]]

(248) *John$_i$ expects [Mary to try [PRO$_i$ to be clever]]

However, alongside these similarities, there are striking differences in the distributions of PRO and standard anaphors. For example, the paradigmatic position for an anaphor—direct object—is unavailable to PRO.

(249) John injured himself

(250) *John injured PRO

Further, even in the kinds of structural positions allowing both PRO and anaphors, as in (243) and (244), the precise distribution is, in general, complementary rather than identical, as seen in the contrast between (243), (244), on one hand, and (251), (252), on the other.

(251) *John believes [PRO to be clever]

(252) *John tries [himself to be clever]

    Thus, there are clear, and well-known, obstacles standing in the way of analyzing PRO simply as an anaphor, and thus determining its distribution and interpretation via Condition A. There have been a number of interesting attempts to overcome these obstacles, some of them involving appeals to the theory of Case, which we will explore in section 1.4.3. Suppose, for example, that *himself* requires Case, since it is lexical, while PRO does not tolerate Case, because it is not. Then (250) is immediately accounted for: PRO is Case-marked. (252) is straightforwardly explained on the standard assumption that *try* cannot "exceptionally" Case-mark; that is, it can Case-mark a complement NP but cannot Case-mark the subject of a complement clause. And (251) is ruled out since *believe* does exceptionally Case-mark, as seen in (243). But there are aspects of the distribution of PRO that cannot be deduced in this way. Consider (253).

(253) *John believes sincerely [Mary to be clever]
      cf. John believes sincerely that Mary is clever

In (253) *Mary* fails to receive Case, perhaps because of the adjacency requirement on Case assignment. But (254) is no better than (251).

(254) *John believes sincerely [PRO to be clever]

Thus, a filter proscribing Case for PRO is insufficient.

Further examples, of the sort that have been widely discussed, indicate additional deficiencies of a purely Case-theoretic account of the distribution of PRO. Since PRO in (255) is not in a configuration of Case assignment (a lexical NP is impossible here), that example might be expected to be grammatical, presumably with an "arbitrary" interpretation for PRO, as in (256).

(255) *it is likely [PRO to solve the problem]

(256) it is important [PRO to solve the problem]

And (257) might be expected to be grammatical with an arbitrary interpretation, or possibly with PRO controlled by *John*, given the general lack (or at least amelioration) of Condition A effects in clauses with expletive subjects, as illustrated in (258).

(257) *John believes [it to be likely [PRO to solve the problem]]

(258) John$_i$ believes [it to be likely [that pictures of himself$_i$ will be on display]]

(259)–(260), discussed in section 1.4.1 (see (139)), display one further configuration in which Case marking is inapplicable, yet PRO is nonetheless impossible.

(259) *my belief [Harry to be intelligent]
      cf. my belief that Harry is intelligent

(260) *my belief [PRO to be intelligent]

In Chomsky 1981a it is argued that the crucial factor determining the distribution of PRO is government. In particular, (261) is offered as a descriptive generalization (see also section 1.4.1).

(261) PRO must be ungoverned.

Under the standard assumption that Case marking requires government, this will entail that PRO will not be Case-marked. But the requirement is now broader, since there is government without Case marking. This is what we find in (254), (255), (257), and (260). The distribution of PRO is thus correctly described.

(261) can itself be deduced from more general properties, namely, Conditions A and B. If we take PRO to be simultaneously both an anaphor and a pronominal, as suggested in section 1.3.1, it will then follow that it will never have a GC, since if it did, contradictory requirements would be in force, given that *free* entails not bound. (261) now follows, since a governed element will always have a GC. The relevance of this to the present discussion is that control must now be independent of Condition A, the condition determining antecedence for (pure) anaphors, since to exist at all, PRO must trivially satisfy Condition A, by virtue of having no GC.

This is widely viewed as an unfortunate, or even intolerable, consequence, and a substantial amount of research has focused on redefining PRO and/or providing alternative characterizations of "governing category." For particularly interesting discussions along these lines, see, for example, Bouchard 1984 and Manzini 1983. We suggest here that control is different enough from anaphor binding that a separate mechanism for antecedent assignment is, in fact, justified. Consider first the familiar observation that in addition to the instances of control by a subject illustrated above, a controller can regularly be an object, as in (262).

(262) John told Mary$_i$ [PRO$_i$ to leave]

Thus far there is no evidence for distinguishing control from binding, since binding too can be by an object.

(263) John told Mary$_i$ about herself$_i$

But at least two differences emerge on closer inspection. First, control is generally by a specifically designated argument. (See Nishigauchi 1984.) (264), with control by a subject instead of an object, is ill formed.

(264) *John$_j$ told Mary [PRO$_j$ to leave]

Binding, on the other hand, has no such constraint in English, as seen in the grammaticality of (265).

(265) John$_j$ told Mary about himself$_j$

Thus, there is an optionality concerning choice of binder that does not regularly exist for choice of controller, a significant difference between the two phenomena.

Now, it is well known that there are languages unlike English with respect to this property of binding. In particular, there are languages where, apparently, only subjects can be binders. Polish is one such language, as illustrated in the following paradigm, from Willim 1982:

(266) Jan$_i$ opowiadał Marii$_j$ o   swoim$_i$ ojcu
        John telling   Mary about self's   father
        'John was telling Mary about his father'

(267) *Jan$_i$ opowiadał Marii$_j$ o   swoim$_j$ ojcu
        John telling   Mary about self's   father
        'John was telling Mary about her father'

These languages display a second difference between binding and control. For, while anaphor binding by a nonsubject is impossible, control by a nonsubject is possible (or even necessary), just as in English.

(268) Jan$_i$ kazał Marii$_j$ [PRO$_{j/*i}$ napisac' artykuł]
        John told   Mary   write   article
        'John told Mary to write an article'

The precise nature of the parameter distinguishing English-type anaphor binding (any c-commander as the binder) from the Polish type (only subject as the binder) is far from clear. But what does seem clear is that this parametric difference does not carry over to control. For this and other reasons, there is considerable evidence for the existence of a distinct control module in the theory of grammar.

1.4.3 Case Theory

In some languages (Sanskrit, Latin, Russian, ...), Case is morphologically manifested, while in others, it has little (English, French, ...) or no (Chinese, ...) overt realization. In line with our general approach, we assume that Case is always present abstractly. In nominative/accusative languages, the subject of a finite clause is assigned *nominative* Case; the object of a transitive verb is assigned *accusative* Case (with some parametric and lexical variation, as discussed by Freidin and Babby (1984), Neidle (1988), among others); and the object of a pre- or postposition is assigned *oblique* Case (again with substantial variation). The basic ideas of Case theory grew out of the investigation of the distribution of overt

NPs, those with morphological content. Chomsky and Lasnik (1977) proposed a set of surface filters to capture this distribution, but Vergnaud (1982) observed that most of their effects could be unified if Case is assigned as indicated just above, and if Case is required for morphological realization, as stated in (269), the *Case Filter*.

(269) Every phonetically realized NP must be assigned (abstract) Case.

Chomsky and Lasnik's filters, and Vergnaud's replacement, were largely concerned with subject position of infinitival clauses. By and large, a lexical NP is prohibited in this position.

(270) *it seems [*Susan* to be here]

(271) *I am proud [*Bill* to be here]

Finite counterparts of these constructions are possible.

(272) it seems [that *Susan* is here]

(273) I am proud [that *Bill* is here]

This is as predicted, since in (272)–(273) the italicized NP is assigned nominative Case, while no Case is available for the corresponding NPs in (270)–(271).

Certain empty categories are permitted in place of the lexical NPs in (270)–(271). In (274) we have the trace of raised *Susan*, instead of the NP *Susan* itself, and in (275) we find PRO in place of *Bill*.

(274) Susan seems [*t* to be here]

(275) I am proud [PRO to be here]

Indeed, as discussed in section 1.3.1, it is the Case requirement that forces the movement producing (274) from an underlying structure like (270). (269) then need not be satisfied at D-Structure, but rather is a condition on a derived level of representation.

(276) displays another construction permitting PRO as subject of an infinitive while disallowing lexical NP.

(276) a. Bill tried [PRO to be here]
      b. *Bill tried [Mary to be here]

In surprising contrast with the complement of *try*, we find just the reverse behavior with *believe*.

(277) a. *Bill believed [PRO to be here]
      b. Bill believed [Mary to be here]

As seen in section 1.4.2, (276a) versus (277a) receives an account in terms of binding theory. The CP complement of *try* is a barrier to government of the subject of the complement, so PRO is allowed, having no GC in this configuration. Under the assumption that *believe*, as a lexical property, takes just an IP complement, PRO in (277a) is governed, hence has a GC. Either Condition A or Condition B is then necessarily violated. However, (277b) is not yet explained. In that example *Mary* is not the subject of a finite clause, the object of a transitive verb, or the object of a preposition, so (269) should be violated. The fact that the example is acceptable indicates that *Mary* does receive Case; (278) indicates that that Case is accusative (or oblique) rather than nominative.

(278) Bill believed [her (*she) to be here]

Further, there is evidence that the Case assigner is the matrix verb *believe(d)*. Perhaps because of the meager overt Case system in English, Case assignment generally conforms to an adjacency requirement, as illustrated in (279).

(279) a.   Bill sincerely believed Sam
        b. *Bill believed sincerely Sam

The same requirement exhibits itself with respect to the subject of the infinitival complement of *believe*.

(280) a.   Bill sincerely believed [Mary to be here]
        b. *Bill believed sincerely [Mary to be here]

Evidently, *believe* can assign accusative Case not only to its object (the core situation) as in (279a), but also to the subject of its infinitival complement, a phenomenon often referred to as *exceptional Case marking* (ECM). Recalling that (277a) shows that there is a government relation in this configuration, we conclude that Case is assigned under government (and, parametrically, adjacency), a slightly weaker requirement than the head-complement relation at its core. We tentatively take nominative Case also to fall under government, in this instance government of the subject by the inflectional head of IP (assuming an m-command definition of government).

In English the lexical heads V and P appear to be Case assigners, while N and A do not. This is why NPs can occur as direct complements of the former, $[-N]$, categories, but not of the latter, $[+N]$, categories, despite the fact that X-bar theory would lead us to expect the same range of complements in both situations. Thus, while *proud* can take a clausal complement, as seen in (273) and (275), it cannot take a bare NP.

(281) *I am proud my students

Likewise, while the verb *criticize* takes an NP complement, its nominalization *criticism* does not.

(282) John criticized the theory

(283) *John's criticism the theory

In place of the NP complements in (281) and (283), we find an apparent prepositional phrase with a semantically null preposition *of*.

(284) I am proud of my students

(285) John's criticism of the theory

It seems that *of* is inserted to provide a Case assigner for a lexical NP that would otherwise be Caseless. Insertion of a pleonastic element to fulfill a morphosyntactic requirement is a rather common process. "*Do*-support" salvages an inflectional affix isolated from V by movement of I to C, as in (286).

(286) did John leave

But there is some reason to question such an account of (284)–(285). In particular, none of the other Case Filter violations enumerated above can be salvaged by the insertion of *of*.

(287) *it seems of *Susan* to be here   (cf. (270))

(288) *I am proud of *Bill* to be here   (cf. (271))

(289) *Bill tried of *Mary* to be here   (cf. (276b))

(290) *Bill believed sincerely of *Sam*   (cf. (279b))

(291) *Bill believed sincerely of *Mary* to be here   (cf. (280b))

To the (271) versus (288) paradigm, with an adjectival head of the construction, could be added (292a) versus (292b), where the head is nominal.

(292) a. *my proof *John* to be here
       b. *my proof of *John* to be here

That *proof* can take a clausal complement is evidenced by (293).

(293) my proof that John is here

Further, it would be expected to take an infinitival complement as an option since the verb to which it is related can.

(294) a. I proved that John is here
      b. I proved John to be here

It is important to note that under other circumstances "*of*-insertion" is available with *proof*, as illustrated in (295).

(295) a. *my proof the theorem
      b.   my proof of the theorem

Two requirements emerge from the data examined so far. First, "*of*-insertion" takes place in the context of a [+N] head (N or A) and not otherwise. And second, *of* is available only for the *complement* of an appropriate head. It is not possible in "exceptional" circumstances. This suggests a different perspective on *of*-insertion. Instead of *of* being inserted, as a sort of last resort, before the complement of an A or N, suppose A and N are, in fact, (genitive) Case assigners, as is overtly visible in German (Van Riemsdijk 1981). *Of* can then be regarded as the realization of this genitive Case in this configuration in English. Following Chomsky (1986b), we then distinguish the *structural Cases* accusative and nominative, which are assigned solely in terms of S-Structure configuration, from *inherent Cases*, including genitive, which are associated with θ-marking. That is, inherent Case is assigned by α to NP only if α θ-marks NP. In (292), then, *John* cannot receive inherent Case from *proof* since it receives no θ-role from it. Structural Case has no such thematic requirement, but *proof*, being a noun, has no structural Case to assign. Thus, *John* receives no Case at all and violates the Case Filter. Note that under the inherent Case approach to *of*-insertion, the abstract Case needed for the satisfaction of the Case Filter can be either structural or inherent.

Passives are another construction in which Case is evidently not available, but where *of*-insertion, now viewed as inherent genitive assignment, still does not obtain. (296) illustrates this for "exceptional" Case.

(296) *it is believed (of) Mary to be here

Compare *Mary is believed to be here* and *it is believed that Mary is here*. These examples show that a passive verb, unlike a preposition or active verb, is not a structural Case assigner. The impossibility of *of* here is not surprising, given the thematic requirement we have seen. (297) is more problematic.

(297) *it is believed (of) Mary
       cf. Mary is believed

Again, structural Case is unavailable, indicating that, as suggested in Chomsky and Lasnik 1977, passive verbs are not [−N]. But since *Mary* is the θ-marked complement of *believed*, inherent genitive Case might be expected. The fact that it is not possible indicates that a passive verb, while not a verb ([+V, −N]), is not an adjective ([+V, +N]) either. Rather, it is a neutralized [+V] category with no marking for the feature [N]. Alternatively, as in Baker, Johnson, and Roberts 1989, the passive morpheme is actually an argument receiving the subject θ-role of the verb and the accusative Case that the verb assigns. Accusative Case is then unavailable for the object of the verb, or for the subject of a clausal infinitival complement.

The Case Filter was originally proposed as a morphological requirement, and while such a requirement might well be at its core, there are relevant phenomena that do not seem amenable to an account in morphological terms. The trace of *wh*-movement generally must conform to the Case Filter; note that virtually all of the contexts examined thus far where a lexical NP is prohibited also disallow a *wh*-trace.

(298) *who does it seem [t to be here]

(299) *who are you proud [t to be here]

(300) *who did Bill try [t to be here]

(301) *who are you proud t

(302) *which theory did you understand the proof t

(303) *who is it believed t

Though traces have features, they have no morphological realization, so (298)–(303) are unexpected. It might be thought that it is actually the *wh*-phrase antecedent of the trace that must satisfy (269), with Case somehow being transmitted from the trace via the links of the movement chain in well-formed *wh*-questions such as (304).

(304) who did you see t

However, the paradigm is replicated in constructions where even the moved operator need not have overt morphological realization, as in the relative clauses in (305) or the complex adjectival constructions in (306).

(305) a. the man (who) I see
      b. *the man (who) it seems to be here
      c. *the man (who) you are proud to be here
      d. *the man (who) Bill tried to be here
      e. *the man (who) I am proud
      f. *the theory (which) you understand the proof
      g. *the man (who) it is believed

(306) a. $Mary_i$ is too clever [Op_i [for us to catch t_i]]
      b. *$Mary_i$ is too reclusive [Op_i [for it to seem t_i to be here]]
      c. *$Bill_i$ is too unpopular [Op_i [for you to try t_i to be here]]

Evidently, both phonetically realized NPs and variables (traces of operator movement) must have abstract Case. Arguably, *pro*, the null pronominal subject in such languages as Italian and Spanish, must also since it typically occurs as the subject of a finite clause. In terms of phonetics and morphology, these three NP types constitute an unnatural class. It is for this reason that we instead might attribute Case Filter effects to θ-theory. As mentioned in section 1.3.1, we assume that an argument must be visible for θ-role assignment, and it is Case that renders it visible. This correctly distinguishes overt NPs, variables, and *pro*, on the one hand, from NP-trace on the other hand. Only the former are arguments.

We now assume, then, that the Case Filter is, in effect, part of the principle of θ-marking: a chain is visible for θ-marking only if it has a Case position. Economy conditions (Last Resort) block further movement if a Case position has been reached in chain formation. Given the interface condition on D-Structures, we derive the Chain Condition: in an argument chain $(\alpha_1, \ldots, \alpha_n)$, α_1 is a Case position and α_n a θ-position.

In discussing the Chain Condition in section 1.3.1, we noted two major problems: concerning expletives and PRO. The former were discussed in section 1.3.3; it remains to deal with the fact that argument PRO appears in non-Case positions, a fact that apparently compels us to adopt a disjunctive version of the Visibility Condition that falls short of a true generalization.

(307) A chain is visible for θ-marking if it contains a Case position
      (necessarily, its head) or is headed by PRO.

The problems concerning PRO are in fact more serious. Thus, PRO is like other arguments in that it is forced to move from a non-Case position, and cannot move from a Case-marked position, facts left unexplained even by the unsatisfactory disjunction (307).

The first problem is illustrated by such constructions as (308).

(308) we never expected [there to be found α]

If α is an indefinite NP, the counterpart to (308) is grammatical in many languages and marginally acceptable in English (more so, with "heavy NPs" such as *a hitherto unknown play by Shakespeare*); at LF, α raises to the position of the expletive, giving a chain that satisfies the Visibility Condition. But with α = PRO, the sentence is completely excluded, though all relevant conditions are satisfied: PRO occupies a θ-position as object of *find*, and choice of arbitrary PRO should satisfy the "definiteness condition," giving the meaning 'we never expected that some arbitrary person would be found'. Overt raising of PRO to the position of *there* is possible, as in (309), but with an entirely different meaning involving control by *we*.

(309) we never expected [PRO to be found *t*]

As a descriptive observation, yet to be explained, we conclude that PRO must move from a non-Case position at S-Structure, while other arguments must move from such a position either at S-Structure or at LF.

To bar (308), we might appeal to the requirement that PRO be ungoverned (see section 1.4.2). We must, however, now assume that this condition applies at S-Structure; if the condition follows from Conditions A and B of the binding theory, then these too apply at S-Structure. To account for (309), we might modify Last Resort to permit movement of PRO from a governed position.

Both the assumption that binding theory applies at S-Structure and the extension of Last Resort are open to question. Furthermore, they are empirically inadequate, because of the second problem: like other arguments, PRO is not permitted to move from a Case-marked position, even to escape government. The problem is illustrated in such forms as (310).

(310) a. α to talk about β
      b. α to strike β [that the problems are insoluble]
      c. α to seem to β [that the problems are insoluble]

Suppose that (310a) is a D-Structure in the context *it is unfair* —, with α = *e* and β = John. Last Resort bars raising of β to position α, yielding

(311a), because the chain (*John*) is already visible for θ-marking without movement. Suppose β = PRO. On the assumptions now under consideration, PRO must raise to the position α to satisfy the nongovernment requirement. But that movement is impermissible, even though α is a legitimate position for PRO in other constructions, as in (311c).

(311) a. *it is unfair [John to talk about *t*]
      b. *it is unfair [PRO to talk about *t*]
      c. it is unfair [PRO to talk about John]

One might argue in this case that there is a θ-theory violation, the subject being an obligatorily θ-marked position (a dubious move, as illustrated by nominalizations in which no external θ-role is assigned; see Chomsky 1981a). But that argument will not suffice for (310b–c) (Lasnik 1992). Here α is in a non-θ-position, so that the sentences are well formed with α = expletive *it* and β = *John* as in (312a–b).

(312) a. it is rare for it to strike John that the problems are insoluble
      b. it is rare for it to seem to John that the problems are insoluble

Still, β = *John* cannot raise to the position α, leaving trace, as in (313).

(313) a. *We want John to strike *t* that the problems are insoluble
      b. *We want John to seem to *t* that the problems are insoluble

In the case of β = *John*, Last Resort accounts for the phenomena, Case being assigned in the trace position and therefore barring further movement. But suppose that β = PRO in (310). The requirement of nongovernment forces movement, to yield (314).

(314) a. PRO to strike *t* [that the problems are insoluble]
      b. PRO to seem to *t* [that the problems are insoluble]

PRO is now in an ungoverned position, heading a θ-marked chain. Hence, all conditions are satisfied. But the constructions are radically ungrammatical, whatever the context.

We conclude, then, that the proposal to impose the nongovernment requirement for PRO at S-Structure and to incorporate this condition in Last Resort did not solve the problem. Even with these questionable moves, the disjunctive formulation of the Visibility Condition remains empirically inadequate, as well as unsatisfactory. Some other principle requires that PRO behave like other arguments, moving from non-Case positions and barred from moving from Case positions.

Notice that these anomalies would be overcome if PRO, like other arguments, has Case, but a Case different from the familiar ones: nominative, accusative, and so on. From the point of view of interpretation, we might regard PRO as a "minimal" NP argument, lacking independent phonetic, referential, or other properties. Accordingly, let us say that it is the sole NP that can bear null Case (though it may have other Cases as well, in nonstandard conditions that we will not review here). It follows that Last Resort applies to PRO exactly as it does to any argument: PRO is permitted to move from a non-Case position to a position where its Case can be assigned or checked, and is not permitted to move from a Case position. The Visibility Condition can now be simplified to (315).

(315) A chain is visible for θ-marking if it contains a Case position.

—necessarily, its head, by Last Resort.

Observe further that in some languages, agreement plays the same role as Case in rendering chains visible (Baker 1988). Thus, abstract Case should include agreement along with standard Case phenomena. The realization of abstract Case will depend on parametric choices for functional categories. Case is a relation of XP to H, H an X^0 head that assigns or checks the Case of XP. Where the feature appears in both XP and H, we call the relation "agreement"; where it appears only on XP, we call it "Case."

In English, Spanish, and other languages with minimal overt Case marking, agreement is often manifest with PRO as well as overt NPs, as in (316), where the predicate necessarily agrees with the subject of the lower clause.

(316) a.   I want [them to be officers]
      b.   *they want [me to be officers]
      c.   they want [PRO to be officers]
      d.   Juan cree   [PRO   estar enfermo]
           Juan believes [(himself) to.be sick]

Thus, PRO includes φ-features for agreement, elements of abstract Case if we construe this category in the manner just indicated. It is a small further step, then, to suppose that like other NPs, PRO contains standard Case as well as agreement features.

Where, then, is null Case assigned or checked (assume the latter, for concreteness)? Recall that nominative Case is standardly checked in

[Spec, IP], where I involves the features of tense and agreement (T, Agr). It is thus a realization of a Spec-head relation, with the head = I, the head of IP. It is natural, then, to take null Case to be a realization of the same relation where I lacks tense and agreement features: the minimal I checks null Case, and the minimal NP alone can bear it. More generally, we may assume that the infinitival element (with null agreement) and the head Ing of gerundive nominals check null Case, so that PRO will appear in such constructions as (317).

(317) a. PRO to VP (to be sick)
      b. PRO Ing VP (being sick)

One striking anomaly still remains in Case theory. We are taking abstract Case to be an expression of an (XP, head) relation. But we still have two distinct relations of head to XP, leaving us still with an unsatisfactory disjunctive formulation: while nominative (and now null) Case is the realization of a Spec-head relation, accusative Case is assigned by V to an NP that it governs. In discussing the matter earlier, we extended government to m-command to incorporate nominative Case assignment; but apart from the Case relation, c-command appears to be the appropriate basis for government. It would be more natural to suppose that structural Case in general is the realization of a Spec-head relation, while inherent Case, which, as we have seen, is associated with θ-marking, is assigned by lexical heads. We have already touched upon this possibility in discussing the inflectional system in section 1.3.2, where we took it to have the form (318) (=(77)).

(318)

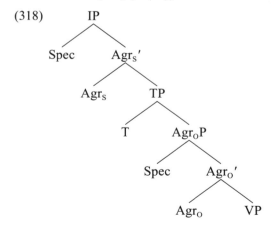

As before, the notations *Agr*$_S$ and *Agr*$_O$ are mnemonics; there is only one element Agr, a collection of φ-features. We continue to omit a possible [Spec, T] and negation, and to assume that at D-Structure the subject occupies the [Spec, VP] position.

Recall further that the V head of VP amalgamates with the heads Agr$_O$, T, and Agr$_S$; and at least by LF, V with its affixes has raised to eliminate all traces not c-commanded by their antecedents. Verbs may or may not have the ability to assign Case, which we may assume to be indicated by a two-valued feature [Case] for accusative and unaccusative verbs (Perlmutter 1978, Burzio 1986). If V has [+Case], then the amalgam [Agr$_O$, V] will also have this feature and will check accusative Case in the position [Spec, Agr$_O$]; if V has [−Case], an NP in [Spec, Agr$_O$] will not have its Case checked and must therefore move to [Spec, Agr$_S$]. The [Agr$_S$, T] amalgam checks either nominative or null Case in the position [Spec, Agr$_S$], depending on whether T has the value [+tense] or [−tense]. Structural Case in general is simply a manifestation of the [Spec, Agr] relation, with realizations as Case or agreement, depending on language-particular morphology.

As we have seen, one standard kind of parametric variation among languages has to do with the position of S-Structure in the derivation of LF from D-Structure. Thus, certain operations that are necessary for satisfying LF conditions may apply before or after the branch point to the PF component. The same is true of the operations that raise NP to the [Spec, Agr] positions for Case checking. Suppose that all the NP-raising operations are at LF and the language is left-headed, with V raising overtly to the inflectional position. Then as noted earlier (section 1.3.2), we have a VSO configuration at S-Structure, V and the inflectional elements having amalgamated and trace of V heading VP in (318), with subject and object remaining in their VP-internal positions. Subject will raise to [Spec, Agr$_S$] and object to [Spec, Agr$_O$] at LF. Suppose that subject raising is overt and object raising covert in the LF component. We then have an SVO configuration at S-Structure, with the VP headed by V or its trace depending on whether the language lowers inflections to V (like English) or raises V to inflection (like French, and English auxiliaries; see section 1.3.1). Suppose that the language is right-headed with overt object raising and covert subject raising; we then have OSV order at S-Structure (scrambling). If both subject and object raise overtly in a right-headed language, we will still have SOV order, but with traces in the original positions in VP. Other options are also possible.

The parameters involved are much like those that differentiate English-type languages that require overt raising of a question phrase from Chinese-type languages that leave all such phrases in situ. As discussed in section 1.3.3, we take the economy principles to prefer covert operations, which do not feed the PF component, to overt operations that do. Hence, unless a language requires that movement be overt, it will apply at LF, as in Chinese-type interrogatives or multiple *wh*-phrases in English-type languages. We might assume that what is involved is a condition on S-Structure Spec-head agreement, where the head is the C to which the *wh*-phrase raises—that is, a condition on Case, in the broad sense now under consideration. The conditions on Agr_S and Agr_O are similar. Only if S-Structure Spec-head agreement (Case, in the broad sense) is required is overt raising permissible: in English, for Agr_S but not Agr_O. For a formulation eliminating the S-Structure condition, see chapter 3.

This approach, which reduces Case agreement to a reflection of the Spec-head relation, requires that we modify the formulation of a number of the basic principles discussed earlier, while leaving their content essentially intact, for example, the Last Resort condition for movement and the associated Chain Condition. Consider the D-Structures (319).

(319) a. we believe [*e* to have [$_{VP}$ John won the election]]
       b. we believe [*e* to have [$_{VP}$ been elected John]]

Assuming the VP-internal subject hypothesis, *John* is within VP in (319a) and must raise to the subject position *e*, as also in (319b), yielding the S-Structure forms (320).

(320) a. we believe [John to have [*t* won the election]]
       b. we believe [John to have [been elected *t*]]

The standard account, reviewed earlier, explains this in terms of the Chain Condition, assuming an S-Structure requirement on Case assignment. Movement is a legitimate last resort operation.

We now cannot appeal to this argument for S-Structure movement. The problem is that the S-Structure forms (320) still do not satisfy the Chain Condition, because Case is checked only at the LF representations (321).

(321) a. we [John believe [*t′* to have *t* won the election]]
       b. we [John believe [*t′* to have been elected *t*]]

This is one of a class of problems relating to the subject position [Spec, IP], a non-θ-position that can be occupied either by an argument (raised from a θ-position) or an expletive, which may in turn be overt (*there*, *it*) or vacuous, that is, nothing but a target for movement. The expletive can be *pro*, if the language permits null subjects. In such a case, analogues to (319) would be acceptable in principle at S-Structure with *e* being *pro*, assuming the satisfaction of other conditions (the indefiniteness condition, etc.). Then LF movement would replace *pro* by its associate in the normal fashion.

Note that these problems arose in a different way in the standard account. In part the problems were conceptual: the standard account was based on the dubious assumption that Case must be checked at S-Structure, though on conceptual grounds we would expect the Visibility Condition, hence the Chain Condition, to apply only at the LF interface. In part the problems were similar to the ones just raised. Thus, in the construction (322), for example, the phrase *an error* is raised at S-Structure even though the target position is not assigned structural Case; this is checked (or assigned) only at LF, after expletive replacement.

(322) there was an error made *t* in the calculation

The problem is similar to the one we now face in the case of (319)–(321).

The EPP (see section 1.3.2) requires, for English, that the [Spec, IP] position be present through the course of a derivation, hence occupied by an expletive at D-Structure. Other optional positions (e.g., [Spec, Agr$_o$]) may be assumed to be inserted in the course of the derivation as part of the movement operation itself, inserting a target for movement in a manner conforming to X-bar theory. Where the expletive is inserted to satisfy the EPP, it must be either *pro* or a vacuous target for movement. English lacks the first option and must therefore accept the second: the vacuous expletive, which is only a target for movement.

A vacuous expletive, being only a target for movement, must be eliminated "as soon as possible." Either it is eliminated by the very movement operation that inserted it as a target, or, if it was inserted at D-Structure to satisfy the EPP, it is eliminated at the first opportunity in the course of derivation, hence surely by S-Structure, in the course of cyclic application of rules from the most deeply embedded structure to the highest category. Indirectly, then, (320) is left as the only option for English. It is necessary to extend this reasoning to other constructions that exhibit a similar range of properties, a matter that requires a closer analysis of the notions of economy and the status of expletives. For discussion within a considerably simplified framework, see chapter 3.

Turning now to the new version of Case theory, we can account for the fact that raising takes place at S-Structure in such constructions as (319). And since English does not require S-Structure checking of accusative Case, overt operations cannot form (321). It remains to provide a new interpretation of the Chain Condition and Last Resort, to conform to the new assumptions.

These revisions are straightforward. The Visibility Condition took Case (now including agreement) to be a condition for θ-marking. We assumed before that this was a condition on chains (the Chain Condition). We now take it to be a condition on *linked chains*, where a linked chain is formed by linking two chains C_1 and C_2 of (323), where $\alpha_n = \beta_1$.

(323) a. $C_1 = (\alpha_1, \ldots, \alpha_n)$
      b. $C_2 = (\beta_1, \ldots, \beta_m)$

The new linked chain C_3, headed by α_1 and terminating in β_m, is the LF object that must satisfy the Chain Condition. In the examples (319)–(321) we have the linked chain (*John, t', t*) at LF, in each case. The account can be simplified further in ways that we will not explore here.

Turning now to Last Resort, its intuitive content was that operations should be permissible only if they form legitimate LF objects. We now relax that requirement, taking an operation to be permissible if it is a *prerequisite* to the formation of a legitimate LF object; had the operation not taken place, the derivation would not have been able to form such an object. S-Structure raising is now a permissible last resort operation because, were it not to apply, the derivation would not yield legitimate LF objects in the case of (320), (322); the latter case indicates that this interpretation of Last Resort was already necessary in the standard account.

In presenting the standard account, we noted that the Case Filter is not satisfied at D-Structure, but rather is a condition on a derived level of representation. Apart from expletive constructions, that level was S-Structure, for English. We have now moved to the conceptually preferable assumption that the Case Filter is satisfied only at the interface level. S-Structure movement, where required, follows from the economy conditions, the EPP, and properties of expletives (including the null subject parameter).

It remains to settle many other questions (see chapter 3). But the basic structure of the system is reasonably clear, and it offers some prospects for unifying the properties of Case theory and integrating it into the general framework in a natural way.

1.5 Further Topics

The review above is sketchy and incomplete, and leaves many important topics virtually or completely unmentioned. A number of examples have been noted, among them the status of morphology, a question with broad implications, however the problems are settled. The discussion of the computational system is also crucially too narrow in that it excludes the PF component. This restriction of scope not only omits major topics (see Chomsky and Halle 1968, Goldsmith 1976, McCarthy 1979, Clements 1985, Dell and Elmedlaoui 1985, Halle and Vergnaud 1988, among many others), but also begs certain questions; as briefly noted earlier, there are open questions as to whether certain operations and properties we have assigned to the LF component do not in fact belong to the PF component (section 1.3.3).

Similar questions arise about the actual "division of labor" between the PF component and the overt syntax. Consider, for example, the "parallelism requirement"—call it PR—that holds of such expressions as (324).

(324) John said that he was looking for a cat, and so did Bill [say that he was looking for a cat]

The first conjunct is several-ways ambiguous. Suppose we resolve the ambiguities in one of the possible ways, say, by taking the pronoun to refer to Tom, and interpreting *a cat* nonspecifically, so that John said that Tom's quest would be satisfied by any cat. The constraint PR requires that the second conjunct be interpreted in the same way as the first—in this case, with *he* referring to Tom and *a cat* understood nonspecifically. The same is true of the elliptical construction (325).

(325) John said that he was looking for a cat, and so did Bill

Here too, the interpretation satisfies PR (Lasnik 1972, Sag 1976, Ristad 1993).

On our assumptions so far, PR applies to the LF representation. If (325) is generated at S-Structure, we must assume that some LF process "regenerates" something like (324), which is then subject to PR. A simple alternative would be to deny that (325) is generated at S-Structure, taking it to be formed by a rule of the PF component that deletes the bracketed material in (324) to form (325), as in earlier versions of generative grammar. That alternative is strengthened by observation of a

distinctive phonetic property of (324): the bracketed phrase has a distinguished low-flat intonation. That property, we assume, is determined
within the PF component. The deletion rule, then, could say simply
that material with this intonational property may optionally delete. Since
such expressions as (324) have their particular status in the language,
they must be generated quite independently of their elliptical counterparts. We are left, then, with a very simple treatment of ellipsis: it reduces to deletion of phonetically marked material by a general principle.
The problems of parallelism, and so on, must still be dealt with for such
examples as (324), but that is true independently of how we handle
ellipsis.

If this approach is correct, then a wide class of elliptical constructions
will be formed within the phonological component, not by operations of
the overt syntax. Numerous problems remain, for example, the status of
such expressions as (326), derived from the presumed underlying forms
(327), which are, however, ill formed in this case.

(326) a. John said that he was looking for a cat, and Bill did too
      b. John likes poetry, but not Bill

(327) a. John said that he was looking for a cat, and Bill did [say he was
         looking for a cat] too
      b. John likes poetry, but not Bill [likes poetry]

The solution to the problem might well involve significant changes in
how inflectional processes and negation are treated in the overt syntax.
We leave the question here, merely noting that an approach to ellipsis
that has considerable initial plausibility involves PF component properties in ways that may have large-scale effects when pursued. In this
respect too, omission of the PF component leaves important questions
unanswered.

The discussion of modules of language is also seriously incomplete.
We have, for example, said virtually nothing about θ-theory and argument structure (see, among many others, Gruber 1965, Jackendoff 1972,
1983, 1987, 1990b, Williams 1981, Bresnan 1982, Higginbotham 1985,
1988, Hale and Keyser 1986, 1991, Wilkins 1988, Grimshaw 1990, Pustejovsky 1992) and have barely mentioned the theory of control, topics that
interact crucially with other aspects of syntax. Further inquiry into these
topics raises the question whether the system of modules is, in fact, a real
property of the architecture of language, or a descriptive convenience.

It is unnecessary to add that this sketch also omits many other major topics that have been the focus of highly productive inquiry and provides only a scattered sample of relevant sources on the topics that have been addressed. As explained at the outset, we have attempted no more than to indicate the kinds of work being pursued within the general P&P framework and to outline some of the thinking that underlies and guides it.

Chapter 2

Some Notes on Economy of Derivation and Representation

The past few years have seen the development of an approach to the study of language that constitutes a fairly radical departure from the historical tradition, more so than contemporary generative grammar at its origins. I am referring to the principles-and-parameters (P&P) approach,[1] which questions the assumption that a particular language is, in essence, a specific rule system. If this approach is correct, then within syntax (excluding phonology)[2] there are no rules for particular languages and no construction-specific principles. A language[3] is not, then, a system of rules, but a set of specifications for parameters in an invariant system of principles of Universal Grammar (UG); and traditional grammatical constructions are perhaps best regarded as taxonomic epiphenomena, collections of structures with properties resulting from the interaction of fixed principles with parameters set one or another way. There remains a derivative sense in which a language L is a "rule system" of a kind: namely, the rules of L are the principles of UG as parameterized for L.

In the course of this recent work. certain unifying concepts have emerged—unifying in the sense that they appear throughout the components of a highly modular system: c-command and government, for example. There also seem to be fairly general principles involving these concepts, with wide-ranging effects. The Empty Category Principle (ECP), belonging to the theory of government, is one such principle, which has been the subject of much fruitful work. Such concepts and principles play a pervasive role in a tightly integrated system; slight modifications

This chapter originally appeared in *Principles and Parameters in Comparative Syntax*, edited by Robert Freidin (Cambridge, Mass.: MIT Press, 1991), and is published here with minor revisions.

in their formulation yield a diverse and often complex array of empirical consequences, which have also been fruitfully explored in a large number of languages. And we may be fairly confident that much remains to be learned about just how they should be expressed.

I think we can also perceive at least the outlines of certain still more general principles, which we might think of as "guidelines," in the sense that they are too vaguely formulated to merit the term "principles of UG." Some of these guidelines have a kind of "least effort" flavor to them, in the sense that they legislate against "superfluous elements" in representations and derivations. Thus, the notion of "Full Interpretation" (FI) requires that representations be minimal in a certain sense. Similarly, the Last Resort condition on movement, which yields a partial explanation for the requirement that A-chains be headed by a Case position and terminate in a θ-position (the "Chain Condition"), has the corresponding effect of eliminating superfluous steps in derivations, thus minimizing their length.[4] What I would like to do here is to search for some areas where we might be able to tease out empirical effects of such guidelines, with a view toward elevating them to actual principles of language, if that is indeed what they are.

2.1 Preliminary Assumptions

Let us begin with a range of assumptions concerning language design, generally familiar though often controversial, which I will adopt without specific argument.

I will assume the familiar Extended Standard Theory (EST) framework, understood in the sense of the P&P approach. We distinguish the lexicon from the computational system of the language, the syntax in a broad sense (including phonology). Assume that the syntax provides three fundamental levels of representation, each constituting an "interface" of the grammatical system with some other system of the mind/brain: D-Structure, Phonetic Form (PF), and Logical Form (LF).

The lexicon is a set of lexical elements, each an articulated system of features. It must specify, for each such element, the phonetic, semantic, and syntactic properties that are idiosyncratic to it, but nothing more; if features of a lexical entry assign it to some category K (say, consonant-initial, verb, or action verb), then the entry should contain no specification of properties of K as such, or generalizations will be missed. The lexical entry of the verb *hit* must specify just enough of its properties to determine its sound, meaning, and syntactic roles through the operation of general principles, parameterized for the language in question. It should not contain redundant information, for example, about the quality of the vowel, properties of action verbs generally, or the fact that together with its complement, it forms a VP.[5]

It has been suggested that parameters of UG relate, not to the computational system, but only to the lexicon. We might take this to mean that each parameter refers to properties of specific elements of the lexicon or to categories of lexical items—canonical government, for example. If this proposal can be maintained in a natural form, there is only one human language, apart from the lexicon, and language acquisition is in essence a matter of determining lexical idiosyncrasies. Properties of the lexicon too are sharply constrained, by UG or other systems of the mind/brain. If substantive elements (verbs, nouns, etc.) are drawn from an invariant universal vocabulary, then only functional elements will be parameterized. The narrower assumption appears plausible; what follows is consistent with it.[6]

The level of D-Structure is directly associated with the lexicon. It is a "pure" representation of θ-structure, expressing θ-relations through the medium of the X-bar-theoretic conditions in accordance with the Projection Principle. It may meet some strong "uniformity condition"[7] and in this sense be invariant across languages. I will assume here a two-level X-bar theory of the conventional sort, perhaps restricted to binary branching in accordance with Kayne's (1984) theory of "unambiguous paths."[8]

The level of PF is the interface with sensorimotor systems, and the level of LF, the interface with systems of conceptual structure and language use.

Each of these levels is a system of representation of a certain type, its properties specified by principles of UG.[9] For a particular language, the choice of D-Structure, PF, and LF must satisfy the "external" constraints of the interface relation. Furthermore, the three levels must be interrelated by mechanisms permitted by the language faculty. The *structural description* of an expression E in language L includes—perhaps *is* —the set $\{\delta, \pi, \lambda\}$, representations at the levels of D-Structure, PF, and LF, respectively, each satisfying the "external" conditions.[10] We may understand the *structure* of L to be the set of structural descriptions, for all expressions E. The language L itself consists of a lexicon, a specific choice of values for parameters of UG, and such rules as there may be, perhaps restricted to phonology. I understand *language* here in the sense of what I have called elsewhere *I-language*, where the terminology is intended to suggest "internalized" and "intensional." Intuitively, a language, so construed, is "a way of speaking and understanding," in a traditional sense; to have such a way of speaking and understanding (that is, to "have a language" or to "know a language") is to have the I-language as a component of the mind/brain. Note that although they are "external" to the computational system of language, the interface constraints are "internal" to the mind/brain. Other interactions—for example, those entering into the study of reference and truth—are a different matter.

In accordance with the general EST framework, I assume that the three levels are related to one another not directly, but only through the intermediary level of S-Structure, which is the sole point of interaction among the three fundamental levels. From this standpoint, S-Structure is a derivative concept. For a specific language L, its properties are determined by those of the fundamental levels, and by the condition that it be related to them by the appropriate principles. The level of S-Structure for L is the system that satisfies these conditions, something like the solution to a certain set of equations. Presumably, the principles of language design require that this "solution" be unique.

Exactly how these principles of interaction among levels should be understood is not entirely clear. I will adopt the general assumption that S-Structure is related to LF by iterated application of the principle Move α (substitution and adjunction), deletion, and insertion—that is, by the principle Affect α in the sense of Lasnik and Saito (1984)—and to PF by this principle and the rules of the phonological component.

The relation of S-Structure to the lexicon has been construed in various ways. I will assume that the relation is mediated by D-Structure, in the manner just outlined, and that D-Structure is related to S-Structure as S-Structure is related to LF and (in part) PF, that is, by iterated application of Affect α. Alternatively, it might be that D-Structure is determined by a chain formation algorithm applying to S-Structure (or perhaps LF), and in this sense is "projected" from S-Structure as a kind of property of S-Structure; this algorithm will then express the relation of S-Structure to the lexicon.

The choice between these two options has been open since the origins of trace theory, before the P&P approach crystallized. It has never been entirely clear that there is a real empirical issue here. There is, at best, a rather subtle difference between the idea that two levels are simply related, and the idea that the relation is a "directional mapping." Similarly, it is a subtle question whether the relation of S-Structure to the lexicon is mediated by a level of D-Structure with independent properties, serving as one of the fundamental "interface" levels. My own rather tentative feeling is that there is an issue, and that there is mounting, if rather subtle and inconclusive, evidence in support of the picture sketched earlier, with three fundamental interface levels and the D- to S-Structure relation interpreted as a directional mapping.[11] I will adopt this interpretation for expository purposes; it is rather generally adopted in practice, with results then sometimes reconstructed in terms of the alternative conception, a suggestive and possibly meaningful fact. Much of what follows is neutral between the several interpretations of this system.

S-Structure may also have to satisfy independent conditions, for example, the binding theory principles, conditions on identification of empty categories, and perhaps X-bar theory.[12]

2.2   Some Properties of Verbal Inflection

Of the many specific areas that might be investigated in an effort to clarify general guidelines of the kind mentioned earlier, I will concentrate on the topic of X^0-movement, a matter of particular interest because of its implications for the study of word formation, though there are other cases, for example, V-movement in the sense of Koopman (1984) and others. With respect to word formation, there are two major categories where the question of X^0-movement arises: complex predicates (causatives, noun incorporation, etc.), and inflectional morphology. There is an ongoing and illuminating debate about whether X^0-movement applies in these cases, and if so, how. I will not consider the first category, but will limit attention to inflection, assuming that it involves syntactic rules such as V-raising to I, and I-lowering to V (affix hopping). I am thus assuming a sharp and principled distinction between inflectional morphology, part of syntax proper, and strictly derivational morphology, part of the lexicon, perhaps subject to such principles as right-headedness in the sense of Edwin Williams and others. I am, then, assuming something like the earliest version of the lexicalist hypothesis.

With respect to X^0-movement, there is one salient descriptive fact— the Head Movement Constraint (HMC)—and one central question

about it: is it reducible, partially or completely, to independently motivated principles of syntactic movement? Assume for now that XP-movement (A- and Ā-movement) is given, with its principles, specifically the
ECP. I will assume that the ECP reduces to the property of antecedent
government, with the requirement that trace be properly governed relating to other conditions that have to do with "identification" of empty
categories.[13] We then ask whether these same principles yield the HMC
as a special case. If so, we have a true reduction of the HMC, and therefore reduction of properties of word formation to independently established principles of syntax.[14]

Let us begin with some recent ideas of Jean-Yves Pollock, based on
work by Joseph Emonds on verbal inflection in English-type and French-
type languages.[15] I will generally follow Pollock's proposals, adapting
some of them in a different way and asking how they might bear on
"least effort" guidelines and the status of the HMC.

Assume the X-bar-theoretic principle that $S = I''$ (IP), so that the basic
structure of the clause is (1).[16]

(1)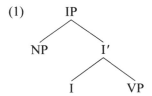

We leave open the question whether the subject NP is base-generated in
place or raised from VP, as proposed in several recent studies, and many
other questions that are not directly relevant.

Emonds's basic idea is that in French-type languages, V raises to I,
whereas in English-type languages, I lowers to V. There is a variety of
empirical evidence supporting this conclusion. Assume it to be correct. It
will then follow that VP-adverbs, which we take to be generated under
VP adjoined to another VP, are preverbal in English and postverbal in
French, as in (2).

(2) a. John often kisses Mary
    b. John completely lost his mind
    c. Jean embrasse souvent Marie
    d. Jean perdit complètement la tête

But the English auxiliaries *have* and *be* behave approximately like ordinary verbs in French, as in (3).

(3) a. John has completely lost his mind

    b. books are often (completely) rewritten for children

Therefore, the distinction is not raising in French versus lowering in English, but some other difference that requires French verbs and English auxiliaries to raise while barring this possibility for other verbs in English.

On other grounds, it has been postulated that the Agr element is "stronger" in French than in English. Assume this to be true. Assume further that weak Agr is unable to "attract" true verbs such as *kiss* or *lose*, though it can attract auxiliaries, whereas strong Agr attracts all verbs.[17]

Why should weak and strong Agr behave in this fashion? One possibility, suggested by Howard Lasnik, is that it is simply a morphological property: only strong Agr can accept a "heavy" element such as a verb, though any Agr can accept a "light" element such as an auxiliary. Another possibility, developed by Pollock, is that the difference reduces to θ-theory: strong Agr allows an adjoined element to head a θ-chain, but weak Agr does not. If the auxiliaries are not θ-markers, then they can raise to Agr without a violation of the θ-Criterion, but raising a true verb to weak Agr will lead to a violation of the θ-Criterion.

Looking at this option more closely, consider the effect of raising Y^0 to adjoin to X^0. This process yields the structure (4), where t is the trace of Y^0.

(4)

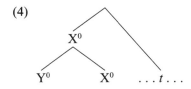

The theory of government must permit Y^0 to govern its trace t in this structure, so as to satisfy the ECP. If the theory of government precludes government of Y^0 from outside of the complex element X^0 formed by adjunction, then successive-cyclic movement of Y^0 will be barred; thus, causative formation, for example, cannot escape the HMC (assuming it to reduce to the ECP) by successive-cyclic movement. I will assume this to be the case, putting a precise formulation aside.

The chain (Y^0, t) will therefore be properly formed in (4) with regard to the ECP. Suppose that Y^0 is a θ-marker. Then t must be able to θ-mark; the θ-marking property of Y^0 must be "transmitted" through the chain. That will be possible if X^0 is strong, but not if it is weak. We will therefore have a θ-Criterion violation if a θ-marker Y^0 is adjoined to weak Agr.

Suppose that instead of raising Y^0 to adjoin to X^0 to yield (4), we lower X^0 to adjoin to Y^0. This process again forms the complex element $[Y^0-X^0]$, but with a structure different from (4)—namely, (5)—t being the trace of X^0.

(5)

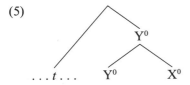

Here the lower Y^0 is the head of the construction, and we may assume that whatever the character of X^0, Y^0 will retain all relevant relations to other elements and will therefore retain the capacity to θ-mark a complement. The normal properties of adjunction, then, have the desired effect, as Pollock observes: lowering of weak Agr to the verb v does not bar θ-marking of the complement, but raising of v to weak Agr does bar θ-marking.

Pollock extends the domain of observation further to negation, proposing the more articulated structure (6) in a Kayne-style unambiguous path analysis.

(6)

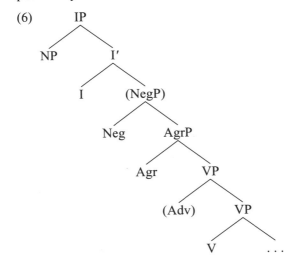

Here I may be [±finite] and Neg is English *not* or French *pas*.[18] This representation, separating I and Agr, eliminates the odd dual-headedness of I in earlier treatments. The assumption is that infinitives have (generally vacuous) Agr.

Suppose that V raises to Agr. Then we have the S-Structure order Verb-Adverb-Object, as with English auxiliaries or French verbs generally. If Agr lowers to V, we have the order Adv-V-Obj, as with English nonauxiliary verbs. If V raises to Agr and the complex then raises further to I, we have such forms as (7).

(7) a. John has not seen Bill
    b. Jean (n') aime pas Marie
       Jean (*ne*) love NEG Marie
       'Jean does not love Marie'

If V raises to Agr but not to I, we have (8) in French, where *sembler* 'seem' in (8a) contrasts with *être* 'be' in (8b).

(8) a. ne pas sembler heureux
       ne NEG seem   happy
       'not to seem happy'
    b. n'être pas heureux
       ne be NEG happy
       'not to be happy'

The properties illustrated in (7) and (8) follow on the assumption that [+finite] is strong and [−finite] is weak. Being strong, [+finite] allows the verb *aime* to adjoin to it, crossing Neg (*pas*), in (7b). Being weak, [−finite] does not permit the verb *sembler* to adjoin to it, crossing Neg, in (8a), though the auxiliary *être* can raise to weak I just as auxiliaries can raise to weak Agr.

Though the V-raising rule in French is obligatory for tensed clauses, it is optional for infinitives. Thus, alongside (8b) we have the option (9a); and alongside the form V-Adv-NP (obligatory for finite verbs as in (2c)) we have (9b).

(9) a. ne pas être heureux
    b. souvent paraître triste
       often   seem   sad

(9a) results from failure of *être* to raise over Neg to [−finite] I, and (9b) from failure of *paraître* to raise over the adverb to Agr in the infinitive.

We return in section 2.3.2 to the question of why raising should be optional just in the case of the infinitive, and in section 2.5 to further questions about the nature of Agr. Tentatively, let us assume the analysis just given, putting aside the optionality with infinitives.

At S-Structure the verb must typically be combined with its various affixes, to yield the proper forms at PF; the various affixes in (6) must form a single complex with a verb. Let us suppose that these affixes share some unique feature to guarantee proper association at S-Structure. Thus, any series of rule applications that separates them is barred by an appropriate S-Structure condition, and we need not be concerned if the rule system permits "wild" applications of rules that would leave affixes improperly scattered among the words of the sentence generated. Note that other improper rule applications are barred by the requirement that items lexically identified as affixes be properly "attached" at S-Structure.

Assuming Pollock's parameter, we have strong and weak inflectional affixes. The [+finite] choice for I (tensed) is strong and the [−finite] choice (infinitive) is weak. Agr is strong in French, weak in English. The basic facts follow, with some idealization of the data.

Pollock observes that earlier stages of English were very much like French, suggesting plausibly that a change in the Agr parameter led to the collection of phenomena that differentiate the languages in their current state. Some of the forms reflect D-Structure directly: for example, (9a–b) in French and their English equivalents. Other forms reflect the consequences of raising of V to Agr or to I, as illustrated. Pollock points out that unitary treatment of the comparative data—with the array of facts involving tense-infinitive, negation and adverbs, verbs and auxiliaries—relies crucially on analysis of Tense and Agreement morphemes "as separate syntactic entities at an abstract level of representation," namely, D-Structure. The analysis, he concludes, provides support for the rigid X-bar-theoretic condition of single-headedness and the consequent distinction between Agr and I, and for the distinction between D-and S-Structure representation.

2.3   A "Least Effort" Account

2.3.1   Minimizing Derivations

Let us now see how an analysis of this nature would bear on the guidelines we have been considering. I will put aside the relation of S-Structure to PF and D-Structure to lexicon. Thus, we are considering the

relations among D-Structure, S-Structure, and LF. For expository convenience, I will refer to the relation of D- to S-Structure as *overt syntax*
(since the consequences of the operations relating these levels are commonly reflected at PF).

The analysis of verbal inflection outlined in section 2.2 relies crucially
on the principle that raising is necessary if possible. This would follow
from the assumption that shorter derivations are always chosen over
longer ones. The reason is that lowering of an inflectional element Inf, as
in the case of English true verbs, yields an improper chain $(t, \dots, \text{Inf})$,
where Inf is adjoined to V at S-Structure to form $[_v \text{V–Inf}]$ and t is the
trace of Inf, which c-commands it. Subsequent LF raising of $[_v \text{V–Inf}]$
to the position of t is therefore required to create a proper chain. The
result is essentially the same as would have been achieved with the
shorter derivation that involves only raising in the overt syntax. Therefore, by a "least effort" condition, only the latter is permissible.

A closer look shows that the "least effort" condition cannot reduce
simply to the matter of counting steps in a derivation. Consider English
interrogatives. Let us assume that an interrogative construction has the
complementizer Q ($[+wh]$) to distinguish it at D-Structure from the
corresponding declarative, triggering the appropriate intonational structure at PF and the proper interpretation at LF. If Q is furthermore an
affix, then it must be "completed" in the overt syntax by X^0-raising. The
D-Structure representation (10) will yield, by lowering, an S-Structure
representation with the verb $[\text{V–Agr–I}]$[19] and traces in the positions of I
and Agr.

(10) Q John I Agr write books

The resulting form is indistinguishable from the declarative at PF and is
furthermore illegitimate (at S-Structure) if Q is a real element, as postulated. To permit an output from the legitimate D-Structure representation (10), English makes use of the dummy element *do* to bear the affix,
so that lowering does not take place; rather, Agr and I adjoin to *do*.
Let us call this process *do*-support, a language-specific process contingent upon the weakness of Agr; for expository purposes, assume it to be
a rule of the overt syntax inserting *do* in the Modal position, hence *do*-
insertion, attracting the raised affixes and then raising to Q. Given this
device, we can form *did John write books* from (10).[20]

The same device, however, permits the illegitimate form *John did write
books* (*do* unstressed) alongside *John wrote books*, both deriving from the

declarative form corresponding to (10) (lacking Q). In fact, this option is not only available but in fact arguably obligatory if shorter derivations are always preferred. The reason is that the illegitimate form requires only the rule of *do*-insertion and raising, whereas the correct form requires overt lowering and subsequent LF raising.

To yield the correct results, the "least effort" condition must be interpreted so that UG principles are applied wherever possible, with language-particular rules used only to "save" a D-Structure representation yielding no output: interrogative forms without modal or non-θ-marking verbs, in this case. UG principles are thus "less costly" than language-specific principles. We may think of them, intuitively, as "wired-in" and distinguished from the acquired elements of language, which bear a greater cost.[21]

Consider now a negative expression with the D-Structure representation (11).

(11) John I Neg Agr write books

The correct derivation involves *do*-insertion and raising of Agr to form the complex verb [*do*–I–Agr], with the S-Structure representation (12).

(12) John did (does) not write books

But again we face a problem: why doesn't I lower to Agr, then to V, yielding the complex verb [V–Agr–I] as in the nonnegated form, so that at S-Structure and PF we have *John not wrote (writes) books*? Then LF raising will apply, eliminating the improper chain, exactly as in the case of the nonnegative counterpart. This process involves only the UG principles of overt lowering and LF raising, avoiding the language-particular rule of *do*-insertion. It is therefore not only a permissible derivation, but is actually required by the "least effort" condition, as just revised.

A partial solution to this problem is provided by the HMC. The process of LF raising has to cross Neg, thus violating the HMC. There is therefore only one legitimate derivation: the one involving *do*-insertion, which is therefore required in these cases.

We are thus assuming that, given a well-formed representation at D-Structure, we necessarily apply the least costly derivation that is legitimate to yield an S-Structure and, ultimately, a PF output.

But several further questions immediately arise. Consider the French counterpart to (11) or, equivalently, the English form (13).

(13) John I Neg Agr have written books

Here the correct derivation requires that the verb *have* raise to Agr, then to I, crossing Neg, to yield (14).

(14) John has not written books

The same will be true of a main verb in French, as in the counterpart to the D-Structure representation (11). If the HMC blocks the unwanted derivation with LF raising over Neg in the case of (11), then why does it not equivalently block the *required* derivation with overt raising over Neg in the case of (14) and the French equivalent to (11)?

Note that a similar question also arises in the case of (11). Thus, the required derivation involves raising of Agr over Neg to I to form the complex verb [*do*–I–Agr] after *do*-insertion. Why, then, does overt raising of Agr over Neg not violate the HMC?[22]

To deal with these questions, we have to consider more carefully the nature of deletion. Clearly, we cannot delete an element if it plays a role at LF: for example, the trace of a verb. But such considerations do not require that the trace of Agr remain at LF, since it plays no role at that level. We might, then, suppose that the trace of Agr is deletable (I will return to this conclusion in a more general setting in section 2.6.2). We must also determine exactly what we intend the process of deletion to be. There are various possible answers to this question, generally not addressed because they go beyond known empirical consequences. In the present context, however, there are empirical consequences, so a specific decision must be reached. One plausible answer is that deletion of an element leaves a category lacking features, which we can designate [*e*]. The deletion leaves a position but no features, in particular, no categorial features. Deletion of [$_{Agr}$ *t*], the trace of Agr, leaves [*e*], and by X-bar-theoretic principles, the dominating category AgrP is now *e*P, an XP with no features.[23] That is a satisfactory conclusion, since AgrP plays no role at LF.

Making these assumptions, let us return to the problems we faced. Consider first the raising of Agr to I over Neg to form [*do*–I–Agr] in the correct derivation from the D-Structure representation (11). This process will, in fact, violate the HMC regarded as a condition on derivations, but there will be no ECP violation at LF once the trace of Agr is deleted. Recall that we are taking the ECP to be a condition on chains, along the lines discussed in Chomsky 1986a, thus not applicable to the empty categories PRO, *pro*, and *e*, but only to trace. We therefore have no ECP violation, though we do have an HMC violation. But if the HMC is reducible to the ECP, then we can dismiss the HMC as a descriptive artifact, valid only insofar as it does in fact reduce to the ECP. The present case would be one in which the HMC does not reduce to the ECP and is therefore inoperative.

Let us now turn to the more general question. Why does LF raising of [V–Agr] to I over Neg violate the HMC, whereas overt raising of [V–Agr] to I over Neg (as in the case of English auxiliaries and all French verbs) does not violate the HMC? To answer this question, we must again consider more closely the structures formed by adjunction.

Let us return to the D-Structure representations (11) and (13), repeated here in (15).

(15) a. John I Neg Agr write books
     b. John I Neg Agr have written books

Lowering of I to Agr forms the element [$_{Agr}$ Agr–I], leaving the trace t_1. Further lowering of the complex element to V forms [$_V$ V [$_{Agr}$ Agr–I]], a verb, leaving the trace t_{Agr}. But this trace deletes, leaving [e], a position lacking features. Applying these processes to (15a), then, we derive the S-Structure representation (16).

(16) John t_1 Neg [e] [$_{VP}$[$_V$ write [$_{Agr}$ Agr–I]] books]

We now turn to LF raising. The complex V raises to the position [e], leaving a V-trace; we may assume this to be substitution, not adjunction, on a natural interpretation of recoverability of deletion. We now raise this element to the position t_1, again leaving a V-trace. The latter is of course undeletable, being part of a chain with substantive content at LF. This step violates the HMC; and its residue, (17), violates the ECP at LF.

(17) John [$_V$ write–Agr–I] Neg t'_V [$_{VP}$ t_V books]

Here antecedent government of t'_V is blocked by the intermediate element Neg, under the Minimality Condition. We therefore have a violation of the ECP at LF. In this case the HMC, reducing to the ECP, is a valid descriptive principle, violated by the derivation.

Note that the situation contrasts with overt raising of V to Agr, then to I over Neg, as in the case of (15b) (and all French verbs). Here raising to Agr is permitted, therefore obligatory by the "least effort" condition. Following the derivation step by step, we first raise V to Agr, leaving V-trace and forming [$_{Agr}$ V–Agr]. We then raise this complex element to

I over Neg, forming [$_I$ V–Agr–I] and leaving Agr-trace; this step violates the HMC. The Agr-trace now deletes, leaving [e]. We thus derive the form (18).

(18) John [$_I$ have–Agr–I] Neg [e] [$_{VP}$ t_V ...]

This representation induces no ECP violation,[24] though the derivation that formed it violates the HMC. Again, we see that the HMC is descriptively valid only insofar as it reduces to the ECP.

The problems that arise therefore receive straightforward solutions when we consider the nature of adjunction, as standardly defined. Note, however, the crucial assumption that "unnecessary elements" delete at LF; we return to the matter in section 2.6.2. Also crucial is the assumption that D-Structure relates to S-Structure by a directional mapping, a step-by-step derivational process. In the S-Structure (and LF) representation (18), *have* is "too far" from its trace t_V for the ECP to be satisfied, but the locality requirement has been satisfied in the course of the derivation from D- to S-Structure.[25]

2.3.2 The Element I

Let us turn to some speculations on the status of IP and the optionality observed earlier in French infinitival constructions. If I is [+finite] (I = T = tense), then it presumably cannot be deleted, since a tensed phrase plays an LF role. Therefore, we have either overt raising to [+finite] or LF raising to the position of its trace.

There is, however, no strong reason to suppose that the same is true of [−finite] (infinitive). If [−finite] and its IP projection play no role at LF, then this element should be deletable, just as Agr (actually, t_{Agr}) is. Suppose that this is the case.[26]

Before considering the consequences, we have to resolve a minor technical question about infinitival inflection: does [−finite] attach to the base form of the verb or does it not? Little is at stake in the present connection; for concreteness, let us adopt the former alternative.

Keeping now to French, consider verbs that can raise to weak inflection, for example, *être* 'be'. Suppose that we have the form (19), with *être* raised to Agr.

(19) ne I pas être heureux

In this construction, *être* may raise further to I in the normal way, yielding the form (20).

(20) n'être pas heureux

But there is also another option. The form *être* may remain in place, with I lowering to [*être*–Agr], leaving not trace but [*e*]. This is permissible on the assumption we are now considering: that [−finite] is deletable, playing no LF role. The resulting form is (21), identical to (19) but with [*e*] in place of I.

(21) ne pas être heureux

Each of these options involves one rule application. Therefore, the two are equally costly and we have genuine alternatives, in conformity with the "least effort" guideline. As observed earlier, these two cases are both permitted in French.

Consider now a true verb, such as *paraître* 'seem'. We know that it cannot raise to I, so I must lower to Agr, leaving [*e*]. Suppose now that *paraître* is in an adverbial construction, as in the D-Structure representation (22).

(22) souvent paraître triste

If paraître raises to Agr in the usual way, we derive the form (23).

(23) paraître souvent triste

Suppose, however, that [Agr–I] lowers to the V position, leaving [*e*] rather than trace. The resulting form is (22) itself, a legitimate form with no ECP violation. Again we have two options, (22) and (23), each involving a single rule, each legitimate. The reason is that Agr and its projection, exactly like [−finite] I and its projection, play no role at LF and are therefore deletable.

We conclude, then, that although there are no options in the finite forms, their infinitival counterparts allow the options illustrated. Along these lines, we might hope to incorporate Pollock's observations about the range of options for infinitives as distinct from tensed clauses.

We have not settled the precise character of LF raising to the trace of [+finite]. What is required is that the finite (tensed) phrase, functioning at LF, not be deleted. The requirement is met under LF raising, which might be either adjunction or substitution. If it is adjunction, the resulting form will be (24), which heads TP, where T = [+finite] (tense).

(24) $[_T [_V \text{ V } [_{\text{Agr}} \text{ Agr–T}] \, t_T]]$

We must then take this to be a legitimate form, with T c-commanding its trace t_T. If the LF raising is substitution, we derive (25) in place of (24) in the I position, now heading VP.

(25) $[_V \text{ V } [_{Agr} \text{ Agr–T}]]$

The question of government of t_T does not now arise, but we must ask just how the element (25) in the I position satisfies the requirement of tense interpretation at LF. The further implications are not clear, and I will leave the question open.

2.4 Summary: On Economy of Derivation

Summarizing, we have selected one particular option available for sharpening the notion of deletion, previously left undetermined; and we have made a distinction between deletable and nondeletable elements on the basis of their LF role. These moves are natural and seem generally unexceptionable. Apart from this, we have kept largely to familiar assumptions along with Pollock's basic analysis, modified in various ways. Attending to the meaning of the formalism for adjunction and other notions, the basic empirical observations follow.

Some more general conclusions are also suggested. First, the HMC is not a principle, though it is largely accurate as a descriptive generalization. The principle is valid only insofar as it reduces to the ECP, and it can be violated when other processes overcome a potential ECP violation by eliminating an "offending trace." Second, we now have a somewhat more specific interpretation of the "least effort" guidelines. The condition requires that the least costly derivation be used, eliminating the S-Structure and PF consequences of more costly derivations. To a first approximation, cost is determined by length; the condition requires the shortest derivation, so that overt raising is required where it is possible. But "cost" has a more subtle meaning: UG principles are less costly than language-specific rules that are contingent upon parameter choices (see note 20); and *do*-insertion, in particular, functions only as a "last resort," to "save" a valid D-Structure representation that otherwise underlies no legitimate derivation.

Other well-known facts suggest further refinement of the notion "least costly derivation." Consider, for example, a standard case of long-distance movement, as in (26).

(26) how do you think that John said [that Bill fixed the car *t*]?

The sentence is well formed by successive-cyclic movement. There is, of course, a shorter—namely, one-step—derivation, in which case, on the general principles so far assumed, the sentence should have a status no different from (27).

(27) how do you wonder why John asked [which car Bill fixed *t*]

The shorter derivation does not bar the longer successive-cyclic one in this case. In fact, the *shorter* derivation is barred; it is not the case that (26) is structurally ambiguous, with one interpretation given by the legitimate derivation and another deviant interpretation given by the illegitimate shorter one. Hence, it must be that the measure of cost prefers short movement to long movement and thus requires the former where possible.

In such ways as these, we may proceed to refine the "least effort" conditions on movement, raising them from the status of imprecise guidelines to actual principles of UG.

Notice that this approach tends to eliminate the possibility of optionality in derivation. Choice points will be allowable only if the resulting derivations are all minimal in cost, as in the case of French infinitival constructions discussed earlier. Any remaining examples of optional rule application would then have to be assigned to some other component of the language system, perhaps a "stylistic" component of the mapping of S-Structure to PF. This may well be too strong a conclusion, raising a problem for the entire approach.

2.5 The Agreement System: Some Speculations

A number of questions arise about the status of Agr in the system just outlined. Following Pollock, we have assumed that Agr is dominated by T(ense). But assuming these elements to be dissociated, one might rather expect Agr to dominate T, since it presumably stands in a government relation with the subject in tensed clauses, to yield the standard subject-verb agreement phenomena. There is morphological evidence, discussed by Belletti (1990), suggesting the same conclusion: in a number of languages where it is possible to obtain relevant evidence, the agreement element is "outside" the tense element in the verbal morphology, as would follow from successive adjunction if Agr dominates T. Nevertheless, facts of the kind just illustrated lead Pollock to postulate a position intermediate between T and VP, what he takes to be the Agr position.

These conflicts might be reconciled by noting that there are actually two kinds of Verb-NP agreement: with subject and with object. Hence, pursuing the basic lines of Pollock's analysis, we should expect to find two Agr elements: the subject agreement element Agr_S and the object agreement element Agr_O. On general assumptions, Agr_O should be close to V, and Agr_S close to the subject, therefore more remote from V.[27] The element Agr in Pollock's structure (6), which we have adopted as the basis for discussion, would therefore be Agr_O, providing an intermediate position for raising. It would then be unnecessary to suppose that infinitives necessarily carry (generally vacuous) subject agreement, though we would now be assuming that Agr_O is present even for nontransitives. Pollock's structure (6) would now be more fully articulated as (28), where $Agr_S = I$, the head of I' and IP, and F is [±finite].

(28)

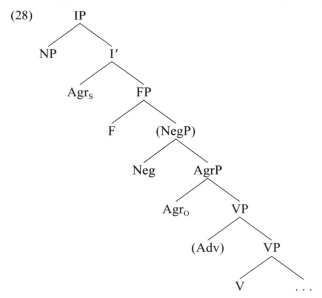

In terms of this proposal, the preceding analysis considered only the structure dominated by FP, which is identical with Pollock's (6) (notations aside).[28]

These conclusions are consistent with Kayne's (1989) analysis of participle agreement in a variety of Romance languages. Kayne assumes an Agr element heading AgrP, with VP as its complement. This element is distinct from the Agr involved in subject agreement; we may take it to be Agr_O. Thus, we have such D-Structure representations as (29), for a French participial construction, putting aside I and Agr_S.

(29) NP V_{aux} [$_{AgrP}$ Agr [$_{VP}$ V-participle NP]]

If the NP object is a *wh*-phrase that undergoes raising, then the participle may or may not agree with it. Kayne assumes that these options correspond to two distinct structures, as in (30), where t, t' are the traces of the *wh*-phrase 'how many tables'.

(30) a. combien   de tables [Paul a   [$_{AgrP}$ t' [$_{AgrP}$ Agr [repeint- t]]]]
        how many (of) tables Paul has   repainted
     b. combien de tables [Paul a [$_{AgrP}$ Agr [repeint- t]]]

The two forms are synonymous, meaning 'how many tables has Paul repainted'. In (30a) the participle surfaces as *repeintes* (plural), in (30b) as *repeint* (lacking agreement).

In the derivation of (30a), the *wh*-phrase raises to the position of the trace t', adjoining to AgrP. In this position, it is in a government relation with Agr (in our terms, Agr_O). The participle thus agrees with its *wh*-phrase object.[29] The underlying assumption is that object agreement is contingent upon a government relation between Agr and an NP, exactly as in the case of subject agreement. In (30b) the *wh*-phrase has not passed through the adjoined position, so there can be no agreement.[30]

Since t', adjoined to AgrP, is in an $\overline{A}$-position, it follows, Kayne observes, that there will be no participial agreement with the *wh*-phrase in the case of an expletive subject (as is the case), on the assumption of expletive replacement, to which we return in section 2.6.3. The reason is that expletive replacement would require improper movement of the trace t' of the *wh*-phrase from an $\overline{A}$- to an A-position.

If an NP remains in the object position, there is no participial agreement, though we again find such agreement in clitic movement, as in (31).

(31) a. Paul a repeint (*repeintes) les tables
     b. Paul les a repeintes

The reason is that the object *les tables* in (31a) is not in the appropriate government relation with Agr_O (the relation is barred by the Minimality Condition on government, since the participle intervenes), whereas in (31b) the clitic has raised to a position governed by Agr, perhaps

[Spec, AgrP]. Kayne argues further that although the two agreement processes (with *wh*-movement and clitics) are not clearly dissociated in French, comparative evidence shows that they are in fact distinct processes and that the clitic does not adjoin to AgrP.

The question arises why the NP object cannot appear in the postulated position associated with Agr, say, its specifier position, as in (32).

(32) *Paul a [les tables repeint(es)]

Base generation is excluded if we take θ-marking to be to the right in French; or, as in recent work that assumes raising of the subject from VP to [Spec, IP], we might assume that θ-marking must be internal to the projection of the θ-marking head, thus impossible in (33).

(33) ... [$_{AgrP}$ NP Agr [$_{VP}$ V]]

Failure of the nonclitic object to raise to the position in (32) follows from the Chain Condition if the participle assigns Case directly to its object, to its right in the base form, as Kayne assumes.[31]

Without reviewing the further consequences that Kayne develops, note that the analysis supports the idea that an Agr position intervenes between T and the V, and that this element is distinct from the subject agreement element. Furthermore, we have evidence that object agreement, like subject agreement, is based upon a government relation between Agr (in this case, Agr$_O$) and the NP.

Koopman (1987) has independently proposed that agreement is always the reflection of a Spec-head relation.[32] We might revise this proposal to accord with Kayne's: agreement with an NP is always the reflection of a government relation between the head Agr and the NP, either the Spec-head relation or the relation of the head to an adjoined element, the Agr typically being associated with the verb at S-Structure by the processes we have been discussing. Koopman suggests further that this idea may relate to her earlier proposal that the order parameters of the X-bar system involve two independent factors: directionality of Case marking and θ-marking (Koopman 1984; see also Travis 1984). If Case marking is to the left and θ-marking to the right, then NP will be in prehead and other θ-marked complements in posthead positions.

We might carry the proposals a step further, supposing that structural Case generally is correlated with agreement and reflects a government relation between the NP and the appropriate Agr elements. Thus, subject-verb agreement is associated with nominative Case and is determined by the relation of the specifier to the Agr_s head of Agr_sP ($=IP$, in (28)), whereas verb-object agreement is associated with accusative Case and is determined by the relation of the NP to the Agr_O head of Agr_OP, either in specifier position or adjoined to Agr_O. The relations might be uniform at LF, parameterized at S-Structure, with Case checking and Case marking perhaps dissociated.

Note finally that if the proposal just outlined is tenable, with Agr_O distinct from Agr_S, then one of the problems discussed earlier in connection with example (11), repeated as (34), does not arise.

(34) John I Neg Agr write books

The problem was to ensure *do*-insertion and raising of Agr to form the complex verb $[_V \, do\text{-}Agr\text{-}I]$ with no violation of the HMC, while barring an alternative derivation with overt lowering. If we were to adopt the structure (28) rather than (6), distinguishing Agr_S from Agr_O, then Agr in (34) is actually Agr_O, which would not raise over Neg, but would lower to V (with subsequent LF raising to the position of the trace of Agr_O to form a proper chain). There is, then, no violation of the HMC, straightforwardly. The more general problems discussed earlier remain, however, still motivating the argument presented.

2.6 Economy of Representation

It has been suggested elsewhere that movement is available only as a "last resort." The preceding discussion suggested that deletion might also be regarded as a "last resort" operation, applicable where necessary, but not otherwise, and that the same is true of whatever is involved in *do*-support: insertion, if that is the proper way to interpret the phenomenon. More generally, then, it may be that the principle Affect α applies only where necessary. This overarching principle, then, expresses a general property of transformational rules—or more properly, of *the* transformational rule, actually a principle of UG. The intuitive meaning is that derivations must be as economical as possible: there is no superfluous rule application. The intuitive content of this idea, however, is spelled out in terms of specific notions of cost that distinguish UG principles from language-particular properties, introduce locality considerations, and so on. We thus have a plausible "least effort" principle, but a principle that is apparently specific to the language faculty in its actual formulation. This is a familiar conclusion elsewhere as well, one that bears on the nature of the language faculty generally.

The analogous principle for representations would stipulate that, just as there can be no superfluous steps in derivations, so there can be no superfluous symbols in representations. This is the intuitive content of the notion of Full Interpretation (FI), which holds that an element can appear in a representation only if it is properly "licensed." Let us proceed now to ask how this intuitive notion might be refined, in an effort to move it too from the status of a guideline toward that of a principle of UG.

It would be natural to expect that FI holds at each of the three fundamental levels that constitute an interface between the computational system of language and other systems: hence, at the levels of D-Structure, PF, and LF. If so, then "licensing" under FI is expressed in terms of conditions relating the syntax, broadly construed, to other systems of the mind/brain.

At D-Structure FI holds by definition, this level simply being a projection of lexical structure in terms of the notions of X-bar theory.[33] At PF it is universally taken for granted, without discussion, that the condition holds in a strong form. That is, a condition on phonetic representation is that each symbol be interpreted in terms of articulatory and perceptual mechanisms in a language-invariant manner; a representation that lacks this property is simply not considered a phonetic representation, but instead is considered a "higher-level" representation, still to be converted to PF. Like D-Structure, PF is understood to be defined by some version of FI. The corresponding notion at LF would be that every element that appears at LF must have a language-invariant interpretation in terms of interactions with the systems of conceptual structure and language use. Let us explore this idea further.

2.6.1 Operators and Variables

One consequence is that vacuous quantification should be forbidden. That is, language should differ from typical formal systems that permit vacuous quantification freely, with the well-formed expression "(x) $(2 + 2 = 4)$" receiving the same interpretation as "$2 + 2 = 4$." Formal systems are designed this way for ease of description and computation, but the design of human language is different. Thus, we cannot have such expressions as (35a) interpreted as 'John saw Bill', or (35b) interpreted as 'some person left'.

(35) a. who John saw Bill
        who did John see Bill
     b. every some person left

Similarly, if a language permits such structures as (36), the vacuous operator interpretation is excluded.

(36) a. who did Mary see him
     b. the man that Mary saw him

These expressions cannot be interpreted to mean 'Mary saw x', 'the man y such that Mary saw x', respectively. If some theory of grammar stipulates specific devices and rules to bar such constructions and interpretations, we conclude that it is the wrong theory: it is generating expressions and structures too accurately and is therefore incorrect. There is nothing paradoxical about this conclusion. The unwanted constructions are excluded on general grounds, in terms of the overarching condition FI; there is no reason to suppose that the mechanisms of language include superfluous devices and rules to achieve, redundantly, the same result in special cases. Similarly, the phonological component contains no rules to express special cases of general properties of universal phonetics or of phonetic representations.

A related question has to do with free variables. What is their status in natural language? Typically, formal systems permit well-formed expressions with free variables, interpreting them as universally quantified or with the free variable treated as an arbitrary name, as in the course of natural deduction and intuitive mathematics generally. One natural-language analogue to a free variable would be an empty category bound by an empty operator. There is quite strong evidence that such constructions exist, for example, in complex adjectival constructions such as (37).

(37) a. John is too clever to catch
     b. John is too clever to expect anyone to catch
     c. *John is too clever to meet anyone who caught
     d. Mary expected John to be too clever to catch

The general properties of these and many other constructions follow from the assumption that the underlying D-Structure representation is as in (38a) (for (37a)) and that empty-operator movement, meeting the usual conditions on $\overline{\text{A}}$-movement, raises the empty category Op to the C position of the bracketed clause (to the specifier position of CP), leaving a trace t in the S-Structure representation (38b).

(38) a. John is too clever [$_{CP}$ PRO to catch Op]
     b. John is too clever [$_{CP}$ Op [PRO to catch t]]

But variables are subject to the property sometimes called "strong binding": a variable must have a range determined by its restricted quantifier (language permitting no unrestricted quantification, as distinct from typical formal systems), or a value fixed by an antecedent that meets certain structural properties: thus *John* but not *Mary* in (37d). The latter condition applies when the operator is an empty category. (37a), for example, cannot mean that John is so clever that he cannot catch everything, or that he cannot catch something (someone) or other, analogous to *John ate*, meaning that John ate something or other. In short, language does not permit free variables: the strong binding property determines the curious semantic properties of these constructions. We might think of this condition as a specific application of the UG condition FI.

In these terms, we would interpret the empty operator binding an empty pronominal, in the sense of Huang's (1984) work on Chinese, as "restricted," in that it is necessarily discourse-related. There are semifree variables such as PRO and *one*, which, however, always appear to have special properties, specifically, human or animate (e.g., *it is easy to roll down a hill* does not refer to a rock). Thus, a true free variable interpretation is disallowed.

2.6.2 Legitimate LF Elements
A further sharpening of the condition FI is suggested by consideration of what counts as a proper element at the LF level. The question here is analogous to the question of what counts as a phonetic element at the PF level. Each relevant element at the LF level is a chain (39), perhaps a one-membered chain.

(39) $(\alpha_1, \ldots, \alpha_n)$

It seems that the following elements are permitted at LF, each a chain (39):

1. Arguments: each element is in an A-position, α_1 Case-marked and α_n θ-marked, in accordance with the Chain Condition.[34]
2. Adjuncts: each element is in an $\overline{\text{A}}$-position.
3. Lexical elements: each element is in an X^0 position.

4. Predicates, possibly predicate chains if there is predicate raising, VP-movement in overt syntax,[35] and other cases.

5. Operator-variable constructions, each a chain (α_1, α_2), where the operator α_1 is in an $\overline{A}$-position and the variable α_2 is in an A-position.

These are the only elements that seem to have an interpretation at LF. Suppose, then, that these are the only elements permitted at LF, in accordance with FI. Then the rule Affect α may apply (and must apply) only to yield such an element, given an illegitimate object. We conclude that Agr-trace (and perhaps the trace of [−finite]) must be eliminated, and V-trace may not be eliminated, as required for the proper functioning of the ECP if the argument sketched earlier is correct.[36]

Consider successive-cyclic $\overline{A}$-movement from an A-position. This will yield a chain that is not a legitimate object; it is a "heterogeneous chain," consisting of an adjunct chain and an $(\overline{A}, A)$ pair (an operator-variable construction, where the $\overline{A}$-position is occupied by a trace). This heterogeneous chain can become a legitimate object—namely, a genuine operator-variable construction—only by eliminating intermediate $\overline{A}$-traces. We conclude, then, that these must be deleted at the point where we reach LF representation.[37] In contrast, intermediate $\overline{A}$-traces formed by successive-cyclic movement from an $\overline{A}$-position need not be deleted, since the chain formed is already a legitimate object—namely, an adjunct; since they need not be deleted, they may not be deleted, by the "least effort" principle for derivations already discussed. The same is true for A-chains (arguments) and X^0-chains (lexical elements). On these natural—though of course not logically necessary—assumptions, we derive, in effect, the basic principle for trace deletion stipulated in Lasnik and Saito's theory of the ECP, now a consequence of the general condition FI, with "may delete" strengthened to "must delete." There are further consequences, and interesting questions arise with regard to the specifier of NPs, which shares some properties of A-positions and other properties of $\overline{A}$-positions, but I will not pursue these matters here.

2.6.3 FI and Expletives

Consider finally the status of expletive elements, such as English *there* or Italian *ci*, or their various counterparts, null or overt, in other languages. This element receives no interpretation and therefore is not licensed as a legitimate LF object. It must therefore somehow be removed. Elsewhere I have suggested that *there* is eliminated by LF substitution.[38] But *there* has specific features, and we might suppose on these grounds that it is undeletable, by the condition on recoverability of deletion—yet to be precisely formulated. Then we must treat *there* as an LF affix; something must adjoin to it.

The expletive *there* has three salient properties. First, an NP must appear in a certain formal relation to *there* in the construction; let us call this element the *associate* of the expletive and take the expletive to be licensed by its presence. Second, number agreement is not with *there* but rather with the associate. Third, there is an alternate form with the associate actually in the subject position after overt raising. Thus, we have (40), with the associate in italics, but not (41).

(40) a.   there is *a man* in the room
   b.   there are *men* in the room
   c.   *a man* is in the room

(41) a.   *there was decided to travel by plane
   b.   *there is unlikely that anyone will agree

These properties are rather naturally explained on the assumption, deriving from FI, that the expletive is an LF affix, with its associate adjoining to it. Since *there* lacks inherent ϕ-features (including number) and category, these features will "percolate" from its associate on usual assumptions. If agreement is checked at LF, then it will already have to have been established at S-Structure between Agr_S and the associate of *there*, as in (40a–b), yielding the observed overt agreement. This analysis fits readily into the framework already outlined, particularly if agreement and Case are treated in the manner suggested: both assigned by S-Structure since they may appear overtly, both checked at LF since they have LF consequences having to do with visibility (the Case Filter) and the Chain Condition.[39] If we assume further that the specifier of IP (Agr_SP, if the speculations of section 2.5 are correct) must be an NP with ϕ-features matching Agr_S, then it will also follow that the associate must be an NP; and it is this NP that raises in overt syntax, as in (40c).

Burzio (1986) argues further that if the expletive is a clitic, it will have to satisfy additional conditions holding generally between a clitic and the position associated with it, specifically, a very restrictive locality condition that, he argues, holds at D-Structure; on this further assumption, he derives an interesting range of phenomena that differentiate English, Italian, French, and Piedmontese expletive constructions. On the general assumptions of the P&P approach, we expect to find that expletive constructions of this type have the same basic properties across languages, with differences explicable in terms of the lexical properties of the elements involved.

For such reasons, then, it is plausible to assume that *there* (and its counterparts) is indeed an LF affix, as required by FI.

In (40a) LF adjunction of the associate to the expletive yields the phrase (42) as subject, the complex constituting an NP by percolation.

(42) [$_{NP}$ there–[$_{NP}$ a man]]

Other well-established principles conspire to guarantee that the only element that can adjoin to the expletive is the associate with the appropriate properties.

Given that *there* must have an NP associate, it follows that some other expletive (in English, *it*) is associated with clauses, as in (43), contrasting with (41).

(43) a. it was decided to travel by plane
     b. it is unlikely that anyone will agree

It should therefore not be necessary to stipulate distributional conditions on *there* and *it* expletives, or their counterparts in other languages, when their lexical properties are considered.[40]

It also follows that at S-Structure an expletive E and its associate A must satisfy all LF chain conditions, since there is a chain ([A–E], ..., t_A]) at LF. Given the Chain Condition holding at LF, it must be that at S-Structure the expletive E is in a Case-marked position and the associate A in a θ-position.[41] Furthermore, if we assume that the binding theory holds at LF, then at S-Structure A and E must be in a relation that satisfies Condition A, since at LF an antecedent-trace relation holds of their S-Structure positions. Similarly, the ECP, a chain condition at LF, will have to hold of the expletive-associate pair at S-Structure. These consequences are largely descriptively accurate, as illustrated in (44).[42]

(44) a. *there* seems that *a man* is in the room   (ECP violation)
     b. *there* seems that John saw *a man*   (Condition A violation)

Similarly, other conditions on movement must be satisfied. Compare the examples in (45).

(45) a. *there* was thought that [pictures of *a man* were on sale]
     b. *we* thought that [pictures of *each other* were on sale]
     c. *a man* was thought that [pictures of *t* were on sale]

The italicized elements are properly related in (45b), but not in (45a) or (45c). The problem with (45a) is not the binding theory, as (45b) shows, but rather a condition on movement (the ECP), as we see from (45c).

Such properties of expletives now follow from FI, without further stipulation. Note that it also follows that the binding theory must apply at LF; whether or not it also applies elsewhere (including S-Structure) is a separate question.

Another consequence has to do with Condition C of the binding theory, which requires that an r-expression, such as the associate of an expletive, be unbound. A long-standing question has been why there is no Condition C violation in the case of an expletive and its related associate. But we now assume that the two simply have different indices.[43] There is, therefore, no need to complicate the binding theory to exclude this case, as in a number of proposals over the past years.

Certain problems of scope of the kind discussed particularly by Edwin Williams also are overcome. Consider the sentences in (46).

(46) a. I haven't met many linguistics students
     b. there aren't many linguistics students here

(46a) has a scopal ambiguity, but in (46b) *many* unambiguously has narrow scope. The LF representation of (46b) is (47).

(47) [$_{NP}$[there [$_A$ many linguistics students]] are not t_A here]

If *many linguistics students* were literally to replace *there*, it would be expected to have scope over *not*, but in (47) no relation is established between the two, and the scope of *many* can be assumed to be narrow, as in *pictures of many students aren't here*.[44]

2.6.4 Further Questions concerning LF Raising
There is one major exception to the generalization that the expletive E and its associate A are in a binding theory (Condition A) relation at S-Structure—namely, raising constructions such as (48).

(48) *there* seems [*a man* to be in the room]

Here the expletive-associate pair satisfies all chain conditions, but the expression is ungrammatical.

A natural explanation of these facts is provided by Belletti's (1988) theory of partitive Case assignment. Taking partitive Case to be oblique, therefore θ-related in accord with the uniformity condition on Case assignment (see Chomsky 1986b), partitive Case will not be assigned to the associate in (48) but will be properly assigned at S-Structure to the associate of the expletive after unaccusatives and, we must assume, copula, as in *there arrived a man, there is a man in the room.* Assume as before that Case must be assigned at S-Structure, given that it appears at PF and is relevant at LF. Then (48) is *, since an S-Structure condition is violated. Note that even with these assumptions, it still follows that *there* must be in a Case-marked position, by the Chain Condition, which requires that an LF chain be headed by a Case-marked position.[45]

If this line of argument is correct, there cannot be a process of Case transmission, for that process would allow (48) to satisfy the Case Filter. Rather, Case must be assigned at S-Structure directly by some Case marker or other device.[46] Lasnik (1989) observes that similar conclusions follow from such examples as (49).

(49) a.   I consider [there to be a solution]
     b. *I consider [there a solution]   (analogous to *I consider John intelligent*)

In (49a) it must be that *be* assigns Case directly to *a solution*; *there* also receives Case (from *consider*), so that the Chain Condition is satisfied after LF raising. There is, it seems, no S-Structure process transmitting Case from the expletive *there* to its associate, the phrase *a solution* in these examples.

Safir (1985) notes the existence of pairs like (50a–b).[47]

(50) a.   [$_{wh}$ how many men] did John say that [there were t_{wh} in the room]
     b. *[$_{wh}$ how many men] did John say that [t_{wh} were in the room]

(50b) is a standard ECP violation; the trace t_{wh} is in a position that is not γ-marked, in Lasnik and Saito's (1984) sense. The question then arises why this is not also true of (50a), if the trace t_{wh}, the associate of the expletive *there*, is raised by LF movement to the position of *there*. Lasnik and Saito's theory provides an explanation, whether we assume LF substitution or, as above, LF adjunction. In either case the trace t_{wh} is γ-marked by the process of *wh*-movement in overt syntax and retains this property when it raises to the position of the expletive, so there is no ECP violation. Similar observations hold with regard to Rizzi's (1982) analysis of *wh*-extraction of subjects in Italian: the subject first extraposes, leaving expletive *pro* subject, and then undergoes normal *wh*-movement, leaving a trace t, γ-marked in overt syntax and then raising at LF to the position of the expletive.

The notion of LF adjunction eliminates much of the motivation for Case transmission theories of expletive-associate relations, and these approaches are still more dubious in the light of the observations just reviewed (see also Pollock 1981 and Kayne 1989). Nevertheless, there is evidence supporting Case transmission.

An indirect though plausible argument for Case transmission is developed by Koopman (1987) in a comparative study of the West African language Bambara and languages of the French-English type. Koopman postulates a parametric difference between languages that have Case chains ($[+CC]$) and those that do not ($[-CC]$). Bambara is $[-CC]$ and English-French, $[+CC]$. Koopman considers three kinds of Case chains.

(51) a. $(V, \ldots, t)$, where V is a Case assigner
   b. $(Op, \ldots, t)$, where Op is an operator and t the variable it binds
   c. $(E, \ldots, NP)$, where E is an expletive and NP its associate

Case (51a) results from V-raising. In a $[+CC]$ language, the trace of V will assign the Case "transmitted" from V through the chain. In a $[-CC]$ language, lacking Case chains, the trace will be unable to assign Case, and raising of transitive verbs will therefore be impossible.

Case (51b) is standard operator movement. Typically, the trace must be in a Case-marked position, and, Koopman assumes, the operator must inherit Case from it to satisfy the Case Filter. This will be possible in a $[+CC]$ language, impossible in a $[-CC]$ language, which will therefore lack overt operator movement.

Case (51c) is the expletive-associate relation. In a $[+CC]$ language, Case can be transmitted from E to NP, as in standard Case transmission theories, and the Case Filter is therefore satisfied. In a $[-CC]$ language, there can be no expletives, for Case transmission will be impossible, Case chains not being permitted.

Koopman observes that in all respects, English-French are of the $[+CC]$ variety, whereas Bambara is of the $[-CC]$ variety. Omitting details, we find in Bambara the following properties. Consider Case chains of type (51a). A verb that does not assign Case raises to I, but a verb that assigns Case remains in place, with a dummy element inserted to bear the affix; the explanation is that the trace could not assign Case if the verb were to raise. In causative formation, an intransitive verb raises to form a complex V-causative construction in the familiar way, but this is impossible for a transitive verb, which allows causative only if the external argument is suppressed, as if prior passivization had taken place. These properties follow on the assumption that the trace of a transitive verb cannot assign Case; since the complex verb assigns its sole Case to the obligatory object, the subject cannot appear.

With regard to property (51b), Bambara has only *wh-* in situ, as predicted. As for (51c), there are no overt expletives; rather, the associate raises overtly to subject position, again as predicted.

We thus have an indirect argument in favor of Case transmission, absent as a device just when Case chains generally are not permitted.

Can we reinterpret these data so as to resolve the conflict between the argument for Case transmission and the evidence against such a process? Suppose we reinterpret Koopman's parameter in the following way, in accord with the plausible and generally applicable principle that parameters are lexical, that is, statable in terms of X^0 elements and X^0 categories only. We then consider the property [C], which an X^0 element may or may not have. A $[+C]$ element can enter into Case relations, either assigning or receiving Case; a $[-C]$ element cannot. Suppose further that X^0 elements with lexical content are always $[+C]$, but that languages can differ with respect to whether other X^0 elements are $[+C]$ or $[-C]$. The parameter is restricted to functional elements, in accordance with the plausible condition discussed earlier. French-English are $[+C]$, meaning that all X^0 elements may enter into Case relations; Bambara is $[-C]$, meaning that only a lexical X^0 enters into such relations.

Turning to the three properties, (51a) follows directly: in Bambara, the trace of V, being $[-C]$, cannot assign Case. As for (51b), the trace of the operator cannot receive Case in Bambara, being $[-C]$, so that we have a typical violation of the Case Filter (or the visibility requirement from which it derives), with a variable heading a (perhaps one-membered) chain that violates the Chain Condition, since it lacks Case. Note that we need not assume that the operator requires Case, an otherwise unmotivated assumption, particularly unnatural for empty operators.

The property that concerns us directly is (51c). Since Bambara is $[-C]$, an expletive cannot receive Case. If the language had expletives, then LF raising (which Koopman assumes) would form a chain headed by an element in a non-Case-marked position, violating the Chain Condition. Consequently, there can be no expletives, and overt raising is required.

There seems, then, to be no strong argument for Case transmission, if this line of argument is viable.[48] We do, however, have evidence for a narrowly specified parametric difference involving Case theory, with a range of interesting consequences. I am not aware of other convincing evidence for Case transmission, so it may be that the property can be eliminated from UG, in favor of LF movement, driven by FI.

2.7 Some Conclusions on Language Design

Summarizing, we have found evidence to support the basic assumptions on language design sketched in section 2.1, the more specific assumptions concerning the separate syntactic status of Tense and Agreement elements, and those of subsequent discussion. There is varied evidence suggesting that both derivations and representations are subject to a certain form of "least effort" condition and are required to be minimal in a fairly well defined sense, with no superfluous steps in derivations and no superfluous symbols in representations. Proceeding in the way indicated, we may hope to raise these "least effort" guidelines to general principles of UG. Notice that although these principles have a kind of naturalness and generality lacking in the specific principles of UG such as the ECP, the binding theory, and so on, nevertheless their formulation is, in detail, specific to the language faculty.

As discussed elsewhere (see Chomsky 1991a), these properties of UG, if indeed they are real, are rather surprising in a number of respects. For one thing, they are the kinds of properties that yield computational difficulties, since structural descriptions have to meet "global" conditions. From the point of view of parsing, suppose that we have a process recovering an S-Structure representation σ from the PF representation π. Then to determine the status of σ, we have to carry out a number of operations. We have to determine whether σ is derived from a properly formed D-Structure representation δ licensed by the lexicon, and whether the derivation from to the LF representation λ is minimal in the required sense, less costly than any other derivation from δ. Furthermore, we have to determine whether λ satisfies the conditions of external licensing, FI, and other properties of LF. In general, these computations may be nontrivial. In these respects, language design appears to be problematic from a parsing-theoretic perspective, though elegant regarded in isolation from considerations of use. The basic assumption that the fundamental levels are those that satisfy the external licensing conditions at the "interface" with other systems already illustrates these properties, and the "least effort" conditions, though natural and plausible in terms of empirical consequences, provide further illustration. The discrepancies between natural-language design and the structure of formal systems constructed for computational efficiency may also be relevant here, as well as other properties of natural language, such as the existence of empty categories, which might also be expected to yield parsing problems. Note that one cannot easily motivate the conditions on economy of representation in terms of processing considerations, since they hold at LF, and only derivatively at S-Structure. Nor does there appear to be any argument that the particular properties of language design are necessary for languagelike systems. These are contingent properties of natural language.

There are "computational tricks" that permit easy determination of the grammatical properties of an S-Structure representation in a large class of cases, broad enough to allow for language to be usable in practice. But language design as such appears to be in many respects "dysfunctional," yielding properties that are not well adapted to the functions language is called upon to perform. There is no real paradox here; there is no reason to suppose, a priori, that the general design of language is conducive to efficient use. Rather, what we seem to discover are some intriguing and unexpected features of language design, not unlike those that have been discovered throughout the inquiry into the nature of language, though unusual among biological systems of the natural world.

Notes

1. This is sometimes called *Government-Binding (GB) Theory*, a misleading term that should be abandoned, in my view; see Chomsky 1988, lecture 2. Generative grammar has engendered a good deal of controversy, sometimes for good reason, often not. There has been a fair amount of plain misunderstanding, beginning with the notion of generative grammar itself. I have always understood a generative grammar to be nothing more than an explicit grammar. Some apparently have a different concept in mind. For example, reviewing Chomsky 1986b, McCawley (1988) notes that I interpret the concept here as meaning nothing more than explicit, as I have always done (see, for instance, Chomsky 1965, 4), and concludes erroneously that this is a "sharp change" in my usage that gives the enterprise an entirely different cast from that of the 1960s, when the task, as he perceives it, was taken to be "specifying the membership of a set of sentences that is identified with a language" (pp. 355–356; McCawley takes the set of sentences to be what I have called the "structure" of the language, that is, the set of structural descriptions). But the characterization he gives does not imply that "generative" means anything more than "explicit"; there is, furthermore, no

change in usage or conception, at least for me, in this regard. The review contains a series of further misunderstandings, and there are others elsewhere, but I will not discuss these matters here.

2. On why phonology alone might be expected to have specific rule structure, see Bromberger and Halle 1989.

3. Or what is sometimes called a *core language*. The core-periphery distinction, in my view, should be regarded as an expository device, reflecting a level of understanding that should be superseded as clarification of the nature of linguistic inquiry advances. See Chomsky 1988.

4. On these notions, see Chomsky 1986b. General conditions of this sort were investigated in some detail in the earliest work in generative grammar, in the context of the study of evaluation procedures for grammars; see Chomsky 1951.

5. The lexical elements are sometimes called *atomic* from the point of view of the computational operations. Taking the metaphor literally, we would conclude that no feature of a lexical item can be modified or even addressed (say, for checking against another matching element) in a computational operation, and no features can be added to a lexical element. The condition as stated is too strong; just how it holds is a theory-internal question that I will put aside.

6. On restriction to functional elements, see Borer 1984 and Fukui 1986, 1988.

7. On this matter, see, among others, Baker 1988.

8. As a matter of notation for X-bar theory, I will use prime instead of bar, X^0 for the lowest-level category, and XP for X'', for each X.

9. I have in mind the notion of "level of representation" discussed in Chomsky 1975a and subsequent work.

10. Some have proposed that certain conditions on syntax hold at PF; see, for example, Aoun et al. 1987. It cannot be, strictly speaking, the level of PF at which these conditions apply, since at this level there is no relevant structure, not even words, in general. Rather, this approach assumes an additional level S-P intermediate between S-Structure and PF, the purported conditions holding at S-P.

11. See Burzio 1986 and Chomsky 1987. Some have felt that there is a profound issue of principle distinguishing "two-level" theories that include a relation of D- to S-Structure from "one-level" approaches, which relate S-Structure to lexical properties in some different way; for some comment, see my (1981b) response to queries in Longuet-Higgins, Lyons, and Broadbent 1981, 63f. and Chomsky 1981a. There may be an issue, but as noted, it is at best a rather subtle one.

12. On X-bar-theoretic conditions at S-Structure, see Van Riemsdijk 1989. In lectures in Tokyo in January 1987, I suggested some further reasons why such conditions might hold at S-Structure.

13. I assume here the general framework of Chomsky 1986a, based essentially on Lasnik and Saito 1984, though further modifications are in order that I will not consider here.

14. Note that there also might be a partial reduction, for example, a formulation of the ECP that expresses a generalization holding of X^0-movement and other cases; that would be the import of a proposal by Rizzi (1990). We should also look into the other possible case of movement: X'-movement. For evidence supporting this option, see Van Riemsdijk 1989. See also Namiki 1979.

15. See Pollock 1989. I will touch upon only a few of the questions that Pollock addresses. See Emonds 1978 and, for more recent development of his approach, Emonds 1985.

16. Order irrelevant, here and below, for abstract formulations.

17. Pollock's terms for *strong* and *weak* are *transparent* and *opaque*, respectively, for reasons that become clear directly.

18. Pollock treats *ne* in the *ne-pas* construction as the clitic head of NegP, raising to a higher position. We might think of it as a kind of scope marker.

19. More explicitly. the verb $[_V \, V \, [_{Agr} \, Agr \, I]]$.

20. The mechanics of how modals and *do* relate to the inflectional affixes remain to be specified. If *do*-support can be shown to be a reflex of parameter fixing (choice of weak Agr, we are assuming), then it is not, strictly speaking, a language-specific rule, though I will continue to use this term for expository purposes. The device of employing dummy elements in this manner is found elsewhere, also plausibly considered to be contingent on parameter fixing; see section 2.6.4 for one example.

21. Note that there are empirical consequences to these assumptions. They entail that at the steady state attained in language acquisition, the UG principles remain distinct from language-particular properties. Suggestive work by Flynn (1987) on second-language acquisition supports this conclusion.

22. There would in fact be a straightforward solution to this particular problem in terms of an analysis to which we return in section 2.5, but I will put that aside here, since it will not bear on the other questions just raised.

23. Note that *e* is regarded here as an actual symbol of mental representation, but lacking φ-features and categorial features. *e* is not to be confused with the identity element of a syntactic level, regarded as an algebraic construction in the manner of Chomsky 1975a.

24. Recall that we are assuming, essentially, Lasnik and Saito's (1984) theory of the ECP, as modified in Chomsky 1986a. Under this theory, t_V in (17) is γ-marked after raising of V to Agr, and subsequent deletion of Agr-trace in this position leaves no ECP violation.

25. On other cases of a similar sort, see Chomsky 1987.

26. Semantic properties of infinitives, then, would be understood as properties of the construction, not its head [−finite].

27. A cursory check suggests that the morphological consequences are as expected, in languages where the hierarchic position of object and subject agreement can be detected.

28. At various points, the reinterpretation would require slight modifications in the exposition and the resulting analysis. I will omit further comment on these matters, which do not seem to raise any serious problem.

29. More precisely, agreement holds between the *wh*-phrase and Agr_O, to which the participle raises so that it agrees with the *wh*-phrase; the same is true of subject-verb agreement.

30. Note that we must assume the two derivations to be "equally costly," each being "minimal" by successive-cyclic movement. This consideration would lead to a further refinement of the notion of "cost."

31. The case of clitic movement depends upon theory-internal assumptions about cliticization, but no new problems appear to arise here. Kayne's argument is slightly different from the above.

32. Koopman is considering the possibility of object raising to [Spec, VP]; alternatively, we might suppose that the process in question is raising to [Spec, AgrP].

33. There are further refinements to be considered. For example, should expletives be present at D-Structure or inserted in the course of derivation? What is the status of functional elements? And so on.

34. If we adopt the approach to NP-raising discussed in Chomsky 1986a, then we will have to distinguish the chain (39) formed by movement from the intermediate "derived chain" that takes part in the process of γ-marking of α_n.

35. An alternative possibility, suggested by certain facts about binding and trace interpretation, is that VP-movement is restricted to the PF component (as an optional "stylistic rule") and possibly also to (obligatory) LF movement, along the lines of a reinterpretation of the barriers framework (Chomsky 1986a) discussed in my lectures at Tokyo in January 1987. This conclusion may indeed follow from the considerations discussed above concerning optionality, within the present framework.

36. Note that further precision is necessary to make explicit just when and how this condition applies.

37. They might be present at earlier stages, where licensing conditions do not yet apply, serving, as Norbert Hornstein observes, to permit the application of principles for the interpretation of anaphors in displaced phrases of the sort proposed by Barss (1986).

38. See Chomsky 1986b. For extensive discussion of expletives, which I will largely follow here, see Burzio 1986. See also Travis 1984 on the typology of expletives. The status of *it* (and its counterparts) in extraposition constructions is more convoluted for various reasons, including the question of whether it occupies a θ-position.

39. See Baker 1988 on the role of both Case and agreement in this connection.

40. Such properties had to be stipulated on the assumptions made in Chomsky and Lasnik 1977, but perhaps they are dispensable along the lines just sketched. For these reasons alone, it seems doubtful that what adjoins to the expletive is a small clause of which it is the subject; thus, I assume that what adjoins is *a man*, not the small clause [*a man in the room*], in (40a). There are other reasons for supposing this to be true. Kayne (1989) observes (see his note 6) that the assumption is required for his explanation of the lack of participle-object agreement with object raising in expletive constructions. Consider, furthermore, such expressions as *there seems to be several men sick*, excluded by lack of agreement between *several men* and *seems*. But the phrase [*several men sick*] can be singular, as in [*several men sick*] *is a sign that the water is polluted* and a range of similar cases discussed by Safir (1987), though many questions remain unsettled. On the possibility of nonagreement between the verb and its associate, see Burzio 1986, 132–133. Note that nothing requires that the two kinds of expletives be morphologically distinct.

41. We assume that Case distributes from a category to its immediate constituents, a process that is often morphologically overt, thus from the category of the complex element [A–E] to the adjoined element A, heading the chain $(A, \ldots, t_A)$. Recall that A adjoined to E does head such a chain, by earlier assumptions.

42. Note that these examples could be accounted for by stipulations on the distribution of expletives, as in Chomsky and Lasnik 1977, but we are now exploring the possibility, which seems plausible, that these are dispensable.

43. Or no linking, in Higginbotham's (1983) sense. Note that we cannot assume the expletive to be unindexed—thus, it might have raised, leaving an indexed trace.

44. To account for scopal properties appropriately, more elaborate assumptions are required, taking into account the position of both the head and the terminal position of the associate chain $(A, \ldots, t)$. In a raising construction such as *there appear (not) to have been many linguistics students here*, we have to ensure that the scope of *many* falls within that of *appear* and *not*; no relation is determined by the proposed LF representation, but such a relation would be established in the correct way if the position of the trace is considered, given that the head of the chain has no relation to the other relevant elements. Just what is entailed by a wider range of considerations remains to be determined. See chapter 4.

45. Similar remarks hold of "quirky Case," assigned at D-Structure under the uniformity condition, but realized in a Case-marked position at S-Structure.

46. See Pollock 1981 for arguments against Case transmission. For additional argument, see Kayne 1989.

47. For discussion of these and the preceding examples, see Shlonsky 1987.

48. Koopman considers other possible Case chains, but the evidence is less convincing.

Chapter 3

A Minimalist Program for Linguistic Theory

3.1 Some General Considerations

Language and its use have been studied from varied points of view. One approach, assumed here, takes language to be part of the natural world. The human brain provides an array of capacities that enter into the use and understanding of language (the *language faculty*); these seem to be in good part specialized for that function and a common human endowment over a very wide range of circumstances and conditions. One component of the language faculty is a generative procedure (an *I-language*, henceforth *language*) that generates *structural descriptions* (SDs), each a complex of properties, including those commonly called "semantic" and "phonetic." These SDs are the *expressions* of the language. The theory of a particular language is its *grammar*. The theory of languages and the expressions they generate is *Universal Grammar* (UG); UG is a theory of the initial state S_0 of the relevant component of the language faculty. We can distinguish the language from a conceptual system and a system of pragmatic competence. Evidence has been accumulating that these interacting systems can be selectively impaired and developmentally dissociated (Curtiss 1981, Yamada 1990, Smith and Tsimpli 1991), and their properties are quite different.

A standard assumption is that UG specifies certain *linguistic levels*, each a symbolic system, often called a "representational system." Each linguistic level provides the means for presenting certain systematic

This chapter originally appeared in *The View from Building 20: Essays in Linguistics in Honor of Sylvain Bromberger*, edited by Kenneth Hale and Samuel Jay Keyser (Cambridge, Mass.: MIT Press, 1993), and is published here with minor revisions.

information about linguistic expressions. Each linguistic expression (SD) is a sequence of representations, one at each linguistic level. In variants of the Extended Standard Theory (EST), each SD is a sequence $(\delta, \sigma, \pi, \lambda)$, representations at the D-Structure, S-Structure, Phonetic Form (PF), and Logical Form (LF) levels, respectively.

Some basic properties of language are unusual among biological systems, notably the property of discrete infinity. A working hypothesis in generative grammar has been that languages are based on simple principles that interact to form often intricate structures, and that the language faculty is nonredundant, in that particular phenomena are not "overdetermined" by principles of language. These too are unexpected features of complex biological systems, more like what one expects to find (for unexplained reasons) in the study of the inorganic world. The approach has, nevertheless, proven to be a successful one, suggesting that the hypotheses are more than just an artifact reflecting a mode of inquiry.

Another recurrent theme has been the role of "principles of economy" in determining the computations and the SDs they generate. Such considerations have arisen in various forms and guises as theoretical perspectives have changed. There is, I think, good reason to believe that they are fundamental to the design of language, if properly understood.[1]

The language is embedded in performance systems that enable its expressions to be used for articulating, interpreting, referring, inquiring, reflecting, and other actions. We can think of the SD as a complex of instructions for these performance systems, providing information relevant to their functions. While there is no clear sense to the idea that language is "designed for use" or "well adapted to its functions," we do expect to find connections between the properties of the language and the manner of its use.

The performance systems appear to fall into two general types: articulatory-perceptual and conceptual-intentional. If so, a linguistic expression contains instructions for each of these systems. Two of the linguistic levels, then, are the *interface levels* A-P and C-I, providing the instructions for the articulatory-perceptual and conceptual-intentional systems, respectively. Each language determines a set of pairs drawn from the A-P and C-I levels. The level A-P has generally been taken to be PF; the status and character of C-I have been more controversial.

Another standard assumption is that a language consists of two components: a lexicon and a computational system. The lexicon specifies the items that enter into the computational system, with their idiosyncratic properties. The computational system uses these elements to generate derivations and SDs. The derivation of a particular linguistic expression, then, involves a choice of items from the lexicon and a computation that constructs the pair of interface representations.

So far we are within the domain of virtual conceptual necessity, at least if the general outlook is adopted.[2] UG must determine the class of possible languages. It must specify the properties of SDs and of the symbolic representations that enter into them. In particular, it must specify the interface levels (A-P, C-I), the elements that constitute these levels, and the computations by which they are constructed. A particularly simple design for language would take the (conceptually necessary) interface levels to be the only levels. That assumption will be part of the "minimalist" program I would like to explore here.

In early work in generative grammar, it was assumed that the interface C-I is the level of T-markers, effectively a composite of all levels of syntactic representation. In descendants of EST approaches, C-I is generally taken to be LF. On this assumption, each language will determine a set of pairs (π, λ) (π drawn from PF and λ from LF) as its formal representations of sound and meaning, insofar as these are determined by the language itself. Parts of the computational system are relevant only to π, not λ: the *PF component*.[3] Other parts are relevant only to λ, not π: the *LF component*. The parts of the computational system that are relevant to both are the *overt syntax*—a term that is a bit misleading, in that these parts may involve empty categories assigned no phonetic shape. The nature of these systems is an empirical matter; one should not be misled by unintended connotations of such terms as "logical form" and "represent" adopted from technical usage in different kinds of inquiry.

The standard idealized model of language acquisition takes the initial state S_0 to be a function mapping experience (primary linguistic data, PLD) to a language. UG is concerned with the invariant principles of S_0 and the range of permissible variation. Variation must be determined by what is "visible" to the child acquiring language, that is, by the PLD. It is not surprising, then, to find a degree of variation in the PF component, and in aspects of the lexicon: Saussurean arbitrariness (association of concepts with phonological matrices), properties of grammatical formatives (inflection, etc.), and readily detectable properties that hold of lexical items generally (e.g., the head parameter). Variation in the overt syntax or LF component would be more problematic, since evidence could only be quite indirect. A narrow conjecture is that there is no such variation: beyond PF options and lexical arbitrariness (which I henceforth ignore), variation is limited to nonsubstantive parts of the lexicon and general properties of lexical items. If so, there is only one computational system and one lexicon, apart from this limited kind of variety. Let us tentatively adopt that assumption—extreme, perhaps, but it seems not implausible—as another element of the Minimalist Program.[4]

Early generative grammar approached these questions in a different way, along lines suggested by long tradition: various levels are identified, with their particular properties and interrelations; UG provides a format for permissible rule systems; any instantiation of this format constitutes a specific language. Each language is a rich and intricate system of rules that are, typically, construction-particular and language-particular: the rules forming verb phrases or passives or relative clauses in English, for example, are specific to *these* constructions in *this* language. Similarities across constructions and languages derive from properties of the format for rule systems.

The more recent principles-and-parameters (P&P) approach, assumed here, breaks radically with this tradition, taking steps toward the minimalist design just sketched. UG provides a fixed system of principles and a finite array of finitely valued parameters. The language-particular rules reduce to choice of values for these parameters. The notion of grammatical construction is eliminated, and with it, construction-particular rules. Constructions such as verb phrase, relative clause, and passive remain only as taxonomic artifacts, collections of phenomena explained through the interaction of the principles of UG, with the values of parameters fixed.

With regard to the computational system, then, we assume that S_0 is constituted of invariant principles with options restricted to functional elements and general properties of the lexicon. A selection Σ among these options determines a language. A language, in turn, determines an infinite set of linguistic expressions (SDs), each a pair (π, λ) drawn from the interface levels (PF, LF), respectively. Language acquisition involves fixing Σ; the grammar of the language states Σ, nothing more (lexical arbitrariness and PF component aside). If there is a parsing system that is invariant and unlearned (as often assumed), then it maps (Σ, π) into a structured percept, in some cases associated with an SD.[5] Conditions on representations—those of binding theory, Case theory, θ-theory, and so on—hold only at the interface, and are motivated by properties of the interface, perhaps properly understood as modes of interpretation by performance systems. The linguistic expressions are the optimal realizations of the interface conditions, where "optimality" is determined by the economy conditions of UG. Let us take these assumptions too to be part of the Minimalist Program.

In early work, economy considerations entered as part of the evaluation metric, which, it was assumed, selected a particular instantiation of the permitted format for rule systems, given PLD. As inquiry has progressed, the presumed role of an evaluation metric has declined, and within the P&P approach, it is generally assumed to be completely dispensable: the principles are sufficiently restrictive so that PLD suffice in the normal case to set the parameter values that determine a language.[6]

Nevertheless, it seems that economy principles of the kind explored in early work play a significant role in accounting for properties of language. With a proper formulation of such principles, it may be possible to move toward the minimalist design: a theory of language that takes a linguistic expression to be nothing other than a formal object that satisfies the interface conditions in the optimal way. A still further step would be to show that the basic principles of language are formulated in terms of notions drawn from the domain of (virtual) conceptual necessity.

Invariant principles determine what counts as a possible derivation and a possible derived object (linguistic expression, SD). Given a language, these principles determine a specific set of derivations and generated SDs, each a pair (π, λ). Let us say that a derivation D *converges* if it yields a legitimate SD and *crashes* if it does not; D *converges at PF* if π is legitimate and *crashes at PF* if it is not; D *converges at LF* if λ is legitimate and *crashes at LF* if it is not. In an EST framework, with SD = $(\delta, \sigma, \pi, \lambda)$ (δ a D-Structure representation, σ an S-Structure representation), there are other possibilities: δ or σ, or relations among $(\delta, \sigma, \pi, \lambda)$, might be defective. Within the Minimalist Program, all possibilities are excluded apart from the status of π and λ. A still sharper version would exclude the possibility that π and λ are each legitimate but cannot be paired for UG reasons. Let us adopt this narrower condition as well. Thus, we assume that a derivation converges if it converges at PF and at LF; convergence is determined by independent inspection of the interface levels—not an empirically innocuous assumption.[7]

The principles outlined are simple and restrictive, so that the empirical burden is considerable; and fairly intricate argument may be necessary to support it—exactly the desired outcome, for whatever ultimately proves to be the right approach.

These topics have been studied and elaborated over the past several years, with results suggesting that the minimalist conception outlined may not be far from the mark. I had hoped to present an exposition in this paper, but that plan proved too ambitious. I will therefore keep to an informal sketch, only indicating some of the problems that must be dealt with.[8]

3.2   Fundamental Relations: X-Bar Theory

The computational system takes representations of a given form and modifies them. Accordingly, UG must provide means to present an array of items from the lexicon in a form accessible to the computational system. We may take this form to be some version of X-bar theory. The concepts of X-bar theory are therefore fundamental. In a minimalist theory, the crucial properties and relations will be stated in the simple and elementary terms of X-bar theory.

An X-bar structure is composed of projections of heads selected from the lexicon. Basic relations, then, will involve the head as one term. Furthermore, the basic relations are typically "local." In structures of the form (1), two local relations are present: the *Spec(ifier)-head* relation of ZP to X, and the *head-complement* relation of X to YP (order irrelevant; the usual conventions apply).

(1)

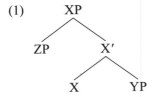

The head-complement relation is not only "more local" but also more fundamental—typically, associated with thematic (θ-) relations. The Spec-head relation, I will suggest below, falls into an "elsewhere" category. Putting aside adjunction for the moment, the narrowest plausible hypothesis is that X-bar structures are restricted to the form in (1); only local relations are considered (hence no relation between X and a phrase included within YP or ZP); and head-complement is the core local relation. Another admissible local relation is *head-head*, for example, the relation of a verb to (the head of) its Noun Phrase complement (selection). Another is *chain link*, to which we will return. The version of a minimalist program explored here requires that we keep to relations of these kinds, dispensing with such notions as government by a head (head government). But head government plays a critical role in all modules of grammar; hence, all of these must be reformulated, if this program is to be pursued.

Take Case theory. It is standardly assumed that the Spec-head relation enters into structural Case for the subject position, while the object position is assigned Case under government by V, including constructions in which the object Case-marked by a verb is not its complement (exceptional Case marking).[9] The narrower approach we are considering requires that all these modes of structural Case assignment be recast in unified X-bar-theoretic terms, presumably under the Spec-head relation. As discussed in chapter 2, an elaboration of Pollock's (1989) theory of inflection provides a natural mechanism, where we take the basic structure of the clause to be (2).

(2)

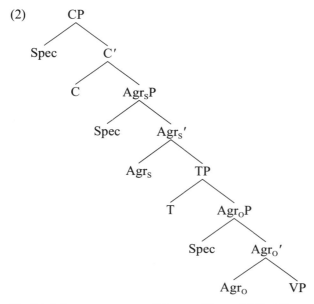

Omitted here are a possible specifier of TP ([Spec, TP]) and a phrase headed by the functional element *Neg(ation)*, or perhaps more broadly, a category that includes an affirmation marker and others as well (Pollock 1989, Laka 1990). Agr_S and Agr_O are informal mnemonics to distinguish the two functional roles of Agr. Agr is a collection of ϕ-features (gender, number, person); these are common to the systems of subject and object agreement, though Agr_S and Agr_O may of course be different selections, just as two verbs or NPs in (2) may differ.[10]

We now regard both agreement and structural Case as manifestations of the Spec-head relation (NP, Agr). But Case properties depend on characteristics of T and the V head of VP. We therefore assume that T raises to Agr_S, forming (3a), and V raises to Agr_O, forming (3b); the complex includes the ϕ-features of Agr and the Case feature provided by T, V.[11]

(3) a. $[_{Agr}$ T Agr]
    b. $[_{Agr}$ V Agr]

The basic assumption is that there is a symmetry between the subject and the object inflectional systems. In both positions the relation of NP to V is mediated by Agr, a collection of ϕ-features; in both positions agreement is determined by the ϕ-features of the Agr head of the Agr complex, and Case by an element that adjoins to Agr (T or V). An NP in the Spec-head relation to this Agr complex bears the associated Case and agreement features. The Spec-head and head-head relations are therefore the core configurations for inflectional morphology.

Exceptional Case marking by V is now interpreted as raising of NP to the Spec of the AgrP dominating V. It is raising to [Spec, Agr_O], the analogue of familiar raising to [Spec, Agr_S]. If the VP-internal subject hypothesis is correct (as I henceforth assume), the question arises why the object (direct, or in the complement) raises to [Spec, Agr_O] and the subject to [Spec, Agr_S], yielding unexpected crossing rather than the usual nested paths. We will return to this phenomenon below, finding that it follows on plausible assumptions of some generality, and in this sense appears to be a fairly "deep" property of language. If parameters are morphologically restricted in the manner sketched earlier, there should be no language variation in this regard.

The same hypothesis extends naturally to predicate adjectives, with the underlying structure shown in (4) (Agr_A again a mnemonic for a collection of ϕ-features, in this case associated with an adjective).

(4)

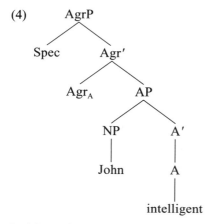

Raising of NP to Spec and A to Agr_A creates the structure for NP-adjective agreement internal to the predicate phrase. The resulting structure is a plausible candidate for the small clause complement of *consider*, *be*, and so on. In the former construction (complement of *consider*), NP raises further to [Spec, Agr_O] at LF to receive accusative Case; in the latter (complement of *be*), NP raises overtly to receive nominative Case and verb agreement, yielding the overt form *John is intelligent* with *John* entering into three relations: (1) a Case relation with [T Agr_S] (hence ultimately the verbal complex [[T Agr_S] V]), (2) an agreement relation with Agr_S (hence the verbal complex), and (3) an agreement relation with Agr of structure (4) (hence the adjectival complex). In both constructions, the NP subject is outside of a full AP in the small clause construction, as required, and the structure is of a type that appears regularly.[12]

An NP, then, may enter into two kinds of structural relations with a predicate (verb, adjective): agreement, involving features shared by NP and predicate; or Case, manifested on the NP alone. Subject of verb or adjective, and object of verb, enter into these relations (but not object of adjective if that is an instance of inherent, not structural, Case). Both relations involve Agr: Agr alone, for agreement relations; the element T or V alone (raising to Agr), for Case relations.

The structure of CP in (2) is largely forced by other properties of UG, assuming the minimalist approach with Agr abstracted as a common property of adjectival agreement and the subject-object inflectional systems, a reasonable assumption, given that agreement appears without Case (as in NP-AP agreement) and Case appears without agreement (as in transitive expletives, with the expletive presumably in the [Spec, Agr_S]

position and the subject in [Spec, T], receiving Case; see note 11). Any appropriate version of the Case Filter will require two occurrences of Agr if two NPs in VP require structural Case; conditions on Move α require the arrangement given in (2) if structural Case is construed as outlined. Suppose that VP contains only one NP. Then one of the two Agr elements will be "active" (the other being inert or perhaps missing). Which one? Two options are possible: Agr_S or Agr_O. If the choice is Agr_S, then the single NP will have the properties of the subject of a transitive clause; if the choice is Agr_O, then it will have the properties of the object of a transitive clause (nominative-accusative and ergative-absolutive languages, respectively). These are the only two possibilities, mixtures apart. The distinction between the two language types reduces to a trivial question of morphology, as we expect.

Note that from this point of view, the terms *nominative, absolutive*, and so on, have no substantive meaning apart from what is determined by the choice of "active" versus "inert" Agr; there is no real question as to how these terms correspond across language types.

The "active" element (Agr_S in nominative-accusative languages and Agr_O in ergative-absolutive languages) typically assigns a less-marked Case to its Spec, which is also higher on the extractability hierarchy, among other properties. It is natural to expect less-marked Case to be compensated (again, as a tendency) by more-marked agreement (richer overt agreement with nominative and absolutive than with accusative and ergative). The C-Command Condition on anaphora leads us to expect nominative and ergative binding in transitive constructions.[13]

Similar considerations apply to licensing of *pro*. Assuming Rizzi's theory (1982, 1986a), *pro* is licensed in a Spec-head relation to "strong" Agr_S, or when governed by certain verbs V*. To recast these proposals in a unitary X-bar-theoretic form: *pro* is licensed only in the Spec-head relation to $[_{Agr} \alpha \text{ Agr}]$, where α is [+tense] or V, Agr strong or V = V*. Licensing of *pro* thus falls under Case theory in a broad sense. Similar considerations extend rather naturally to PRO.[14]

Suppose that other properties of head government also have a natural expression in terms of the more fundamental notions of X-bar theory. Suppose further that antecedent government is a property of chains, expressible in terms of c-command and barriers. Then the concept of government would be dispensable, with principles of language restricted to something closer to conceptual necessity: local X-bar-theoretic relations to the head of a projection and the chain link relation.

Let us look more closely at the local X-bar-theoretic notions, taking these to be fundamental. Assume binary branching only, thus structures limited to (1). Turning to adjunction, on the assumptions of Chomsky 1986a, there is no adjunction to complement, adjunction (at least, in overt syntax) has a kind of "structure-preserving" character, and a segment-category distinction holds.[15] Thus, the structures to be considered are of the form shown in (5), where XP, ZP, and X each have a higher and lower segment, indicated by subscripting (H and X heads).

(5)

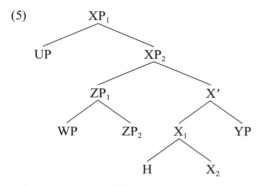

Let us now consider the notions that enter into a minimalist program. The basic elements of a representation are chains. We consider first the case of one-membered chains, construing notions abstractly with an eye to the general case. The structure (5) can only have arisen by raising of H to adjoin to X (we put aside questions about the possible origins of UP, WP). Therefore, H heads a chain $CH = (H, \ldots, t)$, and only this chain, not H in isolation, enters into head-α relations. The categories that we establish are defined for H as well as X, but while they enter into head-α relations for X, they do not do so for H (only for the chain CH), an important matter.

Assume all notions to be irreflexive unless otherwise indicated. Assume the standard notion of domination for the pair (σ, β), σ a segment. We say that the category α *dominates* β if every segment of α dominates β. The category α *contains* β if some segment of α dominates β. Thus, the two-segment category XP dominates ZP, WP, X', and whatever they dominate; XP contains UP and whatever UP and XP dominate; ZP contains WP but does not dominate it. The two-segment category X contains H but does not dominate it.

For a head α, take $\text{Max}(\alpha)$ to be the least full-category maximal projection dominating α. Thus, in (5) $\text{Max}(H) = \text{Max}(X) = [XP_1, XP_2]$, the two-segment category XP.

Take the *domain* of a head α to be the set of nodes contained in $\text{Max}(\alpha)$ that are distinct from and do not contain α. Thus, the domain of X in (5) is {UP, ZP, WP, YP, H} and whatever these categories dominate; the domain of H is the same, minus H.

As noted, the fundamental X-bar-theoretic relation is head-complement, typically with an associated θ-relation determined by properties of the head. Define the *complement domain* of α as the subset of the domain reflexively dominated by the complement of the construction: YP in (5). The complement domain of X (and H) is therefore YP and whatever it dominates.

The remainder of the domain of α we will call the *residue* of α. Thus, in (5) the residue of X is its domain minus YP and what it dominates. The residue is a heterogeneous set, including the Spec and anything adjoined (adjunction being allowed to the maximal projection, its Spec, or its head; UP, WP, and H, respectively, in (5)).

The operative relations have a local character. We are therefore interested not in the sets just defined, but rather in *minimal* subsets of them that include just categories locally related to the heads. For any set S of categories, let us take $\text{Min}(S)$ (minimal S) to be the smallest subset K of S such that for any $\gamma \in S$, some $\beta \in K$ reflexively dominates γ. In the cases that interest us, S is a function of a head α (e.g., S = domain of α). We keep to this case, that is, to $\text{Min}(S(\alpha))$, for some head α. Thus, in (5) the minimal domain of X is {UP, ZP, WP, YP, H}; its minimal complement domain is YP; and its minimal residue is {UP, ZP, WP, H}. The minimal domain of H is {UP, ZP, WP, YP}; its minimal complement domain is YP; and its minimal residue is {UP, ZP, WP}.

Let us call the minimal complement domain of α its *internal domain*, and the minimal residue of α its *checking domain*. The terminology is intended to indicate that elements of the internal domain are typically internal arguments of α, while the checking domain is typically involved in checking inflectional features. Recall that the checking domain is heterogeneous: it is the "elsewhere" set. The minimal domain also has an important role, to which we will turn directly.

A technical point should be clarified. The internal and checking domains of α must be uniquely defined for α; specifically, if α (or one of its elements, if it is a nontrivial chain) is moved, we do not want the internal and checking domains to be "redefined" in the newly formed construction, or we will have an element with multiple subdomains—for example, ambiguous specification of internal arguments. We must therefore understand the notion $Min(S(\alpha))$ *derivationally*, not *representationally*: it is defined for α as part of the process of introducing α into the derivation. If α is a trivial (one-membered) chain, then $Min(S(\alpha))$ is defined when α is lexically inserted; if α is a nontrivial chain $(\beta_1, \ldots, \beta_n)$, then $Min(S(\alpha))$ is defined when α is formed by raising β_1. In (5) the head H has no minimal, internal, or checking domain, because it is raised from some other position to form the chain $CH = (H, \ldots, t)$ and has already been assigned these subdomains in the position now occupied by t; such subdomains are, however, defined for the newly formed chain CH, in a manner to which we will turn directly. Similarly, if the complex [H X] is later raised to form the chain $CH' = ([H\ X], t')$, $Min(S(\alpha))$ will be defined as part of the operation for $\alpha = CH'$, but not for $\alpha = X, H$, or CH.

Returning to (5), suppose X is a verb. Then YP, the sole element of the internal domain of X, is typically an internal argument of X. Suppose X is Agr and H a verb raised to Agr forming the chain $CH = (H, t)$. Then the specifier ZP (and possibly the adjoined elements UP, WP) of the checking domain of X and CH will have agreement features by virtue of their local relation to X, and Case features by virtue of their local relation to CH. H does not have a checking domain, but CH does.[16]

We have so far considered only one-membered chains. We must extend the notions defined to a nontrivial chain CH with $n > 1$ (α_1 a zero-level category), as in (6).

(6) $CH = (\alpha_1, \ldots, \alpha_n)$

Let us keep to the case of $n = 2$, the normal case for lexical heads though not necessarily the only one.[17]

The issue arises, for example, if we adopt an analysis of multiargument verbs along the lines suggested by Larson (1988), for example, taking the underlying structure of (7) to be (8).

(7) John put the book on the shelf

(8)

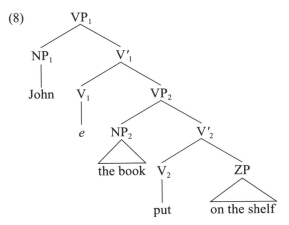

V_2 raises to the empty position V_1, forming the chain (put, t) (subsequently, NP_1 raises (overtly) to [Spec, Agr_S] and NP_2 (covertly) to [Spec, Agr_O]).

The result we want is that the minimal domain of the chain (put, t) is $\{NP_1, NP_2, ZP\}$ (the three arguments), while the internal domain is $\{NP_2, ZP\}$ (the internal arguments). The intended sense is given by the natural generalization of the definitions already suggested. Let us define the domain of CH in (6) to be the set of nodes contained in $Max(\alpha_1)$ and not containing any α_i. The complement domain of CH is the subset of the domain of CH reflexively dominated by the complement of α_1. Residue and $Min(S(\alpha))$ are defined as before, now for $\alpha = CH$. The concepts defined earlier are the special cases where CH is one-membered.

Suppose, for example, that $CH = (put, t)$, after raising of put to V_1 in (8), leaving t in the position V_2. Then the domain of CH is the set of nodes contained in VP_1 ($= Max(V_1)$) and not containing either put or t (namely, the set $\{NP_1, NP_2, ZP\}$ and whatever they dominate); the minimal domain is $\{NP_1, NP_2, ZP\}$. The internal domain of the chain CH is $\{NP_2, ZP\}$ (the two internal arguments), and the checking domain of CH is NP_1, the typical position of the external argument in this version of the VP-internal subject hypothesis (basically Larson's).

Suppose that instead of replacing e, put had adjoined to some nonnull element X, yielding the complex category $[_X \; put \; X]$, as in adjunction of H to X in (5). The domain, internal domain, and checking domain of the chain would be exactly the same. There is no minimal domain, internal domain, or checking domain for put itself after raising; only for the chain CH $= (put, t)$. It is in terms of these minimal sets that the local head-α relations are defined, the head now being the nontrivial chain CH.

In (8), then, the relevant domains are as intended after V-raising to V_1. Note that VP_2 is not in the internal domain of CH $(= (put, t))$ because it dominates t $(= \alpha_n$ of (6)).

The same notions extend to an analysis of lexical structure along the lines proposed by Hale and Keyser (1993a). In this case an analogue of (8) would be the underlying structure for *John shelved the book*, with V_2 being a "light verb" and ZP an abstract version of *on the shelf* $(= [P \ shelf])$. Here *shelf* raises to P, the amalgam raises to V_2, and the element so formed raises to V_1 in the manner of *put* in (7).[18]

So far we have made no use of the notion "minimal domain." But this too has a natural interpretation, when we turn to Empty Category Principle (ECP) phenomena. I will have to put aside a careful development here, but it is intuitively clear how certain basic aspects will enter. Take the phenomena of superiority (as in (9a)) and of relativized minimality in the sense of Rizzi (1990) (as in (9b)).

(9) a. i. $whom_1$ did John persuade t_1 [to visit $whom_2$]
        ii. *$whom_2$ did John persuade $whom_1$ [to visit t_2]
     b. Superraising, the Head Movement Constraint (HMC), [Spec, CP] islands (including *wh*-islands)

Looking at these phenomena in terms of economy considerations, it is clear that in all the "bad" cases, some element has failed to make "the shortest move." In (9aii) movement of $whom_2$ to [Spec, CP] is longer in a natural sense (definable in terms of c-command) than movement of $whom_1$ to this position. In all the cases of (9b) the moved element has "skipped" a position it could have reached by a shorter move, had that position not been filled. Spelling out these notions to account for the range of relevant cases is not a trivial matter. But it does seem possible in a way that accords reasonably well with the Minimalist Program. Let us simply assume, for present purposes, that this task can be carried out, and that phenomena of the kind illustrated are accounted for in this way in terms of economy considerations.[19]

There appears to be a conflict between two natural notions of economy: shortest move versus fewest steps in a derivation. If a derivation keeps to shortest moves, it will have more steps; if it reduces the number of steps, it will have longer moves. The paradox is resolved if we take the basic transformational operation to be not Move α but *Form Chain*, an operation that applies, say, to the structure (10a) to form (10b) in a single step, yielding the chain CH of (10c).

(10) a. *e* seems [*e* to be likely [John to win]]
     b. John seems [*t'* to be likely [*t* to win]]
     c. CH = (*John*, *t'*, *t*)

Similarly, in other cases of successive-cyclic movement. There is, then, no conflict between reducing derivations to the shortest number of steps and keeping links minimal ("Shortest Movement" Condition). There are independent reasons to suppose that this is the correct approach: note, for example, that successive-cyclic *wh*-movement of arguments does not treat the intermediate steps as adjunct movement, as it should if it were a succession of applications of Move α. Successive-cyclic movement raises a variety of interesting problems, but I will again put them aside, keeping to the simpler case.

A number of questions arise in the case of such constructions as (8), considered now in the more abstract form (11).

(11)

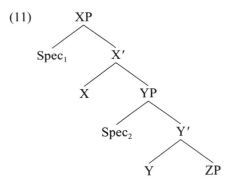

In the particular instance (8), $Spec_1 = NP_1$ (*John*), X = null V_1, $Spec_2 = NP_2$ (*the book*), Y = V_2 (*put*) with ZP its complement (*on the shelf*). Another instance would be object raising to [Spec, Agr] (Agr = Agr_0), as in (12).

(12)

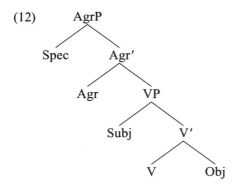

Here Subj is the VP-internal subject (or its trace), and Obj the object. The configuration and operations are exactly those of (8), except that in (12) V *adjoins* to Agr (as in the case of H of (5)), whereas in (8) it *substituted for* the empty position V_1. On our assumptions, Obj must raise to Spec for Case checking, crossing Subj or its trace. (12) is therefore a violation of Relativized Minimality, in effect, a case of superraising, a violation of the "Shortest Movement" Condition.

Another instance of (11) is incorporation in the sense of Baker (1988). For example, V-incorporation to a causative verb has a structure like (12), but with an embedded clause S instead of the object Obj, as in (13).

(13)

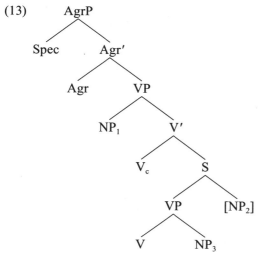

In an example of Baker's, modeled on Chichewa, we take NP_1 = *the baboons*, V_c = *make*, NP_2 = *the lizards*, V = *hit*, and NP_3 = *the children*;

the resulting sentence is *the baboons made-hit the children* [*to the lizards*], meaning 'the baboons made the lizards hit the children'. Incorporation of V to the causative V_c yields the chain (V, t), with V adjoined to V_c. The complex head $[V\ V_c]$ then raises to Agr, forming the new chain $([V\ V_c], t')$, with $[V\ V_c]$ adjoining to Agr to yield $\alpha = [_{Agr}\ [V\ V_c]\ Agr]$. The resulting structure is (14).[20]

(14)

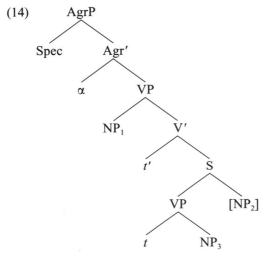

Here NP_3 is treated as the object of the verbal complex, assigned accusative Case (with optional object agreement). In our terms, that means that NP_3 raises to [Spec, α], crossing NP_1, the matrix subject or its trace (another option is that the complex verb is passivized and NP_3 is raised to [Spec, Agr_S]).

In the last example the minimal domain of the chain $([V\ V_c], t')$ is {Spec, NP_1, S}. The example is therefore analogous to (8), in which V-raising formed an enlarged minimal domain for the chain. It is natural to suppose that (12) has the same property: V first raises to Agr, yielding the chain (V, t) with the minimal domain {Spec, Subj, Obj}. The cases just described are now formally alike and should be susceptible to the same analysis. The last two cases appear to violate the "Shortest Movement" Condition.

Let us sharpen the notion "shortest movement" as follows:

(15) If α, β are in the same minimal domain, they are equidistant
     from γ.

In particular, two targets of movement are equidistant if they are in the same minimal domain.

In the abstract case (11), if Y adjoins to X, forming the chain (Y, t) with the minimal domain {$Spec_1$, $Spec_2$, ZP}, then $Spec_1$ and $Spec_2$ are equidistant from ZP (or anything it contains), so that raising of (or from) ZP can cross $Spec_2$ to $Spec_1$. Turning to the problematic instances of (11), in (12) Obj can raise to Spec, crossing Subj or its trace without violating the economy condition; and in the incorporation example (14) NP_3 can raise to Spec, crossing NP_1.

This analysis predicts that object raising as in (12) should be possible only if V has raised to Agr. In particular, overt object raising will be possible only with overt V-raising. That prediction is apparently confirmed for the Germanic languages (Vikner 1990). The issue does not arise in the LF analogue, since we assume that invariably, V raises to Agr_O covertly, if not overtly, therefore "freeing" the raising of object to [Spec, Agr_O] for Case checking.

Baker explains structures similar to (13)–(14) in terms of his Government Transparency Corollary (GTC), which extends the government domain of V_1 to that of V_2 if V_2 adjoins to V_1.[21] The analysis just sketched is an approximate analogue, on the assumption that Case and agreement are assigned not by head government but in the Spec-head relation. Note that the GTC is not strictly speaking a corollary; rather, it is an independent principle, though Baker gives a plausibility argument internal to a specific theory of government. A possibility that might be investigated is that the GTC falls generally under the independently motivated condition (15), on the minimalist assumptions being explored here.

Recall that on these assumptions, we faced the problem of explaining why we find crossing rather than nesting in the Case theory, with VP-internal subject raising to [Spec, Agr_S] and object raising to [Spec, Agr_O], crossing the trace of the VP-internal subject. The principle (15) entails that this is a permissible derivation, as in (12) with V-raising to Agr_O. It remains to show that the desired derivation is not only permissible but obligatory: it is the only possible derivation. That is straightforward. Suppose that in (12) the VP-internal subject in [Spec, VP] raises to [Spec, Agr_O], either overtly or covertly, yielding (16), t_{Subj} the trace of the raised subject Subj.

(16)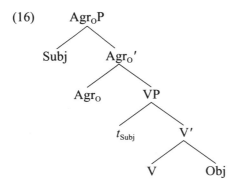

Suppose further that V raises to Agr_O, either overtly or covertly, form-ing the chain (V, t_V) with the minimal domain $\{Subj, t_{Subj}, Obj\}$. Now Subj and its trace are equidistant from Obj, so that Obj can raise to the $[Spec, Agr_O]$ position. But this position is occupied by Subj, blocking that option. Therefore, to receive Case, Obj must move directly to some higher position, crossing $[Spec, Agr_O]$: either to $[Spec, T]$ or to $[Spec, Agr_S]$. But that is impossible, even after the element $[V, Agr_O]$ raises to higher inflectional positions. Raising of $[V, Agr_O]$ will form a new chain with trace in the Agr_O position of (16) and a new minimal domain M. But t_{Subj} is not a member of M. Accordingly, Obj cannot cross t_{Subj} to reach a position in M (apart from the position $[Spec, Agr_O]$ already filled by the subject). Hence, raising of the VP-internal subject to the $[Spec, Agr_O]$ position blocks any kind of Case assignment to the object; the object is "frozen in place."[22]

It follows that crossing and not nesting is the only permissible option in any language. The paradox of Case theory is therefore resolved, on natural assumptions that generalize to a number of other cases.

3.3 Beyond the Interface Levels: D-Structure

Recall the (virtual) conceptual necessities within this general approach. UG determines possible symbolic representations and derivations. A lan-guage consists of a lexicon and a computational system. The computa-tional system draws from the lexicon to form derivations, presenting items from the lexicon in the format of X-bar theory. Each derivation determines a linguistic expression, an SD, which contains a pair (π, λ) meeting the interface conditions. Ideally, that would be the end of the story: each linguistic expression is an optimal realization of interface conditions expressed in elementary terms (chain link, local X-bar-theoretic relations), a pair (π, λ) satisfying these conditions and generated in the most economical way. Any additional structure or assumptions require empirical justification.

The EST framework adds additional structure; for concreteness, take *Lectures on Government and Binding* (*LGB*; Chomsky 1981a). One crucial assumption has to do with the way in which the computational system presents lexical items for further computation. The assumption is that this is done by an operation, call it *Satisfy*, which selects an array of items from the lexicon and presents it in a format satisfying the conditions of X-bar theory. Satisfy is an "all-at-once" operation: all items that function at LF are drawn from the lexicon before computation proceeds[23] and are presented in the X-bar format.

We thus postulate an additional level, D-Structure, beyond the two external interface levels PF and LF. D-Structure is the *internal* interface between the lexicon and the computational system, formed by Satisfy. Certain principles of UG are then held to apply to D-Structure, specifically, the Projection Principle and the θ-Criterion. The computational procedure maps D-Structure to another level, S-Structure, and then "branches" to PF and LF, independently. UG principles of the various modules of grammar (binding theory, Case theory, the *pro* module, etc.) apply at the level of S-Structure (perhaps elsewhere as well, in some cases).

The empirical justification for this approach, with its departures from conceptual necessity, is substantial. Nevertheless, we may ask whether the evidence will bear the weight, or whether it is possible to move toward a minimalist program.

Note that the operation Satisfy and the assumptions that underlie it are not unproblematic. We have described Satisfy as an operation that selects an *array*, not a *set*; different arrangements of lexical items will yield different expressions. Exactly what an array is would have to be clarified. Furthermore, this picture requires conditions to ensure that D-Structure has basic properties of LF. At LF the conditions are trivial. If they are not met, the expression receives some deviant interpretation at the interface; there is nothing more to say. The Projection Principle and the θ-Criterion have no independent significance at LF.[24] But at D-Structure the two principles are needed to make the picture coherent; if the picture is abandoned, they will lose their primary role. These principles are therefore dubious on conceptual grounds, though it remains to account for their empirical consequences, such as the constraint against substitution into a θ-position. If the empirical consequences can be explained in some other way and D-Structure eliminated, then the Projection Principle and the θ-Criterion can be dispensed with.

What is more, postulation of D-Structure raises empirical problems, as noticed at once when EST was reformulated in the more restrictive P&P framework. One problem, discussed in *LGB*, is posed by complex adjectival constructions such as (17a) with the S-Structure representation (17b) (*t* the trace of the empty operator Op).

(17) a. John is easy to please
     b. John is easy [$_{CP}$ Op [$_{IP}$ PRO to please *t*]]

The evidence for the S-Structure representation (17b) is compelling, but *John* occupies a non-θ-position and hence cannot appear at D-Structure. Satisfy is therefore violated. In *LGB* it is proposed that Satisfy be weakened: in non-θ-positions a lexical item, such as *John*, can be inserted in the course of the derivation and assigned its θ-role only at LF (and irrelevantly, S-Structure). That is consistent with the principles, though not with their spirit, one might argue.

We need not tarry on that matter, however, because the technical device does not help. As noted by Howard Lasnik, the *LGB* solution fails, because an NP of arbitrary complexity may occur in place of *John* (e.g., an NP incorporating a structure such as (17a) internally). Within anything like the *LGB* framework, then, we are driven to a version of generalized transformations, as in the very earliest work in generative grammar. The problem was recognized at once, but left as an unresolved paradox. More recent work has brought forth other cases of expressions interpretable at LF but not in their D-Structure positions (Reinhart 1991), along with other reasons to suspect that there are generalized transformations, or devices like them (Kroch and Joshi 1985, Kroch 1989, Lebeaux 1988, Epstein 1991). If so, the special assumptions underlying the postulation of D-Structure lose credibility. Since these assumptions lacked independent conceptual support, we are led to dispense with the level of D-Structure and the "all-at-once" property of Satisfy, relying in its place on a theory of generalized transformations for lexical access —though the empirical consequences of the D-Structure conditions remain to be faced.[25]

A theory of the preferred sort is readily constructed and turns out to have many desirable properties. Let us replace the EST assumptions of *LGB* and related work by an approach along the following lines. The computational system selects an item X from the lexicon and projects it to an X-bar structure of one of the forms in (18), where $X = X^0 = [_X X]$.

(18) a. X
   b. $[_{X'} X]$
   c. $[_{XP} [_{X'} X]]$

This will be the sole residue of the Projection Principle.

We now adopt (more or less) the assumptions of *LSLT*, with a single generalized transformation GT that takes a phrase marker K^1 and inserts it in a designated empty position $\emptyset$ in a phrase marker K, forming the new phrase marker K*, which satisfies X-bar theory. Computation proceeds in parallel, selecting from the lexicon freely at any point. At each point in the derivation, then, we have a structure Σ, which we may think of as a set of phrase markers. At any point, we may apply the operation Spell-Out, which switches to the PF component. If Σ is not a single phrase marker, the derivation crashes at PF, since PF rules cannot apply to a set of phrase markers and no legitimate PF representation π is generated. If Σ is a single phrase marker, the PF rules apply to it, yielding π, which either is legitimate (so the derivation converges at PF) or not (the derivation again crashes at PF).

After Spell-Out, the computational process continues, with the sole constraint that it has no further access to the lexicon (we must ensure, for example, that *John left* does not mean 'they wondered whether John left before finishing his work'). The PF and LF outputs must satisfy the (external) interface conditions. D-Structure disappears, along with the problems it raised.

GT is a substitution operation. It targets K and substitutes K^1 for $\emptyset$ in K. But $\emptyset$ is not drawn from the lexicon; therefore, it must have been inserted by GT itself. GT, then, targets K, adds $\emptyset$, and substitutes K^1 for $\emptyset$, forming K*, which must satisfy X-bar theory. Note that this is a description of the inner workings of a single operation, GT. It is on a par with some particular algorithm for Move α, or for the operation of modus ponens in a proof. Thus, it is invisible to the eye that scans only the derivation itself, detecting only its successive steps. We never see $\emptyset$; it is subliminal, like the "first half" of the raising of an NP to subject position.

Alongside the binary substitution operation GT, which maps (K, K^1) to K*, we also have the singulary substitution operation Move α, which maps K to K*. Suppose that this operation works just as GT does: it targets K, adds $\emptyset$, and substitutes α for $\emptyset$, where α in this case is a phrase marker within the targeted phrase marker K itself. We assume further that the operation leaves behind a trace t of α and forms the chain (α, t). Again, $\emptyset$ is invisible when we scan the derivation; it is part of the inner workings of an operation carrying the derivation forward one step.

Suppose we restrict substitution operations still further, requiring that $\emptyset$ be *external* to the targeted phrase marker K. Thus, GT and Move α extend K to K*, which includes K as a proper part.[26] For example, we can target K = V', add $\emptyset$ to form [$_\beta$ $\emptyset$ V'], and then either raise α from within V' to replace $\emptyset$ or insert another phrase marker K^1 for $\emptyset$. In either case the result must satisfy X-bar theory, which means that the element replacing $\emptyset$ must be a maximal projection YP, the specifier of the new phrase marker VP = β.

The requirement that substitution operations always extend their target has a number of consequences. First, it yields a version of the strict cycle, one that is motivated by the most elementary empirical considerations: without it, we would lose the effects of those cases of the ECP that fall under Relativized Minimality (see (9b)). Thus, suppose that in the course of a derivation we have reached the stage (19).

(19) a. [$_{I'}$ seems [$_{I'}$ is certain [John to be here]]]
 b. [$_{C'}$ C [$_{VP}$ fix the car]]
 c. [$_{C'}$ C [John wondered [$_{C'}$ C [$_{IP}$ Mary fixed what how]]]]

Violating no "Shortest Movement" Condition, we can raise *John* directly to the matrix Spec in (19a) in a single step, later inserting *it* from the lexicon to form *John seems it is certain t to be here* (superraising); we can raise *fix* to adjoin to C in (19b), later inserting *can* from the lexicon to form *fix John can t the car* (violating the HMC); and we can raise *how* to the matrix [Spec, CP] position in (19c), later raising *what* to the embedded [Spec, CP] position to form *how did John wonder what Mary fixed t_{how}* (violating the *Wh*-Island Constraint).[27]

The "extension" version of the strict cycle is therefore not only straightforward, but justified empirically without subtle empirical argument.

A second consequence of the extension condition is that given a structure of the form [$_{X'}$ X YP], we cannot insert ZP into X' (yielding, e.g., [$_{X'}$ X YP ZP]), where ZP is drawn from within YP (raising) or inserted from outside by GT. Similarly, given [$_{X'}$ X], we cannot insert ZP to form [$_{X'}$ X ZP]. There can be no raising to a complement position. We therefore derive one major consequence of the Projection Principle and θ-Criterion at D-Structure, thus lending support to the belief that these notions are indeed superfluous. More generally, as noted by Akira Watanabe, the binarity of GT comes close to entailing that X-bar structures are restricted to binary branching (Kayne's "unambiguous paths"), though a bit more work is required.

The operations just discussed are substitution transformations, but we must consider adjunction as well. We thus continue to allow the X-bar structure (5) as well as (1), specifically (20).[28]

(20) a. $[_X \ Y \ X]$
     b. $[_{XP} \ YP \ XP]$

In (20a) a zero-level category Y is adjoined to the zero-level category X, and in (20b) a maximal projection YP is adjoined to the maximal projection XP. GT and Move α must form structures satisfying X-bar theory, now including (20). Note that the very strong empirical motivation for the strict cycle just given does not apply in these cases. Let us assume, then, that adjunction need not extend its target. For concreteness, let us assume that the extension requirement holds only for substitution in overt syntax, the only case required by the trivial argument for the cycle.[29]

3.4 Beyond the Interface Levels: S-Structure

Suppose that D-Structure is eliminable along these lines. What about S-Structure, another level that has only theory-internal motivation? The basic issue is whether there are S-Structure conditions. If not, we can dispense with the concept of S-Structure, allowing Spell-Out to apply freely in the manner indicated earlier. Plainly this would be the optimal conclusion.

There are two kinds of evidence for S-Structure conditions.

(21) a. Languages differ with respect to where Spell-Out applies in the course of the derivation to LF. (Are *wh*-phrases moved or in situ? Is the language French-style with overt V-raising or English-style with LF V-raising?)
     b. In just about every module of grammar, there is extensive evidence that the conditions apply at S-Structure.

To show that S-Structure is nevertheless superfluous, we must show that the evidence of both kinds, though substantial, is not compelling.

In the case of evidence of type (21a), we must show that the position of Spell-Out in the derivation is determined by either PF or LF properties, these being the only levels, on minimalist assumptions. Furthermore, parametric differences must be reduced to morphological properties if the Minimalist Program is framed in the terms so far assumed. There are strong reasons to suspect that LF conditions are not relevant. We expect languages to be very similar at the LF level, differing only as a reflex of properties detectable at PF; the reasons basically reduce to considerations of learnability. Thus, we expect that at the LF level there will be no relevant difference between languages with phrases overtly raised or in situ (e.g., *wh*-phrases or verbs). Hence, we are led to seek morphological properties that are reflected at PF. Let us keep the conclusion in mind, returning to it later.

With regard to evidence of type (21b), an argument against S-Structure conditions could be of varying strength, as shown in (22).

(22) a. The condition in question *can* apply at LF alone.
     b. Furthermore, the condition sometimes *must* apply at LF.
     c. Furthermore, the condition must *not* apply at S-Structure.

Even (22a), the weakest of the three, suffices: LF has independent motivation, but S-Structure does not. Argument (22b) is stronger on the assumption that, optimally, conditions are unitary: they apply at a single level, hence at LF if possible. Argument (22c) would be decisive.

To sample the problems that arise, consider binding theory. There are familiar arguments showing that the binding theory conditions must apply at S-Structure, not LF. Thus, consider (23).

(23) a. you said he liked [the pictures that John took]
     b. [how many pictures that John took] did you say he liked *t*
     c. who [*t* said he liked [$_\alpha$ how many pictures that John took]]

In (23a) *he* c-commands *John* and cannot take *John* as antecedent; in (23b) there is no c-command relation and *John* can be the antecedent of *he*. In (23c) *John* again cannot be the antecedent of *he*. Since the binding properties of (23c) are those of (23a), not (23b), we conclude that *he* c-commands *John* at the level of representation at which Condition C applies. But if LF movement adjoins α to *who* in (23c), Condition C must apply at S-Structure.

The argument is not conclusive, however. Following the line of argument in section 1.3.3 (see (105)), we might reject the last assumption: that LF movement adjoins α of (23c) to *who*, forming (24), t' the trace of the LF-moved phrase.

(24) [[how many pictures that John took] who] [t said he liked t']

We might assume that the only permissible option is extraction of *how many* from the full NP α, yielding an LF form along the lines of (25), t' the trace of *how many*.[30]

(25) [[how many] who] [t said he liked [[t' pictures] that John took]]

The answer, then, could be the pair (*Bill, 7*), meaning that Bill said he liked 7 pictures that John took. But in (25) *he* c-commands *John*, so that Condition C applies as in (23a). We are therefore not compelled to assume that Condition C applies at S-Structure; we can keep to the preferable option that conditions involving interpretation apply only at the interface levels. This is an argument of the type (22a), weak but sufficient. We will return to the possibility of stronger arguments of the types (22b) and (22c).

The overt analogue of (25) requires "pied-piping" of the entire NP [*how many pictures that John took*], but it is not clear that the same is true in the LF component. We might, in fact, proceed further. The LF rule that associates the in-situ *wh*-phrase with the *wh*-phrase in [Spec, CP] need not be construed as an instance of Move α. We might think of it as the syntactic basis for absorption in the sense of Higginbotham and May (1981), an operation that associates two *wh*-phrases to form a generalized quantifier.[31] If so, then the LF rule need satisfy none of the conditions on movement.

There has long been evidence that conditions on movement do not hold for multiple questions. Nevertheless, the approach just proposed appeared to be blocked by the properties of Chinese- and Japanese-type languages, with *wh*- in situ throughout but observing at least some of the conditions on movement (Huang 1982). Watanabe (1991) has argued, however, that even in these languages there is overt *wh*-movement—in this case movement of an empty operator, yielding the effects of the movement constraints. If Watanabe is correct, we could assume that a *wh*-operator always raises overtly, that Move α is subject to the same conditions everywhere in the derivation to PF and LF, and that the LF operation that applies in multiple questions in English and direct questions in Japanese is free of these conditions. What remains is the question why overt movement of the operator is always required, a question of the category (21a). We will return to that.

Let us recall again the minimalist assumptions that I am conjecturing can be upheld: all conditions are interface conditions; and a linguistic expression is the optimal realization of such interface conditions. Let us consider these notions more closely.

Consider a representation π at PF. PF is a representation in universal phonetics, with no indication of syntactic elements or relations among them (X-bar structure, binding, government, etc.). To be interpreted by the performance systems A-P, π must be constituted entirely of *legitimate PF objects*, that is, elements that have a uniform, language-independent interpretation at the interface. In that case we will say that π satisfies the condition of *Full Interpretation* (FI). If π fails FI, it does not provide appropriate instructions to the performance systems. We take FI to be the convergence condition: if π satisfies FI, the derivation D that formed it converges at PF; otherwise, it crashes at PF. For example, if π contains a stressed consonant or a [+ high, + low] vowel, then D crashes; similarly, if π contains some morphological element that "survives" to PF, lacking any interpretation at the interface. If D converges at PF, its output π receives an articulatory-perceptual interpretation, perhaps as gibberish.

All of this is straightforward—indeed, hardly more than an expression of what is tacitly assumed. We expect exactly the same to be true at LF.

To make ideas concrete, we must spell out explicitly what are the legitimate objects at PF and LF. At PF, this is the standard problem of universal phonetics. At LF, we assume each legitimate object to be a chain $CH = (\alpha_1, \ldots, \alpha_n)$: at least (perhaps at most) with CH a head, an argument, a modifier, or an operator-variable construction. We now say that the representation λ satisfies FI at LF if it consists entirely of legitimate objects; a derivation forming λ converges at LF if λ satisfies FI, and otherwise crashes. A convergent derivation may produce utter gibberish, exactly as at PF. Linguistic expressions may be "deviant" along all sorts of incommensurable dimensions, and we have no notion of "well-formed sentence" (see note 7). Expressions have the interpretations assigned to them by the performance systems in which the language is embedded: period.

To develop these ideas properly, we must proceed to characterize notions with the basic properties of A- and Ā-position. These notions were well defined in the *LGB* framework, but in terms of assumptions that are no longer held, in particular, the assumption that θ-marking is restricted to sisterhood, with multiple-branching constructions. With these assumptions abandoned, the notions are used only in an intuitive sense. To replace them, let us consider more closely the morphological properties of lexical items, which play a major role in the minimalist program we are sketching. (See section 1.3.2.)

Consider the verbal system of (2). The main verb typically "picks up" the features of T and Agr (in fact, both Agr_S and Agr_O in the general case), adjoining to an inflectional element I to form [V I]. There are two ways to interpret the process, for a lexical element α. One is to take α to be a bare, uninflected form; PF rules are then designed to interpret the abstract complex [α I] as a single inflected phonological word. The other approach is to take α to have inflectional features in the lexicon as an intrinsic property (in the spirit of lexicalist phonology); these features are then checked against the inflectional element I in the complex [α I].[32] If the features of α and I match, I disappears and α enters the PF component under Spell-Out; if they conflict, I remains and the derivation crashes at PF. The PF rules, then, are simple rewriting rules of the usual type, not more elaborate rules applying to complexes [α I].

I have been tacitly assuming the second option. Let us now make that choice explicit. Note that we need no longer adopt the Emonds-Pollock assumption that in English-type languages I lowers to V. V will have the inflectional features before Spell-Out in any event, and the checking procedure may take place anywhere, in particular, after LF movement. French-type and English-type languages now look alike at LF, whereas lowering of I in the latter would have produced adjunction structures quite unlike those of the raising languages.

There are various ways to make a checking theory precise, and to capture generalizations that hold across morphology and syntax. Suppose, for example, that Baker's Mirror Principle is strictly accurate. Then we may take a lexical element—say, the verb V—to be a sequence V = (α, $Infl_1$, ..., $Infl_n$), where α is the morphological complex [R-$Infl_1$-...-$Infl_n$], R a root and $Infl_i$ an inflectional feature.[33] The PF rules only "see" α. When V is adjoined to a functional category F (say, Agr_O), the feature $Infl_1$ is removed from V if it matches F; and so on. If any $Infl_i$ remains at LF, the derivation crashes at LF. The PF form α always satisfies the Mirror Principle in a derivation that converges at LF. Other technologies can readily be devised. In this case, however, it is not clear that such mechanisms are in order; the most persuasive evidence for the Mirror Principle lies outside the domain of inflectional morphology, which may be subject to different principles. Suppose, say, that richer morphology tends to be more "visible," that is, closer to the word boundary; if so, and if the speculations of the paragraph ending with note 13 are on the right track, we would expect nominative or absolutive agreement (depending on language type) to be more peripheral in the verbal morphology.

The functional elements T and Agr therefore incorporate features of the verb. Let us call these features *V-features*: the function of the V-features of an inflectional element I is to check the morphological properties of the verb selected from the lexicon. More generally, let us call such features of a lexical item L *L-features*. Keeping to the X-bar-theoretic notions, we say that a position is *L-related* if it is in a local relation to an L-feature, that is, in the internal domain or checking domain of a head with an L-feature. Furthermore, the checking domain can be subdivided into two categories: nonadjoined (Spec) and adjoined. Let us call these positions *narrowly* and *broadly* L-related, respectively. A structural position that is narrowly L-related has the basic properties of A-positions; one that is not L-related has the basic properties of $\overline{\text{A}}$-positions, in particular, [Spec, C], not L-related if C does not contain a V-feature. The status of broadly L-related (adjoined) positions has been debated, particularly in the theory of scrambling.[34] For our limited purposes, we may leave the matter open.

Note that we crucially assume, as is plausible, that V-raising to C is actually I-raising, with V incorporated within I, and is motivated by properties of the (C, I) system, not morphological checking of V. C has other properties that distinguish it from the V-features, as discussed in section 1.4.1.

The same considerations extend to nouns (assuming the D head of DP to have N-features) and adjectives. Putting this aside, we can continue to speak informally of A- and $\overline{\text{A}}$-positions, understood in terms of L-relatedness as a first approximation only, with further refinement still necessary. We can proceed, then, to define the legitimate LF objects $\text{CH} = (\alpha_1, \dots, \alpha_n)$ in something like the familiar way: heads, with α_i an X^0; arguments, with α_i in an A-position; adjuncts, with α_i in an $\overline{\text{A}}$-position; and operator-variable constructions, to which we will briefly return.[35] This approach seems relatively unproblematic. Let us assume so, and proceed.

The morphological features of T and Agr have two functions: they check properties of the verb that raises to them, and they check properties of the NP (DP) that raises to their Spec; thus, they ensure that DP and V are properly paired. Generalizing the checking theory, let us assume that, like verbs, nouns are drawn from the lexicon with all of their morphological features, including Case and φ-features, and that these too must be checked in the appropriate position:[36] in this case, [Spec, Agr] (which may include T or V). This checking too can take place at any stage of a derivation to LF.

A standard argument for S-Structure conditions in the Case module is that Case features appear at PF but must be "visible" at LF; hence, Case must be present by the time the derivation reaches S-Structure. But that argument collapses under a checking theory. We may proceed, then, with the assumption that the Case Filter is an interface condition—in fact, the condition that all morphological features must be checked somewhere, for convergence. There are many interesting and subtle problems to be addressed; reluctantly, I will put them aside here, merely asserting without argument that a proper understanding of economy of derivation goes a long way (maybe all the way) toward resolving them.[37]

Next consider subject-verb agreement, as in *John hits Bill*. The φ-features appear in three positions in the course of the derivation: internal to *John*, internal to *hits*, and in Agr_S. The verb *hits* raises ultimately to Agr_S and the NP *John* to [Spec, Agr_S], each checking its morphological features. If the lexical items were properly chosen, the derivation converges. But at PF and LF the φ-features appear only twice, not three times: in the NP and verb that agree. Agr plays only a mediating role: when it has performed its function, it disappears. Since this function is dual, V-related and NP-related, Agr must in fact have two kinds of features: V-features that check V adjoined to Agr, and NP-features that check NP in [Spec, Agr]. The same is true of T, which checks the tense of the verb and the Case of the subject. The V-features of an inflectional element disappear when they check V, the NP-features when they check NP (or N, or DP; see note 36). All this is automatic, and within the Minimalist Program.

Let us now return to the first type of S-Structure condition (21a), the position of Spell-Out: after V-raising in French-type languages, before V-raising in English-type languages (we have now dispensed with lowering). As we have seen, the Minimalist Program permits only one solution to the problem: PF conditions reflecting morphological properties must force V-raising in French but not in English. What can these conditions be?

Recall the underlying intuition of Pollock's approach, which we are basically assuming: French-type languages have "strong" Agr, which forces overt raising, and English-type languages have "weak" Agr, which blocks it. Let us adopt that idea, rephrasing it in our terms: the V-features of Agr are strong in French, weak in English. Recall that when the V-features have done their work, checking adjoined V, they disappear. If V does not raise to Agr overtly, the V-features survive to PF. Let us now make the natural assumption that "strong" features are visible at PF and "weak" features invisible at PF. These features are not legitimate objects at PF; they are not proper components of phonetic matrices. Therefore, if a strong feature remains after Spell-Out, the derivation crashes.[38] In French overt raising is a prerequisite for convergence; in English it is not.

Two major questions remain: Why is overt raising barred in English? Why do the English auxiliaries *have* and *be* raise overtly, as do verbs in French?

The first question is answered by a natural economy condition: LF movement is "cheaper" than overt movement (call the principle *Procrastinate*). (See section 1.3.3.) The intuitive idea is that LF operations are a kind of "wired-in" reflex, operating mechanically beyond any directly observable effects. They are less costly than overt operations. The system tries to reach PF "as fast as possible," minimizing overt syntax. In English-type languages, overt raising is not forced for convergence; therefore, it is barred by economy principles.

To deal with the second question, consider again the intuition that underlies Pollock's account: raising of the auxiliaries reflects their semantic vacuity; they are placeholders for certain constructions, at most "very light" verbs. Adopting the intuition (but not the accompanying technology), let us assume that such elements, lacking semantically relevant features, are not visible to LF rules. If they have not raised overtly, they will not be able to raise by LF rules and the derivation will crash.[39]

Now consider the difference between SVO (or SOV) languages like English (Japanese) and VSO languages like Irish. On our assumptions, V has raised overtly to I (Agr_S) in Irish, while S and O raise in the LF component to [Spec, Agr_S] and [Spec, Agr_O], respectively.[40] We have only one way to express these differences: in terms of the strength of the inflectional features. One possibility is that the NP-feature of T is strong in English and weak in Irish. Hence, NP must raise to [Spec, [Agr T]] in English prior to Spell-Out or the derivation will not converge. The principle Procrastinate bars such raising in Irish. The Extended Projection Principle, which requires that [Spec, IP] be realized (perhaps by an empty category), reduces to a morphological property of T: strong or weak NP-features. Note that the NP-feature of Agr is weak in English; if it were strong, English would exhibit overt object shift. We are still keeping to the minimal assumption that Agr_S and Agr_O are collections of features, with no relevant subject-object distinction, hence no difference in strength of features. Note also that a language might allow both weak and strong inflection, hence weak and strong NP-features: Arabic is a suggestive case, with SVO versus VSO correlating with the richness of visible verb inflection.

Along these lines, we can eliminate S-Structure conditions on raising and lowering in favor of morphological properties of lexical items, in accord with the Minimalist Program. Note that a certain typology of languages is predicted; whether correctly or not remains to be determined.

If Watanabe's (1991) theory of *wh*-movement is correct, there is no parametric variation with regard to *wh*- in situ: language differences (say, English-Japanese) reduce to morphology, in this case, the internal morphology of the *wh*-phrases. Still, the question arises why raising of the *wh*-operator is ever overt, contrary to Procrastinate. The basic economy-of-derivation assumption is that operations are driven by necessity: they are "last resort," applied if they must be, not otherwise (Chomsky 1986b, and chapter 2). Our assumption is that operations are driven by morphological necessity: certain features must be checked in the checking domain of a head, or the derivation will crash. Therefore, raising of an operator to [Spec, CP] must be driven by such a requirement. The natural assumption is that C may have an operator feature (which we can take to be the Q- or *wh*-feature standardly assumed in C in such cases), and that this feature is a morphological property of such operators as *wh*-. For appropriate C, the operators raise for feature checking to the checking domain of C: [Spec, CP], or adjunction to Spec (absorption), thereby satisfying their scopal properties.[41] Topicalization and focus could be treated the same way. If the operator feature of C is strong, the movement must be overt. Raising of I to C may automatically make the relevant feature of C strong (the V-second phenomenon). If Watanabe is correct, the *wh*-operator feature is universally strong.

3.5 Extensions of the Minimalist Program

Let us now look more closely at the economy principles. These apply to both representations and derivations. With regard to the former, we may take the economy principle to be nothing other than FI: every symbol must receive an "external" interpretation by language-independent rules. There is no need for the Projection Principle or θ-Criterion at LF. A convergent derivation might violate them, but in that case it would receive a defective interpretation.

The question of economy of derivations is more subtle. We have already noted two cases: Procrastinate, which is straightforward, and the Last Resort principle, which is more intricate. According to that principle, a step in a derivation is legitimate only if it is necessary for convergence—had the step not been taken, the derivation would not have converged. NP-raising, for example, is driven by the Case Filter (now assumed to apply only at LF): if the Case feature of NP has already been checked, NP may not raise. For example, (26a) is fully interpretable, but (26b) is not.

(26) a. there is [$_\alpha$ a strange man] in the garden
      b. there seems to [$_\alpha$ a strange man] [that it is raining outside]

In (26a) α is not in a proper position for Case checking; therefore, it must raise at LF, adjoining to the LF affix *there* and leaving the trace *t*. The phrase α is now in the checking domain of the matrix inflection. The matrix subject at LF is [α-*there*], an LF word with all features checked but interpretable only in the position of the trace *t* of the chain (α, *t*), its head being "invisible" word-internally. In contrast, in (26b) α has its Case properties satisfied internal to the PP, so it is not permitted to raise, and we are left with freestanding *there*. This is a legitimate object, a one-membered A-chain with all its morphological properties checked. Hence, the derivation converges. But there is no coherent interpretation, because freestanding *there* receives no semantic interpretation (and in fact is unable to receive a θ-role even in a θ-position). The derivation thus converges, as semigibberish.

The notion of Last Resort operation is in part formulable in terms of economy: a shorter derivation is preferred to a longer one, and if the derivation D converges without application of some operation, then that application is disallowed. In (26b) adjunction of α to *there* would yield an intelligible interpretation (something like 'there is a strange man to

whom it seems that it is raining outside'). But adjunction is not permitted: the derivation converges with an unintelligible interpretation.
Derivations are driven by the narrow mechanical requirement of feature
checking only, not by a "search for intelligibility" or the like.

Note that raising of α in (26b) is blocked by the fact that *its own requirements* are satisfied without raising, even though such raising would
arguably overcome inadequacies of the LF affix *there*. More generally,
Move α applies to an element α only if morphological properties of α
itself are not otherwise satisfied. The operation cannot apply to α to enable some different element β to satisfy *its* properties. Last Resort, then,
is always "self-serving": benefiting other elements is not allowed. Alongside Procrastinate, then, we have a principle of *Greed*: self-serving Last
Resort.

Consider the expression (27), analogous to (26b) but without *there*-
insertion from the lexicon.

(27) seems to [$_\alpha$ a strange man] [that it is raining outside]

Here the matrix T has an NP-feature (Case feature) to discharge, but α
cannot raise (overtly or covertly) to overcome that defect. The derivation
cannot converge, unlike (26b), which converges but without a proper
interpretation. The self-serving property of Last Resort cannot be overridden even to ensure convergence.

Considerations of economy of derivation tend to have a "global"
character, inducing high-order computational complexity. Computational complexity may or may not be an empirical defect; it is a question
of whether the cases are correctly characterized (e.g., with complexity
properly relating to parsing difficulty, often considerable or extreme, as
is well known). Nevertheless, it makes sense to expect language design to
limit such problems. The self-serving property of Last Resort has the
effect of restricting the class of derivations that have to be considered in
determining optimality, and might be shown on closer analysis to contribute to this end.[42]

Formulating economy conditions in terms of the principles of Procrastinate and Greed, we derive a fairly narrow and determinate notion of
most economical convergent derivation that blocks all others. Precise formulation of these ideas is a rather delicate matter, with a broad range of
empirical consequences.

We have also assumed a notion of "shortest link," expressible in terms
of the operation Form Chain. We thus assume that, given two convergent

derivations D_1 and D_2, both minimal and containing the same number of steps, D_1 blocks D_2 if its links are shorter. Pursuing this intuitive idea, which must be considerably sharpened, we can incorporate aspects of Subjacency and the ECP, as briefly indicated.

Recall that for a derivation to converge, its LF output must be constituted of legitimate objects: tentatively, heads, arguments, modifiers, and operator-variable constructions. A problem arises in the case of piedpiped constructions such as (28).

(28) (guess) [[$_{wh}$ in which house] John lived t]

The chain (wh, t) is not an operator-variable construction. The appropriate LF form for interpretation requires "reconstruction," as in (29) (see section 1.3.3).

(29) a. [which x, x a house] John lived [in x]
      b. [which x] John lived [in [x house]]

Assume that (29a) and (29b) are alternative options. There are various ways in which these options can be interpreted. For concreteness, let us select a particularly simple one.[43]

Suppose that in (29a) x is understood as a DP variable: regarded substitutionally, it can be replaced by a DP (the answer can be *the old one*); regarded objectually, it ranges over houses, as determined by the restricted operator. In (29b) x is a D variable: regarded substitutionally, it can be replaced by a D (the answer can be *that* (*house*)); regarded objectually, it ranges over entities.

Reconstruction is a curious operation, particularly when it is held to follow LF movement, thus restoring what has been covertly moved, as often proposed (e.g., for (23c)). If possible, the process should be eliminated. An approach that has occasionally been suggested is the "copy theory" of movement: the trace left behind is a copy of the moved element, deleted by a principle of the PF component in the case of overt movement. But at LF the copy remains, providing the materials for "reconstruction." Let us consider this possibility, surely to be preferred if it is tenable.

The PF deletion operation is, very likely, a subcase of a broader principle that applies in ellipsis and other constructions (see section 1.5). Consider such expressions as (30a–b).

(30) a. John said that he was looking for a cat, and so did Bill
   b. John said that he was looking for a cat, and so did Bill [$_E$ say that he was looking for a cat]

The first conjunct is several-ways ambiguous. Suppose we resolve the ambiguities in one of the possible ways, say, by taking the pronoun to refer to Tom and interpreting *a cat* nonspecifically, so that John said that Tom's quest would be satisfied by any cat. In the elliptical case (30a), a parallelism requirement of some kind (call it *PR*) requires that the second conjunct must be interpreted the same way—in this case, with *he* referring to Tom and *a cat* understood nonspecifically (Lakoff 1970, Lasnik 1972, Sag 1976, Ristad 1993). The same is true in the full sentence (30b), a nondeviant linguistic expression with a distinctive low-falling intonation for E; it too must be assigned its properties by the theory of grammar. PR surely applies at LF. Since it must apply to (30b), the simplest assumption would be that only (30b) reaches LF, (30a) being derived from (30b) by an operation of the PF component deleting copies. There would be no need, then, for special mechanisms to account for the parallelism properties of (30a). Interesting questions arise when this path is followed, but it seems promising. If so, the trace deletion operation may well be an obligatory variant of a more general operation applying in the PF component.

Assuming this approach, (28) is a notational abbreviation for (31).

(31) [$_{wh}$ in which house] John lived [$_{wh}$ in which house]

The LF component converts the phrase *wh* to either (32a) or (32b) by an operation akin to QR.

(32) a. [which house] [$_{wh}$ in t]
   b. [which] [$_{wh}$ in [t house]]

We may give these the intuitive interpretations of (33a–b).

(33) a. [which x, x a house] [in x]
   b. [which x] [in [x house]]

For convergence at LF, we must have an operator-variable structure. Accordingly, in the operator position [Spec, CP], everything but the operator phrase must delete; therefore, the phrase *wh* of (32) deletes. In the trace position, the copy of what remains in the operator position deletes, leaving just the phrase *wh* (an LF analogue to the PF rule just described).

In the present case (perhaps generally), these choices need not be specified; other options will crash. We thus derive LF forms interpreted as (29a) or (29b), depending on which option we have selected. The LF forms now consist of legitimate objects, and the derivations converge.

Along the same lines, we will interpret *which book did John read* either as '[which *x*, *x* a book] [John read *x*]' (answer: *War and Peace*) or as '[which *x*] [John read [*x* book]]' (answer: *that* (*book*)).

The assumptions are straightforward and minimalist in spirit. They carry us only partway toward an analysis of reconstruction and interpretation; there are complex and obscure phenomena, many scarcely understood. Insofar as these assumptions are tenable and properly generalizable, we can eliminate reconstruction as a separate process, keeping the term only as part of informal descriptive apparatus for a certain range of phenomena.

Extending observations of Van Riemsdijk and Williams (1981), Freidin (1986) points out that such constructions as (34a–b) behave quite differently under reconstruction.[44]

(34) a. which claim [that John was asleep] was he willing to discuss

b. which claim [that John made] was he willing to discuss

In (34a) reconstruction takes place: the pronoun does not take *John* as antecedent. In contrast, in (34b) reconstruction is not obligatory and the anaphoric connection is an option. While there are many complications, to a first approximation the contrast seems to reduce to a difference between complement and adjunct, the bracketed clause of (34a) and (34b), respectively. Lebeaux (1988) proposed an analysis of this distinction in terms of generalized transformations. In case (34a) the complement must appear at the level of D-Structure; in case (34b) the adjunct could be adjoined by a generalized transformation in the course of derivation, in fact, after whatever processes are responsible for the reconstruction effect.[45]

The approach is appealing, if problematic. For one thing, there is the question of the propriety of resorting to generalized transformations. For another, the same reasoning forces reconstruction in the case of A-movement. Thus, (35) is analogous to (34a); the complement is present before raising and should therefore force a Condition C violation.

(35) the claim that John was asleep seems to him [$_{IP}$ *t* to be correct]

Under the present interpretation, the trace *t* is spelled out as identical to the matrix subject. While it deletes at PF, it remains at LF, yielding the unwanted reconstruction effect. Condition C of the binding theory requires that the pronoun *him* cannot take its antecedent within the embedded IP (compare *I seem to him [to like John], with *him* anaphoric to *John*). But *him* can take *John* as antecedent in (35), contrary to the prediction.

The proposal now under investigation overcomes these objections. We have moved to a full-blown theory of generalized transformations, so there is no problem here. The extension property for substitution entails that complements can only be introduced cyclically, hence before *wh*-extraction, while adjuncts can be introduced noncyclically, hence adjoined to the *wh*-phrase after raising to [Spec, CP]. Lebeaux's analysis of (34) therefore could be carried over. As for (35), if "reconstruction" is essentially a reflex of the formation of operator-variable constructions, it will hold only for A̅-chains, not for A-chains. That conclusion seems plausible over a considerable range, and yields the right results in this case.

Let us return now to the problem of binding-theoretic conditions at S-Structure. We found a weak but sufficient argument (of type (22a)) to reject the conclusion that Condition C applies at S-Structure. What about Condition A?

Consider constructions such as those in (36).[46]

(36) a. i. John wondered [which picture of himself] [Bill saw *t*]
        ii. the students asked [what attitudes about each other] [the teachers had noticed *t*]
     b. i. John wondered [who [*t* saw [which picture of himself]]]
        ii. the students asked [who [*t* had noticed [what attitudes about each other]]]

The sentences of (36a) are ambiguous, with the anaphor taking either the matrix or embedded subject as antecedent; but those of (36b) are unambiguous, with the trace of *who* as the only antecedent for *himself, each other*. If (36b) were formed by LF raising of the in-situ *wh*-phrase, we would have to conclude that Condition A applies at S-Structure, prior to this operation. But we have already seen that the assumption is unwarranted; we have, again, a weak but sufficient argument against allowing binding theory to apply at S-Structure. A closer look shows that we can do still better.

Under the copying theory, the actual forms of (36a) are (37a–b).

(37) a. John wondered [$_{wh}$ which picture of himself] [Bill saw [$_{wh}$ which picture of himself]]

   b. the students asked [$_{wh}$ what attitudes about each other] [the teachers had noticed [$_{wh}$ what attitudes about each other]]

The LF principles map (37a) to either (38a) or (38b), depending on which option is selected for analysis of the phrase *wh*.

(38) a. John wondered [[which picture of himself] [$_{wh}$ *t*]] [Bill saw [[which picture of himself] [$_{wh}$ *t*]]]

   b. John wondered [which [$_{wh}$ *t* picture of himself]] [Bill saw [which [$_{wh}$ *t* picture of himself]]]

We then interpret (38a) as (39a) and (38b) as (39b), as before.

(39) a. John wondered [which *x*, *x* a picture of himself] [Bill saw *x*]

   b. John wondered [which *x*] [Bill saw [*x* picture of himself]]

Depending on which option we have selected, *himself* will be anaphoric to *John* or to *Bill*.[47]

The same analysis applies to (37b), yielding the two options of (40) corresponding to (39).

(40) a. the students asked [what *x*, *x* attitudes about each other] [the teachers had noticed *x*]

   b. the students asked [what *x*] [the teachers had noticed [*x* attitudes about each other]]

In (40a) the antecedent of *each other* is *the students*; in (40b) it is *the teachers*.

Suppose that we change the examples of (36a) to (41a–b), replacing *saw* by *took* and *had noticed* by *had*.

(41) a. John wondered [which picture of himself] [Bill took *t*]

   b. the students asked [what attitudes about each other] [the teachers had]

Consider (41a). As before, *himself* can take either *John* or *Bill* as antecedent. There is a further ambiguity: the phrase *take...picture* can be interpreted either idiomatically (in the sense of 'photograph') or literally ('pick up and walk away with'). But the interpretive options appear to correlate with the choice of antecedent for *himself*: if the antecedent is

John, the idiomatic interpretation is barred; if the antecedent is *Bill*, it is permitted. If *Bill* is replaced by *Mary*, the idiomatic interpretation is excluded.

The pattern is similar for (41b), except that there is no literal-idiomatic ambiguity. The only interpretation is that the students asked what attitudes each of the teachers had about the other teacher(s). If *the teachers* is replaced by *Jones*, there is no interpretation.

Why should the interpretations distribute in this manner?

First consider (41a). The principles already discussed yield the two LF options in (42a–b).

(42) a. John wondered [which x, x a picture of himself] [Bill took x]
    b. John wondered [which x] [Bill took [x picture of himself]]

If we select the option (42a), then *himself* takes *John* as antecedent by Condition A at LF; if we select the option (42b), then *himself* takes *Bill* as antecedent by the same principle. If we replace *Bill* with *Mary*, then (42a) is forced. Having abandoned D-Structure, we must assume that idiom interpretation takes place at LF, as is natural in any event. But we have no operations of LF reconstruction. Thus, *take ... picture* can be interpreted as 'photograph' only if the phrase is present as a unit at LF —that is, in (42b), not (42a). It follows that in (42a) we have only the nonidiomatic interpretation of *take*; in (42b) we have either. In short, only the option (42b) permits the idiomatic interpretation, also blocking *John* as antecedent of the reflexive and barring replacement of *Bill* by *Mary*.

The same analysis holds for (41b). The two LF options are (43a–b).

(43) a. the students asked [what x, x attitudes about each other]
      [the teachers had x]
    b. the students asked [what x] [the teachers had [x attitudes about each other]]

Only (43b) yields an interpretation, with *have ... attitudes* given its unitary sense.

The conclusions follow on the crucial assumption that Condition A *not* apply at S-Structure, prior to the LF rules that form (42).[48] If Condition A were to apply at S-Structure, *John* could be taken as antecedent of *himself* in (41a) and the later LF processes would be free to choose either the idiomatic or the literal interpretation, however the reconstruction phenomena are handled; and *the students* could be taken as antecedent of *each other* in (41b), with reconstruction providing the interpretation of *have ... attitudes*. Thus, we have the strongest kind of argument against an S-Structure condition (type (22c)): Condition A *cannot* apply at S-Structure.

Note also that we derive a strong argument for LF representation. The facts are straightforwardly explained in terms of a level of representation with two properties: (1) phrases with a unitary interpretation such as the idiom *take ... picture* or *have ... attitudes* appear as units; (2) binding theory applies. In standard EST approaches, LF is the only candidate. The argument is still clearer in this minimalist theory, lacking D-Structure and (we are now arguing) S-Structure.

Combining these observations with the Freidin-Lebeaux examples, we seem to face a problem, in fact a near-contradiction. In (44a) either option is allowed: *himself* may take either *John* or *Bill* as antecedent. In contrast, in (44b) reconstruction appears to be forced, barring *Tom* as antecedent of *he* (by Condition C) and *Bill* as antecedent of *him* (by Condition B).

(44) a.   John wondered [which picture of himself] [Bill saw *t*]
      b. i.   John wondered [which picture of Tom] [he liked *t*]
         ii. John wondered [which picture of him] [Bill took *t*]
         iii. John wondered [what attitude about him] [Bill had *t*]

The Freidin-Lebeaux theory requires reconstruction in all these cases, the *of*-phrase being a complement of *picture*. But the facts seem to point to a conception that distinguishes Condition A of the binding theory, which does not force reconstruction, from Conditions B and C, which do. Why should this be?

In our terms, the trace *t* in (44) is a copy of the *wh*-phrase at the point where the derivation branches to the PF and LF components. Suppose we now adopt an LF movement approach to anaphora (see section 1.4.2), assuming that the anaphor or part of it raises by an operation similar to cliticization—call it *cliticization*$_{LF}$. This approach at least has the property we want: it distinguishes Condition A from Conditions B and C. Note that cliticization$_{LF}$ is a case of Move α; though applying in the LF component, it necessarily precedes the "reconstruction" operations that provide the interpretations for the LF output. Applying cliticization$_{LF}$ to (44a), we derive either (45a) or (45b), depending on whether the rule applies to the operator phrase or its trace TR.[49]

(45) a. John self-wondered [which picture of t_{self}] [NP saw [$_{TR}$ which
        picture of himself]]
     b. John wondered [which picture of himself] [NP self-saw [$_{TR}$ which
        picture of t_{self}]]

We then turn to the LF rules interpreting the *wh*-phrase, which yield the
two options (46a–b) (α = either t_{self} or *himself*).

(46) a. [[which picture of α] t]
     b. [which] [t picture of α]

Suppose that we have selected the option (45a). Then we cannot select
the interpretive option (46b) (with $\alpha = t_{self}$); that option requires deletion of [t *picture of* t_{self}] in the operator position, which would break the
chain (*self*, t_{self}), leaving the reflexive element without a θ-role at LF. We
must therefore select the interpretive option (46a), yielding a convergent
derivation without reconstruction:

(47) John self-wondered [which x, x a picture of t_{self}] NP saw x

In short, if we take the antecedent of the reflexive to be *John*, then only
the nonreconstructing option converges.

   If we had *Tom* or *him* in place of *himself*, as in (44b), then these issues
would not arise and either interpretive option would converge. We thus
have a relevant difference between the two categories of (44). To account
for the judgments, it is only necessary to add a preference principle for
reconstruction: Do it when you can (i.e., try to minimize the restriction
in the operator position). In (44b) the preference principle yields reconstruction, hence a binding theory violation (Conditions C and B). In
(44a) we begin with two options with respect to application of cliticiza-
tion$_{LF}$: either to the operator or to the trace position. If we choose
the first option, selecting the matrix subject as antecedent, then the
preference principle is inapplicable because only the nonpreferred case
converges, and we derive the nonreconstruction option. If we choose
the second option, selecting the embedded subject as antecedent, the
issue of preference again does not arise. Hence, we have genuine options
in the case of (44a), but a preference for reconstruction (hence the
judgment that binding theory conditions are violated) in the case of
(44b).[50]

   Other constructions reinforce these conclusions, for example,
(48).[51]

(48) a. i.   John wondered what stories about us we had heard
      ii'.   *John wondered what stories about us we had told
      ii''. John wondered what stories about us we expected Mary
             to tell
     b. i'.   John wondered what opinions about himself Mary had
               heard
      i''.   *John wondered what opinions about himself Mary had
      ii'.   they wondered what opinions about each other Mary had
             heard
      ii''. *they wondered what opinions about each other Mary had
     c. i.   John wondered how many pictures of us we expected Mary
              to take
      ii.   *John wondered how many pictures of us we expected to
             take   (idiomatic sense)

Note that we have further strengthened the argument for an LF level
at which all conditions apply: the LF rules, including now anaphor raising, provide a crucial distinction with consequences for reconstruction.

The reconstruction process outlined applies only to operator-variable
constructions. What about A-chains, which we may assume to be of the
form $CH = (\alpha, t)$ at LF (α the phrase raised from its original position t,
intermediate traces deleted or ignored)? Here t is a full copy of its antecedent, deleted in the PF component. The descriptive account must capture the fact that the head of the A-chain is assigned an interpretation in
the position t. Thus, in *John was killed t*, *John* is assigned its θ-role in
the position t, as complement of *kill*. The same should be true for such
idioms as (49).

(49) several pictures were taken t

Here *pictures* is interpreted in the position of t, optionally as part of the
idiom *take ... pictures*. Interesting questions arise in the case of such
constructions as (50a–b).

(50) a. the students asked [which pictures of each other] [Mary took t]
     b. the students asked [which pictures of each other] [t' were taken t
         by Mary]

In both cases the idiomatic interpretation requires that t be [x *pictures
of each other*] after the operator-variable analysis ("reconstruction"). In
(50a) that choice is blocked, while in (50b) it remains open. The examples reinforce the suggested analysis of $\overline{A}$-reconstruction, but it is now

necessary to interpret the chain (t', t) in (50b) just as the chain (*several pictures, t*) is interpreted in (49). One possibility is that the trace t of the A-chain enters into the idiom interpretation (and, generally, into θ-marking), while the head of the chain functions in the usual way with regard to scope and other matters.

Suppose that instead of (44a) we have (51).

(51) the students wondered [$_{wh}$ how angry at each other (themselves)] [John was t]

As in the case of (44a), anaphor raising in (51) should give the interpretation roughly as 'the students each wondered [how angry at the other John was]' (similarly with reflexive). But these interpretations are impossible in the case of (51), which requires the reconstruction option, yielding gibberish. Huang (1990) observes that the result follows on the assumption that subjects are predicate-internal (VP-, AP-internal; see (4)), so that the trace of *John* remains in the subject position of the raised operator phrase *wh*-, blocking association of the anaphor with the matrix subject (anaphor raising, in the present account).

Though numerous problems remain unresolved, there seem to be good reasons to suppose that the binding theory conditions hold only at the LF interface. If so, we can move toward a very simple interpretive version of binding theory as in (52) that unites disjoint and distinct reference (D the relevant local domain), overcoming problems discussed particularly by Howard Lasnik.[52]

(52) A. If α is an anaphor, interpret it as coreferential with a c-commanding phrase in D.
    B. If α is a pronominal, interpret it as disjoint from every c-commanding phrase in D.
    C. If α is an r-expression, interpret it as disjoint from every c-commanding phrase.

Condition A may be dispensable if the approach based upon cliticization$_{LF}$ is correct and the effects of Condition A follow from the theory of movement (which is not obvious); and further discussion is necessary at many points. All indexing could then be abandoned, another welcome result.[53]

Here too we have, in effect, returned to some earlier ideas about binding theory, in this case those of Chomsky 1980a, an approach superseded largely on grounds of complexity (now overcome), but with empirical advantages over what appeared to be simpler alternatives (see note 52).

I stress again that what precedes is only the sketch of a minimalist program, identifying some of the problems and a few possible solutions, and omitting a wide range of topics, some of which have been explored, many not. The program has been pursued with some success. Several related and desirable conclusions seem within reach.

(53) a. A linguistic expression (SD) is a pair (π, λ) generated by an optimal derivation satisfying interface conditions.
   b. The interface levels are the only levels of linguistic representation.
   c. All conditions express properties of the interface levels, reflecting interpretive requirements.
   d. UG provides a unique computational system, with derivations driven by morphological properties to which syntactic variation of languages is restricted.
   e. Economy can be given a fairly narrow interpretation in terms of FI, length of derivation, length of links, Procrastinate, and Greed.

Notes

I am indebted to Samuel Epstein, James Higginbotham, Howard Lasnik, and Alec Marantz for comments on an earlier draft of this paper, as well as to participants in courses, lectures, and discussions on these topics at MIT and elsewhere, too numerous to mention.

1. For early examination of these topics in the context of generative grammar, see Chomsky 1951, 1975a (henceforth *LSLT*). On a variety of consequences, see Collins 1994a.

2. Not literal necessity, of course; I will avoid obvious qualifications here and below.

3. On its nature, see Bromberger and Halle 1989.

4. Note that while the intuition underlying proposals to restrict variation to elements of morphology is clear enough, it would be no trivial matter to make it explicit, given general problems in selecting among equivalent constructional systems. An effort to address this problem in any general way would seem premature. It is a historical oddity that linguistics, and "soft sciences" generally, are often subjected to methodological demands of a kind never taken seriously in the far more developed natural sciences. Strictures concerning Quinean indeterminacy and formalization are a case in point. See Chomsky 1990, 1992b, Ludlow 1992. Among the many questions ignored here is the fixing of lexical concepts; see Jackendoff 1990b for valuable discussion. For my own views on some general aspects of the issues, see Chomsky 1992a,b, 1994b,c, 1995.

5. Contrary to common belief, assumptions concerning the reality and nature of I-language (competence) are much better grounded than those concerning parsing. For some comment, see references of preceding note.

6. Markedness of parameters, if real, could be seen as a last residue of the evaluation metric.

7. See Marantz 1984, Baker 1988, on what Baker calls "the Principle of PF Interpretation," which appears to be inconsistent with this assumption. One might be tempted to interpret the class of expressions of the language L for which there is a convergent derivation as "the well-formed (grammatical) expressions of L." But this seems pointless. The class so defined has no significance. The concepts "well-formed" and "grammatical" remain without characterization or known empirical justification; they played virtually no role in early work on generative grammar except in informal exposition, or since. See *LSLT* and Chomsky 1965; and on various misunderstandings, Chomsky 1980b, 1986b.

8. Much additional detail has been presented in class lectures at MIT, particularly in fall 1991. I hope to return to a fuller exposition elsewhere. As a starting point, I assume here a version of linguistic theory along the lines outlined in chapter 1.

9. In Chomsky 1981a and other work, structural Case is unified under government, understood as m-command to include the Spec-head relation (a move that was not without problems); in the framework considered here, m-command plays no role.

10. I will use *NP* informally to refer to either NP or DP, where the distinction is playing no role. *IP* and *I* will be used for the complement of C and its head where details are irrelevant.

11. I overlook here the possibility of NP-raising to [Spec, T] for Case assignment, then to [Spec, Agr_S] for agreement. This may well be a real option. For development of this possibility, see Bures 1992, Bobaljik and Carnie 1992, Jonas 1992, and sections 4.9 and 4.10 of this book.

12. Raising of A to Agr_A may be overt or in the LF component. If the latter, it may be the trace of the raised NP that is marked for agreement, with further raising driven by the morphological requirement of Case marking (the Case Filter); I put aside specifics of implementation. The same considerations extend to an analysis of participial agreement along the lines of Kayne 1989; see chapter 2 and Branigan 1992.

13. For development of an approach along such lines, see Bobaljik 1992a,b. For a different analysis sharing some assumptions about the Spec-head role, see Murasugi 1991, 1992. This approach to the two language types adapts the earliest proposal about these matters within generative grammar (De Rijk 1972) to a system with inflection separated from verb. See Levin and Massam 1985 for a similar conception.

14. See chapter 1.

15. I put aside throughout the possibility of moving X′ or adjoining to it, and the question of adjunction to elements other than complement that assign or receive interpretive roles at the interface.

16. This is only the simplest case. In the general case V will raise to Agr_O, forming the chain $CH_V = (V, t)$. The complex [V, Agr_O] raises ultimately to adjoin to Agr_S. Neither V nor CH_V has a new checking domain assigned in this position. But V is in the checking domain of Agr_S and therefore shares relevant features with it, and the subject in [Spec, Agr_S] is in the checking domain of Agr_S, hence agrees indirectly with V.

17. To mention one possibility, V-raising to Agr_O yields a two-membered chain, but subsequent raising of the [V, Agr_O] complex might pass through the trace of T by successive-cyclic movement, finally adjoining to Agr_S. The issues raised in note 11 are relevant at this point. I will put these matters aside.

18. Hale and Keyser make a distinction between (1) operations of lexical conceptual structure that form such lexical items as *shelve* and (2) syntactic operations that raise *put* to V_1 in (8), attributing somewhat different properties to (1) and (2). These distinctions do not seem to me necessary for their purposes, for reasons that I will again put aside.

19. Note that the ECP will now reduce to descriptive taxonomy, of no theoretical significance. If so, there will be no meaningful questions about conjunctive or disjunctive ECP, the ECP as an LF or PF phenomenon (or both), and so on. Note that no aspect of the ECP can apply at the PF interface itself, since there we have only a phonetic matrix, with no relevant structure indicated. The proposal that the ECP breaks down into a PF and an LF property (as in Aoun et al. 1987) therefore must take the former to apply either at S-Structure or at a new level of "shallow structure" between S-Structure and PF.

20. Note that the two chains in (14) are ([V V_c], t′) and (V, t). But in the latter, V is far removed from its trace because of the operation raising [V V_c]. Each step of the derivation satisfies the HMC, though the final output violates it (since the head t′ intervenes between V and its trace). Such considerations tend to favor a derivational approach to chain formation over a representational one. See chapters 1 and 2. Recall also that the crucial concept of minimal subdomain could only be interpreted in terms of a derivational approach.

21. For an example, see Baker 1988, 163.

22. Recall that even if Obj is replaced by an element that does not require structural Case, Subj must still raise to [Spec, Agr_S] in a nominative-accusative language (with "active" Agr_S).

23. This formulation allows later insertion of functional items that are vacuous for LF interpretation, for example, the *do* of *do*-support or the *of* of *of*-insertion.

24. This is not to say that θ-theory is dispensable at LF, for example, the principles of θ-discharge discussed in Higginbotham 1985. It is simply that the θ-Criterion and Projection Principle play no role.

25. I know of only one argument against generalized transformations, based on restrictiveness (Chomsky 1965): only a proper subclass of the I-languages (there called "grammars") allowed by the *LSLT* theory appear to exist, and only these are permitted if we eliminate generalized transformations and T-markers in favor of a recursive base satisfying the cycle. Elimination of generalized transformations in favor of cyclic base generation is therefore justified in terms of explanatory adequacy. But the questions under discussion then do not arise in the far more restrictive current theories.

26. A modification is necessary for the case of successive-cyclic movement, interpreted in terms of the operation Form Chain. I put this aside here.

27. Depending on other assumptions, some violations might be blocked by various "conspiracies." Let us assume, nevertheless, that overt substitution operations satisfy the extension (strict cycle) condition generally, largely on grounds of conceptual simplicity.

28. In case (19b) we assumed that V adjoins to (possibly empty) C, the head of CP, but it was the substitution operation inserting *can* that violated the cycle to yield the HMC violation. It has often been argued that LF adjunction may violate the "structure-preserving" requirement of (20), for example, allowing XP-incorporation to X^0 or quantifier adjunction to XP. Either conclusion is consistent with the present considerations. See also note 15.

29. On noncyclic adjunction, see Branigan 1992 and section 3.5 below.

30. See Hornstein and Weinberg 1990 for development of this proposal on somewhat different assumptions and grounds.

31. The technical implementation could be developed in many ways. For now, let us think of it as a rule of interpretation for the paired *wh*-phrases.

32. Technically, α raises to the lowest I to form $[_I \ \alpha \ I]$; then the complex raises to the next higher inflectional element; and so on. Recall that after multiple adjunction, α will still be in the checking domain of the "highest" I.

33. More fully, Infl_i is a collection of inflectional features checked by the relevant functional element.

34. The issue was raised by Webelhuth (1989) and has become a lively research topic. See Mahajan 1990 and much ongoing work. Note that if I adjoins to C, forming $[_C \ I \ C]$, [Spec, C] is in the checking domain of the chain (I, t). Hence, [Spec, C] is L-related (to I), and non-L-related (to C). A sharpening of notions is therefore required to determine the status of C after I-to-C raising. If C has L-features, [Spec, C] is L-related and would thus have the properties of an A-position, not an Ā-position. Questions arise here related to proposals of Rizzi (1990) on agreement features in C, and his more recent work extending these notions; these would take us too far afield here.

35. Heads are not narrowly L-related, hence not in A-positions, a fact that bears on ECP issues. See section 1.4.1.

36. I continue to put aside the question whether Case should be regarded as a property of N or D, and the DP-NP distinction generally.

37. See section 1.4.3 for some discussion.

38. Alternatively, weak features are deleted in the PF component so that PF rules can apply to the phonological matrix that remains; strong features are not deleted so that PF rules do not apply, causing the derivation to crash at PF.

39. Note that this is a reformulation of proposals by Emmon Bach and others in the framework of the Standard Theory and Generative Semantics: that these auxiliaries are inserted in the course of derivation, not appearing in the semantically relevant underlying structures. See Tremblay 1991 for an exploration of similar intuitions.

40. This leaves open the possibility that in VSO languages subject raises overtly to [Spec, TP] while T (including the adjoined verb) raises to Agr_S; for evidence that that is correct, see the references of note 11.

41. Raising would take place only to [Spec, CP], if absorption does not involve adjunction to a *wh*-phrase in [Spec, CP]. See note 31. I assume here that CP is not an adjunction target.

42. See chapter 2 and Chomsky 1991b. The self-serving property may also bear on whether LF operations are costless, or simply less costly.

43. There are a number of descriptive inadequacies in this overly simplified version. Perhaps the most important is that some of the notions used here (e.g., objectual quantification) have no clear interpretation in the case of natural language, contrary to common practice. Furthermore, we have no real framework within which to evaluate "theories of interpretation"; in particular, considerations of explanatory adequacy and restrictiveness are hard to introduce, on the standard (and plausible) assumption that the LF component allows no options. The primary task, then, is to derive an adequate descriptive account, no simple matter; comparison of alternatives lacks any clear basis. Another problem is that linking to performance theory is far more obscure than in the case of the PF component. Much of what is taken for granted in the literature on these topics seems to me highly problematic, if tenable at all. See *LGB* and the references of note 4 for some comment.

44. The topicalization analogues are perhaps more natural: *the claim that John is asleep* (*that John made*), . . . The point is the same, assuming an operator-variable analysis of topicalization.

45. In Lebeaux's theory, the effect is determined at D-Structure, prior to raising; I will abstract away from various modes of implementing the general ideas reviewed here. For discussion bearing on these issues, see Speas 1990, Epstein 1991. Freidin (1994) proposes that the difference has to do with the difference between LF representation of a predicate (the relative clause) and a complement; as he notes, that approach provides an argument for limiting binding theory to LF (see (22)).

46. In all but the simplest examples of anaphora, it is unclear whether distinctions are to be understood as tendencies (varying in strength for different

speakers) or sharp distinctions obscured by performance factors. For exposition, I assume the latter here. Judgments are therefore idealized, as always; whether correctly or not, only further understanding will tell.

47. Recall that LF *wh*-raising has been eliminated in favor of the absorption operation, so that in (36b) the anaphor cannot take the matrix subject as antecedent after LF raising.

48. I ignore the possibility that Condition A applies irrelevantly at S-Structure, the result being acceptable only if there is no clash with the LF application.

49. I put aside here interesting questions that have been investigated by Pierre Pica and others about how the morphology and the raising interact.

50. Another relevant case is (i),

(i) (guess) which picture of which man he saw *t*

a Condition C violation if *he* is taken to be bound by *which man* (Higginbotham 1980). As Higginbotham notes, the conclusion is much sharper than in (44b). One possibility is that independently of the present considerations, absorption is blocked from within [Spec, CP], forcing reconstruction to (iia), hence (iib),

(ii) a. which x, he saw [x picture of which man]
     b. which x, y, he saw x picture of [$_{NP}$ y man]

a Condition C violation if *he* is taken to be anaphoric to NP (i.e., within the scope of *which man*). The same reasoning would imply a contrast between (iiia) and (iiib),

(iii) a.   who would have guessed that proud of John, Bill never was
      b. *who would have guessed that proud of which man, Bill never was

(with absorption blocked, and no binding theory issue). That seems correct; other cases raise various questions.

51. Cases (48ai), (48aii) correspond to the familiar pairs *John (heard, told) stories about him*, with antecedence possible only in the case of *heard*, presumably reflecting the fact that one tells one's own stories but can hear the stories told by others; something similar holds of the cases in (48b).

52. See the essays collected in Lasnik 1989; also section 1.4.2.

53. A theoretical apparatus that takes indices seriously as entities, allowing them to figure in operations (percolation, matching, etc.), is questionable on more general grounds. Indices are basically the expression of a relationship, not entities in their own right. They should be replaceable without loss by a structural account of the relation they annotate.

Chapter 4

Categories and Transformations

The chapters that precede have adopted, modified, and extended work in the principles-and-parameters (P&P) model. In this final chapter I will take the framework for Universal Grammar (UG) developed and presented there as a starting point, extending it to questions that had been kept at a distance, subjecting it to a critical analysis, and revising it step by step in an effort to approach as closely as possible the goals of the Minimalist Program outlined in the introduction. The end result is a substantially different conception of the mechanisms of language.

Before proceeding, let us review the guiding ideas of the Minimalist Program.

4.1 The Minimalist Program

A particular language L is an instantiation of the initial state of the cognitive system of the language faculty with options specified. We take L to be a generative procedure that constructs pairs (π, λ) that are interpreted at the articulatory-perceptual (A-P) and conceptual-intentional (C-I) interfaces, respectively, as "instructions" to the performance systems. π is a PF representation and λ an LF representation, each consisting of "legitimate objects" that can receive an interpretation (perhaps as gibberish). If a generated representation consists entirely of such objects, we say that it satisfies the condition of Full Interpretation (FI). A linguistic expression of L is at least a pair (π, λ) meeting this condition—and under minimalist assumptions, at most such a pair, meaning that there are no levels of linguistic structure apart from the two interface levels PF and LF; specifically, no levels of D-Structure or S-Structure.

The language L determines a set of *derivations* (computations). A derivation *converges* at one of the interface levels if it yields a representation satisfying FI at this level, and *converges* if it converges at both interface levels, PF and LF; otherwise, it *crashes*. We thus adopt the (nonobvious) hypothesis that there are no PF-LF interactions relevant to convergence —which is not to deny, of course, that a full theory of performance involves operations that apply to the (π, λ) pair. Similarly, we assume that there are no conditions relating lexical properties and interface levels, such as the Projection Principle. The question of what counts as an interpretable legitimate object raises nontrivial questions, some discussed in earlier chapters.

Notice that I am sweeping under the rug questions of considerable significance, notably, questions about what in the earlier Extended Standard Theory (EST) framework were called "surface effects" on interpretation. These are manifold, involving topic-focus and theme-rheme structures, figure-ground properties, effects of adjacency and linearity, and many others. Prima facie, they seem to involve some additional level or levels internal to the phonological component, postmorphology but prephonetic, accessed at the interface along with PF (Phonetic Form) and LF (Logical Form).[1] If that turns out to be correct, then the abstraction I am now pursuing may require qualification. I will continue to pursue it nonetheless, merely noting here, once again, that tacit assumptions underlying much of the most productive recent work are far from innocent.

It seems that a linguistic expression of L cannot be defined just as a pair (π, λ) formed by a convergent derivation. Rather, its derivation must be *optimal*, satisfying certain natural economy conditions: locality of movement, no "superfluous steps" in derivations, and so on. Less economical computations are blocked even if they converge.

The language L thus generates three relevant sets of computations: the set D of derivations, a subset D_C of convergent derivations of D, and a subset D_A of admissible derivations of D. FI determines D_C, and the economy conditions select D_A. In chapters 1–3 it was assumed that economy considerations hold only among convergent derivations; if a derivation crashes, it does not block others. Thus, D_A is a subset of D_C. The assumption, which I continue to adopt here, is empirical; in the final analysis, its accuracy depends on factual considerations. But it has solid conceptual grounds, in that modifications of it entail departures from minimalist goals. On natural assumptions, a derivation in which an operation applies is less economical than one that differs only in that the operation does not apply. The most economical derivation, then, applies no operations at all to a collection of lexical choices and thus is sure to crash. If nonconvergent derivations can block others, this derivation will block all others and some elaboration will be needed, an unwelcome result. In the absence of convincing evidence to the contrary, then, I will continue to assume that economy considerations hold only of convergent derivations: D_A is a subset of D_C.

Current formulation of such ideas still leaves substantial gaps and a range of plausible alternatives, which I will try to narrow as I proceed. It is, furthermore, far from obvious that language should have anything at all like the character postulated in the Minimalist Program, which is just that: a research program concerned with filling the gaps and determining the answers to the basic questions raised in the opening paragraph of the introduction, in particular, the question "How 'perfect' is language?"

Suppose that this approach proves to be more or less correct. What could we then conclude about the specificity of the language faculty (modularity)? Not much. The language faculty might be unique among cognitive systems, or even in the organic world, in that it satisfies minimalist assumptions. Furthermore, the morphological parameters could be unique in character, and the computational system C_{HL} biologically isolated.

Another source of possible specificity of language lies in the conditions imposed "from the outside" at the interface, what we may call *bare output conditions*. These conditions are imposed by the systems that make use of the information provided by C_{HL}, but we have no idea in advance how specific to language their properties might be—quite specific, so current understanding suggests. There is one very obvious example, which has many effects: the information provided by L has to be accommodated to the human sensory and motor apparatus. Hence, UG must provide for a phonological component that converts the objects generated by the language L to a form that these "external" systems can use: PF, we assume. If humans could communicate by telepathy, there would be no need for a phonological component, at least for the purposes of communication; and the same extends to the use of language generally. These requirements might turn out to be critical factors in determining the inner nature of C_{HL} in some deep sense, or they might turn out to be "extraneous" to it, inducing departures from "perfection" that are satisfied in an optimal way. The latter possibility is not to be discounted.

This property of language might turn out to be one source of a striking departure from minimalist assumptions in language design: the fact that objects appear in the sensory output in positions "displaced" from those in which they are interpreted, under the most principled assumptions about interpretation. This is an irreducible fact about human language, expressed somehow in every contemporary theory of language, however the facts about displacement may be formulated. It has also been a central part of traditional grammar, descriptive and theoretical, at least back to the Port-Royal *Logic* and *Grammar*. We want to determine why language has this property (see section 4.7) and how it is realized (our primary concern throughout). We want to find out how well the conditions that impose this crucial property on language are satisfied: "as well as possible," we hope to find. Minimalist assumptions suggest that the property should be reduced to morphology-driven movement. What is known about the phenomena seems to me to support this expectation.

These "displacement" properties are one central syntactic respect in which natural languages differ from the symbolic systems devised for one or another purpose, sometimes called "languages" by metaphoric extension (formal languages, programming languages); there are other respects, including semantic differences.[2] The displacement property reflects the disparity—in fact, complementarity—between morphology (checking of features) and θ-theory (assignment of semantic roles), an apparent fact about natural language that is increasingly highlighted as we progress toward minimalist objectives. See section 4.6.

The Minimalist Program bears on the question of specificity of language, but in a limited way. It suggests where the question should arise: in the nature of the computational procedure C_{HL} and the locus of its variability (formal-morphological features of the lexicon, I am assuming); in the properties of the bare output conditions; and in the more obscure but quite interesting matter of conceptual naturalness of principles and concepts.

It is important to distinguish the topic of inquiry here from a different one: to what (if any) extent are the properties of C_{HL} expressed in terms of output conditions—say, filters of the kind discussed in Chomsky and Lasnik 1977, or chain formation algorithms in the sense of Rizzi 1986b in syntax, or conditions of the kind recently investigated for phonology in terms of Optimality Theory (Prince and Smolensky 1993, McCarthy and Prince 1993)? The question is imprecise: we do not know enough about the "external" systems at the interface to draw firm conclusions about conditions they impose, so the distinction between bare output conditions and others remains speculative in part. The problems are nevertheless empirical, and we can hope to resolve them by learning more about the language faculty and the systems with which it interacts. We proceed in the only possible way: by making tentative assumptions about the external systems and proceeding from there.

The worst possible case is that devices of both types are required: both computational processes that map symbolic representations to others and output conditions. That would require substantial empirical argument. The facts might, of course, force us to the worst case, but we naturally hope to find that C_{HL} makes use of processes of only a restricted type, and I will assume so unless the contrary is demonstrated.

A related question is whether C_{HL} is derivational or representational: does it involve successive operations leading to (π, λ) (if it converges), or does it operate in one of any number of other ways—say, selecting two such representations and then computing to determine whether they are properly paired, selecting one and deriving the other, and so on?[3] These questions are not only imprecise but also rather subtle; typically, it is possible to recode one approach in terms of others. But these questions too are ultimately empirical, turning basically on explanatory adequacy. Thus, filters were motivated by the fact that simple output conditions made it possible to limit considerably the variety and complexity of transformational rules, advancing the effort to reduce these to just Move α (or Affect α, in the sense of Lasnik and Saito 1984) and thus to move toward explanatory adequacy. Vergnaud's theory of abstract Case, which placed a central part of the theory of filters on more solid and plausible grounds, was a substantial further contribution. Similarly, Rizzi's proposals about chain formation were justified in terms of explaining facts about Romance reflexives and other matters.

My own judgment is that a derivational approach is nonetheless correct, and the particular version of a minimalist program I am considering assigns it even greater prominence, though a residue of filters persists in the concept of morphologically driven Last Resort movement, which has its roots in Vergnaud's Case theory. There are certain properties of language, which appear to be fundamental, that suggest this conclusion. Viewed derivationally, computation typically involves simple steps expressible in terms of natural relations and properties, with the context that makes them natural "wiped out" by later operations, hence not visible in the representations to which the derivation converges. Thus, in syntax, crucial relations are typically local, but a sequence of operations may yield a representation in which the locality is obscured. Head movement, for example, is narrowly "local," but several such operations may leave a head separated from its trace by an intervening head. This happens, for example, when N incorporates to V, leaving the trace t_N and the [$_V$ V–N] complex then raises to I, leaving the trace t_V: the chain (N, t_N) at the output level violates the locality property, and further operations (say, XP-fronting) may obscure it even more radically, but locality is observed by each individual step.

In segmental phonology, such phenomena are pervasive. Thus, the rules deriving the alternants *decide-decisive-decision* from an invariant lexical entry are straightforward and natural at each step, but the relevant contexts do not appear at all in the output; given only output conditions, it is hard to see why *decision* should not rhyme with *Poseidon* on the simplest assumptions about lexical representations, output conditions, and matching of input-output pairings. Similarly, intervocalic spirantization and vowel reduction are natural and simple processes that derive, say, Hebrew *ganvu* 'they stole' from underlying *g-n-B*, but the context for spirantization is gone after reduction applies; the underlying form might even all but disappear in the output, as in *hitu* 'they extended', in which only the /t/ remains from the underlying root /ntC/ (C a "weak" consonant).[4,5]

It is generally possible to formulate the desired result in terms of outputs. In the head movement case, for example, one can appeal to the (plausible) assumption that the trace is a copy, so the intermediate V-trace includes within it a record of the local N → V raising. But surely this is the wrong move. The relevant chains at LF are (N, t_N) and (V, t_V), and in these the locality relation satisfied by successive raising has been lost. Similar artifice could be used in the phonological examples, again improperly, it appears. These seem to be fundamental properties of language, which should be captured, not obscured by coding tricks, which are always available. A fully derivational approach both captures them straightforwardly and suggests that they should be pervasive, as seems to be the case.

I will continue to assume that the computational system C_{HL} is strictly derivational and that the only output conditions are the bare output conditions determined "from the outside," at the interface.

We hope to be able to show that for a particular (I-)language L, the phenomena of sound and meaning for L are determined by pairs (π, λ) formed by admissible (maximally economical) convergent derivations that satisfy output conditions—where "determined," of course, means 'insofar as the cognitive system of the language faculty is responsible'.[6] The computation C_{HL} that derives (π, λ) must, furthermore, keep to computational principles that are minimalist in spirit, both in their character and in the economy conditions that select derivations. Another natural condition is that outputs consist of nothing beyond properties of items of the lexicon (lexical features)—in other words, that the interface levels consist of nothing more than arrangements of lexical features. To the extent that this is true, the language meets a condition of *inclusiveness*.[7] We assume further that the principles of UG involve only elements that function at the interface levels; nothing else can be "seen" in the course of the computation, a general idea that will be sharpened as we proceed.

In pursuing a minimalist program, we want to make sure that we are not inadvertently sneaking in improper concepts, entities, relations, and conventions. The point of the occasional forays into formalism below is to clarify just how closely C_{HL} keeps to minimalist conditions, with principles and conventions derived where valid. The more spare the assumptions, the more intricate the argument is likely to be.

4.2   The Cognitive System of the Language Faculty

4.2.1   The Computational Component

A linguistic expression (π, λ) of L satisfies output conditions at the PF and LF interfaces. Beyond that, π and λ must be *compatible*: it is not the case that any sound can mean anything. In particular, π and λ must be based on the same lexical choices. We can, then, think of C_{HL} as mapping some array A of lexical choices to the pair (π, λ). What is A? At least, it must indicate what the lexical choices are and how many times each is selected by C_{HL} in forming (π, λ). Let us take a *numeration* to be a set of pairs (LI, i), where LI is an item of the lexicon and i is its index, understood to be the number of times that LI is selected. Take A to be (at least) a numeration N; C_{HL} maps N to (π, λ). The procedure C_{HL} selects an item from N and reduces its index by 1, then performing permissible computations. A computation constructed by C_{HL} does not count as a derivation at all, let alone a convergent one, unless all indices are reduced to zero.

Viewing the language L as a derivation-generating procedure, we may think of it as applying to a numeration N and forming a sequence S of symbolic elements $(\sigma_1, \sigma_2, \ldots, \sigma_n)$, terminating only if σ_n is a pair (π, λ)

and N is reduced to zero (the computation may go on). S formed in this way is a derivation, which converges if the elements of σ_n satisfy FI at PF and LF, respectively. Economy considerations select the admissible convergent derivations.

Given the numeration N, the operations of C_{HL} recursively construct *syntactic objects* from items in N and syntactic objects already formed. We have to determine what these objects are and how they are constructed. Insofar as the condition of inclusiveness holds, the syntactic objects are rearrangements of properties of the lexical items of which they are ultimately constituted. We consider now just the computation $N \to \lambda$, for reasons that will become clearer as we proceed and that tend to support the view that there is indeed something "extraneous" about the conditions imposed on language at the A-P (sensorimotor) interface.

Suppose that the derivation has reached the stage Σ, which we may take to be a set $\{SO_1, \ldots, SO_n\}$ of syntactic objects. One of the operations of C_{HL} is a procedure that selects a lexical item LI from the numeration, reducing its index by 1, and introduces it into the derivation as SO_{n+1}. Call the operation *Select*. At the LF interface, Σ can be interpreted only if it consists of a single syntactic object. Clearly, then, C_{HL} must include a second procedure that combines syntactic objects already formed. A derivation converges only if this operation has applied often enough to leave us with just a single object, also exhausting the initial numeration. The simplest such operation takes a pair of syntactic objects (SO_i, SO_j) and replaces them by a new combined syntactic object SO_{ij}. Call this operation *Merge*. We will return to its properties, merely noting here that the operations Select and Merge, or some close counterparts, are necessary components of any theory of natural language.

Note that no question arises about the motivation for application of Select or Merge in the course of a derivation. If Select does not exhaust the numeration, no derivation is generated and no questions of convergence or economy arise. Insufficient application of Merge has the same property, since the derivation then fails to yield an LF representation at all; again, no derivation is generated, and questions of convergence and economy do not arise. The operations Select and Merge are "costless"; they do not fall within the domain of discussion of convergence and economy.[8] Similarly, we do not have to ask about the effect of illegitimate operations, any more than proof theory is concerned with a sequence of lines that does not satisfy the formal conditions that define "proof," or a chess-playing algorithm with evaluation of improper moves.

Within the framework just outlined, there is also no meaningful question as to why one numeration is formed rather than another—or rather than none, so that we have silence. That would be like asking that a theory of some formal operation on integers—say, addition—explain why some integers are added together rather than others, or none. Or that a theory of the mechanisms of vision or motor coordination explain why someone chooses to look at a sunset or reach for a banana. The problem of choice of action is real, and largely mysterious, but does not arise within the narrow study of mechanisms.[9]

Suppose the lexical item LI in the numeration N has index i. If a derivation is to be generated, Select must access LI i times, introducing it into the derivation. But the syntactic objects formed by distinct applications of Select to LI must be distinguished; two occurrences of the pronoun *he*, for example, may have entirely different properties at LF. l and l' are thus marked as distinct for C_{HL} if they are formed by distinct applications of Select accessing the same lexical item of N. Note that this is a departure from the inclusiveness condition, but one that seems indispensable: it is rooted in the nature of language, and perhaps reducible to bare output conditions.

We want the initial array A, whether a numeration or something else, not only to express the compatibility relation between π and λ but also to fix the *reference set* for determining whether a derivation from A to (π, λ) is optimal—that is, not blocked by a more economical derivation. Determination of the reference set is a delicate problem, as are considerations of economy generally. As a first approximation, let us take the numeration to determine the reference set: in evaluating derivations for economy, we consider only alternatives with the same numeration.

Selection of an optimal derivation in the reference set determined from the numeration N poses problems of computational complexity too vast to be realistic. We can reduce the problem with a more "local" interpretation of reference sets. At a particular stage Σ of a derivation, we consider only continuations of the derivation already constructed—in particular, only the remaining parts of the numeration N. Application of the operation OP to Σ is barred if this set contains a more optimal derivation in which OP does not apply to Σ. The number of derivations to be considered for determining whether OP may apply reduces radically as the derivation proceeds. At least this much structure seems to be required, presumably more. See section 4.9 for some empirical evidence supporting this construal of reference sets (which, in any event, is to be preferred)—in fact, an even more stringent condition.

An elementary empirical condition on the theory is that expressions "usable" by the performance systems be assigned interface representations in a manner that does not induce too much computational complexity. We want to formulate economy conditions that avoid "exponential blowup" in construction and evaluation of derivations. A local interpretation of reference sets is a step in this direction. Where "global" properties of derivations have to be considered, as in determining the applicability of the principle Procrastinate of earlier chapters, we expect to find some ready algorithm to reduce computational complexity. In the case of Procrastinate, it typically suffices to see if a strong feature is present, which is straightforward—and even easier under an interpretation of "strength" to which we return directly. But we are still a long way from a comprehensive theory of economy, a topic that is now being explored for the first time within a context of inquiry that is able to place explanatory adequacy on the research agenda.

Given the numeration N, C_{HL} computes until it forms a derivation that converges at PF and LF with the pair (π, λ), after reducing N to zero (if it does). A "perfect language" should meet the condition of inclusiveness: any structure formed by the computation (in particular, π and λ) is constituted of elements already present in the lexical items selected for N; no new objects are added in the course of computation apart from rearrangements of lexical properties (in particular, no indices, bar levels in the sense of X-bar theory, etc.; see note 7). Let us assume that this condition holds (virtually) of the computation from N to LF $(N \rightarrow \lambda)$; standard theories take it to be radically false for the computation to PF.[10]

As already noted, the inclusiveness condition is not fully met. Distinguishing selections of a single lexical item is a (rather narrow) departure. Another involves the deletion operation (Delete α). Let us assume that this operation marks some object as "invisible at the interface"; we will sharpen it as we proceed, assuming for the moment that material deleted, though ignored at the interface, is still accessible within C_{HL}.[11] The question turns out to have interesting ramifications.

A core property of C_{HL} is feature checking, the operation that drives movement under the Last Resort condition. A large part of our concern will be to examine these notions. We can begin by reducing feature checking to deletion: a checked feature is marked "invisible at the interface.[12] Even a cursory look shows that this cannot be the whole story, but let us take it as a starting point, returning to a more careful analysis in section 4.5.2.

Output conditions show that π and λ are differently constituted. Elements interpretable at the A-P interface are not interpretable at C-I, and conversely. At some point, then, the computation splits into two parts, one forming π and the other forming λ. The simplest assumptions are (1) that there is no further interaction between these computations and (2) that computational procedures are uniform throughout: any operation can apply at any point. We adopt (1), and assume (2) for the computation from N to λ, though not for the computation from N to π; the latter modifies structures (including the internal structure of lexical entries) by processes very different from those that take place in the N $\rightarrow$ λ computation. Investigation of output conditions should suffice to establish these asymmetries, which I will simply take for granted here.

We assume, then, that at some point in the (uniform) computation to LF, there is an operation Spell-Out that applies to the structure Σ already formed. Spell-Out strips away from Σ those elements relevant only to π, leaving the residue Σ_L, which is mapped to λ by operations of the kind used to form Σ. Σ itself is then mapped to π by operations unlike those of the N $\rightarrow$ λ computation. We call the subsystem of C_{HL} that maps Σ to π the *phonological component*, and the subsystem that continues the computation from Σ_L to LF the *covert component*. The pre-Spell-Out computation we call *overt*. Let us assume further that Spell-Out delivers Σ to the module Morphology, which constructs word-like units that are then subjected to further phonological processes that map it finally to π, and which eliminates features no longer relevant to the computation. I will have little to say about the phonological component here, except for some comments about morphological structure and linear ordering.

The special properties of the phonological component relate to the need to produce instructions for sensorimotor systems, for production and perception. As noted, this requirement may be the source of other imperfections of C_{HL}, and in this sense "extraneous" to language, possibilities we will explore.

Given these fairly elementary assumptions about the structure of C_{HL}, we distinguish two types of lexical feature: those that receive an interpretation only at the A-P interface (phonological) and those that receive an interpretation only at the C-I interface. I assume further that these sets are disjoint, given the very special properties of the phonological component and its PF output.

It is reasonable to suppose that overt operations do not delete phonological features; otherwise, there would be little reason for them to appear in a lexical item at all. Suppose this to be so. By the assumption of uniformity of C_{HL}, it follows that covert operations cannot do so either; if any phonological features enter the covert component (after Spell-Out), the derivation will crash at LF, violating FI. We will make the still stronger assumption that overt operations cannot detect phonological features at all—such features cannot, for example, distinguish one overt operation from another.[13] Thus, the phonological matrix of a lexical item is essentially *atomic*, as far as overt operations are concerned. It is the form in which the instructions for certain rules of the phonological component are "coded" in the lexical item. For the $N \rightarrow \lambda$ computation, nothing would change if the phonological properties of *book* were coded in the lexicon as *23*, with a rule of the phonological component interpreting *23* as the phonological matrix for *book*.

Among the features that appear in lexical entries, we distinguish further between *formal* features that are accessible in the course of the computation and others that are not: thus, between the formal features $[\pm N]$ and $[\pm \text{plural}]$, and the semantic feature [artifact]. The basis for the distinction and its effects raise substantial questions,[14] among the many that I will put aside here. Such features also function differently in the phonological component. Since we take computation to LF to be uniform, we cannot stipulate that certain features are eliminable only after Spell-Out; but the mapping to PF has completely different properties and eliminates features in ways not permitted in the $N \rightarrow \lambda$ computation —in particular, it eliminates formal and semantic features.

The lexical entry for *airplane*, for example, contains three collections of features: phonological features such as [begins with vowel], semantic features such as [artifact], and formal features such as [nominal]. The phonological features are stripped away by Spell-Out and are thus available only to the phonological component; the others are left behind by Spell-Out, and the formal ones may continue to be accessed by the covert computation to LF. Within the phonological component, non-phonological features are eliminated in the course of the computation, though they may be relevant to its operation—at least its earlier parts, within the morphological subcomponent.

The collection of formal features of the lexical item LI I will call *FF(LI)*, a subcomplex of LI. Thus, FF(*airplane*) is the collection of features of *airplane* that function in the N → λ computation, excluding the phonological and (purely) semantic features. Some of the features of FF(LI) are *intrinsic* to it, either listed explicitly in the lexical entry or strictly determined by properties so listed. Others are *optional*, added as LI enters the numeration. We will return to this matter in section 4.2.2. Insofar as we are considering properties of the computation from numeration to LF, we restrict attention to formal features, though bare output conditions at the A-P interface sometimes force a departure from this desideratum; see section 4.4.4.

In the case of *airplane*, the intrinsic properties include the categorial feature [nominal], the person feature [3 person], and the gender feature [−human]. Its optional properties include the noncategorial features of number and Case. The intrinsic properties of *build* include the categorial feature [verbal] and the Case feature [assign accusative], but its φ-features and tense are optional (if internal to the item). Choices of lexical item LI with different optional features are distinct members of the numeration. If (*airplane, i*) is in the numeration, its first term must include the categorial feature [nominal] and the noncategorial features [3 person], [−human], as well as one or another choice among number and Case features—perhaps [plural] and [accusative], in which case it may appear in a convergent derivation for *we build airplanes*. Further analysis reveals additional distinctions and complexity that do not seem to relate to the computational procedure C_{HL}, at least those aspects of it to which I will limit attention, along with a host of further questions about boundaries, substructure, and interaction with semantic features, which I ignore here for the same reason—perhaps improperly, as further inquiry may reveal.

A guiding intuition of the Minimalist Program is that operations apply anywhere, without special stipulation, the derivation crashing if a "wrong choice" is made. Let us assume this to be true of Spell-Out, as of other operations. After Spell-Out, the phonological component cannot select from the numeration any item with semantic features, and the covert component cannot select any item with phonological features. That is a requirement for any theory on the weakest empirical assumptions; otherwise, sound-meaning relations would collapse.[15]

It is unnecessary to add stipulations to this effect. For the phonological component, the question does not arise. It has rules of a special nature, distinct from those of the N → λ computation, and these only modify forms already presented to them. Accordingly, Select is inoperative in the phonological component: no items can be selected from the numeration in the computation from Spell-Out to PF.

The operation Select is available to the covert component, however, assuming the uniformity condition on the N → λ computation. But if an item with phonological features is selected, the derivation will crash at LF. Selection of LI must be overt, unless LI has no phonological features. In this case LI can be selected covertly and merged (at the root, like overt merger, for simple reasons to which we return). We will see that this conceptual possibility may well be realized.

One interesting case concerns strong features: can a (phonologically null) lexical item with a strong feature be selected covertly?

To clarify the issues, we have to settle the status of the strength property. Feature strength is one element of language variation: a formal feature may or may not be strong, forcing overt movement that violates Procrastinate. A look at cases suggests that the [±strong] dimension is narrowly restricted, perhaps to something like the set of options (1).

(1) If F is strong, then F is a feature of a nonsubstantive category and F is checked by a categorial feature.

If so, nouns and main verbs do not have strong features, and a strong feature always calls for a certain *category* in its checking domain (not, say, Case or φ-features). It follows that overt movement of β targeting α, forming [Spec, α] or [$_α$ β α], is possible only when α is nonsubstantive and a categorial feature of β is involved in the operation.[16] Thus, the Extended Projection Principle (EPP) plausibly reduces to a strong D-feature of I, and overt *wh*-raising to a strong D-feature of C (assuming *wh*- to be a variant of D (Determiner)). Other cases would include overt N-raising to D (Longobardi 1994, and sources cited), and I-to-C raising, now understood as involving not Agr or T but a true modal or V adjoined to I, an idea that will make more sense as we proceed. Adjunction of nominals to transitive verbs will target a [*v*–V] complex formed by raising of the main verb V to a light verb, and verb-incorporation would also be to a weak verb. Let us assume that something like this is the case.

For ease of exposition, I sometimes speak of a functional category as strong when I mean, more explicitly, that one of its features is strong. I am also glossing over a possibly significant distinction between D-features and N-features, that is, among three variants of the EPP: (1) requiring a DP as specifier, (2) requiring an NP, (3) requiring a nominal category, whether NP or DP. The differences may be significant; I will return to them in sections 4.9 and 4.10. Until then, references to the EPP will be expressed in terms of strong D-features, but the intention is to remain neutral among the choices (1), (2), (3).

A strong feature has two properties. First, it triggers an overt operation, before Spell-Out. Second, it induces cyclicity: a strong feature cannot be "passed" by α that would satisfy it, and later checked by β; that would permit Relativized Minimality violations (*Wh*-Island, superraising). In chapter 3 the pre-Spell-Out property was stated in terms of convergence at PF (a strong feature crashes at PF and therefore must be removed before Spell-Out), but that formulation was based on a stipulation that we have now dropped: that lexical access takes place before Spell-Out. The cyclic property was left only partially resolved in chapter 3 (and in Chomsky 1994a).

Apart from its problems and limitations, formulation of strength in terms of PF convergence is a restatement of the basic property, not a true explanation. In fact, there seems to be no way to improve upon the bare statement of the properties of strength. Suppose, then, that we put an end to evasion and simply define a strong feature as one that a derivation "cannot tolerate": a derivation $D \rightarrow \Sigma$ is canceled if Σ contains a strong feature, in a sense we must make precise. A strong feature thus triggers a rule that eliminates it: [strength] is associated with a pair of operations, one that introduces it into the derivation (actually, a combination of Select and Merge), a second that (quickly) eliminates it.

Cyclicity follows at once.[17] We also virtually derive the conclusion that a strong feature triggers an *overt* operation to eliminate it by checking. This conclusion follows with a single exception: covert merger (at the root) of a lexical item that has a strong feature but no phonological features—an option noted earlier, to which we return.

It is perhaps worth mentioning in this connection that the Minimalist Program, right or wrong, has a certain therapeutic value. It is all too easy to succumb to the temptation to offer a purported explanation for some phenomenon on the basis of assumptions that are of roughly the order of complexity of what is to be explained. If the assumptions have broader scope, that may be a step forward in understanding. But sometimes they do not. Minimalist demands at least have the merit of highlighting such moves, thus sharpening the question of whether we have a genuine explanation or a restatement of a problem in other terms.

We have to determine in what precise sense a strong feature cannot be included within a legitimate derivation. The intuitive idea is that the strong feature merged at the root must be eliminated before it becomes part of a larger structure by further operations. The notion "part of" can be understood in various ways. There are four possibilities, based on the two ways of building new structures (substitution, adjunction)[18] and the two options for projection (either the category with the strong feature or the one joined with it can project).

To illustrate, take the case of T (Tense) with a strong V-feature and a strong D-feature (as in French), forcing overt V-raising to T (adjunction) and overt DP-raising to [Spec, T] (substitution). We want to know how T and some category K can be joined to form a larger category L, consistent with the strength of T.

Suppose T and K are joined and T projects. Suppose the operation is substitution, forming $L = [_{TP}\ T\ K]$ with head T and complement K, the strong feature of T remaining in the larger structure. Plainly that is admissible; in fact, it is the only way T can enter a convergent derivation. Projection of strong T, then, permits the derivation to continue when T and K are joined: the projection of T can tolerate embedded strong T.

Suppose that T and K are joined and K projects. Then T is either the specifier or complement of K (substitution), or an adjunct of K (adjunction). For reasons that will be clarified as we proceed, subsequent joining of L to T (by adjunction or substitution) is barred. In general, then, we will try to establish the principle (2).

(2) Nothing can join to a nonprojecting category.

That is, nothing can join to an adjunct, specifier, or complement. Hence, we need not consider the case of nonprojecting strong T, for if a strong feature does not project, the operation required to eliminate strength will never apply.

If this is the correct interpretation of the options, then the descriptive property of strength is (3). Suppose that the derivation D has formed Σ containing α with a strong feature F. Then

(3) D is canceled if α is in a category not headed by α.

The cases just reviewed follow, as do others. Note that this is not a principle governing strength but a descriptive observation about it, if (2) holds.

Suppose K adjoins to TP, forming the two-segment category M = [$_{TP}$ K TP]. By (3), the derivation tolerates the strong features of T, which can be satisfied by later operations. This is the right result. Suppose K is an adverbial. Then TP can be extended to M = [$_{TP}$ K TP] by adjunction of the adverbial K, and M can be further extended to N = [$_{TP}$ DP M] by insertion of DP as [Spec, T] to satisfy the EPP, yielding such expressions as *John probably has left already, there probably will be snow tomorrow.* In fact, the NP-I' break is a typical position for merger of adverbials.

Suppose we have formed TP with head T and complement K, and the strong D-feature of T (EPP) has not yet been checked. Suppose we next merge TP with C, forming CP with head C and complement TP. That is excluded by (3); the derivation will crash. Again, this is the right result quite generally, required to avoid Relativized Minimality violations, as mentioned earlier.

These cases are typical. We therefore assume (3) to hold for strong features.

While Merge is costless for principled reasons, movement is not: the operation takes place only when forced (Last Resort); and it is overt, violating Procrastinate, only when that is required for convergence. If α has a strong feature F, it triggers an operation OP that checks F before the formation of a larger category that is not a projection of α. The operation OP may be Merge or Move.

4.2.2 The Lexicon

I will have little to say about the lexicon here, but what follows does rest on certain assumptions that should be made clear. I understand the lexicon in a rather traditional sense: as a list of "exceptions," whatever does not follow from general principles. These principles fall into two categories: those of UG, and those of a specific language. The latter cover aspects of phonology and morphology, choice of parametric options, and whatever else may enter into language variation. Assume further that the lexicon provides an "optimal coding" of such idiosyncrasies.

Take, say, the word *book* in English. It has a collection of properties, some idiosyncratic, some of varying degrees of generality. The lexical entry for *book* specifies the idiosyncrasies, abstracting from the principles of UG and the special properties of English. It is the optimal coding of information that just suffices to yield the LF representation and that allows the phonological component to construct the PF representation; the asymmetry reflects the difference between the $N \rightarrow \lambda$ computation and the phonological component, the former (virtually) satisfying and the latter radically violating the principles of uniformity and inclusiveness.

One idiosyncratic property of *book* coded in the lexical entry is the sound-meaning relation. The lexical entry also either lists, or entails, that it has the categorial feature [N]; we overlook open questions of some interest here.[19] But the lexical entry should not indicate that *book* has Case and φ-features; that follows from its being of category N (presumably, by principles of UG). It should also not specify phonetic or semantic properties that are universal or English-specific: predictable interactions between vowel and final consonant, or the fact that *book* can be used to refer to something that is simultaneously abstract and concrete, as in the expression *the book that I'm writing will weigh 5 pounds.* That is a property of a broad range of nominal expressions, perhaps all —one of the many reasons why standard theories of reference are not applicable to natural language, in my opinion (see note 2).

For the word *book*, it seems the optimal coding should include a phonological matrix of the familiar kind expressing exactly what is not predictable, and a comparable representation of semantic properties, about which much less is known. And it should include the formal features of *book* insofar as they are unpredictable from other properties of the lexical entry: perhaps its categorial feature N, and no others. The fact that Case and φ-features have to be assigned to *book* follows from general principles, and nothing intrinsic to the lexical entry *book* tells us that a particular occurrence is singular or plural, nominative or accusative (though its person feature is presumably determined by intrinsic semantic properties). In some cases such features might be idiosyncratic (e.g., the plural feature of *scissors*, or grammatical gender). More important, in some languages the system works very differently: for example, Semitic, with root-vowel pattern structure. But lexical entries are determined on the same general grounds.

Suppose that *book* is chosen as part of the array from which a derivation proceeds to form PF and LF representations. I have described the choice of *book* as a two-step process: (1) form a numeration that includes (*book*, *i*), with index *i*, and (2) introduce *book* into the derivation by the operation Select, which adds *book* to the set of syntactic objects generated and reduces its index by 1. The optional features of a particular occurrence of *book* (say, [accusative], [plural]) are added by either step (1) or step (2)—presumably by step (1), a decision that reduces reference sets and hence computability problems. Suppose so. Then the numeration N will include [*book*, [accusative], [plural], 2], in this case (assuming index 2). The fact that these features are present is determined (we assume) by UG, but the choice among them is not.

Recall that we are concerned here only with mechanisms, not with choices and intentions of speakers. Over the class of derivations, then, the mapping from lexicon to numeration is random with regard to specification of *book* for Case and φ-features, and the index of that collection of properties, though UG requires that there is always some choice of Case, φ-features, and index.

This much seems fairly clear. It is hardly plausible that Case and φ-features of *book* are determined by its position in a clausal configuration. If the word is used in isolation, these features will be fixed one way or another, though there is no structure. One could say that there is a "presupposed structure," some representation of the intentions of the speaker or (possibly) shared assumptions in some interchange. But that is surely the wrong course to pursue. It is possible (and has been proposed) that nouns are automatically selected along with broader nominal configurations (involving Case, perhaps φ-features). That is a possibility, but would require positive evidence. I will assume here the null hypothesis: Case and φ-features are added arbitrarily as a noun is selected for the numeration.

The same conclusions are appropriate in other cases. Take such constructions as (4).

(4) as far as John is concerned, [$_{CP}$ I doubt that anyone will ever want to speak to the fool again]

Here some formal properties of *John* and *a fool* are related, but not by the mechanisms of C_{HL}. The example falls together with use of CP in isolation on the background assumption that John is under discussion (perhaps provided by discourse context, perhaps not). The same might be true of the more interesting case of nominal expressions in languages that express arguments as adjuncts associated with pronominal elements within words (see Baker 1995 and section 4.10.3). The particular form taken by such adjuncts may depend on the association, but might not be expressible in terms of local relations of the kind admitted in C_{HL} (typically, H-α relations, where H is a head and α is in its checking domain).

In the numeration, then, Case and φ-features of nouns are specified, whether by the lexical entry (intrinsic features) or by the operation that forms the numeration (optional features). Larger structures are relevant, but only for checking of features of the noun that are already present in the numeration.

Consider verbs, say, *explain*. Its lexical entry too represents in the optimal way the instructions for the phonological component and for interpretation of the LF representation: a phonological matrix, and some array of semantic properties. It must also contain whatever information is provided by the verb itself for the operations of C_{HL}. The lexical entry must suffice to determine that *explain* has the categorial property V, perhaps by explicit listing. What about its selectional features? Insofar as these are determined by semantic properties, whether by UG or by specific rules of English, they will not be listed in the lexicon. The fact that *explain* has tense and ϕ-features will not be indicated in the lexical entry, because that much is determined by its category V (presumably by UG). The particular specification of such features, however, is not part of the lexical entry. The verb also has a Case-assigning property, which is intrinsic: either determined by properties of the lexical entry (its semantic features) or listed as idiosyncratic. Features that are associated with the verb but not predictable from the lexical entry have two possible sources: they might be chosen arbitrarily as the verb enters the numeration, or they might be the result of operations that form complex words by association with other elements (e.g., adjunction to T). These could be operations of the overt syntax or the phonological component (including morphology). If overt syntactic operations are involved, the categories involved will be marked (in the lexicon, or the transition to the numeration) as allowing or requiring affixation.

The decisions are less clear than for nouns, but the principles are the same. Whatever information feeds the phonological rules must be available for the computation as the item is introduced into the derivation, but the specific character of this information has to be discovered, as well as whether it is provided by optional choice of feature values as the item enters the numeration or by overt syntactic operations. Take inflected *explain*. Its tense and ϕ-features might be chosen optionally and assigned to the word as it enters the numeration, or they might result from overt V-raising to Agr and T. Or the word might reach the phonological component uninflected, the PF form resulting from interaction with functional elements within the phonological component. The answers could vary across or within languages.[20] The questions have to be answered case by case.

For my specific purposes here, it does not matter much which choices turn out to be correct, until section 4.10, when the status of functional categories is reassessed. For concreteness (and with an eye in part to that later reassessment), I will assume that tense and φ-features of verbs (say, inflected *explain*) are chosen optionally as the item enters the numeration, then matched by other processes. But alternatives are compatible with much of what follows.

A separate question is the form in which the information should be coded in the lexical entry. Thus, in the case of *book*, the optimal representation in the lexicon could include the standard phonological matrix PM, or some arbitrary coding (say, *23*) interpreted within the phonological component as PM—presumably the former, unless there is strong independent reason for the latter. Similarly, in the case of [past tense], the fact that it is typically dental could be represented by a phonological matrix [dental], or by an arbitrary coding (say, *47*) interpreted in the phonological component as [dental] (with whatever complications have to be coded in the entries of irregular verbs)—again, presumably the former, unless there is strong independent reason to the contrary. I will put these matters aside, assuming that they have to be settled case by case, though in a manner that will not matter for what follows.

On the simplest assumptions, the lexical entry provides, once and for all, the information required for further computations—in particular, for the operations of the phonological component (including morphology, we assume). There seems to be no compelling reason to depart from the optimal assumption.

I have kept to the easiest cases. Let us move to the opposite extreme. Suppose the PF form of a lexical entry is completely unpredictable: the English copula, for example. In this case the lexical coding will provide whatever information the phonological rules need to assign a form to the structure [copula, {F}], where {F} is some set of formal features (tense, person, etc.). It does not seem to matter (for our purposes here, at least) how this information is presented: as a list of alternants, each with its formal features, or by some coding that allows the phonological component to pick the alternant ("late insertion").

This is the worst possible case. Plainly, it would be a methodological error to generalize the worst case to all cases—to infer from the fact that the worst case exists that it holds for all lexical items.

There are many intermediate cases. Take the lexical element *come-came*. Some regularity can be extracted and presented as a phonological matrix, perhaps /kVm/. But the choice of vowel is not rule-governed and therefore must be coded in one or another way. Structural linguistics devoted much energy to whether the information should be coded in the form of morpheme alternants, item-and-process rules that change one form to another, and so on. As in the case of pure suppletion, it is not clear that there even is an empirical issue. There are similar problems, real or illusory, concerning semantic features (idiom structure, etc.).

With regard to functional categories, the same general considerations apply, though new problems arise. It is clear that the lexicon contains substantive elements (nouns, verbs, ...) with their idiosyncratic properties. And it is at least reasonably clear that it contains some functional categories: complementizer (C), for example. But the situation is more obscure in the case of other possible functional categories, in particular, T, Agr, specific φ-features, a Case category K, and so on, which is why theories about these matters have varied so over the years. Postulation of a functional category has to be justified, either by output conditions (phonetic and semantic interpretation) or by theory-internal arguments. It bears a burden of proof, which is often not so easy to meet.

The functional categories that concern us particularly here are T, C, D, and Agr; their formal properties are the primary focus throughout. T, D, and C have semantic properties; Agr does not. Thus, T is [±finite], with further subdivisions and implications about event structure and perhaps other properties. D may be the locus of what is loosely called "referentiality."[21] C is basically an indicator of mood or force (in the Fregean sense): declarative, interrogative, and so on. The choice among the options of a given type is arbitrary, part of the process of forming a numeration from the lexicon, as (I am tentatively assuming) in the case of φ-features of verbs, and Case and (some) φ-features of nouns.

Functional categories may also have phonological properties. Thus, English T is dental and declarative C is *that* (with a null option) (we will return to interrogative C = Q); Japanese Cases are phonologically invariant; and so on. The lexical entry, again, provides an optimal coding for what is not predictable.

We expect different decisions in different cases, depending on details of the phonological component, the lexical inventory for the language, and perhaps more. Suppose, for example, that specific morphological properties of a language constrain the phonetic correlate of formal features: say, that verbs indicate person with prefixes and number with suffixes, or that exactly n slots are available for spelling out formal features. Then the lexical entries will abstract from these properties, presenting just the information that they do not determine. It appears to be the case for some languages that "templatic" conditions are required for morphological structure. If so, the option is universally available, as are adjunction operations, along with whatever else the empirical facts may require.

In all cases the principle is clear, though the answers to specific questions are not: the lexicon provides the optimal coding for "exceptions." Though important typological differences doubtless exist, there seems little reason to expect much of any generality, among languages or often within them. Perhaps Jespersen was correct in holding that "no one ever dreamed of a universal morphology," to any far-reaching degree, morphology being a primary repository of exceptional aspects of particular languages.

I am keeping to the optimal assumption: that for each lexical item in a particular language, the idiosyncratic codings are given in a unified lexical entry. There are more complex theories that scatter the properties. One might propose, for example, that formal features, instructions for phonological rules, and instructions for LF interpretation appear in distinct sublexicons, which are accessible at different points in the computational process. Such elaborations might also involve new levels and relations among various parts of the derivation, to ensure proper matching of (PF, LF) pairs. The burden of proof is always on the proposal that the theory has to be made more complex, and it is a considerable one. I will keep to the optimal assumptions, which seem to be about as just indicated—stressing, however, that the serious questions of implementation and perhaps general theoretical issues are scarcely even touched in these remarks.

I have said nothing about other major components of the theory of word formation: compound forms, agglutinative structures, and much more. This is only the barest sketch, intended for no more than what follows.

4.3 Phrase Structure Theory in a Minimalist Framework

The development of X-bar theory in the 1960s was an early stage in the effort to resolve the tension between explanatory and descriptive adequacy. A first step was to separate the lexicon from the computations, thus removing a serious redundancy between lexical properties and phrase structure rules and allowing the latter to be reduced to the simplest (context-free) form. X-bar theory sought to eliminate such rules altogether, leaving only the general X-bar-theoretic format of UG. The primary problem in subsequent work was to determine that format, but it was assumed that phrase structure rules themselves should be eliminable, if we understood enough about the matter—which, needless to say, we never do, so (unsurprisingly) many open questions remain, including some that are quite central to language.[22]

In earlier papers on economy and minimalism (chapters 1–3), X-bar theory is presupposed, with specific stipulated properties. Let us now subject these assumptions to critical analysis, asking what the theory of phrase structure should look like on minimalist assumptions and what the consequences are for the theory of movement.

At the LF interface, it must be possible to access a lexical item LI and its nonphonological properties LF(LI): the semantic properties and the formal properties that are interpreted there. Accordingly, LI and LF(LI) should be available for C_{HL}, on the natural minimalist assumption, discussed earlier, that bare output conditions determine the items that are "visible" for computations. In addition, C_{HL} can access the formal features FF(LI), by definition. It is also apparent that some larger units constructed of lexical items are accessed, along with their types: noun phrases and verb phrases interpreted, but differently, in terms of their type, and so on. Of the larger units, it seems that only maximal projections are relevant to LF interpretation. Assuming so,[23] bare output conditions make the concepts "minimal and maximal projection" available to C_{HL}. But C_{HL} should be able to access no other projections.

Given the inclusiveness condition, minimal and maximal projections are not identified by any special marking, so they must be determined from the structure in which they appear; I follow Muysken (1982) in taking these to be relational properties of categories, not properties inherent to them. (See section 1.3.2, below (64).) There are no such entities as XP (X^{max}) or X^{min} in the structures formed by C_{HL}, though I continue to use the informal notations for expository purposes, along with X′ (X-bar) for any other category. A category that does not project any further is a maximal projection XP, and one that is not a projection at all is a minimal projection X^{min}; any other is an X′, invisible at the interface and for computation.[24] As we proceed, I will qualify the conclusion somewhat for X^0 categories, which have a very special role.

A further goal is to show that computation keeps to local relations of α to terminal head. All principles of UG should be formulated in these terms—which have to be made precise—and only such relations should be relevant at the interface for the modules that operate there.[25]

Given the numeration N, C_{HL} may select an item from N (reducing its index) or perform some permitted operation on the syntactic objects already formed. As discussed earlier, one such operation is necessary on conceptual grounds alone: an operation that forms larger units out of those already constructed, the operation Merge. Applied to two objects α and β, Merge forms the new object K, eliminating α and β. What is K? K must be constituted somehow from the two items α and β; the only other possibilities are that K is fixed for all pairs (α, β) or that it is randomly selected, neither worth considering. The simplest object constructed from α and β is the set $\{\alpha, \beta\}$, so we take K to involve at least this set, where α and β are the *constituents* of K. Does that suffice? Output conditions dictate otherwise; thus, verbal and nominal elements are interpreted differently at LF and behave differently in the phonological component. K must therefore at least (and we assume at most) be of the form $\{\gamma, \{\alpha, \beta\}\}$, where γ identifies the type to which K belongs, indicating its relevant properties. Call γ the *label* of K.

For the moment, then, the syntactic objects we are considering are of the following types:

(5) a. lexical items
    b. $K = \{\gamma, \{\alpha, \beta\}\}$, where α, β are objects and γ is the label of K

Objects of type (5a) are complexes of features, listed in the lexicon. The recursive step is (5b). Suppose a derivation has reached state $\Sigma = \{\alpha, \beta, \delta_i, \ldots, \delta_n\}$. Then application of an operation that forms K as in (5b) converts Σ to $\Sigma' = \{K, \delta_i, \ldots, \delta_n)$, including K but not α, β. In a convergent derivation, iteration of operations of C_{HL} maps the initial numeration N to a single syntactic object at LF.

We assume further that the label of K is determined derivationally (fixed once and for all as K is formed), rather than being derived representationally at some later stage of the derivation (say, LF). This is, of course, not a logical necessity; Martian could be different. Rather, it is an assumption about how *human* language works, one that fits well with

the general thesis that the computational processes are strictly derivational, guided by output conditions only in that the properties available
for computational purposes are those interpreted at the interface. The
proper question in this case is whether the assumption (along with the
more general perspective) is empirically correct, not whether it is logically necessary; of course it is not.

Suppose that the label for $\{\alpha, \beta\}$ happens to be determined uniquely
for α, β in language L, meaning that only one choice yields an admissible
convergent derivation. We would then want to deduce that fact from
properties of α, β, L—or, if it is true for α, β in language generally, from
properties of the language faculty. Similarly, if the label is uniquely determined for arbitrary α, β, L, or other cases. To the extent that such
unique determination is possible, categories are representable in the
more restricted form $\{\alpha, \beta\}$, with the label uniquely determined. I will
suggest below that labels are uniquely determined for categories formed
by the operation Move α, leaving the question open for Merge, and
indicating labels throughout for clarity of exposition, even if they are
determined.

The label γ must be constructed from the two constituents α and β.
Suppose these are lexical items, each a set of features.[26] Then the
simplest assumption would be that γ is either

(6) a. the intersection of α and β
    b. the union of α and β
    c. one or the other of α, β

The options (6a) and (6b) are immediately excluded: the intersection of
α, β will generally be irrelevant to output conditions, often null; and the
union will be not only irrelevant but "contradictory" if α, β differ in
value for some feature, the normal case. We are left with (6c): the label γ
is either α or β; one or the other *projects* and is the *head* of K. If α
projects, then K $= \{\alpha, \{\alpha, \beta\}\}$.

For expository convenience, we can depict a constructed object of type
(5b) as a more complex configuration involving additional elements such
as nodes, bars, primes, XP, subscripts and other indices, and so on.
Thus, we might represent K $= \{\alpha, \{\alpha, \beta\}\}$ informally as (7) (assuming
no order), where the diagram is constructed from nodes paired with
labels and pairs of such labeled nodes, and labels are distinguished by
subscripts.

(7)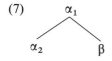

This, however, is informal notation only: empirical evidence would be required to postulate the additional elements that enter into (7) beyond lexical features, and the extra sets. (See note 7.) I know of no such evidence and will therefore keep to the minimalist assumption that phrase structure representation is "bare," excluding anything beyond lexical features and objects constructed from them as in (5) and (6c), with some minor emendations as we move toward a still more principled account.

The terms *complement* and *specifier* can be defined in the usual way, in terms of the syntactic object K. The head-complement relation is the "most local" relation of an XP to a terminal head Y, all other relations within YP being head-specifier (apart from adjunction, to which we turn directly). In principle, there might be a series of specifiers, a possibility with many consequences to which we return. The principles of UG, we assume, crucially involve these local relations.

Further projections satisfy (6c), for the same reasons. Any such category we will refer to as a *projection* of the head from which it ultimately projects, restricting the term *head* to terminal elements drawn from the lexicon, and taking complement and specifier to be relations to a head.

To review notations, we understand a *terminal element* LI to be an item selected from the numeration, with no parts (other than features) relevant to C_{HL}. A category X^{min} is a terminal element, with no categorial parts. We restrict the term *head* to terminal elements. An X^0 (zero-level) category is a head or a category formed by adjunction to the head X, which projects. The head of the projection K is H(K). If H = H(K) and K is maximal, then K = HP. We are also commonly interested in the maximal zero-level projection of the head H (say, the T head of TP with V and perhaps more adjoined). We refer to this object as H^{0max}.

If constituents α, β of K have been formed in the course of computation, one of the two must project—say, α. At the LF interface, maximal K is interpreted as a phrase of the type α (e.g., as a nominal phrase if H(K) is nominal); and it behaves in the same manner in the course of computation. It is natural, then, to take the label of K to be not α itself but rather H(K), a decision that also leads to technical simplification. Assuming so, we take K = {H(K), {α, β}}, where H(K) is the head of α and its label as well, in the cases so far discussed. We will keep to the assumption that the head determines the label, though not always through strict identity.

The operation Merge(α, β) is asymmetric, projecting either α or β, the head of the object that projects becoming the label of the complex formed. If α projects, we can refer to it as the *target* of the operation, borrowing the notion from the theory of movement in the obvious way. There is no such thing as a nonbranching projection. In particular, there is no way to project from a lexical item α a subelement H(α) consisting of the category of α and whatever else enters into further computation, H(α) being the actual "head" and α the lexical element itself; nor can such "partial projections" be constructed from larger elements. We thus dispense with such structures as (8a) with the usual interpretation: *the*, *book* taken to be terminal lexical items and D+, N+ standing for whatever properties of these items are relevant to further computation (perhaps the categorial information D, N; Case; etc.). In place of (8a) we have only (8b).

(8) a.

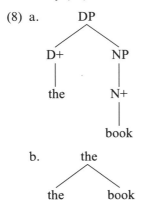

Standard X-bar theory is thus largely eliminated in favor of bare essentials.

Suppose that we have the structure represented informally as (9), with *x*, *y*, *z*, *w* terminals.

(9)

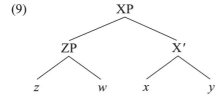

Here ZP = $\{z, \{z, w\}\}$, X′ = $\{x, \{x, y\}\}$, XP = $\{x, \{ZP, X′\}\}$; more accurately, the tree with ZP as root corresponds to $\{z, \{z, w\}\}$, and so on, the labels of the roots having no status, unlike standard phrase markers. Note that w and y are both minimal and maximal; z and x are minimal only.

The functioning elements in (9) are at most the configurations corresponding to (the trees rooted at) the nodes of the informal representation: that is, the lexical terminals z, w, x, y; the intermediate element X′ and its sister ZP; and the root element XP. Represented formally, the corresponding elements are z, w, x, y; $\{x, \{x, y\}\} = P$ and its sister $\{z, \{z, w\}\} = Q$; and the root element $\{x, \{P, Q\}\}$. These alone can be functioning elements; call them the *terms* of XP. More explicitly, for any structure K,

(10) a. K is a term of K.

   b. If L is a term of K, then the members of the members of L are terms of K.

For the case of substitution, terms correspond to nodes of the informal representations, where each node is understood to stand for the subtree of which it is the root.[27]

In (9) x is the head of the construction, y its complement, and ZP its specifier. Thus, (9) could be, say, the structure VP with the head *saw*, the complement *it*, and the specifier *the man* with the label *the*, as in (11).

(11)

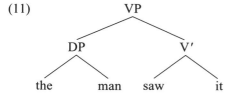

Here V′ = VP = *saw*, and DP = *the*.

Note that this very spare system fails to distinguish unaccusatives from unergatives, a distinction that seems necessary. The simplest solution to the problem would be to adopt the proposal of Hale and Keyser (1993a) that unergatives are transitives; I will assume so.

We assumed earlier that Merge applies at the root only. In the bare system, it is easy to see why this is expected. Suppose that the derivation has reached stage Σ, with objects α and β. Then Merge may eliminate α and β from Σ in favor of the new object $K = \{\gamma, \{\alpha, \beta\}\}$, with label γ. That is the simplest kind of merger. We might ask whether C_{HL} also permits a more complex operation: given α and β, select K within β (or within α; it is immaterial) and construct the new object $\{\gamma, \{\alpha, K\}\}$, which replaces K within β. That would be an application of Merge that embeds α within some construction β already formed. Any such complication (which could be quite serious) would require strong empirical motivation. I know of none, and therefore assume that there is no such operation. Merge always applies in the simplest possible form: at the root.

The situation is different for Move; we will return to this matter.

To complete the minimalist account of phrase structure, we have to answer several questions about adjunction. Let us keep to the simplest (presumably only) case: adjunction of α to β, forming a two-segment category.

That adjunction and substitution both exist is not uncontroversial; thus, Lasnik and Saito (1992) reject the former while Kayne (1993) largely rejects the latter, (virtually) assimilating specifiers and adjuncts (see section 4.8 and Chomsky 1994a). Nevertheless, I will assume here that the distinction is real: that specifiers are distinct in properties from adjuncts, and A- from $\overline{\text{A}}$-positions (a related though not identical distinction).

Substitution forms $L = \{H(K), \{\alpha, K\}\}$, where $H(K)$ is the head (= the label) of the projected element K. But adjunction forms a different object. In this case L is a two-segment category, not a new category. Therefore, there must be an object constructed from K but with a label distinct from its head $H(K)$. One minimal choice is the ordered pair $\langle H(K), H(K)\rangle$. We thus take $L = \{\langle H(K), H(K)\rangle, \{\alpha, K\}\}$. Note that $\langle H(K), H(K)\rangle$, the label of L, is not a term of the structure formed. It is not *identical* to the head of K, as before, though it is constructed from it in a trivial way. Adjunction differs from substitution, then, only in that it forms a two-segment category rather than a new category. Along these lines, the usual properties of segments versus categories, adjuncts versus specifiers, are readily formulated.

Suppose that α adjoins to K and the target K projects. Then the resulting structure is $L = \{\langle H(K), H(K)\rangle, \{\alpha, K\}\}$, which replaces K within the structure Σ containing K: Σ itself, if adjunction is at the root. Recall that it is the *head* that projects; the head either *is* the label or, under adjunction, determines it trivially.

We thus have the outlines of a "bare phrase structure" theory that derives fairly strictly from natural minimalist principles. The bare theory departs from conventional assumptions in several respects: in particular, categories are elementary constructions from properties of lexical items, satisfying the inclusiveness condition; there are no bar levels and no distinction between lexical items and "heads" projected from them (see (8)). A consequence is that an item can be both an X^0 and an XP. Does this cause problems? Are there examples that illustrate this possibility? I see no particular problems, and one case comes to mind as a possible illustration: clitics. Under the DP hypothesis, clitics are Ds. Assume further that a clitic raises from its θ-position and attaches to an inflectional head. In its θ-position, the clitic is an XP; attachment to a head requires that it be an X^0 (on fairly standard assumptions). Furthermore, the movement violates the Head Movement Constraint (HMC),[28] indicating again that it is an XP, raising by XP-adjunction until the final step of X^0-adjunction. Clitics appear to share XP and X^0 properties, as we would expect on minimalist assumptions.

If the reasoning sketched so far is correct, phrase structure theory is essentially "given" on grounds of virtual conceptual necessity in the sense indicated earlier. The structures stipulated in earlier versions are either missing or reformulated in elementary terms satisfying minimalist conditions, with no objects beyond lexical features. Stipulated conventions are derived. Substitution and adjunction are straightforward. At least one goal of the Minimalist Program seems to be within reach: phrase structure theory can be eliminated entirely, it seems, on the basis of the most elementary assumptions. If so, at least this aspect of human language is "perfect" (but see note 22).

4.4 The Operation Move

4.4.1 Movement and Economy
The structure (11) will yield the sentence *the man saw it* when further inflectional elements are added by Merge and the specifier of the VP is

raised (assuming this form of the predicate-internal subject hypothesis). The construction so formed involves the second operation that forms categories: Move (Move α). What is this operation? We have so far assumed that it works like this.

Suppose we have the category Σ with terms K and α. Then we may form Σ' by *raising* α to *target* K. That operation replaces K in Σ by $L = \{\gamma, \{\alpha, K\}\}$. In the optimal theory, nothing else will change in Σ, and γ will be predictable. We take human language to be optimal in the former sense: there are no additional mechanisms to accommodate further changes in Σ. As for predictability of γ, we hope to establish the standard convention that the target projects (within the class of convergent derivations), so that γ is H(K) or $\langle H(K), H(K) \rangle$, depending on whether the operation is substitution or adjunction. The question does not arise for Merge, but it does for Move; we will return to this matter. The only other operation for the moment is Delete (Delete α), which we have assumed to leave the structure unaffected apart from an indication that α is not "visible" at the interface.

The operation Move forms the chain CH = $(\alpha, t(\alpha))$, $t(\alpha)$ the trace of α.[29] Assume further that CH meets several other conditions (C-Command, Last Resort, and others), to be spelled out more carefully as we proceed.

In forming the IP derived from (11), the subject is raised to the root of the category Σ, targeting the projection of I and becoming [Spec, I]. But raising of the object *it* targets an embedded inflectional category K that is a proper substructure of Σ. We have taken this to be covert raising of the object to [Spec, Agr$_o$], for Case and agreement. Prior to this operation we have (in informal notation) the structure (12a) embedded in the larger structure (12b).

(12) a.

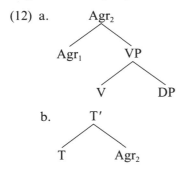

Here T′ is {T, {T, K}}, where K (namely, (12a)) is {Agr, {Agr,VP}}, VP = {V, {V, DP}}.[30] If we target K, merging DP and K and projecting Agr as intended, we form (13), with the raised DP the specifier of AgrP (Agr^{max}).

(13)

Here AgrP is {Agr, {DP, K}} = L, and the term T′ immediately dominating it is {T, {T, L}}, not {T, {T, K}} as it was before Move raised DP.

Under the copy theory of movement (section 3.5), a two-element chain is a pair ⟨α, β⟩, where α = β. Since we distinguish among distinct selections of a single item from the lexicon, we can be sure that such pairs arise only through movement. Suppose, for example, that we have constructed the object (14), β a head, and we derive (15) from it by raising α, targeting and projecting β.

(14)
(15)

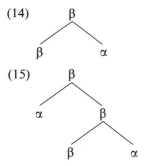

Let K, L be the objects represented informally in (14), (15), respectively. Thus, K = {β, {β, α}} and L = {β, {α, K}}. We are now interested in two of the terms of L, call them τ_1 and τ_2, where τ_1 is the term of L such that L = {β, {τ_1, K}} and τ_2 is the term of L such that K = {β, {β, τ_2}}. Here, $\tau_1 = \tau_2 = α$. We wish to construct the chain CH that will serve as the LF object formed from these two terms of L, which we call α and the trace of α, respectively. The operation that raises α introduces α a second time into the syntactic object that is formed by the operation, the only case in which two terms can be identical. But we want to distinguish the two elements of the chain CH formed by this operation. The natural way to do so is by inspection of the context in which the term appears. Given the way syntactic objects are formed, it suffices to consider the co-constituent (sister) of a term, always distinct for α and its trace. Suppose, then, that α raises to target M in Σ, so that the result of the operation is Σ', formed by replacing M in Σ by $\{N, \{\alpha, M\}\}$, N the label. The element α now appears twice in Σ', in its initial position and in the raised position. We can identify the initial position of α as the pair $\langle \alpha, \beta \rangle$ (β the co-constituent of α in Σ), and the raised position as the pair $\langle \alpha, K \rangle$ (K the co-constituent of the raised term α in Σ'). Actually, β and K would suffice; the pair is simply more perspicuous. Though α and its trace are identical, the two positions are distinct. We can take the chain CH that is the object interpreted at LF to be the pair of positions. In (14) and (15) the position POS_1 of τ_1 is $\langle \alpha, K \rangle$ and the position POS_2 of τ_2 is $\langle \alpha, \beta \rangle$. POS_1 and POS_2 are distinct objects constituting the chain $CH = \langle POS_1, POS_2 \rangle$ formed by the operation; the chain is actually (K, β), if we adopt the more austere version. We refer to CH informally as $(\alpha, t(\alpha))$. I omit a more precise account, the point being clear enough for our purposes.

The c-command relations are determined by the manner of construction of L. Chains are unambiguously determined in this way.

It may, however, be correct to allow a certain ambiguity. Recall the earlier discussion of ellipsis as a special case of "copy intonation," the special intonation found in the bracketed phrase of (16a) (= (324) of chapter 1; see sections 1.5 and 3.5).

(16) a. John said that he was looking for a cat, and so did Bill [say that he was looking for a cat]
     b. John said that he was looking for a cat, and so did Bill

Here (16b) is derived from (16a) by deletion of the bracketed phrase in the phonological component. At some point in the derivation, the bracketed element must be marked as "subject to parallelism interpretation." Assume that this takes place before Spell-Out.[31] The marking could be removal of the distinctions indicated by numeration, in which case the bracketed element is in a certain sense nondistinct from the phrase it "copies" (the latter still marked by the numeration). Such a configuration might be interpreted at PF as assigning copy intonation to the bracketed expression, and at LF as imposing the parallelism interpretations (a complex and intriguing matter, which has only been very partially investigated). Suppose that numeration markings on the copy are changed to those of the first conjunct instead of being deleted. Then the antecedent and its copy are strictly identical and constitute a chain, if a chain is understood as (constructed from) a pair of terms (α_1, α_2) that are identical in constitution. It will follow, then, that the copy deletes, by whatever mechanism deletes traces in the phonological component. At LF the two kinds of constructions will be very similar, though not quite identical. It will then be necessary to demonstrate that legitimate LF objects, in the sense of earlier chapters, can be uniquely identified, with chains that constitute arguments (etc.) properly distinguished from those involved in parallelism structures.

Without pursuing intricacies here, there are strong reasons to suppose that the strict copy (with PF deletion) generally involves the same kind of interpretation at the interface as the nondistinct copy (with copy intonation) but somewhat strengthened, and that the latter falls under far more general conditions that hold for a wide range of other constructions as well and that go far beyond sentence grammar or discourse.

Similar ideas might accommodate the notion of linked chains (in the sense of section 1.4.3) and chains formed by successive-cyclic movement. We will return to these questions.

A chain $CH = (\alpha, t(\alpha))$ formed by Move meets several conditions, which we take to be part of the definition of the operation itself. One of these is the C-Command Condition: α must c-command its trace, so that there cannot be an operation that lowers α or moves it "sideways"; movement is raising, in the specific sense defined by c-command. A second requirement, which seems natural, is that chains meet the uniformity condition (17),[32] where the *phrase structure status* of an element is its (relational) property of being maximal, minimal, or neither.

(17) A chain is uniform with regard to phrase structure status.

A third requirement is that Move must meet the Last Resort condition on movement, which expresses the idea that Move is driven by feature checking, a morphological property. We will return to the proper interpretation of Last Resort and to empirical consequences of the conditions that we take to define Move. Note that if deletion forms chains, as suggested earlier, these may not meet any of the conditions that hold of the operation Move.

It is meaningless to ask whether the conditions that constitute the definition of Move can be "overridden" for convergence, or to ask how economy considerations apply to them. That is true whatever the proper conditions turn out to be. However formulated, these conditions are part of the definition of the algorithm C_{HL}. Violating them would be on a par with making an illegitimate move in a game of chess or adding a line illegitimately to a proof. In such cases further questions about the object being constructed (convergence, economy, shortest game or proof, etc.) do not arise. If the proper conditions are C-Command, uniformity, and Last Resort, then there is no meaningful question about the effects of violating these conditions (or whatever others may be introduced).

The computational system C_{HL} is based on two operations, Merge and Move. We have assumed further that Merge always applies in the simplest possible form: at the root. What about Move? The simplest case again is application at the root: if the derivation has reached the stage Σ, then Move selects α and targets Σ, forming $\{\gamma, \{\alpha, \Sigma\}\}$. But covert movement typically embeds α and therefore takes a more complex form: given Σ, select K within Σ and raise α to target K, forming $\{\gamma, \{\alpha, K\}\}$, which substitutes for K in Σ. The more complex operation is sometimes induced by economy considerations, namely, Procrastinate, which requires that some operations be covert, hence (typically) operations that embed. Furthermore, even overt X^0-adjunction of α to β is within the category β^{max} headed by β, hence not strictly speaking at the root even if β^{max} is the root category.

For overt movement, targeting of an embedded category is obviously not forced by Procrastinate, or by feature strength (see (3)). Overt movement therefore always targets the root, with the minor qualification noted in the case of head adjunction, and is invariably cyclic.

It would be interesting to strengthen this conclusion: that is, to show that overt targeting of an embedded category (hence lowering and non-cyclic raising) is not possible, hence a fortiori not necessary. Arguments to this effect have been proposed (Kawashima and Kitahara 1994, Erich Groat, personal communication), based on two assumptions: (1) that c-command plays a crucial role in determining linear order in accord with Kayne's theory of ordering, to which we will return in section 4.8; (2) that the only relations that exist for C_{HL} are those established by the derivational process itself (Epstein 1994). Specifically, in Epstein's theory, c-command is just the relation that holds between α and elements of β when α is attached to β by Merge or Move. If so, then if α is attached to an embedded category by an operation, α will enter into no c-command relation with any "higher" element β, so no order is established between α and β and the derivation crashes at PF. It follows that overt operations are never of the more complex type that involves an embedded category, hence must be cyclic and must be raising (not lowering) operations. But covert operations might not meet these conditions, the ordering requirement being irrelevant for LF convergence.[33]

There are a number of questions about checking theory that remain open, which we will have to resolve as we proceed. One has to do with checking in structure (18), where F is a functional category with α adjoined.

(18)

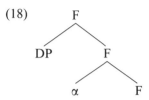

Suppose F is Agr and α is T or V, and we are interested in Case checking. DP is in the checking domain of both α and F. Its Case could therefore be checked either by features of α or by features of F. It is reasonable to suppose that α has the Case-assigning feature as an intrinsic property: either listed in its lexical entry or determined by the entry. It would suffice, then, to consider only the checking domain of α to determine whether the Case of DP has been properly selected (accusative if α is V, nominative if α is T). A more complex alternative is that F and α necessarily share all features relevant to checking, and that DP is checked against F. That would mean that in the numeration, F has the Case-assigning property, which matches that of α. As usual, I will adopt the simpler assumption in the absence of evidence to the contrary. We will see later that the conclusion is also empirically well motivated (also as usual, an interesting fact).

Whether the same conclusion holds for φ-features is a matter of fact, not decision, depending on the answers to a question raised in section 4.2.2: how are φ-features associated with verbs and adjectives? I have tentatively assumed that the assignment is optional, in the transition from lexicon to numeration. If so, then Case and φ-features function alike; they are not properties of the functional category Agr (F, of (18)), and there is no matching relation between F and α. I will continue to assume, then, that the features of T and V that check Case or φ-features of DP appear only in these categories, not in Agr, which lacks such features. The decision is of little relevance until section 4.10.

4.4.2 Projection of Target

Consider again (11), embedded in higher inflectional categories, as in (19) ($I = [Agr_S, T]$).

(19)

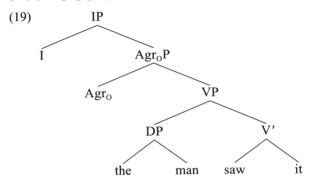

We assume that the DP *the man* then raises overtly, targeting IP, while *it* raises covertly, targeting Agr_OP, each of the raised elements becoming the specifier of the targeted category. As noted, there is another option: the phrase that is raised might itself have projected. If it is internally complex, then it becomes an X′, with the AgrP its specifier; if it is an X^0, then it becomes the head of the new projection, with the AgrP its complement. Thus, if the raised DP projects, the targeted IP becomes the specifier of the D head of *the man*, which is now a D′; and the targeted Agr_OP becomes the complement of *it*, which heads a new DP. After raising and projecting, neither *the man* nor *it* is a DP, as they were before the operation took place. In pre–Minimalist Program work, these obviously unwanted options were excluded by conditions on transformations and stipulated properties of X-bar theory. But we no longer can, or wish to, make recourse to these, so we hope to show that the conventional assumptions are in fact derivable on principled grounds—that it is impossible for Move to raise α, targeting K, then projecting α rather than K.

Note that these questions arise only for Move, not Merge, for which the conclusion is true by definition. Let us begin with substitution, turning to adjunction later.

Recall the guiding assumption: movement of α targeting K is permitted only if the operation is morphologically driven, by the need to check some feature (Last Resort). This idea can be formulated in a number of ways. Consider three interpretations of Last Resort, adapted from the literature.[34]

(20) α can target K only if
   a. a feature of α is checked by the operation
   b. a feature of either α or K is checked by the operation
   c. the operation is a necessary step toward some later operation in which a feature of α will be checked.[35]

There are various unclarities here, which will be resolved as we proceed. Recall that Last Resort, however it is finally interpreted, is to be understood as part of the definition of the operation Move—that is, as an attempt to capture precisely the intuitive idea that movement is driven by morphological checking requirements.

Suppose that α raises to target K, forming $L = \{H(\alpha), \{\alpha, K\}\}$, L a projection of α with label $H(\alpha)$ = head of α. Since the operation is substitution, we have two cases to consider.

(21) a. α is the head of L and K its complement.
     b. K is the specifier of $H(\alpha)$.

Suppose case (21a). The operation is not permitted under versions (20a) or (20b) of Last Resort. No property P can be checked in the head-complement structure that has been formed. The operation might be allowed only under interpretation (20c): raising of α is permitted so as to allow it to reach some position from which it can then raise further to target K', where P will be satisfied. However, any position accessible from the newly formed position of head of $[_L \ \alpha \ K]$ would also have been accessible from the position of its trace; the HMC cannot be overcome in this way, nor can any other condition, it seems. Thus, the case should not arise. Since I will later propose a version of Last Resort that excludes this option on principled grounds, eliminating (20c), I will not pursue the questions any further here.

Projection of *it* after it raises to [Spec, Agr_O] is therefore barred in (19), along with many other cases; thus, it is impossible to raise V, targeting K, V projecting to form $[_{VP} \ V \ K]$ with head V and complement K.

The only possibility, then, is case (21b): after raising, $K = [Spec, H(\alpha)]$. α is therefore nontrivial α^{max} (otherwise, K would be its complement); in the chain $CH = (\alpha, t(\alpha))$ formed by the operation, $t(\alpha)$ is an X^{max}. But α projects after raising, so it is an X' category. This new X' category cannot itself be moved further, being invisible to the computational system C_{HL}; thus, interpretation (20c) is not directly relevant—and in any event, we may put the matter aside, anticipating elimination of this option. Keeping to (20a) and (20b), the question is whether the operation forming

L = {H(α), {α, K}}, with K = [Spec, H(α)] and α heading the chain CH, is legitimate. We hope to show that it is not.

There are two lines of argument that could bar this operation. One approach is to question the legitimacy of the chain CH = (α, $t(\alpha)$) that is formed by the operation. In fact, CH violates the uniformity condition (17), which requires that α and $t(\alpha)$ have the same phrase structure status, since $t(\alpha)$ is maximal and α is not.

Assuming this condition, then, we conclude that nonmaximal α cannot raise by substitution, targeting K, whichever element projects. If K projects, then α is maximal and its trace is not, violating the uniformity condition. If α projects, the uniformity condition is satisfied but K is the complement of α, and the operation is barred under case (21a). The unwanted interpretations of (19) are thus ruled out, by case (21a) for DP = D and by case (21b) for DP $\neq$ D. Similarly, the D head of nontrivial DP cannot raise, targeting XP (say, an AgrP), leaving the residue of the DP behind, whether D or the target projects; and the V head of nontrivial VP cannot raise, targeting K, whether V or K projects.

A different approach to case (21b) considers not the chain CH but the structure L that is formed by projection of the raised element α. In L, the target K = [Spec, H(α)] is in the checking domain of H(α), but α and its constituents are not in the checking domain of H(K) (the head of K). Returning to (19), if *the man* raises, targeting IP, and the raised DP projects, then the elements of IP are in the checking domain of the D head of *the man*, but *the man* is not in the checking domain of the head of IP. We might ask whether a proper checking relation is established in this case.

To answer this question, we have to resolve an ambiguity about checking that has not been sorted out carefully. The intuitive idea is that operations involving Case and agreement are asymmetric. The traditional intuition is that a verb assigns Case to its object, not conversely. That asymmetry is carried over only in part to some of the earlier approaches based on government: a transitive verb assigns Case to the DP it governs, and the head agrees with its specifier for checking of ϕ-features—but nominative Case is assigned in the Spec-head relation. With a uniform interpretation of Case as a Spec-head relation, falling together with agreement, the asymmetry intuition is again expressible, but not captured. The informal description is that the V or T head checks the Case of the DP in Spec, not that the DP checks the head; and the ϕ-features of the head are determined by those of the DP in Spec—the verb agrees with the subject, not the subject with the verb. Similarly, it has been standard to speak of the *wh*-phrase raised to [Spec, C] as being licensed by a Q-feature of the complementizer C, not of the latter being licensed by the raised *wh*-phrase. The intuitive basis for the distinctions is fairly clear. Case is an intrinsic property of a verb or I element, not of the DP that "receives" Case in a certain position; and ϕ-features are properties of the DP, not of the verb or adjective that assumes these features in a Spec-head configuration. The question we now face is whether these intuitions actually play a role in the computational process C_{HL} or whether, like others of ancient vintage (grammatical construction, etc.), they dissolve into taxonomic artifacts.

If the Spec-head relation really is asymmetric in the manner supposed in informal description, then the fact that K is in the checking domain of $H(\alpha)$ in the construction L formed by raising the moved element α would not establish a checking relation, since it is $H(K)$ that must check the features of α, while $H(\alpha)$ cannot check the features of K. If the intuition is not relevant to C_{HL}, then a checking relation is established and the illegitimate construction L is not barred on these grounds.

These two approaches are not logically equivalent, but they overlap for standard cases, forcing the target to project. The redundancy suggests that at least one is incorrect. The approach in terms of uniformity has advantages: it extends to other cases and is conceptually much simpler, and we do not have to introduce a notion of asymmetry expressed ultimately in terms of intrinsic properties of heads—and not in any simple way, as will become even clearer below. There is, so far as I know, no reason to suppose that the property [intrinsic] plays any role in C_{HL}. For these reasons, I will assume the uniformity approach.

Summarizing, there are good reasons why the target, not the raised element, should project under substitution.

In special cases there are other arguments that lead to the same conclusion. Keeping to substitution, suppose that the target K is a constituent of the category $N = \{H(K), \{K, M\}\}$ projected from K. Note that K is an X^0 category; otherwise, it is an X' category, not a visible target. Thus, K is either $H(K)$ or an X^0 projection of $H(K)$ formed by adjoining elements to $H(K)$, with M its complement.

Suppose that α raises, targeting K and projecting to form $L = \{H(\alpha), \{\alpha, K\}\}$. L now replaces the term K in N, forming $N' =$

$\{H(K), \{L, M\}\}$. The head of N' is H(K), the head of L is H(α), and the head of M is H(M), all distinct; the head of N' is distinct from the head of either of its constituents. N' is not a legitimate syntactic object of the sort permitted by the recursive procedure (5). The derivation therefore is canceled.

The argument extends directly to adjunction of α to K, so that the label of L is $\langle H(\alpha), H(\alpha) \rangle$. It is still the case that replacement of the term K in N by L yields an illegitimate syntactic object. This case is of particular interest in the light of the role of X^0-adjunction in computation, which becomes even more central as we proceed.

To summarize, we have the following answers to the question about projection after Move. Suppose that α, K are categories in Σ, and α raises to target K. If the operation is substitution, K must project for convergence, whether K is embedded in Σ (covert raising) or K = Σ (overt raising). Suppose the operation is adjunction to H^0 within N = $\{H, \{H^0, M\}\} = [_{HP} H^0 M]$, with head H and complement M. Again, the target X^0 must project when α adjoins to H^0. Furthermore, adjunction of nonmaximal α to XP (including root Σ) is barred by the uniformity condition.

The only cases still not covered are adjunction of α to K in an adjunction structure N = [K, M], where M is adjoined to nonminimal K or M projects. In such cases either α, K, and M are all nonminimal (XPs), or they are all nonmaximal (X^0s); we will return to details. We will see that YP-adjunction to XP has a dubious status, and this marginal case even more so. We therefore ignore it, restricting attention to N = [K, M] with α, K, and M all X^0s, and M projecting to form L = $\{\langle H(M), H(M) \rangle, \{K, M\}\}$. This case violates plausible morphological conditions. K can adjoin to M only if M has a morphological feature $[-K]$ requiring it to take K as an affix. If $[-K]$ is strong, adjunction of K is overt; otherwise, it is covert. Suppose that α adjoins to K and α projects, forming N = $\{\langle H(\alpha), H(\alpha) \rangle, \{K, \alpha\}\}$. N replaces K in L, forming L'. The category L' is a legitimate syntactic object, in this case, but the feature $[-K]$ of M is not satisfied, since M now has α rather than K as its affix—assuming, now, that K and α differ morphologically in a relevant way. The derivation therefore crashes, for morphological reasons. If so, this case does not exist.

There are, then, fairly solid grounds for assuming that the target of movement projects, whether the operation is substitution or adjunction, overt or covert.

4.4.3   Last Resort: Some Problems

So far we have found no special reason to adopt interpretation (20c) of Last Resort, the version that is most problematic. This was one component of the principle Greed assumed in the preceding chapters and Chomsky 1994a, holding in the form (22).

(22) Move raises α only if morphological properties of α itself would not otherwise be satisfied in the derivation.

On this assumption, we cannot, for example, derive (23b) from (23a) by raising, with the meaning (23c), violating Greed to satisfy the EPP (the strong D-feature of I); and (24a) cannot be interpreted as something like (24b), with covert raising.[36]

(23) a.   seems [(that) John is intelligent]
      b.   *John seems [(that) t is intelligent]
      c.   it seems (that) John is intelligent

(24) a.   *there seem [(that) [$_A$ a lot of people] are intelligent]
      b.   it seems (that) a lot of people are intelligent

Assuming Greed, the unwanted computations are barred; all relevant properties of *John* and *a lot of people* are satisfied without raising.

These computations are, however, legitimate under interpretation (20b) of Last Resort, since a feature of the target K is satisfied by the operation: in (23) the strong D-feature of matrix I (EPP) is checked by raising of the DP *John*; and in (24) covert raising of the associate A satisfies the Case or agreement features of matrix I (or both), or some property of *there*.

Raising of α targeting K is barred by (22) unless some property of α is satisfied by its moving to, or through, this position, and that property would not have been satisfied had this operation not applied. Consistent with Greed, such movement would be permitted if there were no other way for α to reach a position where its features would eventually be satisfied. One can think of circumstances under which this eventuality might arise, though computational problems are not inconsiderable. Instead of pursuing the matter, let us see if there is a simpler way to proceed.

4.4.4   Move F

The proper formulation of Greed poses complicated questions, which, one might suspect, do not arise if the theory of movement is properly formulated. Let us therefore consider a narrower conception that eliminates the whole range of options permitted by interpretation (20c) of Last Resort, thereby avoiding these questions entirely.

So far I have kept to the standard assumption that the operation Move selects α and raises it, targeting K, where α and K are categories constructed from one or more lexical items. But on general minimalist assumptions, that is an unnatural interpretation of the operation. The underlying intuitive idea is that the operation Move is driven by morphological considerations: the requirement that some feature F must be checked. The minimal operation, then, should raise just the feature F: we should restrict α in the operation Move α to lexical features. Let us investigate what happens if we replace the operation Move α by the more principled operation Move F, F a feature.

We now extend the class of syntactic objects available to the computational system. Along with those permitted by the procedure (5), we allow also (25).

(25) $K = \{\gamma, \{\alpha, \beta\}\}$, where α, β are features of syntactic objects already formed.

The extension holds only for Move; it is vacuous for Merge. So far we have considered only one case of the form (25), namely, $K = \{\gamma, \{F, \beta\}\}$, where F is raised to target β. We will see that the extension is even narrower: if α raises to target β, then β must be a full-fledged category and α may (and in a certain deeper sense *must*) be a feature.

One question arises at once: when F is raised to target K, why does F not raise alone to form $\{\gamma, \{F, K\}\}$? Suppose that the subject raises to [Spec, IP]. The simplest assumption would be that only the formal features of the head involved in feature checking raise to this position, leaving the rest of the DP unaffected. Why is this not the case? The answer should lie in a natural economy condition.

(26) F carries along just enough material for convergence.

The operation Move, we now assume, seeks to raise just F. Whatever "extra baggage" is required for convergence involves a kind of "generalized pied-piping." In an optimal theory, nothing more should be said about the matter; bare output conditions should determine just what is carried along, if anything, when F is raised.

For the most part—perhaps completely—it is properties of the phonological component that require such pied-piping. Isolated features and other scattered parts of words may not be subject to its rules, in which case the derivation is canceled; or the derivation might proceed to PF with elements that are "unpronounceable," violating FI. There may be a morphological requirement that features of a single lexical item must be within a single X^0 (see McGinnis 1995). In any event, properties of the phonological component have a major (perhaps the total) effect on determining pied-piping.

To take a concrete example, suppose that the words *who, what* have three components: the *wh*-feature, an abstract element underlying indefinite pronouns, and the feature [±human].[37] Suppose interrogative C (= Q) is strong, as in English. The *wh*-feature cannot overtly raise alone to check Q because the derivation will crash at PF. Therefore, at least the whole word *who, what* will be pied-piped in overt raising. Suppose that *who* appears in the phrase *whose book*, which we assume to have the structure (27), with D the possessive element and *book* its complement.

(27)

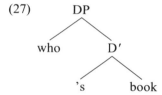

Suppose that Move F seeks to raise the *wh*-feature to check strong Q, pied-piping *who* and leaving the residue *-'s book*. That too crashes at PF (at least). And *whose* cannot raise because it is not a syntactic object at all, hence not subject to movement. Therefore, the smallest category that can be raised by the operation Move [*wh*-] in this case is the phrase *whose book*—though as far as the computational procedure is concerned, it is only the feature [*wh*-] that is raising; the rest is automatically carried along by virtue of the economy condition (26).

PF convergence is determined in this case by a morphological property of the determiner D = Possessive. Suppose that these properties of D did not bar extraction of the *wh*-phrase. Then violation of the Left-Branch Condition should be permitted. Uriagereka (1988) found a correlation between left-branch extraction and "richness" of D, in a sense he characterizes: the Left-Branch Condition holds for languages with D rich. The correlation follows, he observes, if the reasoning outlined here is correct.

Just how broadly considerations of PF convergence might extend is unclear, pending better understanding of morphology and the internal structure of phrases. Note that such considerations could permit raising without pied-piping even overtly, depending on morphological structure, as in the theory of overt raising of empty operators in Japanese developed by Watanabe (1992).

Pied-piping might in principle depend as well on factors that constrain movement: barriers, Empty Category Principle (ECP) considerations, the Minimal Link Condition (MLC) that requires "shortest moves," or whatever turns out to be the right story for this much-studied but still murky area. In the case of all such principles, one open question has been whether violation causes a derivation to crash or allows it to converge as deviant (say, a Subjacency violation vs. an ECP violation). The question could have an answer in the terms now being considered. Thus, if pied-piping is forced by the need to satisfy some principle P, we conclude that violation of P causes the derivation to crash so that it does not bar less economical derivations without pied-piping—for example, the principle P that sometimes bars preposition stranding.

Any further elaboration would be a departure from minimalist assumptions, hence to be adopted only insofar as that is forced on empirical grounds: never, in the best case. A host of problems arise that look difficult. The basic task is to determine how much of a departure (if any) is required from these optimal assumptions to account for "generalized pied-piping"; how PF and LF considerations enter into the picture; what these considerations imply about the structure of phrases and the status and nature of conditions on movement; and how language variation is determined.

As noted by Hisa Kitahara and Howard Lasnik, the proposed economy principle provides a further rationale for the principle Procrastinate: nothing at all is the least that can be carried along for convergence, and that is possible only if raising is covert, not entering the phonological component.

Consider now the case of covert movement. Questions of PF convergence do not arise, so generalized pied-piping could only be required by conditions on movement. Earlier discussion of Move α assumed that the principles that govern the operation hold only for categories, since only categories were assumed to move. If that happens to be true, then these principles hold only of overt movement, which has to carry along whole categories for PF convergence. The conclusion could well be true for other reasons even if the assumption is false. If the conclusion is true (for whatever reason), then covert raising is restricted to feature raising. The operation Move F carries along "excess baggage" only when it is "heard" in the phonetic output. I will assume that to be the case. The assumption accords well with the general minimalist perspective, and it has no obvious empirical flaw.

We tentatively assume, then, that only PF convergence forces anything beyond features to raise. If that turns out to be the case, or to the extent that it does, we have further reason to suspect that language "imperfections" arise from the external requirement that the computational principles must adapt to the sensorimotor apparatus, which is in a certain sense "extraneous" to the core systems of language as revealed in the $N \rightarrow \lambda$ computation.

When the feature F of the lexical item LI raises without pied-piping of LI or any larger category α, as always in covert raising, does it literally raise alone or does it automatically take other formal features along with it? There are strong empirical reasons for assuming that Move F automatically carries along FF(LI), the set of formal features of LI. We therefore understand the operation Move F in accord with (28), where FF[F] is FF(LI), F a feature of the lexical item LI.

(28) Move F "carries along" FF[F].

This much pied-piping is automatic, reflecting the fact that Move relates to checking of formal features. Broader pied-piping is as required for convergence—"extraneous," insofar as PF convergence is the driving factor, which we tentatively assume to mean "always."

Applied to the feature F, the operation Move thus creates at least one and perhaps two "derivative chains" alongside the chain $CH_F = (F, t_F)$ constructed by the operation itself. One is $CH_{FF} = (FF[F], t_{FF[F]})$, consisting of the set of formal features FF[F] and its trace; the other is $CH_{CAT} = (\alpha, t_\alpha)$, α a category carried along by generalized pied-piping and including at least the lexical item LI containing F. CH_{FF} is always constructed, CH_{CAT} only when required for convergence. The computational system C_{HL} is really "looking at" CH_F, but out of the corner of its eye it can "see" the other two as well. Each enters into operations. Thus, CH_{CAT} determines the PF output, and CH_{FF} enters into checking operations in a manner to which we will return. As noted, CH_{CAT} should be completely dispensable, were it not for the need to accommodate to the sensorimotor apparatus.

The empirical questions that arise are varied and complex, and it is easy enough to come up with apparent counterevidence. I will put these problems aside for now, simply assuming the best outcome, namely, that UG settles the matter—hardly an innocuous step, needless to say. I assume, then, that the operation Move raises F and derivatively raises FF[F] as well, carrying along a phrase containing F only when the movement is overt, as required for convergence. The general approach is natural if not virtually obligatory on minimalist grounds, and it confers a number of advantages, as we will see.

Note that we continue to rely on the assumption that only convergent derivations are compared for economy—that the admissible derivations D_A are a subset of the convergent ones D_C. Thus, raising without pied-piping is more "economical" in some natural sense, but that is irrelevant if the derivation does not converge.

We have already considered a special case that resembles the economy principle (26): namely, such operations as *wh*-movement. As discussed in section 3.5, the entire *wh*-phrase need not raise covertly for feature checking and scope determination, and perhaps does not; thus, we found good reason to believe that nothing more than *how many* raises covertly from within the phrase *how many pictures of John*. A natural extension of that analysis is that only the *wh*-feature raises in the covert operation, the rest of the phrase remaining in situ.

The revision of Move α to Move F extends this reasoning to all cases. It also permits a way to capture the essence of Last Resort (to be revised) as a property of the operation Move F.

(29) F is unchecked and enters into a checking relation.

Thus, the variable F in Move F ranges over unchecked features, and the result of the operation is that it enters into a checking relation, either checking a feature of the target or being checked itself.[38]

We are now tentatively assuming that if all features of some category α have been checked, then α is inaccessible to movement, whether it is a head or some projection. But if some feature F is as yet unchecked, α is free to move. Economy conditions exclude "extra" moves and anything more than the minimal pied-piping required for convergence. In covert movement, features raise alone. Procrastinate expresses the preference for the covert option.

This simple and natural reinterpretation of Move α, already motivated for *wh*-movement, allows us to eliminate the complexities of interpretation (20c) of Last Resort entirely, a welcome outcome. We can dispense with (20b) as well: the raised feature F must enter into a checking relation, which is only possible if the target K has an as-yet-unchecked feature. Thus, we have a very narrow and restrictive interpretation of Greed, incorporated straightforwardly into the definition of Move. We will return to further improvements, resolving ambiguities and imprecision and bringing in crucial properties so far overlooked.

In the cases just discussed, the intended consequences follow directly. The first problem was to bar movement of α targeting K, with α rather than K projecting. The argument given before carries over without change. We therefore retain the conclusion that the target projects. Such cases as (23)–(24) also fall into place: though the target is legitimate, having an unchecked feature, the category to be raised is invisible to movement, having no unchecked features (an analysis to be revised below). Raising under ECM is permitted if some feature is checked: the strong feature of the embedded I that yields the EPP, in this case. The principle of Greed seems dispensable, except insofar as it is incorporated within (29).

Consider successive-cyclic *wh*-movement. It is allowed under this approach only where there is a morphological reflex. Sometimes this is visible at PF, as in Irish and Ewe (see Collins 1993); it remains an open question whether such visibility is only an accident of morphology, revealing the workings of a process that is more general, perhaps universal, even if morphological reflexes are not detected in the PF output.

Adjunction to nonminimal XP is now barred unless some feature is thereby checked (see Oka 1993, for development of this possibility); successive-cyclic adjunction is even more problematic. The condition could be restricted to A-movement, or perhaps modified to include satisfaction of the MLC alongside feature checking, though consequences are rather complex. See Collins 1994b for further discussion; we will return to questions about XP-adjunction.

Among the matters still to be clarified is the status of the MLC. The preferred conclusion would be that the MLC is part of the definition of Move: Move F must observe this condition, making the "shortest move" permissible. If that can be established, it will sharply reduce the computational complexity of determining whether a particular operation OP in the course of a derivation is legitimate. In contrast, if the MLC is an economy condition selecting among derivations, OP will be permissible only if no other convergent derivation has shorter links. It is hard to see even how to formulate such a condition, let alone apply it in some computationally feasible way; for example, how do we compare derivations with shorter links in different places? But the question does not arise if violation of the MLC is not a legitimate move in the first place. Following the usual minimalist intuition, let us assume that violation of the MLC is an illegitimate move, exploring the issues as we proceed.

Suppose that F raises, carrying along the rest of a category α, targeting K. By version (29) of Last Resort, the operation is permitted only if it satisfies a checking relation. We therefore have to have an elementary way to determine the features of α and K that enter into this checking relation, no matter how deeply embedded these are in α and K.

For the raised element α, the question does not arise. It is the feature F itself that must enter into the checking relation, by (29); other features of FF[F] may also enter into checking relations as "free riders," carried along in the derivative chain $CH_{FF} = (FF, t_{FF})$ that is automatically constructed, but that is easily detectable, given F. If a checking relation is established by merger of α in the checking domain of β, then the relevant features in the new checking domain are those of the head of α, which are immediately determined by its label.[39] Questions arise, then, only with regard to the category K that is the target of movement, gaining a checking domain (either an adjunct or a specifier) by virtue of the operation.

Suppose that $K = \{\gamma, \{L, M\}\}$ is the target of movement. Then a feature F_K of K may enter into a checking relation if it is within the zero-level projection H^{0max} of the head H of K. H and H^{0max} are constructed trivially from the label γ, which is immediately determined by inspection of K. F_K will be a feature either of H itself, or of some element adjoined to H, and so on; this will be simplified even further in section 4.10. Recall that we are keeping to the optimal assumption that not only H but also features adjoined to it can enter into a checking relation with α in the checking domain (see end of section 4.4.1).

For the target, then, determination of the relevant features is also trivial: these are the features associated with the label, which we may call *sublabels*.

(30) A sublabel of K is a feature of $H(K)^{0max}$.

That is, it is a feature of the zero-level projection of the head H(K) of K. When Move F raises F to target K, some sublabel of K must legitimize the operation by entering into a checking relation with F, and features of

FF[F] may also enter into checking relations with sublabels of K as free riders.

The features that legitimize the operation raising α to target K are therefore determined straightforwardly, however deeply embedded they may be in α and K: for example, the *wh*-feature in *pictures of whose mother did you think were on the mantelpieces*. The computation "looks at" only F and a sublabel of K, though it "sees" more. The elementary procedure for determining the relevant features of the raised element α is another reflection of the strictly derivational approach to computation.

To take a concrete case, suppose that at LF the head of IP is T with the verbal element α adjoined to it, assuming all other functional categories to be irrelevant at this point (we will return to this assumption).

(31)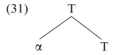

The operation Move F forming (31) raises the categorial feature v of the verb V, carrying FF[v] along automatically in a derivative chain. If the operation is covert, as in English, then nothing else happens: α in (31) is v. If the operation is overt, as in French, then α is V itself, pied-piped to allow convergence at PF. In either case v must enter into a checking relation with the affixal feature $[-v]$ ("takes verbal affix") of T, and any other feature of FF[v] can in principle enter into a checking relation with a feature of T ($= T^{0max}$, before raising, by assumption). The sublabels of IP, so formed, are the features of T and of α.

Similarly, when the Case feature of LI is raised by Move F, so are the ϕ-features of LI, and any of these free riders may also enter into a (derivative) checking relation with a sublabel of the target. For example, raising of DP for Case checking carries along ϕ-features, which may happen to check agreement features of the target. We will return to various consequences.

Bringing these ideas together, we have the following theory of the operation Move. Move raises feature F to target K in Σ only if (32) holds, with (33a) and (33b) as automatic consequences, and (33c) a further consequence (assumed, but not fully established).

(32) a. F is an unchecked feature.
     b. F enters into a checking relation with a sublabel of K as a result of the operation.

(33) a. FF[F] raises along with F.

    b. A category α containing F moves along with F only as required for convergence.

    c. Covert operations are pure feature raising.

Other features of FF[F] may check a sublabel of K as free riders. (32a) and (32b) incorporate Last Resort.

Let us turn now to several issues that come to the fore when we formulate movement theory as Move F.

The recursive step in the definition (5) of admissible objects permitted the construction of $L = \{\gamma, \{\alpha, \beta\}\}$, where α, β are syntactic objects and γ is the label of L. In earlier discussion we kept to the case where α, β are lexical items or larger phrases constructed from them, but we have now been considering a more general case, with the variables allowed to range over features as well. Specifically, we allow an object $L = \{\gamma, \{F, K\}\}$, F a feature, formed by raising F to target K without pied-piping of a category α. Several questions arise, including the following:

(34) a. Can the operation be substitution?

    b. Must the target project?

    c. Can K be a feature rather than a category?

The answers depend on how we interpret such notions as "X^{max}" and "head," which so far have been defined only for phrases constructed from lexical items, not for features. But these notions have no clear sense for features. Suppose, then, that the definitions given earlier carry over without change. If so, the questions of (34) are settled.

Suppose the feature F is raised, targeting K and forming $\{\gamma, \{F, K\}\}$.

The answer to question (34a) is negative. F cannot become a complement for reasons already discussed. It must therefore be a specifier of K, hence an X^{max} by definition. The statement is meaningless if the notions X^{max} (etc.) are not defined for X a feature. If they were defined, then F would be a new kind of X^{max} and the chain formed would violate the uniformity condition (17), under any natural interpretation. In either case, then, the operation must be adjunction of F to K. Move F can be substitution only in overt movement, with a category pied-piped for convergence.

As for question (34b), the target must project; γ cannot be (or be constructed from) the head of F if the notion "head of F" is not defined. Question (34c) is also answered: K cannot be a feature; if it is, the object constructed will have no label.

On plausible assumptions, the class of permissible objects is extended only very slightly by extending (5) to (25), permitting the variables α, β to range over features in the recursive step of the characterization of syntactic objects $K = \{\gamma, \{\alpha, \beta\}\}$. In fact, the only new objects allowed are those formed by covert adjunction of features to a head—which amounts to saying that a formal property of a lexical item can covertly enter the checking domain of a category, the question of PF convergence being irrelevant.[40] Furthermore, we see that the target always projects in this case, as desired.

From a more fundamental point of view, the class of permissible objects is radically limited by these revisions. The only "real" syntactic objects are lexical items and $L = \{\gamma, \{F, K\}\}$, F a feature, K a projecting category, and γ constructed from H(K). This view captures rather closely the concept of movement (transformations) toward which work in generative grammar has been converging for many years: "last resort" operations driven by morphological requirements, which vary within a narrow range, yielding crucial typological differences. Other objects are formed only as required for convergence—perhaps only PF convergence, illustrating again the "extraneous" character of the link to sensorimotor systems.

Suppose that the target K is nonminimal. A reasonable conjecture is that the object formed, with a feature adjoined to a pure (nonminimal) maximal projection, would be uninterpretable at LF; independently, we will see that there are empirical reasons to suppose that an element adjoined to nonminimal K is not in the checking domain of its head H(K), so that the operation would be barred by Last Resort. Assuming this, we conclude that pure feature raising—hence all covert raising—is adjunction of a feature to a head, which projects. The only new objects $L = \{\gamma, \{F, K\}\}$ allowed are those constructed by adjoining the feature F to the head K, which projects, so that γ gives the "type" of K.

We have already found that in the case of category movement, the target always projects. The conclusion is now general, covering all cases of movement, with questions remaining only for YP-adjunction to XP.

The picture is very simple and straightforward, and the arguments follow on assumptions that seem conceptually natural and in accord with the Minimalist Program. If it is close to accurate, then human language is surprisingly close to "perfect," in the sense described. Whether the conclusions are empirically correct is another question, hardly a trivial one.

4.4.5 Covert Raising

The shift of perspective just outlined has broader consequences. In the case of *wh*-movement, if the operator feature [wh-] is unchecked, it raises to an appropriate position, covertly if possible (by Procrastinate) and thus without pied-piping. If raising is overt, then pied-piping will be determined (we hope) by PF convergence and morphological properties of the language. Similarly, if the grammatical object Obj raises for checking of Case or some other formal feature, then the features FF[F] of its head raise derivatively, and the operation carries along a full category only if the movement is overt. If raising is overt, then Obj becomes [Spec, Agr$_O$]. If it is covert, then the features FF[F] raise alone, adjoining to Agr$_O$, which has V (or its relevant features) already adjoined to it.[41]

The same should hold for raising of subject Subj. Its unchecked features are eligible for raising. The operation is substitution with pied-piping if overt (say, to satisfy the EPP), and it is adjunction to the appropriate head without pied-piping if covert (perhaps in VSO languages).

Subj and Obj should function in much the same way at LF whether they have raised overtly as full categories or covertly as features. In either case the raised element contains at least FF(LI), LI the head of Subj or Obj. FF(LI) includes the categorial feature of the nominal phrase and should have argument (A-position) properties, including the ability to serve as a controller or binder. In their reanalysis and extension of observations of Postal (1974), Lasnik and Saito (1991) argue that this is true for object raising: Obj raised covertly to [Spec, Agr$_O$] for Case checking has basically the same properties as an overt object in this regard, as illustrated for example in (35), with judgments somewhat idealized.

(35) a. the DA [proved [the defendants to be guilty] during each other's trials]

   b. *the DA [proved [that the defendants were guilty] during each other's trials]

   c. the DA [accused the defendants during each other's trials]

For the conclusions to carry over to the Move F theory, it must be that the features adjoined to Agr$_O$ also have A-position properties, c-commanding and binding in the standard way. There is every reason to assume this to be true.

Consider such expletive constructions as (36a–b).[42]

(36) a. there is a [book missing from the shelf]

   b. there seem [*t* to be some books on the table]

Agreement is with the associate of the expletive (namely, *book-books*), which in our terms requires that the φ-features of the associate raise to the checking domain of matrix I. But the operation is covert. Therefore, it is not the associate that raises but its unchecked features, leaving the rest in situ. The natural assumption, once again, is that these features adjoin to I, not to its specifier *there*.[43]

Interpretations of (37) would therefore be roughly as in the paired cases (38)—though only roughly, because on this analysis, only formal features of the associate raise, leaving its semantic features behind.

(37) a. there is considerable interest (in his work)
     b. there aren't many pictures (on the wall)
     c. there are pictures of many presidents (on the wall)

(38) a. interest is considerable (in his work)
     b. pictures aren't many (on the wall)
     c. pictures are of many presidents (on the wall)

Similarly in other cases. The general conclusions about expletive constructions follow. Specifically, the associate must have unchecked features in order to be accessible for raising, so that we account for such standard examples as (24a) (see also note 36); we will return to some other locality effects. The HMC is largely inoperative, however it is understood to apply to feature movement.[44]

It also follows that the expletive *there* cannot have checked all the features of I; if it had, I would not be a legitimate target for the associate. Plainly, *there* checks the strong feature of I (EPP); otherwise, expletive constructions such as (37) would not exist in the first place. But *there* must lack Case or φ-features, or both; otherwise, all features of I will be checked and the associate will not raise. There will be no way to express agreement of matrix verb and associate; (39a) will have the same status as (39b).

(39) a. *there seem to be a man in the room
     b.   there seems to be a man in the room

Covert raising to Agr$_S$ places the features of the associate in a structural position with the essential formal properties of [Spec, Agr$_S$]. We therefore expect the associate to have the binding and control properties of the overt subject, analogously to the case of covert object raising to Agr$_O$ (see (35)). The issues take a somewhat sharper form in a null subject language. Here we expect that the counterparts to such expressions as (40) should be admissible, contrasting with (41).

(40) a. there arrived three men (last night) without identifying
         themselves
     b. there arrived with their own books three men from England

(41) a. *I met three men (last night) without identifying themselves
     b. *I found with their own books three men from England

That appears to be correct. Thus, we find the following contrasts between Italian (42a–b) and French (42c–d):[45]

(42) a. sono entrati tre   uomini senza   identificarsi
         are entered three   men   without identifying themselves
         'three men entered without identifying themselves'
     b. ne   sono entrati tre   t senza dire una parola
         of. them are entered three   without saying anything
         'of-them three entered without saying anything'
     c. *il   est entré   trois hommes sans   s'annoncer
         there is entered three men   without identifying
         themselves
     d. *il   en   est entré   trois t sans   s'annoncer
         there of. them is   entered three   without identifying
         themselves

In Italian, with null subject expletive sharing the relevant properties of
English *there*, LF raising to I of Subj (actually, its formal features) assigns A-position properties to Subj for binding and control, including
the case of *ne*-extraction that makes it clear that Subj is overtly in the
internal domain of the verb ("object position," basically). In French,
with the full NP expletive *il* analogous to English *it*, the LF operation is
barred, all features of the matrix I-phrase, the potential target, having
already been checked by the expletive. Accordingly, there is no covert
raising, hence no binding or control.
  Consider the German analogue (43).

(43) es   sind gestern   viele Leute angekommen, ohne
     there are yesterday many people arrived   without
     sich   zu identifizieren
     themselves to identify
     'many people arrived yesterday without identifying themselves'

Here agreement is with the associate, not the expletive, and the binding
and control properties are as in (42), as predicted.[46]

Agreement with the associate, then, appears to correlate with matrix-subject binding and control properties for the associate, as expected on the minimalist assumption that Case and agreement are local Spec-head relations and that features raise under Last Resort, covertly if possible. We will return to a closer look at the factors involved.

Note that the entire discussion relies on the assumption that Case and ϕ-features of a noun N are part of its internal constitution, either intrinsic to it or added optionally as N is selected from the lexicon for the numeration. Therefore, these features form part of FF[N] and function within the "package" of formal features that drive computation, raising as a unit. We have seen that the conclusion is motivated on independent grounds; it is confirmed by the central role it plays within the computational system, which will be further confirmed as we proceed. Abandonment of the conclusion (say, by taking Case or ϕ-features of N to be separate lexical categories with their own positions in phrase markers) would cause no slight complication.

Though core predictions appear to be verified, many questions arise. One immediate problem is that the raised associate *cannot* be a binder in such expressions as (44), where *t* is the trace of *there* (see Lasnik and Saito 1991).

(44) *there seem to each other [*t* to have been many linguists given good job offers]

We know that this is an expletive-associate construction with associate agreement, as shown by replacing of *each other* with *us*. That leaves us with an apparent direct contradiction: the associate both can and cannot bind.

The solution to the paradox might lie within binding theory. Suppose that an LF movement approach of the kind mentioned in chapter 3, and developed in detail elsewhere in the literature, proves correct. Then the head of the matrix clause of (44), at LF, would have the structure (45a) or (45b), depending on how covert operations are ordered, where An is the anaphor and α is the X^0 complex formed from I and the matrix V.

(45) a. $[_I$ An [FF(*linguists*) α]]
     b. $[_I$ FF(*linguists*) [An α]]

On reasonable assumptions, neither of these structures qualifies as a legitimate binding-theoretic configuration, with An taking FF(*linguists*) as its antecedent. No such problem would arise in the examples (40) and (42), or in such standard examples as (46).

(46) they seemed to each other [t to have been angry]

   These phenomena provide further evidence that the features of the associate raise to I rather than adjoining to the expletive, over and above the fact that this operation is the normal one while adjunction from the associate position to the expletive would be without any analogue. If adjunction were in fact to the expletive, then there might be no relevant difference between (44) and (46). The phenomena also provide additional evidence for an LF movement analysis of anaphora.

   Overt raising of Subj and Obj to Spec yields an A-chain. What about the covert analogue? Is the position of the adjoined features of Subj and Obj also an A-position? It is not clear that it matters how (or if) the question is decided; though A- and $\overline{\text{A}}$-positions differ in the usual properties, it is not clear that they have more than a taxonomic role in the Minimalist Program. But suppose that an answer is required. Then we conclude that covert adjunction of features of Subj and Obj establishes an A-chain: the concept "A-position" should cover the position occupied by the formal features of Subj and Obj both before and after the adjunction operation. We have taken A-positions to be those narrowly L-related to a head H. Adapting the terminology of section 1.3.2, let us add all sublabels of H^{max} to the positions narrowly L-related to H, including H itself, features of H, and any feature adjoined to H.[47]

   These conclusions appear to accord with binding and control properties of covertly raised object and subject, on standard assumptions. It also follows that relativized minimality effects (in Rizzi's (1990) sense) should be those of A-chains, though that may well follow from independent considerations.

4.5   Interpretability and Its Consequences

We have now reached the point where distinctions among the various kinds of formal features of FF(LI) are becoming important. Let us take a closer look at these, continuing to assume that F automatically carries along FF[F] and, if overt, a full category α as required for convergence (perhaps just PF convergence).

4.5.1 Types of Features

Along with others, the following distinctions among features are worth noting:

(47) a. categorial features
 b. φ-features
 c. Case features
 d. strong F, where F is categorial

As discussed earlier, there are further distinctions that cross-cut those of (47): some features are intrinsic, either listed in the lexical item LI or determined by listed features; others are optional, added arbitrarily as LI enters the numeration.

Suppose we have a convergent derivation for (48).

(48) we build airplanes

Intrinsic features of the three lexical items include the categorial features, [1 person] in FF(*we*), [3 person] and [−human] in FF(*airplanes*), [assign accusative Case] in FF(*build*), and [assign nominative Case] in FF(T). Optional features include [plural] for the nouns and the φ-features of *build*.

As already discussed, these distinctions enter into informal descriptive usage. The distinctions also correlate more or less with other facts. Thus, the φ-features of a DP specifier commonly show up both on the DP and on the verbal head, but the Case feature of DP does not appear on the head. There is at least a tendency for φ-features to be overtly manifested when raising to the checking domain is overt rather than covert, as in verbal agreement with subject versus object in nominative-accusative languages with the EPP, or visible participial agreement in French as a reflex of overt raising. In the Move F theory, the difference reduces to [Spec, H] versus [$_H$ F H] constructions, φ-features tending to be overt on H in the former but not the latter. Let us tentatively assume this to be the case, though a principled explanation is lacking, and the empirical facts plainly require much closer scrutiny over a far broader range.

The intrinsic-optional distinction plays virtually no role here, but there is a much more important distinction that has so far been overlooked. Evidently, certain features of FF(LI) enter into interpretation at LF while others are uninterpretable and must be eliminated for convergence. We therefore have a crucial distinction ±interpretable. Among the Interpretable features are categorial features and the φ-features of nominals.[48]

The operations that interpret (48) at the LF interface will have to know that *build* is a V and *airplanes* an N with the φ-features [plural], [−human], [3 person]. On the other hand, these operations have no way to interpret the Case of *airplane* or the agreement features of *build*, which must therefore be eliminated for LF convergence.

Interpretability at LF relates only loosely to the intrinsic-optional distinction. Thus, the optional feature [±plural] of nouns is Interpretable, hence not eliminated at LF. The Case features of V and T are intrinsic but −Interpretable, hence eliminated at LF (assuming that they are distinguished from the semantic properties that they closely reflect). It follows that these features of the head must be checked, or the derivation crashes. The Interpretable features, then, are categorial features generally and φ-features of nouns.[49] Others are −Interpretable.

Interpretability does relate closely to the formal asymmetry of the checking relation, which holds between a feature F of the checking domain of the target K and a sublabel F′ of K. F′ is always −Interpretable: strength of a feature, affixal features, the Case-assigning feature of T and V, φ-features of verb and adjective. The target has Interpretable features, such as its categorial features, but these never enter into checking relations. F in the checking domain, however, can be an Interpretable feature, including categorial and φ-features. These differences between checker (within the target) and checked (within the checking domain) play a certain role in computation. They give some meaning to the intuitive asymmetry, though with only weak correlation to informal usage, as the notion "agreement" shows.

These descriptive observations raise two obvious questions: (1) Why is a sublabel F′ of the target that enters a checking relation invariably −Interpretable? (2) Being −Interpretable, why is F′ present at all? Question (2) is part of a more fundamental one: why does language have the operation Move? If it does, and if the operation is morphology-driven as we assume, then there must be feature checkers in the targeted category. The fact that these are always −Interpretable again highlights the special role of the property of displacement of categories that is characteristic of human language: the sole function of these feature checkers is to force movement, sometimes overtly. These questions begin to fall into place as we look more closely at the theory of movement.

Case differs from φ-features in that it is always −Interpretable, for both terms of the checking relation. Case is therefore the formal feature par excellence, and it is not surprising that this entire line of inquiry has its origins in Vergnaud's Case Filter.

4.5.2 Checking Theory

Interpretability at LF is determined by bare output conditions and is clearly an important property of features. Attending to it, we see at once that the notion of checking so far proposed is defective in fundamental ways, and the same is true of earlier versions. These were unclear about the status of a checked feature, but did not differentiate among the cases. We see, however, that there are crucial differences depending on Interpretability. In earlier sections here, we took checking to be deletion. A checked feature, then, is accessible to the computational system, but not visible for interpretation at LF. But that cannot be correct. Some features remain visible at LF even after they are checked: for example, φ-features of nouns, which are interpreted. And some plainly are not accessible to the computational system when checked: the Case feature of nouns, for example, which cannot be accessed after checking.

We therefore have to give a more nuanced analysis of the relation between visibility at LF and accessibility to the computational system. The two properties are related by the descriptive generalization (49).

(49) a. Features visible at LF are accessible to the computation C_{HL} throughout, whether checked or not.

    b. Features invisible at LF are inaccessible to C_{HL} once checked.

Case (49a) holds without exception; (49b) only in part, in an interesting way.

The valid part of the generalization follows at once from a slight modification of the theory of checking, actually an improvement that was needed anyway. The checking operation taken over from earlier work has a number of odd features. For one thing, it seems redundant: the relevant properties are determinable by algorithm from the LF representation itself. But we now see that the proposal is untenable. Is there a way, then, to dispense with the checking operation entirely?

Suppose that we do so, keeping just to the relation from which the operation is derived: the checking relation that holds between features of the checking domain and of the target (features that are readily detected, as we have seen). We have so far assumed that the operation Move F is defined in terms of the conditions in (32), repeated here.

(50) a. F is an unchecked feature.

b. F enters into a checking relation with a sublabel of K as a result
of the operation.

The point of (50a) was to prevent a nominal phrase that has already
satisfied the Case Filter from raising further to do so again in a higher
position. The conclusion is correct, but the formulation of the principle
must be revised to yield the condition (49). We now have the means to
do so quite straightforwardly.

The key to the problem is the hitherto neglected property $\pm$ Interpretable. This property is determined by bare output conditions, hence
available "free of charge." We can therefore make use of it to restate
(50), without cost. As throughout, we restrict attention to formal features in this inquiry into the computational system. To begin with, let us
simplify (50) by eliminating (a) entirely, allowing the variable F in Move
F to range over formal features freely. We then replace (50b) by (51), the
final version here of Last Resort.

(51) *Last Resort*

Move F raises F to target K only if F enters into a checking
relation with a sublabel of K.

But we still have to capture the intended effects of (50a): crucially, that a
[−Interpretable] feature is "frozen in place" when it is checked, Case
being the prototype.

Continuing to understand "deleted" as "invisible at LF but accessible
to the computation," we now reformulated the operations of checking
and deletion as in (52).

(52) a. A checked feature is deleted when possible.

b. Deleted α is erased when possible.

Erasure is a "stronger form" of deletion, eliminating the element entirely
so that it is inaccessible to any operation, not just to interpretability at
LF.[50]

"Possibility" in (52) is to be understood relative to other principles.
Thus, deletion is "impossible" if it violates principles of UG. Specifically, a checked feature cannot be deleted if that operation would
contradict the overriding principle of recoverability of deletion, which
should hold in some fashion for any reasonable system: Interpretable
features cannot delete even if checked. The question of erasure, then,
arises only for a −Interpretable feature F, which is erased by (52b)

unless that operation is barred by some property P of F. P should be readily detected, to avoid excessive computational complexity. One such property is parametric variation: F could be marked as not erased when deleted, a possibility that will be explored below in connection with multiple-Spec constructions. Tentatively, let us assume that this is the only relevant property of F.

Erasure is also barred if it creates an illegitimate object, so that no derivation is generated. That too is trivially determined. The crucial case has to do with erasure of an entire term α of a syntactic object Σ. Let $N = \{\gamma, \{\alpha, \beta\}\}$. Erasure of α replaces N by $N' = \{\gamma, \{\beta\}\}$, which is not a legitimate syntactic object (see (24)). We conclude that

(53) A term of Σ cannot erase.

Erasure of a full category cancels the derivation. In the parallelism cases discussed earlier, for example, deletion is not followed by erasure in the $N \to \lambda$ computation, under (52); what happens in the phonological component, which has a wholly different character, is a separate matter. But illegitimate objects are not formed by erasure *within* some term (see note 12). Hence, such erasure is not barred for this reason.

We have now dispensed with the checking operation. The problems about interpretability skirted in earlier discussion dissolve, and the descriptive generalization (49) follows at once insofar as it is valid. Case (49a) is true without exception: Interpretable features cannot be deleted (a fortiori, erased) and therefore remain accessible to the computation and visible at LF. Case (49b) holds unless erasure of the −Interpretable checked feature erases a term or is barred by a parametrized property *P* of the feature. Though examples exist, they are few; thus, case (49b) holds quite generally. For expository purposes, I will speak of deletion as erasure except when the issue arises.

The revision of checking theory is without effect for −Interpretable features in the checking domain, such as Case of an argument. It is these features that must be inaccessible after checking; the examples discussed are typical in this regard. Erasure of such features never creates an illegitimate object, so checking is deletion and is followed by erasure without exception. Features of the target are always −Interpretable, for reasons yet to be explained. The revised checking theory deletes them without exception, and typically erases them. One might ask what happens when all features of FF(LI) are −Interpretable and it raises to the checking domain of K: raising of the associate of an expletive or covert object agreement, for example. Not all of FF(LI) could erase; if it did, an illegitimate object would be formed. But we need not solve the problem, because it does not arise. FF(LI) always contains Interpretable features: the categorial and φ-features of the argument.

The only exception to the conclusions of the last paragraph is pure expletives, to which we will return.

To illustrate the consequences, let us return to sentence (48), *we build airplanes*. When the subject *we* is introduced into the derivation within the verb phrase, FF(*we*) includes D and specific choices of φ-features and Case. Since I has a strong D-feature (EPP), the categorial feature of *we* raises overtly to its checking domain, pied-piping the entire DP; therefore, the operation is substitution in [Spec, I]. There are two ways in which *we* could have raised in this case, depending on how F is selected for the Move F operation. If F = D, then a checking relation is established between the raised categorial feature of *we* and the strong D-feature of I. The Case feature of *we* is checked by T as a free rider, as are the φ-features, after covert raising of the verb establishes the required checking relation. F could also be Case, which would mean that the EPP is satisfied by the categorial feature as a free rider. But F could not be a φ-feature in this case, because the verb raises only covertly so that the checking relation between φ-features is only established later; Last Resort (51) would be violated if φ-features of *we* were accessed in overt raising. The Case feature of *we* is −Interpretable, therefore erased when checked. The φ-features, however, are Interpretable, hence accessible to further operations, as is the categorial feature D.

Note that the EPP is divorced from Case. Thus, we assume that all values of T induce the EPP in English, including infinitives, though only control infinitives assign (null) Case; raising infinitives do not (see section 1.4.3).

We can now return to a question that was left open: why are the features of the target that enter into checking relations invariably −Interpretable? Suppose that a sublabel F′ of the target category K is Interpretable. Suppose the feature F that is accessed by the operation OP and raised to the checking domain of F′ is Interpretable, entering into a checking relation with F′. Both features are Interpretable, hence unchanged by the operation. The operation OP is "locally superfluous," not required by the features that enter into the checking relation that drives it. But OP might nonetheless contribute to convergence. For example, a free rider of FF[F] might enter into a checking relation with another sublabel of the target, one or the other being affected (erased or deleted); or OP might be a necessary step toward a later operation that does delete and perhaps erase — Interpretable features, allowing convergence. Such possibilities abound, considerably extending the class of possible derivations and thus making it harder to compute economy, perhaps also allowing derivations too freely (as might not be easy to determine). Preferably, OP should be excluded. It is, if F′ is necessarily — Interpretable, hence always affected by the operation. If F raises to target K, then, the sublabel that is checked by F deletes and typically erases.

This property of feature checkers eliminates the possibility of "locally superfluous" movement operations. It reinforces the minimalist character of the computational system, permitting its operations to be formulated in a very elementary way without proliferation of unwanted derivations. To put it differently, the "imperfection" of language induced by the displacement property is restricted by language design so as to avoid excessive computational complexity.

Consider successive-cyclic raising as in (54).

(54) we are likely [t_3 to be asked [t_2 to [t_1 build airplanes]]]

Overt raising of *we* from t_1 to t_2 accesses D to satisfy the EPP in the most deeply embedded clause, the only possibility since the raising infinitival does not assign Case. D is Interpretable, therefore unaffected by checking. It is accessed again to raise *we* to t_3, satisfying the EPP in the medial clause. Further raising from t_3 to the matrix subject can access any of the features that enter into a checking relation there.

Consider a different case of successive-cyclic raising, the simple adjectival construction (55).

(55) John is [$_{AgrP}$ t_2 Agr [$_{AP}$ t_1 intelligent]]

John raises from the predicate-internal subject position t_1 to [Spec, Agr] (t_2) for agreement with the adjective, raised to Agr.[51] By virtue of Last Resort (51), the operation must access the φ-features of *John*, which check agreement. They are Interpretable, therefore unaffected. *John* then raises to matrix subject position, satisfying the EPP, Case, and agreement. Here any of the relevant features may be accessed, since all enter into checking relations (one accessed, the others as free riders). *John* thus enters into double agreement: with each of the two Agr nodes, hence with the copula and the adjective. What shows up at PF depends on morphological particulars.[52]

The example illustrates the fact that agreement can be assigned with or without Case—in the higher and lower [Spec, Agr] positions, respectively. Since the categorial and φ-features of DP remain accessible after checking while the Case feature does not, a single DP can enter into multiple satisfaction of the EPP and multiple agreement, but not multiple Case relations. The latter option is the core example that we want to exclude under Last Resort, and its ancestors back to Vergnaud's Case Filter. But the other two definitely should be permitted, as they now are.

In (55) all features of the subject have been checked and the −Interpretable ones erased. Suppose that (55) is embedded, as in (56).

(56) I(nfl) seems [that John is intelligent]]

Though the Case feature of *John* has been erased, its categorial and φ-features are unchanged. Therefore, *John* can raise to matrix subject ([Spec, I]), satisfying the EPP and matrix agreement and yielding (23b), repeated here.

(57) *John [I(nfl) seems [that *t* is intelligent]]

But *John* offers no Case feature to be checked, so the derivation crashes rather than converging with the interpretation 'it seems that John is intelligent'. In (56) *John* is effectively "frozen in place," as in the examples that originally motivated Greed (see note 36), though not for the reasons given in earlier theories. These reasons were defective in a fundamental way, failing to take account of the property ±Interpretable and its relation to accessibility to the computational system.

We conclude that the intrinsic Case feature of T is dissociated not only from its (parametrically varying) EPP feature, but also from the (perhaps invariant) semantic properties it reflects. Being −Interpretable, the Case feature must be checked for the derivation to converge. Since it is not checked in (57), the derivation crashes.

Suppose that matrix I in (56) is [−tense]. If the structure is a control infinitive, the derivation crashes again, for Case reasons. If it is a raising infinitival, the construction is barred as it stands, presumably for selectional reasons: a nonembedded infinitival can be a control structure with arbitrary PRO (in some languages and constructions), but not a raising infinitival with no relevant properties other than the strong D-feature (EPP). Further embedding in raising structures reintroduces the same problem, so that *John* remains "frozen in place" in (56) with infinitival I as well.[53]

Suppose that a language were to allow the construction (56), but with only agreement checked in the embedded clause, not Case. Then raising should be possible. The categorial and φ-features of *John* are Interpretable, hence accessible even when checked; and the Case feature is unchecked, hence still available for checking. Raising *John* to matrix subject, we derive (57), again with double agreement and double satisfaction of the EPP, but with only one Case relation: in the matrix clause. Such constructions have been reported in a number of languages, first (in this context) in modern Greek (Ingria 1981). Assuming the descriptions to be correct, they are (and have been regarded as) prima facie violations of the Case Filter. They fall into place in the manner just described. We expect the matrix subject in (57) to have the Case required in this position, which could in principle be distinct from nominative: in an ECM construction, for example. If that is so, it confirms the conclusion that Case was not assigned in the lower clause, which would have caused Case conflict.[54]

Successive-cyclic movement raises further questions, to which we will return after the groundwork has been laid.

One consequence of this reanalysis of the theory of movement is that Interpretable features need not enter checking relations, since they survive to LF in any event. In particular, categorial and φ-features of NP need not be checked. The conclusion resolves an outstanding problem concerning inherent Case: it has never been clear how the φ-features of the nominal receiving inherent Case can be checked, in the absence of any plausible functional category; but the question does not arise if they need not be checked. The same consideration overcomes the problem of checking of φ-features in dislocation or coordination, as in *John and his friends are here*.[55]

Consider α incorporated into β (say, a noun incorporated into a verb), so that α has the morphological feature [affix] that allows the operation. If this feature is −Interpretable, excorporation of α will be impossible because the feature will have been erased and will thus be unavailable for further checking; α will be unable to adjoin to a second head, even though its other properties are intact.

The improved theory of movement has consequences for multiple-Spec constructions, which are permitted in principle on minimalist assumptions about phrase structure theory, as noted earlier. If this option is realized, we have the structure (58), with possible further proliferation of Spec.

(58)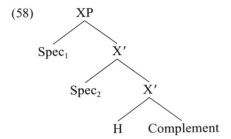

Here we may tentatively assume $Spec_1$ and $Spec_2$ to be equidistant targets for movement, being within the same minimal domain.[56]

Suppose a language permits (58) for some construction. Suppose further that a −Interpretable feature F of H is not necessarily erased when checked and deleted, a parameterized property. F can then check each Spec, optionally erasing at some point to ensure convergence. If F is a Case feature, it could assign the same Case repeatedly; such an account has been proposed for multiple Case checking in Japanese and other languages (see note 56). Watanabe's (1993a) layered Case theory as restated in note 49 could also be formulated in these terms. In section 4.10 we will see that similar ideas have interesting consequences in areas of more central concern here.

$Spec_1$ also allows an escape hatch for Relativized Minimality violations and scrambling with A-position properties (binding, obviating weak crossover effects, etc.), unlike scrambling to an $\overline{A}$-position, which, under earlier assumptions, involves full reconstruction; the idea was introduced by Reinhart (1981) to account for *Wh*-Island violations in Hebrew. Ura (1994) holds that superraising, A-scrambling, and multiple Case assignment correlate in many languages. If so, that would lend further empirical support to the conclusion that (58) is an option that a language may have.[57]

4.5.3 Expletives

Suppose that a derivation has reached the construction (56) and the numeration contains an expletive, so that we can derive, for example, (24a), repeated here.[58]

(59) *there seem [that [$_{Subj}$ a lot of people] are intelligent]

The expletive *there* checks the strong feature of I (EPP), but it fails to check some feature of H = [I, *seem*] that is −Interpretable and must be erased for convergence. The −Interpretable features of H are its Case and φ-features. Once again, we see that the expletive must lack Case or φ-features, or both (see discussion of (39)).

Suppose that *there* has Case, so that only the φ-features of H remain unchecked. But the φ-features of Subj are Interpretable, so Subj (actually, the formal features of its head) can raise covertly, checking the φ-features of H and allowing the derivation to converge—incorrectly, with an interpretation similar to 'it seems that a lot of people are intelligent'. It follows that *there* must lack Case.

Suppose that the expletive has φ-features. Suppose that these do not match the features of its associate, as in (39a), repeated here, with *there* plural and its associate *a man* singular, and the raising verb plural, matching *there*.

(60) *there seem to be [a man] in the room

The φ-features of *seem* are erased in the Spec-head relation with *there*. The φ-features of *there*, being −Interpretable for an expletive, are also erased under this checking relation. The Case feature of *seem* is erased by raising of the associate *a man*. Since the φ-features of *a man* are Interpretable, they need not be checked. The derivation of (60) therefore converges, incorrectly.

We conclude, then, that the expletive has neither Case nor φ-features. FF(*there*) contains only D, which suffices to satisfy the EPP: the expletive has no formal features apart from its category.

Notice that agreement is overtly manifested on the verb that has *there* as subject. Earlier we considered the suggestion that overt manifestation of φ-features is a reflection of the [Spec, H] rather than [$_H$ F H] relation. The observation about agreement with expletives is consistent with this proposal, but it would conflict with the alternative idea that the distinction reflects overt rather than covert agreement. The two suggestions are empirically distinct in this case, perhaps only this case.

Suppose that *there* is a pure expletive lacking semantic features as well as formal features apart from its category D. We therefore expect it to be invisible at LF, to satisfy FI. We know that *there* cannot be literally erased when checked; that would violate the fundamental condition (53), forming an illegitimate syntactic object that would cancel the derivation. By the general principle of deletion-erasure, (52), it follows that the categorial feature of *there* is only deleted when checked, not erased, along with those of its traces (see note 12).

Since the expletive necessarily lacks Case, it must be the associate that provides the Case in ordinary expletive constructions such as (61a–c).

(61) a. there is a book on the shelf
     b. there arrived yesterday a visitor from England
     c. I expected [there to be a book on the shelf]

The associate must therefore have the Case that would be borne by DP in the constructions (62a–c), respectively.

(62) a. DP is ...   (DP = nominative)
     b. DP arrived ...   (DP = nominative)
     c. I expected [DP to be ...]   (DP = accusative)

We therefore cannot accept the partitive Case theory of Belletti (1988), contrary to the assumption in chapter 2.

There is a distinction between expletives that have Case and φ-features and the "pure expletives" that lack these features: in English, *it* and *there*, respectively. The distinction is neither clear nor sharp, but it is adequate for our limited purposes.[59] The former satisfy all properties of the I-V head they check, erasing the relevant features, and therefore bar associate raising. The latter do not erase the −Interpretable features of the I-V head. Therefore, raising is permitted, targeting this element; and it is required for convergence.

Two consequences follow. The direct prediction is that expletive constructions will manifest verbal agreement with the associate just in case the expletive lacks Case and φ-features: English *there*, German *es*, and Italian *pro*—but not English *it* and French *il*, which have a full complement of features. Note that the distinction is only partially related to overt manifestation.[60] A more interesting prediction, and one that will be more difficult to confirm if true, is that just in case the expletive lacks Case and φ-features, the associate will bind and control as if it were in the surface subject position. We have seen some reason to believe that this is true.

We might ask why languages should have overt expletives lacking Case and φ-features rather than *pro*. In part, the reason may reduce to the null subject parameter, but more seems to be involved. Thus, Icelandic and German both have null expletives, but Icelandic is a null subject language and German is not. In these languages the lexical entry for the expletive specifies two forms, null and overt. Their distribution seems to be complementary, determined by structural factors. The optimal result would be that the overt variant is used only when this is required for convergence: PF convergence, since the two forms are identical within the covert component. That could be true if the presence of the overt expletive reduces to the V-second property, which could belong to the phonological component if there is no ordering in the core $N \rightarrow \lambda$ computation, as we have assumed. That seems promising. In both languages it seems that the overt expletive is used only where the V-second property otherwise holds. If that turns out to be correct, then the expletive may well be null—nothing beyond the categorial feature [D]—throughout the $N \rightarrow \lambda$ computation. The overt features are then added only in the course of the phonological operations, though coded in the lexicon.[61]

Though a serious development of the theory of expletives requires much more careful examination, including a far broader range of cases, some conclusions follow even from fairly weak considerations, as we have already seen and will continue to find as we proceed.

4.5.4 Clause Type

Let us turn to the formal features of the functional category C (complementizer) that determines clause type,[62] for example, the feature Q for interrogative clauses in the construction (63).

(63) Q [$_{IP}$ John gave DP to Mary]

Q is plainly Interpretable; therefore, like the ϕ-features of a nominal, it need not be checked—unless it is strong, in which case it must be checked before Spell-Out if a derivation is to be constructed.[63] As is well known, languages differ in strength of Q. The strong Q feature is satisfied by a feature F_Q.

For English, Q is strong. Therefore, when Q is introduced into the derivation, its strong feature must be eliminated by insertion of F_Q in its checking domain before Q is embedded in any distinct configuration (see (3)). F_Q may enter the checking domain by Merge or Move, by substitution or adjunction.

Consider the Merge option. Since it is overt, a full category α must be inserted in the checking domain of Q. If the operation is substitution, α becomes [Spec, Q]; if adjunction, α is an X^0 category. In English the two cases are illustrated by (64).

(64) a. (I wonder) [$_{CP}$ whether Q [he left yet]]
      b. (I wonder) [$_{CP}$ [$_Q$ if Q] [he left yet]]

F_Q is often called the *wh*-feature, which we can take to be a variant of D.

Notice that a checking relation can be established by Merge, though the notions have so far been discussed only for Move. We will return to the question after improving the theory of movement.

Let us turn to the second and more intricate possibility: F_Q enters the checking domain of Q by raising. Again, the options are substitution or adjunction. The substitution option is realized by raising of F_Q to [Spec, Q] by overt *wh*-movement, which pied-pipes a full category for PF convergence. The adjunction option is realized by I → Q raising. If this is in fact raising of a verbal feature, as proposed earlier (see (1)), then F_Q in this case is [V]. There are generalizations and language-specific properties,[64] but any account that departs from minimalist assumptions can be considered explanatory only insofar as it has independent justification.

Under raising, (63) yields two legitimate outputs, (65a) and (65b), depending on whether the strong feature of Q is checked by adjunction or substitution (we abstract from the contrast between embedded and root forms).

(65) a. did [$_{IP}$ John give a book to Mary]
     b. (guess) which book [$_{IP}$ John gave to Mary]
     c. (guess) which x, x a book, John gave x to Mary

In (65a) DP of (63) is *a book, did* adjoins to Q, and the construction is interpreted as a yes-or-no question. In (65b) DP of (63) is *which book*, and the construction is interpreted as something like (65c), along the lines sketched in section 3.5.

F_Q is Interpretable and hence need not be checked. It therefore raises to the checking domain of Q only if this option is selected to eliminate the strong feature of Q, in which case an entire *wh*-phrase or I-complex is pied-piped, substituted in [Spec, Q] or adjoined to Q, respectively.

Suppose that DP is *which book* and the strong feature of Q in (63) is satisfied by adjunction of I alone, as in (65a), so that what surfaces is (66).

(66) did John give which book to Mary

Covert raising of the *wh*-feature is unnecessary and hence impossible, by economy conditions (see note 64). The interpretation of (66) is not (65c), as it would be if the *wh*-feature raised covertly to adjoin to Q. (66) converges, with whatever interpretation it has—perhaps gibberish (I put aside interpretations with focus and echo questions, irrelevant here).

Suppose (63) is embedded and DP = *which book*. The I → Q option is now unavailable (alternatively, it is available, and yields an embedded yes-or-no question, interpreted as gibberish). The *wh*-phrase, however, may raise overtly to the embedded [Spec, Q], yielding (67), with (65b) embedded.

(67) they remember [which book Q [John gave *t* to Mary]]

Suppose that the matrix clause is also interrogative, with the complementizer Q′. Again, there are two ways to check its strong feature, I-raising or *wh*-movement, yielding either (68a) or (68b) (again abstracting from the root-embedded distinction).

(68) a. do they remember which book John gave to Mary
      b. (guess) which book [they remember [*t*′ Q [John gave *t* to Mary]]]

The second option is available, because the *wh*-feature is Interpretable in (67), hence accessible to the computation.

(68a) is unproblematic: it is a yes-or-no question with an embedded indirect question. (68b) converges with the interpretation (69).

(69) (guess) which *x*, *x* a book, they remember [Q John gave *x* to Mary]

Here the embedded clause is interpreted as a yes-or-no question, presumably gibberish, but in any event different from the interpretation of (70), which results if embedded Q is replaced by declarative C (perhaps mildly deviant because of the factive character of the embedded clause).

(70) (guess) which book they remember that John gave to Mary

Whether the operation that forms (70) is successive cyclic depends on the answer to a question raised earlier (see p. 267). Interpretations fall out as they do, depending on the nature of the complementizer.

Suppose that a language has weak Q. In that case the structure (63) will reach PF without essential change. If DP = *which book*, it will remain in situ at PF, (and also at LF, apart from covert raising for Case). The *wh*-feature does not adjoin to Q; both are Interpretable and need not be checked for convergence. If the language has only the interpretive options of English, it will have no intelligible *wh*-questions and presumably no evidence for a *wh*-feature at all. But languages commonly have *wh*- in situ with the interpretation of (65c). They must, then, employ an alternative interpretive strategy for the construction Q[... *wh*- ...], interpreting it, perhaps, as something like unselective binding.

On different grounds, Reinhart (1993) proposes a similar analysis. The same basic conclusions are reached by Tsai (1994), in a study of typologically diverse languages that carries further the effort to use morphological properties to account for some of the problems opened to investigation by Huang (1982). The essence of this theory seems to be a fairly direct consequence of minimalist assumptions, strictly pursued.[65]

In discussing the operation Merge in section 4.2.1, we came to the conclusion that it must be overt, with a single exception: covert insertion of an item α lacking phonological features, necessarily at the root. We can restrict attention to α a complementizer C. The option left open is that phonologically null C may be inserted covertly at the root. C could in principle be strong, in which case it triggers an immediate operation to erase the strength feature. Since the triggered operation is covert, it cannot be substitution in [Spec, C], but must be feature adjunction to C. Do such cases exist?

Consider first declarative C, which is weak. Can its null variant be inserted covertly in a root clause? There is good reason to believe that it can. Declarative C is one of the force indicators and therefore must be present for interpretation at the C-I interface. But it never appears overtly: at the root we have (71a), not (71b) (understood as a declarative assertion).

(71) a. John left
     b. *that John left

The natural conclusion is that C is indeed introduced, but covertly. Furthermore, covert insertion is necessary on grounds of economy, if we assume that Procrastinate holds of Merge as well as Move.[66]

Discourse properties confirm these conclusions. We do indeed find such root clauses as (71b) or (72) with overt complementizer, but not with declarative forces.

(72) that John leave

Thus, (71b) and (72) could be the answers to the questions (73a) and (73b), respectively, but not (73c), which calls for a declarative assertion.

(73) a. what did he tell you
     b. what would you prefer
     c. what happened yesterday

Consider interrogative C, say, English Q, which we still take to be strong. Suppose it is inserted covertly, at the root, to yield (74).

(74) Q [DP$_{Subj}$ will see DP$_{Obj}$]

We can rule out the possibility that this is the variant of Q satisfied by F$_Q$ = [V], yielding a yes-or-no question with I → Q raising in the overt case. That variant has phonological properties that determine rising intonation; if it is inserted covertly, the derivation will therefore crash at LF. The only possibility, then, is that Q requires interpretation as a *wh*-question, which has no phonological properties, leaving intonation unchanged.

We might ask why the variant of Q satisfied by adjunction of F$_Q$ = [V] does not have a null alternant, like declarative C. There could be structural reasons: perhaps some barrier against a null element with an affixal feature (Agr is an exception, but the problem will be overcome in section 4.10; *if*-adjunction to Q is a more serious counterexample). There are also functional motivations. Thus, if there were a null alternant for Q with strong V-feature, the sentence *John will see Bill* would be ambiguously interpreted as declarative or interrogative.

We restrict attention, then, to covert introduction of Q, still assuming it to be strong in English. Covert substitution is impossible, so the strong feature has to be satisfied by adjunction: the strong feature of Q must be checked by F$_Q$ = [wh-].

The structure must therefore contain a *wh*-phrase with a *wh*-feature that adjoins covertly to Q. The *wh*-phrase might be the subject, the object, or an adjunct, as in (75), an IP lacking C at the point of Spell-Out but interpreted as a *wh*-question at LF (declarative intonation throughout).

(75) a. Q [$_{IP}$ who will fix the car]
     b. Q [$_{IP}$ John will fix what]
     c. Q [$_{IP}$ John will fix the car how (why)]

For (75a), the conclusion accords reasonably well with the facts, which have always been puzzling: why should a construction that seems to have all the overt syntactic properties of IP be interpreted as a *wh*-question?

Case (75b) yields the interpretation 'what will John fix'. That is allowed in some languages (French), but is dubious at best in English. Case (75c) should be interpreted as 'how (why) will John fix the car'. That is excluded generally. The main results follow if we assume that strong features cannot be inserted covertly, so that some variant of the in-situ strategy has to be employed (possible for (75a) and (75b), blocked for (75c), which allows no variable formation in the *wh*-phrase; see note 65).

Let us assume, then, that covert insertion of strong features is indeed barred. One might suspect that the possibility is excluded because of paucity of evidence. To put it differently, the interface representations (π, λ) are virtually identical whether the operation takes place or not. The PF representations are in fact identical, and the LF ones differ only trivially in form, and not at all in interpretation. Suppose there is an economy principle (76).

(76) α enters the numeration only if it has an effect on output.

With regard to the PF level, *effect* can be defined in terms of literal identity: two outputs are the same if they are identical in phonetic form, and α is selected only if it changes the phonetic form. At the LF level the condition is perhaps slightly weaker, allowing a narrow and readily computable form of logical equivalence to be interpreted as identity.[67] Under (76), the reference set is still determined by the numeration, but output conditions enter into determination of the numeration itself; they affect the operation that constructs the numeration from the lexicon.

Covert insertion of complementizer has an LF effect and therefore is not barred by (76). The status of strength is somewhat different. Insofar as its presence is motivated only by PF manifestation, it cannot be inserted covertly, under (76), or it would not have been in the numeration at all. There is a good deal more to say about these questions. We will return to some of their aspects in a broader framework in section 4.10.

With regard to covert insertion of lexical elements, we are fairly close to what seem to be the basic facts, on only minimalist assumptions and with some apparent language variation that seems rather peripheral, though a good deal remains to be explained.

4.5.5 The Minimal Link Condition

Suppose that *whom* replaces *Mary* in (67), yielding (77).

(77) they remember [which book Q [John gave *t* to whom]]

Suppose that (77) is interrogative, with the complementizer Q′. If it is a root construction, the strong feature of Q′ can be eliminated by adjunction of I to Q′ or substitution of a *wh*-phrase in [Spec, Q′]; if it is embedded, as in (78), only the latter option is available.

(78) guess [Q′ they remember [which book Q [John gave *t* to whom]]]

Embedded or not, there are two *wh*-phrases that are candidates for raising to [Spec, Q'] to check the strong feature: *which book* and *(to-)whom*, yielding (79a) and (79b).

(79) a. (guess) [which book Q' [they remember [*t'* Q [to give *t* to whom]]]]
    b. (guess) [[to whom]$_2$ Q' [they remember [[which book]$_1$ Q [to give *t*$_1$ *t*$_2$]]]]

(79b) is a *Wh*-Island violation. It is barred straightforwardly by the natural condition that shorter moves are preferred to longer ones—in this case, by raising of *which book* to yield (79a). This operation is permissible, since the *wh*-feature of *which book* is Interpretable, hence accessible, and the raising operation places it in a checking relation with Q', erasing the strong feature of Q'. The option of forming (79a) bars the "longer move" required to form (79b). But (79a), though convergent, is deviant, as in the case of (69).

Let us interpret the Minimal Link Condition (MLC) as requiring that at a given stage of a derivation, a longer link from α to K cannot be formed if there is a shorter legitimate link from β to K. In these terms, the $\overline{A}$-movement cases of relativized minimality can be accommodated (to a first approximation; we will return to further comment). It is not that the island violation is deviant; rather, there is no such derivation, and the actual form derived by the MLC is deviant.

What about the A-movement cases (superraising)? Suppose we have constructed (80).

(80) seems [$_{IP}$ that it was told John [$_{CP}$ that IP]]

Raising of *John* to matrix subject position is a Relativized Minimality (ECP) violation, but it is barred by the "shorter move" option that raises *it* to this position. Raising of *it* is a legitimate operation: though its Case feature has been erased in IP, its D-feature and ϕ-features, though checked, remain accessible.

There are differences between the A- and $\overline{A}$-movement cases that have to be dealt with, but these aside, both kinds of Relativized Minimality violation fall together naturally under the MLC.[68]

Closer analysis of formal features thus allows us to resurrect an idea about island violations that has been in the air for some years: they involve a longer-than-necessary move and thus fall under an approach that has sometimes been suggested to account for superiority phenomena.[69]

The idea ran into two problems. Suppose a derivation had reached the "intermediate stage" Σ of (78) and (80), with an intermediate category (*which book*, *it*) closer to the intended target than the one we hope to prevent from raising. The first problem is that the intermediate category has its features checked, so it should be frozen in place. The second problem has to do with the range of permissible operations at stage Σ: there are so many of these that it is hard to see why raising of the intermediate category is the "shortest move." That problem was in fact more general: thus, it was far from clear why raising of *John* to [Spec, I] in (81) is the "shortest move."[70]

(81) I(nfl) was told John (that IP)

Both problems are now overcome, the first by attention to interpretability of features, the second by a radical narrowing of the class of permissible operations under (51) (Last Resort).

Let us turn now to the differences between the $\overline{\text{A}}$- and A-movement violations (*Wh*-Island, superraising). In the former case, the derivation satisfying the MLC converges; in the latter, it does not. Raising of embedded *it* to matrix subject satisfies the EPP and the φ-features of [I, *seem*], but not the Case feature. But matrix T has a −Interpretable Case feature, which, unless checked and erased, causes the derivation to crash.[71] In the case of A-movement, unlike $\overline{\text{A}}$-movement, the "shortest move" does not yield a convergent derivation.

For the account of the superraising violation to go through, we must take the MLC to be part of the definition of Move, hence inviolable, not an economy condition that chooses among convergent derivations: "shortest moves" are the only ones there are. As noted earlier, that has always been the preferred interpretation of the MLC for purely conceptual reasons, and perhaps the only coherent interpretation (see p. 268). We are now in a position to adopt it, having eliminated many possible operations that would appear to undermine the condition.

We therefore add to the definition of Move the condition (82), expressing the MLC, where *close* is (tentatively) defined in terms of c-command and equidistance, as discussed in chapter 3.

(82) α can raise to target K only if there is no legitimate operation Move β targeting K, where β is closer to K.

A "legitimate operation" is one satisfying (51).

Before proceeding, let us review the status of the superraising violation (80) in the light of economy considerations. Suppose that the derivation D with the initial numeration N has reached stage Σ. The reference set within which relative economy is evaluated is determined by (N, Σ): it is the set $R(N, \Sigma)$ of convergent extensions of the derivation $N \rightarrow \Sigma$, using what remains of N. At Σ, the operation OP is blocked if OP' yields a more economical derivation in $R(N, \Sigma)$.

Considerations of economy arise at stage Σ of the derivation only if there is a convergent extension. But in the case of (80), there is none. The problem is not with the initial numeration N: there is a convergent derivation that takes a different path from N, leading to (83), with *it* inserted in matrix subject position.

(83) it seems [that John was told *t* [that IP]]

Superraising from (80) is not barred by economy considerations that reject the outcome in favor of (83), because (80) is not a stage on the way to a convergent derivation at all. Unless the shortest-move requirement is part of the definition of Move, there will be a convergent derivation from (80), namely, the one that involves superraising. But things work out as desired if the MLC is part of the definition of Move, as preferred for other reasons.[72]

As is well known, the superraising violation is far more severe than the *Wh*-Island violation involving arguments, and there are many related problems that have been the topic of much investigation.[73] The conclusions here shed no further light on them.

4.5.6 Attract/Move
The formulation of the MLC is more natural if we reinterpret the operation of movement as "attraction": instead of thinking of α as raising to target K, let us think of K as attracting the closest appropriate α.[74] We define *Attract F* in terms of the condition (84), incorporating the MLC and Last Resort (understood as (51)).

(84) K *attracts* F if F is the closest feature that can enter into a
      checking relation with a sublabel of K.

If K attracts F, then α merges with K and enters its checking domain, where α is the minimal element including FF[F] that allows convergence: FF[F] alone if the operation is covert. The operation forms the chain (α, t).

For expository purposes, I will sometimes use the familiar terminology of the theory of movement (*target*, *raise*, etc.), though assuming that the correct interpretation is in terms of attraction, referring to the operation generally as Attract/Move.

The notion "equidistance" defined in chapter 3 carries over to Attract F without essential change, though we can simplify it and generalize it to crucial cases not considered there. Let us consider the matter step by step, beginning with the earlier notion.

In chapter 3 we considered several instances of the structure (85) (= (11) of chapter 3, modified as required in the present framework), t the trace of Y, which is adjoined to X to form [Y–X].

(85)

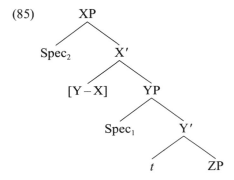

$Spec_1$ and $Spec_2$ are both in the minimal domain of the chain CH = (Y, t) and are therefore *equidistant* from α = ZP or within ZP. Move can therefore raise α to target either $Spec_1$ or $Spec_2$, which are equally close to α. Reformulating the notion of equidistance in terms of Attract, we say that $Spec_1$, being in the same minimal domain as $Spec_2$, does not prevent the category X' (= {X, {X, YP}}) from attracting α to $Spec_2$.

But note that (85) is only a special case: another possibility is that α attaches to the higher target X', skipping $Spec_1$, not by substitution as in (85) but by adjunction, either adjunction to X' or head adjunction to [Y–X]. The case did not arise in chapter 3, but it does now, particularly with regard to feature raising (hence all covert movement). We want to extend the notion of closeness to include this possibility.

Let us review the basic notions of domain and minimal domain of α defined earlier (section 3.2), as a prelude to what will be a considerable simplification. The notions were defined for heads (either alone, or heading chains). We now extend them to features as well. Recall that we have modified them slightly; see note 47.

Suppose α is a feature or an X^0 category, and CH is the chain (α, t) or (the trivial chain) α. Then

(86) a. Max(α) is the smallest maximal projection including α.
  b. The *domain* δ(CH) of CH is the set of categories included in Max(α) that are distinct from and do not contain α or t.
  c. The *minimal domain* Min(δ(CH)) of CH is the smallest subset K of δ(CH) such that for any γ ∈ δ(CH), some β ∈ K reflexively dominates γ.

Recall that *domain* and *minimal domain* are understood derivationally, not representationally. They are defined "once and for all" for each CH: at the point of lexical insertion for CH = α, and when CH is formed by movement for nontrivial CH.

The domain δ(α) and the minimal domain Min(δ(α)) of α are as defined for CH = α, t now being irrelevant.

Turning to "closeness," we are concerned with the maximal projection HP headed by H with γ adjoined to form H^{0max} (the zero-level projection of H), γ heading the chain CH = (γ, t).

(87) β is *closer to* HP than α if β c-commands α and is not in the minimal domain of CH.

γ may be an X^0 category or a feature.

In effect, the minimal domain of CH determines a "neighborhood of H" that can be ignored when we ask whether a feature F is attracted by HP; β within the neighborhood of H is not closer to HP than α. Note that the neighborhood is determined only by γ that is an immediate constituent of H^{0max}, not by a more deeply embedded sublabel; this is necessary, or virtually all categories will be equidistant with I at LF after V-raising. This issue will dissolve later on, so it need not be analyzed further.

The definition incorporates equidistance in the former sense and straightforwardly extends it to the case of adjunction. We will see in section 4.10 that the notions "closeness" and "equidistance" can be further simplified. Unclarities remain about a zero-level projection of H with more than one γ adjoined. I will leave the problems unsettled for the moment; they will be reduced considerably as we proceed.

In the light of this more principled approach to the theory of movement, let us return to the phenomenon of successive cyclicity, that is, raising of the head α of a chain CH = (α, t) to form a new chain CH' = (α, t'). A number of problems arise if this is a permissible process.

Suppose that α is an argument that raises successive-cyclically to form (54), repeated here.

(88) we are likely [t_3 to be asked [t_2 to [t_1 build airplanes]]]

Here the traces are identical in constitution to *we*, but the four identical elements are distinct terms, positionally distinguished (see discussion of (14) and (15)). Some technical questions remain open. Thus, when we raise α (with co-constituent β) to target K, forming the chain CH $=$ (α, t), and then raise α again to target L, forming the chain CH' $=$ (α, t'), do we take t' to be the trace in the position of t or α of CH? In the more precise version, do we take CH' to be $(\langle \alpha, L \rangle, \langle \alpha, K \rangle)$ or $(\langle \alpha, L \rangle, \langle \alpha, \beta \rangle)$? Suppose the latter, which is natural, particularly if successive-cyclic raising is necessary in order to remove all $-$Interpretable features of α (so that the trace in the initial position will then have all such features deleted). We therefore assume that in (88), the element α in t_1 raises to position t_2 to form the chain CH_1 of (89), then raises again to form CH_2, then again to form CH_3.

(89) a. $\text{CH}_1 = (t_2, t_1)$
     b. $\text{CH}_2 = (t_3, t_1)$
     c. $\text{CH}_3 = (we, t_1)$

In more precise terms, t_1 of (89a) is $\langle we, [build\ airplanes] \rangle$ and t_2 is $\langle we, [to\ [we\ build\ airplanes]] \rangle$ (or simply the co-constituents themselves); and so on.

But a problem arises: only CH_3 is a legitimate LF object, with the $-$Interpretable Case feature eliminated from t_1. The other two chains violate the Chain Condition, so the derivation should crash.

The problem has been recognized for years, along with others concerning successive-cyclic movement to A-positions, in which medial links might be expected to have properties of adjunct movement (see section 3.2). Various proposals have been put forth. It was suggested in chapter 1 that the chains formed by successive-cyclic movement become a single "linked chain." In chapter 3 we assumed that a single Form Chain operation yields a multimembered chain; but that proposal does not fit easily into the current framework, and the motivation has largely disappeared with the revision of the theory of movement to incorporate the MLC.

In the present framework, the natural proposal is to eliminate the chains CH_1 and CH_2, leaving only the well-formed chain CH_3. That result would be achieved if the traces formed by raising of the head of a chain are invisible at LF. Why might that be the case?

In the phonological component, traces delete. We have found no reason to extend that convention to the $N \rightarrow \lambda$ computation, and indeed cannot; were we to do so, θ-positions would be invisible at LF and argument chains would violate the Chain Condition (analogous considerations hold for other chains). But we can extend the convention partially, stipulating that raising of α heading the chain $CH = (\alpha, t)$ deletes the trace formed by this operation—that is, marks it invisible at LF. Suppose we do so. At LF, then, all that is "seen" is the chain CH_3, which satisfies the Chain Condition.

Can the deleted traces erase under the deletion-erasure principle (52)? We know that they cannot fully erase: they are terms, and terms cannot erase (see (53)). But the intermediate deleted traces do not enter into interpretation. Therefore, the economy condition (52b), which erases deleted formal features where possible, allows erasure of formal features of the intermediate traces if something remains. The phonological features do not remain; they have been stripped away by Spell-Out. But in the case of an argument, semantic features remain. These are not subject to the operations of checking theory (including (52)), which are restricted to formal features. Therefore, a formal feature F of an intermediate trace of an argument may erase, and indeed must erase if possible. We therefore conclude that formal features of the intermediate trace of A-movement erase. We can now informally think of the set of chains so produced as a single "linked chain," along the lines of chapter 1, with "defective" intermediate traces.

Filling in the details of this outline, we have a theory of successive-cyclic movement that fits into the broader framework. Intermediate traces are invisible at LF; the only chain subjected to interpretation is the pair (α, t), α in the highest position of raising and t in the position of lexical insertion—which for convenience I will continue to call the *base position*, borrowing the term from EST. In an argument chain, formal features of intermediate traces are erased.[75] We derive the property (90).

(90) The intermediate trace t of an argument cannot be attracted; hence, t does not prevent attraction of an element that it c-commands.

The argument extends to traces of A-movement generally. Thus, the head α of such a chain can freely raise, but the properties of the trace t left by the operation will depend on the feature composition of α.

If α has semantic features, all formal features of *t* erase; if α is a pure expletive, its sole formal feature [D] remains, though it is deleted (invisible at LF).

Language design must therefore be such that the trace of a raised expletive can never be attracted improperly or bar attraction required for convergence. That is indeed the case. The only relevant construction would be (91), in which an expletive has raised, leaving a trace.

(91) there seem [*t* to be some books on the table]

The Case and φ-features of *book* must raise to matrix I, though *t* is closer to this position. The problem is overcome if *t* lacks relevant features, that is, features that can enter into a checking relation with matrix I. If so, matrix I attracts the features of the associate *book*, as required. But we already know that the trace of the expletive lacks such features. Its only formal feature is its category [D], which is irrelevant, the EPP having already been satisfied by the expletive itself. This is, furthermore, the only kind of construction in which the problem of attracting expletive trace could arise. We therefore conclude that the trace of an expletive does not enter into the operation Attract/Move; it is immobile and cannot bar raising. Once again, strict observance of minimalist assumptions yields the correct array of facts, without redundancy or other imperfection.

We have restricted attention to intermediate traces of argument chains. But the notion "intermediate trace" is imprecise. Further questions arise when the head of an argument chain is raised to an $\overline{\text{A}}$-position, as in (92).

(92) a. what did John see *t*
      b. what [*t* was seen *t'*]
      c. (guess) what there is *t* in the room

In all cases the trace *t* (= *what*) heads an argument A-chain and is raised further by *wh*-movement. In (92a,c) features of *t* (which could head a nontrivial argument chain, as in (92b)) must still be accessible for Case checking and associate raising, respectively. These are not what we think of intuitively as "intermediate traces" of successive-cyclic movement, but the computational system does not make the intuitive distinctions (unless modified to do so). We therefore have to ask what happens to the features of the traces in these constructions: are their formal features deleted and erased, as in the case of successive-cyclic raising?

One possibility is to sharpen the notion "intermediate trace" to exclude these cases, but a more attractive one is to extend the discussion to them. If so, a host of questions arise. Thus, in (92a), or the more complex structure *what did John expect t to be seen t'* in which *t* heads a nontrivial chain, can the Case feature F of *t* raise covertly for Case checking, or must the *wh*-phrase have passed through [Spec, Agr$_O$] overtly? If the former, then F must not have been erased, or presumably even deleted, when *wh*-movement took place. A convention is then needed requiring erasure of F throughout the array of chains containing F, so that no −Interpretable feature remains in the operator position; questions of some potential interest also arise about the position of reconstruction.

This line of reasoning suggests a narrow modification of the preceding account of feature deletion under movement: formal features of trace are deleted (hence erased) if they are not necessary for the formation of legitimate LF objects that satisfy FI. There are two kinds of objects that concern us here: argument chains satisfying the Chain Condition and operator-variable constructions with the variable heading an argument chain. When A-chains are formed, no formal features in the trace position are necessary; the argument chain is well formed without them. But when *wh*-movement or some other form of operator raising takes place, the trace left behind heads an argument chain and must have the full complement of features: Interpretable features required for interpretation of the argument at LF, and −Interpretable features that have not yet been checked (otherwise, the Case feature is never checked, remaining in the operator, and the derivation crashes). We conclude, then, that in A-movement the formal features of the trace are deleted and erased, but in *wh*-movement (and other operator movement), these features remain intact.

The earlier discussion is unaffected. As for (92a), the revised formulation permits the Case feature F in the argument chain headed by *t* to raise covertly for Case checking, which now deletes and erases it in both positions of the chain (F, t_F) formed by the operation (and in the operator). (92c) falls out the same way. There are a variety of other cases to consider. I will leave the matter here, pending closer study. The general idea, then, should be that formal features of a trace are deleted and erased if they are unnecessary, and that some version of (90) holds for traces of A-movement generally.

It also seems natural to expect (90) to extend to (93).[76]

(93) Trace is immobile.

The operation Attract/Move can "see" only the head of a chain, not its second or later members. Though it is not forced, the natural more general principle is that traces also cannot be targets, so that we have (94), with the qualifications already noted.

(94) Only the head of a chain CH enters into the operation Attract/Move.

If (94) holds, we settle a question that was left unresolved in the case of V-raising: do the features of the object Obj adjoin to the head of the V-chain or to its trace? Suppose, say, that V-raising is overt, as in French-type languages. Do the features FF(Obj) adjoin to the trace of [V, Agr_0], a copy of the raised V–Agr complex, or to the I complex of which V is a part? The latter must be the case if (94) is correct, as I will assume. We will return to supporting evidence in section 4.10.

Summarizing, minimalist assumptions lead to (something like) the conditions (95) on Attract/Move. Where CH is a (possibly trivial) chain headed by α,

(95) a. α can raise, leaving the trace t, a copy of α.
    b. Formal features of the trace of A-movement are deleted and erased.
    c. The head of CH can attract or be attracted by K, but traces cannot attract and their features can be attracted only under narrow conditions reviewed (and left partially open).

A problem is posed, once again, by such constructions as (46), which appear in preraising form as (96).

(96) I(nfl) seem [$_{PP}$ to γ] Cl

There is good evidence that γ c-commands into the infinitival clause Cl. Suppose that γ = *him* and CL = *they to like John*, so that the preraising structure is (97), yielding *they seem to him to like John* after raising.

(97) I(nfl) seem [to him] [$_{Cl}$ they to like John]

Then a Condition C violation results if γ (= *him*) takes *John* as antecedent. It follows that γ must also c-command *they*.

Why, then, does I in (96) attract the subject *they* of Cl rather than γ, which c-commands it, an apparent Relativized Minimality violation?

In (96) *seem* has two internal arguments: PP and Cl. On present assumptions, that requires an analysis as a Larsonian shell, with *seem* raising to the light verb *v* and subsequent operations yielding (98) (internal structure of I omitted).

(98)
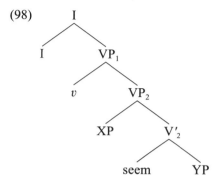

Since PP is the optional argument and Cl the obligatory one in (96), it is likely that Cl is the complement YP and PP the specifier XP, which yields the observed order directly.[77]

When *seem* raises to adjoin to *v*, it forms the chain CH = (*seem*, *t*). PP is in the minimal domain of CH, but this does not suffice to place PP within the neighborhood of I that can be ignored when we ask whether *they* in (97) is close enough to IP to be attracted by IP. It is not, because nothing has adjoined to I at the point when *they* raises.[78] Therefore, $\gamma = him$ is closer to IP and has features that can enter into a checking relation with I (e.g., its D-feature). We expect, then, that *they* should not raise in (97), contrary to fact.

In some languages, the facts generally accord with these expectations. In French, for example, raising is barred in the counterpart to (97), unless PP is a clitic, which raises, presumably leaving a trace.[79]

(99) a. *Jean semble à   Marie [t_j avoir   du talent]
          Jean seems to Marie   to.have talent
     b. Jean lui   semble t_1 [t_j avoir   du talent]
          Jean to.her seems   to.have talent
          'Jean seems to her to have talent'

The results are as predicted. *Marie* is closer to IP than the embedded subject *Jean* in the position t_j of (99a) and therefore bars raising. The Case of *Jean* is not checked and erased, so the derivation crashes. In

(99b) the trace of the clitic cannot be attracted, by (95). Therefore, raising is permitted and the derivation converges.

If PP in such structures could be raised by $\overline{A}$-movement (topicalization, *wh*-movement), it would leave the structure (100).

(100) V *t* Cl

According to the principle (95), the effects should be as in (99b). The evidence appears to be partial and somewhat obscure, however. The status of the English constructions still remains unexplained, along with many other related questions.

In (96) γ receives its inherent Case and θ-role internally to the construction [*seem to* ——], in terms of properties of *seem*. Could there be a verb SEEM, like *seem* except that it selects DP instead of PP and assigns a θ-role but no Case? We would then be able to derive the structure (101), which would yield the outputs (102a–c), among others.

(101) I [[SEEM-v] [$_{VP}$ DP [$_{VP'}$ t_s Cl]]]

(102) a. Bill SEEMs t_B [that it is raining]
       b. there SEEMs someone [that it is raining]
       c. there SEEMs someone [John to be likely that *t* is intelligent]

Presumably, no such verb as SEEM can exist, perhaps because of some interaction between inherent Case and θ-role of internal argument for which we have no natural expression and which, to my knowledge, remains unexplained and largely unexplored. There are many similar questions.[80]

Consider the ECM constructions in (103).

(103) a. I expected [there to be a book on the shelf]
       b. I expected [there to seem [*t* to be a book on the shelf]]

In earlier chapters we assumed that the expletive *there* raises to [Spec, Agr$_O$] to have its accusative Case checked by the transitive verb *expect* and that the associate *book* then adjoins to the raised expletive. We have now rejected that view. The associate raises not to *there* but to the matrix verbal element Vb (= [*expect*, Agr$_O$]) itself (not to its Spec). Furthermore, the expletive is pure and therefore cannot raise to [Spec, Agr$_O$] at all,[81] though it can raise overtly to subject, as in (91), to satisfy the EPP. Matrix Vb attracts an appropriate feature F of the associate *book* (Case or φ-feature), this being the closest F that can enter into a checking relation with Vb. (103b) is accounted for along the same lines.

Attraction of the associate in these cases radically violates the HMC. The status of this condition remains unresolved. It always fit rather uneasily into the theories of locality of movement, requiring special assumptions. The empirical motivation for the HMC is also not entirely clear, and there seem to be fairly clear counterexamples to it. Can the HMC fall within the framework just outlined? That seems doubtful.

We can restrict attention to adjunction of an X^0 element α to another X^0 element β. Suppose we could establish that β attracts only the closest such α, meaning: a feature F of α is the closest feature that enters into a checking relation with a sublabel of β^{max}. But that is not enough to yield the HMC. Specifically, there is nothing to prevent α from skipping some head γ that offers no features to be checked. Consider, for example, the construction (104).

(104)

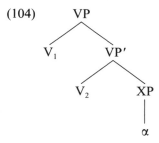

Here $\beta = V_1$ and $\gamma = V_2$ (perhaps a causative construction). Suppose only V_1 allows incorporation. Does V_1 attract α, violating the HMC?

If $\alpha = V$, so that V_1 requires a verbal affix, then we might argue that V_1 attracts the closer verb V_2, barring attraction of α. But that seems implausible if $\alpha = N$ and V_1 requires noun incorporation. It is easy enough to add further conditions, in effect stipulating the HMC; but we need strong arguments for that undesirable conclusion. The problem might be overcome if noun incorporation involves a θ-relation, not a structural configuration (see Di Sciullo and Williams 1988). But it is still necessary to bar unwanted cases of long head raising in other cases. The situation remains unsatisfactory.

Given the central role of feature checking in the minimalist approach, we want to be clear about just what it means. Category K attracts F only if F enters into a checking relation with a sublabel of K. But earlier discussion skirted an important problem: what happens in the case of feature mismatch?

Two related questions arise.

(105) a. In a configuration for feature checking, are features checked if they fail to match?

   b. If a feature is not checked, does the derivation crash?

Suppose, for example, that DP has nonnominative Case (accusative, null, or something else) and has been raised to [Spec, T], T finite, where nominative Case is assigned. Then question (105a) asks which of (106a) or (106b) is correct.

(106) a. The feature is checked in this configuration so that Case can no longer be accessed by the computation, and the derivation crashes by virtue of feature incompatibility.

   b. This is not a checking configuration at all, so that Case is still accessible.

As for (105b), suppose that a verb such as *want* takes a complement that may or may not have Case (*want – a book, want – to leave*). Then (105b) asks whether the verb must have two distinct lexical entries, or may have only one, the Case feature simply not being assigned if there is no object.

The tacit assumption of earlier work has been that the answer to (105a) is positive (i.e., (106a), not (106b)) and that the answer to (105b) is negative. In the illustrative example, if DP is in [Spec, T] but has accusative or null Case, then it cannot raise to check this still unmatched feature; and a verb like *want* can have a single lexical entry, with the Case feature assigned or not.

We now know that the assumption about (105b) was incorrect. If a feature that is −Interpretable is not checked, the derivation crashes. As discussed, all formal features of heads that create checking domains (that is, all their formal features apart from category) are −Interpretable (Case and ϕ-features of verbs and adjectives, strong features, etc.). Therefore, all must be checked, and the answer to (105b) is definitely positive.

Assuming that, suppose we also replace (105a) by its negation (essentially following Ura 1994).

(107) Features cannot be checked under feature mismatch.

Then in the example of Case conflict, DP will be able to move further to receive Case, but the derivation will crash because T fails to assign its Case-assigning feature. And verbs with optional objects will have distinct lexical entries, one with and one without the Case feature.

Considerations of conceptual naturalness seem to favor (107) over the alternative, in part because of the answer to (105b). We will return to some further support for the same conclusion.

To show that all unwanted constructions are barred by the condition (107) combined with the positive answer to (105b), it is necessary to survey a broad range of possibilities: thus, the subject might have its (improper) accusative Case checked in the checking domain of V raised to T, while the (improper) nominative Case feature of the object raises to T for checking nominative Case. Both subject and T might raise to higher positions for Case checking. Options proliferate, and it is no simple matter to show that all are blocked for one or another reason. It is therefore reasonable to refine (107) to bar these possibilities across the board: feature mismatch cancels the derivation. The complexity of the computations required to determine whether a derivation will converge is therefore sharply reduced, a desideratum quite generally. Furthermore, as we will see in section 4.10, this step is necessary on empirical grounds as we refine the framework in accord with the Minimalist Program.

I will therefore strengthen (107) to (108).

(108) Mismatch of features cancels the derivation.

A configuration with mismatched features is not a legitimate syntactic object.[82] We distinguish mismatch from nonmatch: thus, the Case feature [accusative] mismatches $F' = $ [assign nominative], but fails to match $F' = I$ of a raising infinitival, which assigns no Case. I have left the notion "match" somewhat imprecise pending a closer analysis. But its content is clear enough for present purposes: thus, the categorial feature D of DP matches the D-feature of I; ϕ-features match if they are identical; and so on.

Notice that cancellation of a derivation under mismatch should be distinguished from nonconvergence. The latter permits a different convergent derivation to be constructed, if possible. But the point here is literally to bar alternatives. A canceled derivation therefore falls into the category of convergent derivations in that it blocks any less optimal derivation; mismatch cannot be evaded by violation of Procrastinate or other devices. If the optimal derivation creates a mismatch, we are not permitted to pursue a nonoptimal alternative.

Suppose, for example, that a series of applications of Merge has formed a verb phrase α with DP_1 as specifier and DP_2 as complement, bearing accusative and nominative Case, respectively. We will see that the optimal derivation from that point leads to mismatch. Since mismatch is equivalent to convergence from an economy-theoretic point of view, we cannot construct a less optimal derivation from α that might converge, with the thematic subject bearing accusative Case and the thematic object nominative Case. The interpretation is motivated on purely conceptual grounds: it sharply reduces computational complexity. Again, conceptual and empirical considerations converge.

We now distinguish between a checking *configuration* and a checking *relation*. Suppose that K attracts F, which raises to form {H(K), {α, K}}; here α = F if the operation is covert, and α includes whatever is required for convergence if the operation is overt. Each feature of FF[F] (including F) is in the checking domain of each sublabel f of K.[83] We now say that

(109) Feature F′ of FF[F] is in a *checking configuration* with f; and F′ is in a *checking relation* with f if, furthermore, F′ and f match.

If F′ and f fail to match, no problem arises; if they mismatch (conflict), the derivation is canceled with an illegitimate object.

In the illustrative example, if DP has nonnominative Case and has been raised to [Spec, T], the Case feature [CF] of DP is in a checking configuration with the Case feature of T, but not in a checking relation with it. Hence, the target TP did not attract [CF], because no checking relation is established. It does, however, attract the categorial feature [D] of DP, to satisfy the EPP. But then [CF] is in a mismatching checking configuration with f, and the derivation is canceled.

Suppose that f is the Case-assigning feature of K, α and β have the unchecked Case features F_α and F_β (respectively), and F_α but not F_β matches f. Suppose that β is closer to K than α. Does β prevent K from attracting α? The Case feature F_β of β does not do so; it is not attracted by K and is therefore no more relevant than some semantic feature of β. Suppose, however, that β has some other feature F'_β that *can* enter into a checking relation with a sublabel of K. Then β is attracted by K, which cannot "see" the more remote element α. A mismatching relation is created, and the derivation is canceled: α cannot be attracted.

Consider again the superraising example (80) (= *I(nfl)* seems [*that it was told John* ...]). The intermediate DP *it* is able to check the D-feature but not the Case feature of matrix I; the more remote DP *John* can check all features of I. But I cannot "see" beyond *it*, so only that intervening element can raise, causing the derivation to crash. Had *John* been permitted to raise, the derivation would wrongly converge.

The definition (82) of the MLC therefore has the somewhat sharper form (110) as a consequence of the refinement of the concept "checking relation."

(110) *Minimal Link Condition*

K attracts α only if there is no β, β closer to K than α, such that K attracts β.

The definition of the operation Attract/Move incorporates this property, yielding the MLC in what seems to be the required form. I leave this here as the final version of the MLC, apart from a refinement of the notion "closeness" in section 4.10.

Consequences ramify, and merit further thought.

The notions of checking theory have been defined only for Attract/ Move, but we have seen that that may be too narrow. Thus, checking domains are established by Merge in (64), repeated here as (111), and in simple expletive constructions such as (112).

(111) a. (I wonder) [$_{CP}$ whether Q [he left yet]]
      b. (I wonder) [$_{CP}$ [$_Q$ if Q] [he left yet]]

(112) there is a book on the table

In these cases *whether*, *if*, and *there* remain in their base positions, but satisfy the strong features of Q, I. The operations are closely analogous to raising of a *wh*-phrase, I, or DP to become [Spec, I], checking the strong features in the same way.

These cases of merger will fall under checking theory if we extend the notion "close" to distinct syntactic objects α and K, taking the categorial feature CF of the head H(α) to be *close to* K. K attracts α, then, if CF enters into a checking relation with a sublabel of K, in which case α becomes [Spec, H(K)] or adjoins to H(K) (or its zero-level projection, if elements have already adjoined to H(K)). The result is as intended for (111) and (112), but is too broad elsewhere. Thus, it would cover merger of the subject Subj with V' within any version of the VP-internal subject hypothesis and would thus force the subject to have the accusative Case and object agreement features of the transitive main verb of the VP (perhaps raised to the light verb *v* of which Subj is the specifier).

The required distinction can be made in various ways. One is to extend Attract/Move only to merger of nonarguments, keeping strictly to the conception of Attract/Move as the formal expression of the feature-checking property of natural language. That has some plausibility.

Arguments (and operator phrases constructed from them) satisfy the Chain Condition nontrivially; an argument is a nontrivial chain CH = (α, t), where α has raised for feature checking and t is in a θ-position. In contrast, the elements *whether*, *if*, and *there* of (111) and (112) do not satisfy the Chain Condition at all.

A second approach is to allow the categorial feature CF of α to be attracted by a distinct object K only if it enters into a checking relation with a *strong* sublabel of K. The rationale is that Merge creates a checking domain only when overt insertion is forced, violating Procrastinate in the case of Move—hence a special case for both Merge and Move.

I will adopt the first option, though without strong reasons at this point. Some will be suggested in section 4.10, though they rely on specific choices about mechanisms that, while reasonable, are not well grounded. The choice is therefore highly tentative.

4.6 Movement and θ-Theory

Under any approach that takes Attract/Move to be driven by morphological features—whether Move F, Move α, and Greed, or some other variant—there should be no interaction between θ-theory and the theory of movement. θ-roles are not formal features in the relevant sense; typically they are assigned in the internal domain, not the checking domain, and they differ from the features that enter into the theory of movement in numerous other respects. The conclusion is immediate in Hale and Keyser's (1993a) configurational approach to θ-theory, implicit in some others (though rejected in theories that permit percolation, transmission, and other operations on θ-features). Let us assume it to be valid.

In fundamental respects, θ-theory is virtually complementary to the theory of checking, a fact expressed in part as a descriptive generalization in the Chain Condition: in the chain CH = $(\alpha_1, \ldots, \alpha_n)$, α_n receives a θ-role and α_1 enters into a checking relation. Furthermore, only α_n can assign a θ-role, so that only the base position is "θ-related," able to assign or receive a θ-role (see note 75). The properties of α_1 follow from Last Resort movement. Consider the properties of α_n, that is, the fact that movement takes place from a position that is θ-related to one that is not: for an argument, from a θ-position to a non-θ-position; for a head (or predicate), from a position in which a θ-role is assigned to one in which it is not.

With regard to assignment of θ-roles, the conclusion is natural in Hale and Keyser's theory. A θ-role is assigned in a certain structural configuration; β assigns that θ-role only in the sense that it is the head of that configuration (though the properties of β or its zero-level projection might matter). Suppose β raises, forming the chain CH = $(\beta, \ldots, t)$. The trace t remains in the structural configuration that determines a θ-role and can therefore function as a θ-role assigner; but the chain CH is not in a configuration at all, so cannot assign a θ-role. In its raised position, β can function insofar as it has internal formal features: as a Case assigner or a binder. But in a configurational theory of θ-relations, it makes little sense to think of the head of a chain as assigning a θ-role.[84]

With regard to receipt of θ-roles, similar reasoning applies. If α raises to a θ-position Th, forming the chain CH = (α, t), the argument that must bear a θ-role is CH, not α. But CH is not in any configuration, and α is not an argument that can receive a θ-role. Other conditions too are violated under earlier assumptions or others like them, but I will not spell out the problems further.

We conclude, then, that a raised element cannot receive or assign a θ-role. θ-relatedness is a "base property," complementary to feature checking, which is a property of movement. More accurately, θ-relatedness is a property of the position of merger and its (very local) configuration. The same considerations bar raising-to-object, even if the object is a specifier in a Larsonian shell. We thus derive the P&P principle that there is no raising to a θ-position—actually in a somewhat stronger form, since θ-relatedness generally is a property of "base positions."

Thus, DP cannot raise to [Spec, VP] to assume an otherwise unassigned θ-role. There can be no words HIT or BELIEVE sharing the θ-structure of *hit* and *believe* but lacking Case features, with *John* raising as in (113) to pick up the θ-role, then moving on to [Spec, I] to check Case and agreement features.

(113) a. John [$_{VP}$ t' [HIT t]]
　　　b. John [$_{VP}$ t' [BELIEVE [t to be intelligent]]]

Surely no strong feature of the target is checked by raising to the [Spec, HIT] position, so overt raising is barred; in fact, no checking relation is established.[85] The only possibility is direct raising to [Spec, I]. The resulting sentences *John HIT* and *John BELIEVES to be intelligent* are therefore deviant, lacking the external argument required by the verb.

The deviance of (113a) sheds some light on the question left open about θ-role assignment in a configuration headed by unraised α to which β has adjoined, yielding the complex [$_α$ β α]; see note 84. Can β, which heads a chain, participate in θ-role assignment in the configuration headed by α? Suppose so. In the illegitimate *John I HIT t*, the argument chain CH = (*John*, *t*) satisfies the Chain Condition: *John* receives Case in [Spec, I] and *t* receives a θ-role within the VP. HIT then raises to I, so that *John* falls into its checking domain. If *John* can receive the subject θ-role in the configuration [Spec, I] headed by the complex [$_I$ HIT I] formed by V-raising to I, then all properties are satisfied and the expression should be well formed, with *John* bearing a double θ-role. Assuming that the expression is deviant, HIT cannot contribute to assigning a θ-role when it adjoins to I. The principle that θ-relatedness is a "base property," restricted to configurations of lexical insertion, has to be understood in an austere form.

What is the nature of the deviance in the derivation of (113)? More generally, what is the status of a violation of the θ-Criterion, whether it involves an unassigned θ-role or an argument lacking a θ-role? No relevant performance tests are available, but economy conditions might provide evidence. Thus, if the derivation converges, it could block others under economy conditions, so the deviance would have to be a case of nonconvergence if that result is empirically wrong.[86]

To illustrate these possibilities, suppose that the theory of economy entails that shorter derivations block longer ones. The assumption seems plausible.[87] Kitahara (1994) observes that the condition can be invoked to deduce Procrastinate, if we assume that application of phonological rules counts in determining length of derivation; trace deletion is required only if an operation is overt, so covert operations are always preferred, if they yield convergence. The economy condition receives independent confirmation in section 4.10.

Now consider any simple sentence, say, (114a) with structure (114b), before Spell-Out.

(114) a. John likes Bill
      b. [John I VP]

There is a derivation in which *John* is inserted directly in [Spec, I], not raising from VP. If the VP-internal subject hypothesis is correct, as so far assumed, that derivation must crash, or it will block the less economical derivation with raising of *John* to [Spec, I]; the two begin with the same numeration, but the desired one has an extra step. All formal features are checked.[88] Insertion of *John* satisfies the EPP, and other features are checked as or by free riders. The only defects of the unwanted derivation lie in θ-theory: the argument *John* lacks a θ-role, and *like* does not assign its external θ-role. If either of these properties constitutes a violation of FI, the derivation crashes, and the problem disappears.

The "shortest derivation" condition, then, entails that a violation of the θ-Criterion causes the derivation to crash, by failure to satisfy FI. Still open is the question whether the problem is the failure of an argument to receive a θ-role, or the failure of a θ-assigning head to assign its θ-role, or both. Independent reasons for the first, at least, are given in section 4.9: an argument without a θ-role violates FI, causing the derivation to crash. Note that these questions about violation of the θ-Criterion have no relation to the conclusion that θ-role is not a formal property that permits Last Resort movement, as Case and agreement features do.

The form of the VP-internal subject hypothesis has so far been left vague. We have, however, generally assumed a version of the Hale-Keyser approach to θ-theory that has certain consequences for the hypothesis.[89] In particular, if a verb has several internal arguments, then we have to postulate a Larsonian shell, as in (98) or (115), where v is a light verb to which V overtly raises.

(115)

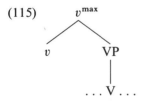

The internal arguments occupy the positions of specifier and complement of V. Accordingly, the external argument cannot be lower than [Spec, v]. If it is [Spec, v], as I will assume, then the v–VP configuration can be taken to express the causative or agentive role of the external argument. It would be natural to extend the same reasoning to transitive verb constructions generally, assigning them a double-VP structure as in (115), the agent role being understood as the interpretation assigned to the v–VP configuration. A V–object construction is therefore maximal, not V'. The conclusion gains further support if such constructions may assign a partially idiosyncratic semantic role (See Marantz 1984). If intransitive (unergative) verbs are hidden transitives, as Hale and Keyser suggest, then only unaccusatives lacking agents would be simple VP structures. The analysis, which is natural in the present framework, also has welcome empirical consequences, as we will see. I will assume it in what follows.

In these terms, failure of a transitive verb to assign an external θ-role could be interpreted as simply meaningless. The external role is a property of the v–VP configuration, and a specifier bearing this role is therefore a necessary part of the configuration; a transitive verb assigns an external θ-role by definition.[90] The question of the nature of the deviance in (113) would therefore not arise: there are no such objects. The only remaining question is whether failure of an argument to receive a θ-role is a case of nonconvergence or deviant convergence. Presumably it is the former, under the natural interpretation of FI—the conclusion we will reach in section 4.9.

The spirit of this analysis requires that there be no AgrP intervening between the light verb v and its VP complement in (115), contrary to what is assumed in the most extensive development of the complex-VP analysis of transitives (see Koizumi 1993, 1995). The issue takes a different form under refinements introduced in section 4.10. We will return to the whole issue in sections 4.9 and 4.10.

4.7   Properties of the Transformational Component

4.7.1   Why Move?

We have so far considered two operations, Merge and Move, each with two cases, substitution and adjunction. The operation Merge is inescapable on the weakest interface conditions, but why should the computational system C_{HL} in human language not be restricted to it? Plainly, it is not. The most casual inspection of output conditions reveals that items commonly appear "displaced" from the position in which the interpretation they receive is otherwise represented at the LF interface.[91] There is no meaningful controversy about the basic facts. The only questions are, what are the mechanisms of displacement, and why do they exist? As for their nature, on minimalist assumptions we want nothing more than an indication at LF of the position in which the displaced item is interpreted; that is, chains are legitimate objects at LF. Since chains are not introduced by selection from the lexicon or by Merge, there must be another operation to form them: the operation Attract/Move.

The second question—why do natural languages have such devices?—arose in the early days of generative grammar. Speculations about it invoked considerations of language use: facilitation of parsing on certain assumptions, the separation of theme-rheme structures from base-determined semantic (θ) relations, and so on.[92] Such speculations involve "extraneous" conditions of the kind discussed earlier, conditions imposed on C_{HL} by the ways it interacts with external systems. That is where we would hope the source of "imperfections" would lie, on minimalist assumptions.

Our concern here is to determine how spare an account of the operation Attract/Move the facts of language allow. The best possible result is that bare output conditions are satisfied in an optimal way.

This question was a second focus of the effort to resolve the tension between descriptive and explanatory adequacy, alongside the steps that led to X-bar theory in the 1960s. The central concern was to show that the operation Move α is independent of α; another, to restrict the variety of structural conditions for transformational rules. These efforts were motivated by the usual dual concerns: the empirical demands posed by the problems of descriptive and explanatory adequacy, and the conceptual demands of simplicity and naturalness. Proposals motivated by these concerns inevitably raise the new leading problem that replaces the old: to show that restricting the resources of linguistic theory preserves (and we hope, even enhances) descriptive adequacy while explanation deepens. The efforts have met with a good deal of success,[93] though minimalist assumptions would lead us to expect more.

4.7.2 Departures from the Best Case
The properties that motivate Attract/Move have to be captured somehow in the theory of human language, but we would like to show, if possible, that no further departure from minimalist assumptions is required. That is the problem that comes into sharper focus as explanatory adequacy begins to take its place on the research agenda.

Consider first the independence of Move α from choice of α. Although this currently seems a reasonable supposition, it has been necessary to distinguish various kinds of movement: XP-movement from X^0-movement and (among XPs) A-movement from $\overline{A}$-movement. Various kinds of "improper movement" have been ruled out in various ways (e.g., head raising to an $\overline{A}$-position followed by raising to Spec). One goal is to eliminate any such distinctions, demonstrating on general grounds that the "wrong kinds" of movement crash—not an easy problem, though it is by now substantially reduced.

Some of the general constraints introduced to reduce the richness of descriptive apparatus also had problematic aspects. An example is Emonds's influential structure-preserving hypothesis (SPH) for substitution operations. As has been stressed particularly by Jan Koster, the SPH introduces an unwanted redundancy in that the target of movement is somehow "there" before the operation takes place; that observation provides one motive for nonderivational theories that construct chains by computation on LF (or S-Structure) representations. The minimalist approach overcomes the redundancy by eliminating the SPH: with D-Structure gone, it is unformulable, its consequences derived—we hope to show—by the general properties of Merge and Attract/Move.

It has also been proposed that something like the SPH holds of adjunction: bar levels are matched within adjunctions. This extended SPH introduces no redundancy and is not affected by the Minimalist Program, though we would like to deduce it from more elementary considerations.

The descriptive facts are not entirely clear, but they might be as just described: only YP can adjoin to XP and only Y^0 can adjoin to X^0, though covert operations may have the apparent effect of adjoining YP to nonmaximal X^0 (e.g., VP-adjunction to causative V_c, which we now take to be adjunction of formal features of the main verb to V_c). We then have several problems to deal with.

(116) a. Why does the SPH hold at all?
       b. Why is there a difference before and after Spell-Out, apparently violating the (optimal) uniformity assumption on C_{HL}?
       c. Why does the target K project after adjunction?

Under the feature movement theory we are now assuming, the questions are narrower still. All covert raising is adjunction of features, so question (116b) dissolves and (116c) arises only for overt adjunction. In that case it has already been answered for adjunction to X^0 and to projecting XP. Furthermore, under the interpretation of Last Resort and checking domain that we are now assuming (see (51) and note 47), it is unclear that adjunction to nonminimal XP is possible at all; let us assume so nevertheless and see what problems arise.

What remains, then, is question (116a) and three cases of question (116c) for overt movement: adjunction of YP to XP that is

(117) a. the root
      b. a specifier
      c. itself an adjunct

Consider question (116a). In the case of overt movement, the answer may lie in part in properties of the morphological component. At Spell-Out, the structure Σ already formed enters Morphology, a system that presumably deals only with wordlike elements, which we may take to be X^0s—that is, either an item H selected from the lexicon or such an item with elements adjoined to it to form H^{0max}. Suppose we assume the property (118).

(118) Morphology deals only with X^0 categories and their features.

The morphological component gives no output (so the derivation crashes) if presented with an element that is not an X^0 or a feature.

On this natural assumption, the largest phrases entering Morphology are X^0s, and if some larger unit appears within an X^0, the derivation crashes.

Question (116a) remains, then, only for adjunction of nonmaximal α (either a feature or a category) to nonminimal XP—XP with at least a head H(XP) and a complement. Both cases are barred under the condition (119) on checking domains (see note 47).

(119) α adjoined to nonminimal K is not in the checking domain of H(K).

If so, the operation we are trying to eliminate cannot take place. We will see directly that there is reason to believe that (119) holds. Then question (116a) is fully answered, and we are left with the three cases (117) of question (116c).

All cases of (117) are barred by Last Resort if checking domains are construed as in (119). A number of special cases are barred for independent reasons.

Summarizing, the asymmetry of projection after movement has solid grounds: it is only the target that can project, whether movement is substitution or adjunction. The only obvious problem is that the constraints appear to be too strong, barring YP adjunction to XP entirely.

We have found a number of reasons to question the status of YP adjunction to XP. There are others. Suppose we suspend the barriers to the operation already found, thus allowing adjunction of α to nonminimal K, as in (120).

(120)

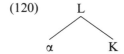

Suppose that α projects so that L = α and the category formed is [α, α]. We have to determine what is the head of the chain formed by the adjunction operation: is it α, or the two-segment category [α, α]? The latter choice is ruled out by the uniformity condition (17). But the former leaves us with a category [α, α] that has no interpretation at LF, violating FI. It cannot be, then, that the raised element α projects, if it requires an interpretation. The same problem would have arisen, this time for α, had we taken the head of the chain to be [α, α]. Similar questions arise about the target, if it projects. Once again, adjunction to non-minimal XP leads to complications however we construe the structure formed, raising further questions about its status.

Still assuming such adjunction to be possible, consider the special case of self-attachment, as in (121).

(121)

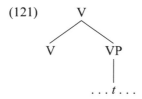

Thus, suppose we have the VP *read the book* and we adjoin to it the head *read*, forming the two-segment category [*read* [*t the book*]]. Under the intended interpretation of (121), with the target projected, we have formed the object (122), where γ is the target VP = {*read*, {*read*, *the book*}} (omitting further analysis).

(122) {⟨read, read⟩, {read, γ}},

Suppose, however, that we had projected the adjunct V (*read*) in (121), yielding (123).

(123)

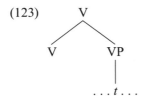

But this too is an informal representation of (122), just as (121) is, though the intended interpretations differ: in (121) we have projected the target, in (123) the adjunct. Furthermore, the latter interpretation should be barred.

The same question would arise if the operation were substitution, not adjunction. Suppose, for example, that we raise the head N of NP to [Spec, N], NP nonminimal (necessarily, or there is no operation to discuss). Then we construct the same formal object whether we think of NP or Spec as projecting.

We might conclude that this is exactly the right result, with such ambiguity interpreted as a crashed derivation. Then such operations of "self-attachment" (whether adjunction or substitution) are barred on grounds independent of those already discussed.

Let us turn now to the case of raising of V in a complex verb structure, as in (115), repeated here.

(124)
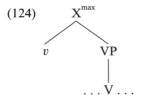

For several reasons already discussed, the operation cannot have targeted VP, either as adjunction or as substitution. It must be, then, that X^{max} is not a projection of the raised verb V but rather a verb phrase distinct from VP, as we have so far assumed. Thus, V raises to an already filled position occupied by the light verb v that has been selected from the lexicon and heads its own projection, v^{max}. V adjoins to v, forming $[_v \text{ V } v]$; the v position is not "created" by the raising operation. (For independent evidence, see Collins and Thráinsson 1994.) The operation is permissible if the target v is a light verb requiring a verbal affix. Independently, these conclusions are required by the properties of θ-theory discussed earlier.[94]

We have so far sidestepped a problem that arises in the case of ordinary head adjunction. Take α, K to be X^0s in (120), with α raising to target K, which projects, forming L = {⟨H(K), H(K)⟩, {α, K}}. Since K projects, α is maximal. Thus, α is both maximal and minimal. If that is true of t as well (e.g., the case of clitic raising), then CH satisfies the uniformity condition (17). But suppose t is nonmaximal, as is common in the case of V-raising to I or to V. Then under a natural interpretation, (17) is violated; CH is not a legitimate object at LF, and the derivation crashes. That is obviously the wrong result. We therefore assume that at LF, wordlike elements are "immune" to the algorithm that determines phrase structure status, as stated in (125),

(125) At LF, X^0 is submitted to independent word interpretation processes WI.

where WI ignores principles of C_{HL}, within X^0.[95] WI is a covert analogue of Morphology, except that we expect it to operate compositionally, unlike Morphology, on the assumption that the $N \rightarrow$ LF mapping is uniform throughout.

Suppose that (120) = L = $\{\gamma, \{\alpha, K\}\}$ is formed by adjunction with K projecting, so that $\gamma = \langle H(K), H(K) \rangle$. So far, there are two ways in which L could have been formed: by strict merger of α, K (without movement), or by raising of α, forming the chain CH, α then merging with K. In either case we form the structure L with the three terms α, K, L. Each of these is a category that is "visible" at the interface, where it must receive some interpretation, satisfying FI. The adjunct α poses no problem. If it heads CH, it receives the interpretation associated with the trace position; if it is added by strict merger, it is presumably a predicate of K (e.g., an adverbial adjunct to a verb). But there is only one role left at LF for K and L (a problem already mentioned). Note that the label $\gamma = \langle H(K), H(K) \rangle$ is not a term, hence receives no interpretation.

If L is nonmaximal, the problem is obviated by (125) under a natural interpretation of WI. This should suffice to account for, say, noun incorporation to verbs, or verb incorporation to causatives or light verbs. What is interpreted as covert incorporation of X^{max} to a pure head is permitted straightforwardly by the Move F theory.

Suppose L is nonminimal—again, we suspend the barriers to this questionable case of adjunction to investigate the problems further. We now have two terms, L and K, but only one LF role. The structure would be permissible if K lacks a θ-role, as in covert adjunction to an expletive (a case that we now assume does not exist). The only other possibility is that the adjunct α is deleted at LF, leaving just K. When would this take place?

One case is when α is the trace of successive-cyclic movement of the type that permits intermediate trace deletion, say, along the lines sketched in section 1.4.1—for example, *wh*-movement to [Spec, CP] with intermediate adjunction, as in (126).[96]

(126) which pictures of John's brother did he expect that [t' [you would buy t]]

Another case is full reconstruction at LF, eliminating the adjunct entirely, thus a structure of the type (127) interpreted only at the trace.

(127) [$_{YP}$ XP [$_{YP}$ ... t ...]]]

An example would be "scrambling" interpreted by reconstruction, argued to be uniformly the case by Saito (1989, and subsequent work). Similarly, it would follow that such constructions as (128) must be Condition C violations (under the relevant interpretation), and we predict a difference in status between (129) and (126), the latter escaping the violation because the head of the chain is not an adjunct.

(128) a. meet John in England, he doesn't expect that I will
      b. pictures of John, he doesn't expect that I will buy

(129) pictures of John's brother, he never expected that you would buy

The conclusions are plausible as a first approximation, though we enter here into a morass of difficult and partially unsolved questions (see Barss 1986, Freidin 1986, Lebeaux 1988, and earlier work; and chapter 3 for some discussion).

On strictly minimalist assumptions, these should be the only possibilities for adjunction:

(130) a. word formation
      b. semantically vacuous target
      c. deletion of adjunct (trace deletion, full reconstruction)

Apart from (130c), there should be no adjunction to a θ-related phrase (a θ-role assigner or an argument, a predicate or the XP of which it is predicated). Since (130c) is irrelevant to strict merger, the options for the current counterpart to "base adjunction" are even narrower. We will consider adjoined adverbials further in section 4.7.5.[97]

Adjunction therefore remains an option under natural minimalist assumptions, but a very limited one with special properties. The primary and perhaps only case is α-adjunction to X^0, α a feature or (if the operation is overt) an X^0. Adjunction of YP to XP does not fit easily into this general approach, and if allowed at all, has a very restricted range.

4.7.3 XP-Adjunction and the Architecture of Linguistic Theory

Adjunction of YP to XP has had a central place in transformational generative grammar from its origins. That is understandable: it provides the most obvious examples of "displacement" of phrases from the positions in which they are interpreted. But as theoretical understanding has evolved, two distinct paths can be discerned. One path focused on the operations formulated as Move NP and Move *wh*, later Move α and Affect α, now Attract F if what precedes is correct. For these, XP-adjunction was marginal, introduced primarily for theory-internal reasons related to the ECP and so on. Another path sought to understand such operations as extraposition, right-node raising, VP-adjunction, scrambling, and whatever "rearrangements" are involved in forming such expressions as (131),

(131) I took a lot of pictures out of the attic yesterday of my children
       and their friends

with two parts of the phrase *took out* ... separated by an element *a lot of pictures* that should not be a phrase at all, and two parts of the unitary phrase *a lot of* [*pictures of DP*] separated by an element of much wider scope. As the two paths increasingly diverge, it becomes more and more reasonable to suppose that the processes and structures they address do not belong together; furthermore, the latter category appears to be heterogeneous. As already observed, the former path does not readily incorporate even elementary structures of many kinds; see notes 22, 93.

The divide has been sharpened further by inquiry into languages of the sort that Baker (1995) describes in terms of his "polysynthesis parameter," with the syntax in large part word-internal and arguments attached as adjuncts associated with internal elements. One might conjecture that such properties of UG appear in some manner in languages for which the principle is not of a fundamental nature. Consider, say, scrambling in Japanese, which seems to share some of those properties, the scrambled element being a kind of adjunct, external to the major syntactic structure, associated with an internal position that determines the semantic interpretation (hence the obligatory "reconstruction"). Related issues are currently being investigated in widely differing languages (see Barbosa 1994). We will return to the matter in section 4.10.

In early transformational grammar, a distinction was sometimes made between "stylistic" rules and others. Increasingly, the distinction seems to be quite real: the core computational properties we have been considering differ markedly in character from many other operations of the language faculty, and it may be a mistake to try to integrate them within the same framework of principles. The problems related to XP-adjunction are perhaps a case in point: they may not really belong to the system we are discussing here as we keep closely to the first of the two courses just outlined, the one that is concerned with Last Resort movement driven by feature checking within the $N \rightarrow \lambda$ computation. It is within this core component of the language that we find the striking properties highlighted by minimalist guidelines. It seems increasingly reasonable to distinguish this component of the language faculty.

These speculations again raise the narrower technical question whether checking domains include YP adjoined to XP, both nonminimal. The most direct empirical motivation for defining checking domains to allow this case was a version of Kayne's (1989) theory of participial agreement (see sections 2.3.2, 3.2). Its basic assumption is that in passive and unaccusative, the object passes through the [Spec, Agr_O] position (A-movement), checking agreement with the participle, and then raises to subject, driven by Case; and in operator movement, the object adjoins to the AgrP ($\overline{A}$-movement), again checking agreement in the checking domain of Agr, then raising ultimately to [Spec, CP], driven by the operator feature. In particular, Kayne found dialect differences associated with the two kinds of participial agreement.

Dominique Sportiche and Philip Branigan have observed that the operator movement case is problematic because of such long-distance movement constructions as French (132).[98]

(132) la   lettre [qu'il   a   [$_{AgrP}$ t' [$_{AgrP}$ dit [que Pierre lui   a
       the   letter that he has   said that Pierre to.him has
       [envoyé t]]]]]
       sent
       'the letter that he said that Pierre sent to him'

Raising of the operator from t to t' (perhaps with intermediate steps) and then to [Spec, CP] is legitimate successive-cyclic $\overline{A}$-movement and should yield participial agreement with *dit* in the higher clause, incorrectly. This suggests that agreement (hence, presumably, Case as well) should be restricted to the specifier position, with "long movement" barred by the same principles that bar object raising to a remote position; there are various possible accounts, depending on other aspects of the theory of movement. The dialect differences noted by Kayne remain unexplained, however.

If these conclusions are correct, we restrict the checking domain of α to positions included in (rather than contained in) $Max(\alpha)$—including the A-positions adjoined to α, we have assumed. In brief, we accept the principle (119), which has useful consequences independently, as already discussed.

4.7.4 Other Improprieties

Let us return to the problem of improper movement. We want to show that the wide variety of such cases are excluded on principled grounds. Some fall into place: for example, such standard cases as improper raising of *John* from t_1 to t_2 to matrix subject as in (133), even if adjunction of *John* to IP is permitted.

(133) *John is illegal [$_{IP}$ t_2 [$_{IP}$ t_1 to leave]]

The complement of *illegal* requires PRO (*it is illegal to leave*), so that (null) Case is assigned to the subject of the infinitive. Since *John* cannot have null Case, the derivation is canceled by mismatch (see (108)).[99]

Consider cases of the type (134), with t_2 adjoined to IP, again putting aside reservations about such processes.

(134) *John seems [that [t_2 [it was told t_1 [that . . .]]]]

We do not want to permit the intermediate (offending) trace t_2 to delete, unlike what happens in (126). The distinction suggests a different approach to intermediate trace deletion: perhaps it is a reflex of the process of reconstruction, understood in minimalist terms as in chapter 3. The basic assumption here is that there is no process of reconstruction; rather, the phenomenon is a consequence of the formation of operator-variable constructions driven by FI, a process that may (or sometimes must) leave part of the trace—a copy of the moved element—intact at LF, deleting only its operator part. The reconstruction process would then be restricted to the special case of $\overline{A}$-movement that involves operators.

That reconstruction should be barred in A-chains is thus plausible on conceptual grounds. It has some empirical support as well. Under the relevant interpretation, (135) can only be understood as a Condition B violation, though under reconstruction the violation should be obviated, with *him* interpreted in the position of *t*, c-commanded by *me*; as we have seen, the latter c-commands α.

(135) John expected [him to seem to me [$_\alpha$ t to be intelligent]]

That the raised subject does not fully reconstruct is shown as well by the quasi-agentive status commonly conferred in "surface subject" position (e.g., for PRO in (136)).

(136) [PRO to appear [t to be intelligent]] is harder than one might think

Other reasons to question whether there is reconstruction in A-chains arise from consideration of "lowering effects" of the kind first discussed by Robert May.

(137) a. (it seems that) everyone isn't there yet
      b. I expected [everyone not to be there yet]
      c. everyone seems [t not to be there yet]

Negation can have wide scope over the quantifier in (137a), and it seems in (137b) but not in (137c). If so, that indicates that there is no reconstruction to the trace position in (137c).[100]

The quantifier interactions could result from adjunction of the matrix quantifier to the lower IP (c-commanding the trace of raising and yielding a well-formed structure if the trace of quantifier lowering is deleted, along the lines of May's original proposal). But reconstruction in the A-chain does not take place, so it appears.

Some other cases of improper movement are eliminated within the framework outlined here, such as XP-movement passing through or adjoining to a pure Y^0 position, the trace then deleting. The status of scrambling might be reconsidered, and the (apparent) distinction in status between such structures as (126) and (129) as well. The general topic merits a comprehensive review.

So far we have (virtually) kept to the minimalist assumption that the computational procedure C_{HL} is uniform from N to LF; any distinction before and after Spell-Out is a reflex of other factors. I have said little so far about the "extension condition" of chapter 3, which guarantees cyclicity. The condition is empirically motivated for substitution before Spell-Out by relativized minimality effects and others, and it does not hold after Spell-Out if the Case agreement theory of the minimalist approach is correct. It also cannot hold strictly for adjunction, which commonly (and in the case of head adjunction, always) targets an element within a larger projection. It would be desirable to show that these consequences are deducible, not stipulated.[101]

With regard to Merge, there is nothing to say. It satisfies the extension condition for elementary reasons already discussed (see below (11)). Questions arise only in connection with Attract/Move. The operation targets K, raising α to adjoin to K or to become the specifier of K, K projecting in either case. K may be a substructure of some structure L already formed. That is a necessary option in the covert component but not allowed freely before Spell-Out—as a result of other conditions, we hope to show.

With regard to overt cyclicity, there are several cases to consider. One type is illustrated by such standard examples as (138).

(138) *who was [$_\alpha$ a picture of t_{wh}] taken t_α by Bill

This is a Condition on Extraction Domain (CED) violation in Huang's (1982) sense if passive precedes *wh*-movement, but it is derivable with no violation (incorrectly) if the operations apply in countercyclic order, with passive following *wh*-movement. In this case cyclicity is induced directly by strength. Unless passive precedes *wh*-movement, the derivation is canceled by violation of strength of T (the EPP). Independently, economy conditions might make the relevant distinction between the competing derivations. Passive is the same in both; *wh*-movement is "longer" in the illicit one in an obvious sense, object being more "remote" from [Spec, CP] than subject in terms of number of XPs crossed. The distinction might be captured by a proper theory of economy of derivation— though the issue is nontrivial, in part, because we are invoking here a "global" notion of economy of the sort we have sought to avoid. Such problems would be avoided in the approach proposed by Kawashima and Kitahara and by Groat, briefly sketched in section 4.4.1 (see also Collins 1994a,b, Kitahara 1994, 1995). We will return in section 4.10 to the possibility of excluding the countercyclic operation under a strict interpretation of the principle (95).

Another class of cases are the relativized minimality constructions, for which the standard account is Rizzi's (1990). These fall into three categories: (1) head movement (the HMC); (2) A-movement; (3) $\overline{\text{A}}$-movement. As discussed, the status of the HMC is unclear. In each case we have two situations to rule out: (I) skipping an already filled position; (II) countercyclic operations (i.e., movement that skips a "potential" position that is later filled). Situation (I) falls under the MLC, which is incorporated into the definition of Move/Attract. As for (II), category (1) is not a problem; head insertion is affected necessarily by pure merger, which satisfies the extension condition. The problem also cannot arise for strong features. Questions still remain; they will be reformulated and simplified in section 4.10.

It may be, then, that there is no need to impose the extension condition of chapter 3 on overt operations. Furthermore, neither the phonological nor the covert component can access the lexicon, for reasons already discussed. The Morphology module indirectly allows variation before and after Spell-Out, as do strength of features and such properties of language as the PF conditions on movement that induce generalized pied-piping. All of these conditions reflect properties of the A-P interface. It seems possible to maintain the conclusion that the computational system C_{HL} is uniform from N to LF, in that no pre- versus post-Spell-Out distinction is stipulated. And perhaps we can approach the optimal conclusion that bare output conditions are satisfied as well as possible.

4.7.5 Adjuncts and Shells

We have so far said little about such structures as (139), with an adverbial adjoined to XP to form the two-segment category [XP, XP], projected from X.

(139)

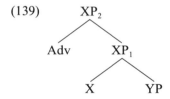

We may, perhaps, assume that the construction is barred if XP has a semantic role at LF (see (130) and note 97)—say, if XP is a predicate (AP or VP), as in the v^{max} structure (140a) underlying (140b), if the analysis of transitive constructions in (115) is correct.

(140) a.   John [$_v$ [$_{VP}$ often [$_{VP}$ reads $\begin{Bmatrix} \text{books} \\ \text{to his children} \end{Bmatrix}$]]]

b.   *John reads often (books, to his children)

Such structures as (139) could have been derived either by Merge or by Move. The latter possibility can perhaps be ruled out in principle: adverbs seem to have no morphological properties that require XP-adjunction (even if it is possible, a dubious idea, as noted). The empirical evidence also suggests that adverbs do not form chains by XP-adjunction (see p. 48). Thus, an adverb in pre-IP position cannot be interpreted as if it had raised from some lower position.[102]

The only option, then, is Merge. The question is whether and how "base adjunction" (in the EST sense) operates above the level of word formation. We have speculated that it is barred if XP is semantically active, as in (140a). Irrespective of the status of the word sequences, the structure assigned in (140a) is not permitted.

As a first approximation, at least, adverbials cannot be adjoined by Merge to phrases that are θ-related (arguments or predicates). If so, they can be "base-adjoined" only to X′ or to phrases headed by v or functional categories. Adjunction to X′ by merger does not conflict with the conclusion that X′ is invisible to C_{HL}; at the point of adjunction, the target is an XP, not X′.

Such constructions as (140a) have played a considerable role in linguistic theory since Emonds's (1978) studies of differences between V-raising and nonraising languages (French, English). The basic phenomena, alongside (140a), are illustrated by (141a–b) (both well formed in French).

(141) a.   John reads often to his children
       b.   *John reads often books

A proposal sometimes entertained is that V raises from the underlying structure (140a) to form (141a), but such raising is barred in (141b) for Case reasons; accusative Case is assigned to *books* by *read* under an adjacency condition of the kind proposed by Stowell (1981). French differs in the adjacency property or in some other way.

Apart from the fact that the source construction (140a) is barred if the discussion earlier is accurate,[103] the general approach is problematic on minimalist grounds. This framework has no natural place for the condition of adjacency. Furthermore, if Case is assigned by raising to a [Spec, head] position, as we assume, adjacency should be irrelevant in any event. It is also unclear why the verb should raise at all in (141), or where it is raising to. It seems that either the proposed analysis is wrong, or there is a problem for the minimalist framework.

In fact, the empirical grounds for the analysis are dubious. Consider such adverbial phrases as *every day* or *last night*, which cannot appear in the position of *often* in (140a).

(142) *John every day reads to his children

Nevertheless, we still find the paradigm of (141).

(143) a.   John reads every day to his children
      b.   *John reads every day books

Furthermore, similar phenomena appear when raising is not an option at all, as in (144).

(144) a.   John made a decision (last night, suddenly) to leave town
      b.   John felt an obligation (last night, suddenly) to leave town

Here the adverbial may have matrix scope, so that it is not within the infinitival clause. It can appear between the N head and its complement, though the N cannot have raised in the manner under discussion. The examples indicate that at least in structures of the form (145), we cannot conclude from the matrix scope of Adv that α has raised out of the embedded phrase β.

(145) [... [$_\beta$ α Adv [to-VP]] ...]

   In general, it is doubtful that raising has anything to do with the relevant paradigms.

   The phenomena suggest a Larsonian solution. Suppose that we exclude (140a) from the paradigm entirely, assuming that *often* appears in some higher position and thus does not exemplify (139) with XP = VP. The structure underlying (141) and (143) is (146); that is true even if α is absent, under assumptions about transitive verb structures adopted earlier (see discussion of (115)).

(146)

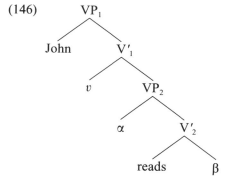

Here VP$_1$ and V$'_1$ are projections of the light verb v, VP$_2$ and V$'_2$ are projections of *read*, and *reads* raises to adjoin to v.

   Suppose that α in (146) is the adverbial *often*. Then if $\beta = $ *to the children*, there is no problem. But if $\beta = $ *books*, the derivation will crash; *books* cannot raise to [Spec, Agr] to have its Case checked because there are two closer intervening elements: the subject *John* and *often*.[104] The Relativized Minimality violations are not overcome by V-raising to v, then v-raising to Agr$_0$; the combined operations leave α closer to Agr$_0$ than β = *books*. Recall that *books* cannot raise to [Spec, v], for reasons already discussed.

Under this analysis, the basic facts follow with no special assumptions. There is a Case solution, but it does not involve adjacency. The problem of optional raising is eliminated, along with those suggested by (143) and (144).

Questions remain about other matters, among them: What is the basis for the French-English distinction, and is it somehow reducible to overt V-raising? Why do the *wh*-variants of the adverbials in question behave like adjuncts, not arguments?[105] What about CED effects in the case of such adjuncts as Adj in (147), which might be in a complement position if the analysis generalizes?

(147) they [read the book [$_{Adj}$ after we left]]

I leave such questions without any useful comment.

Another class of questions has to do with the scope of adverbials in ECM constructions. Consider the sentences in (148).

(148) a. I tell (urge, implore) my students every year (that they should get their papers in on time, to work hard)
      b. I would prefer for my students every year to (get their papers in on time, work hard)
      c. I believe my students every year to (work hard, have gotten their papers in on time)

Under the Larsonian analysis just outlined, *every year* should have matrix scope in (148a), and (148c) should have the marginal status of (148b), with embedded scope if interpretable at all. The differences seem to be in the expected direction, though they are perhaps not as sharp as one might like. We would incidentally expect the distinction to be obviated in a V-raising language such as Icelandic, as appears to be the case (Dianne Jonas, personal communication).

The same analysis predicts that matrix scope should be marginal at best in (149) and (150).

(149) a. I hear [him often talk to his friends]
      b. I've proved [him repeatedly a liar]

(150) I've proved [him repeatedly to be a liar]

The cases of (149) come out about as expected, but such examples as (150) have been cited since Postal's early raising-to-object work (1974) to illustrate matrix scope. We are left with some unclarity about the proper idealization of the data with extraneous factors removed.

A plausible conclusion seems to me that the scope of the embedded element is narrow, as in (148) and (149), and that (150) involves the kind of "rearrangement" that has been called "extraposition" in the past, but that may not belong at all within the framework of principles we are considering; see section 4.7.3. The wide scope interpretation may then fall together with such cases as (131) and (144)–(145), in which overt raising to a higher position is hardly likely.[106] This is speculative, however.

Similar qualifications may well be in order with regard to multiple-adjunct structures such as (151a), particularly if they also involve multiple rearrangement, as in (151b) and (131).

(151) a. John watched a documentary with great interest yesterday twice in a Boston theater
       b. John watched a documentary yesterday that he really enjoyed about the French revolution by the author we met of the most interesting novels that any of us had ever read

Whatever may be involved in such cases, it is unlikely that proliferation of shells is relevant. Even if that analysis is assumed for multiple adjuncts, there is little reason to suppose that the verb raises repeatedly from deep in the structure; rather, if a shell structure is relevant at all, the additional phrases might be supported by empty heads below the main verb, which might be no more deeply embedded than in (146). Pending better understanding of this whole range of topics, it seems premature to speculate.

The same kind of analysis seems appropriate for a wide range of complex verbal structures, whether or not elements of the internal domain are NP arguments. Consider such constructions as *they looked angry to him*. Here *angry* and *to him* are within the internal domain of *looked*, though their relative position is unclear; surface order may be misleading, for reasons discussed. Suppose that on the analogy of *seem to* constructions (see discussion of (98)), *angry* is the complement. The structure would then be (152).

(152)

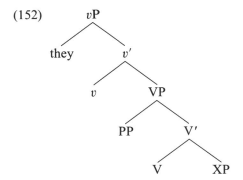

Here V = *looked*, PP = *to him*, XP = *angry*, and V adjoins to the light
verb *v*.

It is possible that a similar approach might cover part of the territory
assigned to a process of "reanalysis" in earlier work. Compare (153a)
and (153b).

(153) a. this road was recently driven on
      b. *this road was driven recently on

Preposition stranding of the kind illustrated in (153a) has varying degrees of acceptability, but examples degrade rapidly when an adverb intervenes as in (153b), a phenomenon that has been used to support the
idea that V–P constructions sometimes "reanalyze" as a new verb V'. An
analysis along the lines of (146) yields the same results—without, however, addressing other familiar questions, for example, why are such sentences as *which road did John drive recently on* also degraded, and why
do we sometimes find idiomatic interpretations in the "reanalyzed" cases?

4.8 Order

Nothing has yet been said about ordering of elements. There is no clear
evidence that order plays a role at LF or in the computation from N to
LF. Let us assume that it does not. Then ordering is part of the phonological component, a proposal that has been put forth over the years in
various forms. If so, then it might take quite a different form without
affecting C_{HL} if language use involved greater expressive dimensionality
or no sensorimotor manifestation at all.

It seems natural to suppose that ordering applies to the output of
Morphology, assigning a linear (temporal, left-to-right) order to the ele-

ments it forms, all of them X^0s though not necessarily lexical items. If correct, these assumptions lend further reason to suppose that there is no linear order in the $N \rightarrow LF$ computation, assuming that it has no access to the output of Morphology.

The standard assumption has been that order is determined by the head parameter: languages are basically head-initial (English) or head-final (Japanese), with further refinements. Fukui has proposed that the head parameter provides an account of optional movement, which otherwise is excluded under economy conditions apart from the special case of equally economical alternative derivations. He argues that movement that maintains the ordering of the head parameter is "free"; other movement must be motivated by Greed (Last Resort). Thus, in head-final Japanese, leftward movement (scrambling, passive) is optional, while in head-initial English, such operations must be motivated by feature checking; and rightward extraposition is free in English, though barred in Japanese.[107]

Kayne (1993) has advanced a radical alternative to the standard assumption, proposing that order reflects structural hierarchy universally by means of the Linear Correspondence Axiom (LCA), which states that asymmetric c-command (ACC) imposes a linear ordering of terminal elements; any category that cannot be totally ordered by LCA is barred. From Kayne's specific formulation, it follows that there is a universal specifier-head-complement (SVO) order and that specifiers are in fact adjuncts. A head-complement structure, then, is necessarily an XP, which can be extended—exactly once, on Kayne's assumptions—to a two-segment XP.

The general idea is very much in the spirit of the Minimalist Program and consistent with the speculation that the essential character of C_{HL} is independent of the sensorimotor interface. Let us consider how it might be incorporated into the bare phrase structure theory. That is not an entirely straightforward matter, because the bare theory lacks much of the structure of the standard X-bar theory that plays a crucial role in Kayne's analysis.[108]

Kayne offers two kinds of arguments for the LCA: conceptual and empirical, the latter extended in subsequent work (see particularly Zwart 1993 and Kayne 1994). The conceptual arguments show how certain stipulated properties of X-bar theory can be derived from the LCA. The empirical arguments can largely be carried over to a reformulation of the LCA within the bare theory, but the conceptual ones are problematic.

First, the derivation of these properties relies crucially not just on the LCA, but on features of standard X-bar theory that are abandoned in the bare theory. Second, the conclusions are for the most part immediate in the bare theory without the LCA.[109]

Let us ask how a modified LCA might be added to the bare theory. There is no category-terminal distinction, hence no head-terminal distinction and no associated constraints on c-command. Suppose we have the structure (154), which is the bare-theory counterpart to several of the richer structures that Kayne considers.

(154)

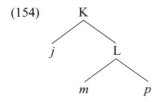

Here L is either m or p, K is either j or L. K may be either a separate category or a segment of either [K, j] or [K, L], depending on which projects. The heads are the terminal elements j, m, p. Assuming that L is not formed by adjunction, either m or p is its head and the other is both maximal and minimal; say m is the head, for concreteness, so L is mP.

Suppose that K is a separate category and L projects, so that j is a specifier in an A-position. ACC holds (j, m) and (j, p), so j must precede m and p. But it would hold of (m, p) only if the single-terminal p (the complement of the head m) were replaced by a complex category. Hence, we have the order specifier-head-complement, though only for nontrivial complement.

Suppose that instead of terminal j we had branching J, with constituents α, β. L is an X′, neither maximal nor minimal, so it does not c-command.[110] Therefore, the ACC relations are unchanged.

Suppose that K is a separate category and j projects, so that it is the head of K with complement L. ACC holds as before.

Suppose that K is a segment, either j or L. There is no particular problem, but adjunct-target order will depend on the precise definition of c-command.

In brief, the LCA can be adopted in the bare theory, but with somewhat different consequences. The segment-category distinction (and the related ones) can be maintained throughout. We draw Kayne's basic conclusion about SVO order directly, though only if the complement is more complex than a single terminal.

Let us return to the case of $L = mP$ with the single-terminal complement p, both minimal and maximal. Since neither m nor p asymmetrically c-commands the other, no ordering is assigned to m, p; the assigned ordering is not total, and the structure violates the LCA. That leaves two possibilities. Either we weaken the LCA so that nontotal orderings (but not "contradictory" orderings) are admissible under certain conditions, or we conclude that the derivation crashes unless the structure $N = [_L \; m \; p]$ has changed by the time the LCA applies so that its internal structure is irrelevant; perhaps N is converted by Morphology to a "phonological word" not subject internally to the LCA, assuming that the LCA is an operation that applies after Morphology.

Consider the first possibility: is there a natural way to weaken the LCA? One obvious choice comes to mind: there is no reason for the LCA to order an element that will disappear at PF, for example, a trace. Suppose, then, that we exempt traces from the LCA, so that (154) is legitimate if p has overtly raised, leaving a trace that can be ignored by the LCA. The second possibility can be realized in essentially the same manner, by allowing the LCA to delete traces. Under this interpretation, the LCA may eliminate the offending trace in (154), if p has raised.

In short, if the complement is a single-terminal XP, then it must raise overtly. If $XP = DP$, then its head D is a clitic, either demonstrative or pronominal, which attaches at a higher point (determined either generally, or by specific morphological properties).[111] If $XP = NP$, then N must incorporate to V (and we must show that other options are blocked). Clitics, then, are bare Ds without complements, and noun incorporation must be restricted to "nonreferential NPs" (as noted by Hagit Borer), assuming the quasi-referential, indexical character of a noun phrase to be a property of the D head of DP, NP being a kind of predicate. Within DP, the N head of NP must raise to D (as argued in a different manner by Longobardi (1994)).[112]

We therefore expect to find two kinds of pronominal (similarly, demonstrative) elements, simple ones that are morphologically marked as affixes and must cliticize, and complex ones with internal structure, which do not cliticize: in French, for example, the determiner D (*le*, *la*, etc.) and the complex element *lui-même* 'himself'. In Irish the simple element is again D, and the complex one may even be discontinuous, as in *an teach sin* 'that house', with determiner *an-sin* (Andrew Carnie, personal communication). A phenomenon that may be related is noted by Esther

Torrego. In Spanish the Case marker *de* can be omitted in (155a), but not in (155b).

(155) a. cerca de la plaza 'near the plaza'
      b. cerca de ella 'near it'

When *de* is deleted in (155a), D = *la* can incorporate in *cerca*, satisfying the Case Filter; but that is impossible in (155b) if the complex pronominal *ella* is not D but a word with richer structure, from which the residue of D cannot be extracted.

Since the affixal property is lexical, simple pronominals cliticize even if they are not in final position (e.g., a pronominal object that is a specifier in a Larsonian shell). If focus adds more complex structure, then focused (stressed) simple pronominals could behave like complex pronominals. If English-type pronouns are simple, they too must cliticize, though locally, not raising to I as in Romance (perhaps as a reflex of lack of overt V-raising). The barrier to such structures as *I picked up it* might follow. English determiners such as *this* and *that* are presumably complex, with the initial consonant representing D (as in *the*, *there*, etc.) and the residue a kind of adjective, perhaps. Various consequences are worth exploring.

Although apparently not unreasonable, the conclusions are very strong: thus, every right-branching structure must end in a trace, on these assumptions.

What about ordering of adjuncts and targets? In Kayne's theory, adjuncts necessarily precede their targets. Within the bare theory, there is no really principled conclusion, as far as I can see. Ordering depends on exactly how the core relations of phrase structure theory, *dominate* and *c-command*, are generalized to two-segment categories.

Consider the simplest case, with α attached to K, which projects.

(156)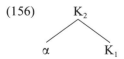

Suppose that K_2 is a new category, α the specifier or complement, so that (156) = L = {H(K), {α, K}}. Take *dominate* to be an irreflexive relation with the usual interpretation. Then L dominates α and K; informally, K_2 dominates α and K_1.

Suppose, however, that the operation was adjunction, forming the two-segment category [K_2, K_1] = {⟨H(K), H(K)⟩, {α, K}}. Are α and

K_1 dominated by the category $[K_2, K_1]$? As for c-command, let us assume that α c-commands outside of this category; thus, if it heads a chain, it c-commands its trace, which need not be in K_1 (as in head raising).[113] But what about further c-command relations, including those within (156) itself?

The core intuition underlying c-command is that

(157) X c-commands Y if (a) every Z that dominates X dominates Y
       and (b) X and Y are disconnected.

For categories, we take X and Y to be disconnected if $X \neq Y$ and neither dominates the other. The notions "dominate" and "disconnected" (hence "c-command") could be generalized in various ways for segments.

These relations are restricted to *terms*, in the sense defined earlier: in the case of (156), to α, K $(= K_1)$, and the two-segment category $[K_2, K_1]$. K_2 has no independent status. These conclusions comport reasonably well with the general condition that elements enter into the computational system C_{HL} if they are "visible" at the interface. Thus, K_1 may assign or receive a semantic role, as may α (or the chain it heads, which must meet the Chain Condition). But there is no "third" role left over for K_2; the two-segment category will be interpreted as a word by Morphology and WI (see (125)) if K is an X^0, and otherwise falls under the narrow options discussed earlier.[114]

If that much is correct, we conclude that in (156), $[K_2, K_1]$ dominates its lower segment K_1, so that the latter does not c-command anything (including α, not dominated by $[K_2, K_1]$ but only contained in it).

Turning next to c-command, how should we extend the notion "disconnected" of (157b) to adjuncts? Take adjunction to a nonmaximal head ((16) in Kayne 1993, reduced to its bare counterpart).

(158)

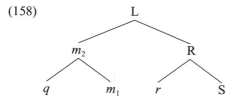

Here q is adjoined to the head m to form the two-segment category $[m_2, m_1]$, a nonmaximal X^0 projecting to and heading the category L, which has label m. R is the complement of m and r its head, and S (which may be complex) is the complement of r. What are the c-command relations for the adjunct structure?

The lowest Z that dominates q and m_1 is L, which also dominates $[m_2, m_1]$. Therefore, q and $[m_2, m_1]$ asymmetrically c-command r and S, however we interpret "disconnected." What are the c-command relations within $[m_2, m_1]$? As noted, m_1 does not c-command anything. The other relations depend on the interpretation of "disconnected" in (158b). Kayne interprets it as "X excludes Y." Then q (asymmetrically) c-commands $[m_2, m_1]$, which dominates m_1, so that q precedes m_1; and in general, an adjunct precedes the head to which it is adjoined. If X, Y are taken to be "disconnected" if no segment of one contains the other, then q c-commands m_1 but not $[m_2, m_1]$, and again q precedes m_1.[115] If "disconnected" requires still further dissociation of X, Y—say, that neither is a segment of a category that contains the other—then no ordering is determined for q, m_1 by the LCA.

I do not see any principled way to choose among the various options.

If m_1 is not a head but the complex category $[_m m \text{ P}]$, so that q is an XP for reasons already discussed, then q c-commands the constituents of m_1 under all interpretations of "disconnect," and the adjunct precedes the target (whether q is internally complex or not).

Left open, then, is the case of adjunction of a head to another head, that is, ordering within words. Whether order should be fixed here depends on questions about inflectional morphology and word formation that seem rather obscure and may have no general answer.

Summarizing, it seems that Kayne's basic intuition can be accommodated in a straightforward way in the bare theory, including the major empirical conclusions, specifically, the universal order SVO and adjunct-target (at least for XP adjuncts). In the bare theory, the LCA gains no support from conceptual arguments and therefore rests on the empirical consequences. We take the LCA to be a principle of the phonological component that applies to the output of Morphology, optionally ignoring or deleting traces. The specifier-adjunct (A-$\overline{\text{A}}$) distinction is maintained, along with the possibility of multiple specifiers or adjuncts, though the options for adjunction are very limited for other reasons. There are further consequences with regard to cliticization and other matters, whether correct or not, I do not know.

4.9 Expletives and Economy

The evidence reviewed so far has led us to postulate two functional categories within IP for simple constructions, Tense (T) and Agr. Occurrence of T is motivated by bare output conditions because of its semantic properties, and also for structural reasons: it checks the tense feature of V and the Case of the subject, and it provides a position for overt nominals, either raised or merged (EPP). Agr is motivated only structurally: it is involved in checking of features of subject and object, and it provides a position for overt object raising.[116]

Several gaps in the paradigm remain to be explained. There are three functional categories, but so far only two positions for overt specifiers: subject and object. Furthermore, the [Spec, I] position contains either an expletive or a raised nominal, but only the latter appears in [Spec, Agr_O].

The first gap would be eliminated if there were structures with both of the predicted [Spec, I] positions occupied. More interesting still are constructions with all three of the possible specifier positions: IPs of the form (159), where Nom is a nominal phrase, DP or NP.

(159) [$_{AgrP}$ Nom Agr_S [$_{TP}$ Nom T [$_{AgrP}$ Nom Agr_O VP]]]

Recall that the subscripts on Agr are mnemonics with no theoretical status, indicating the position of the functional category.

The structure (159) is illustrated by transitive expletive constructions (TECs) as analyzed by Jonas and Bobaljik (1993), Jonas (1994, forthcoming). Jonas and Bobaljik concentrate on Icelandic, which has structures of the following type (English words), according to their analysis:

(160) [$_{AgrP}$ there painted [$_{TP}$ a student t_T [$_{AgrP}$[the house VP]]]]

The meaning is something like 'a student painted the house', or the intelligible but unacceptable English counterpart (161).

(161) there painted the house a student (who traveled all the way from India to do it)

In (160) the expletive is in [Spec, Agr_S]; *painted* is the verbal head of VP raised in stages to T, which then raises to Agr_S, leaving the trace t_T; the subject *a student* is raised to [Spec, t_T] and the object *the house* to [Spec, Agr_O]; and VP contains only traces. The pre-VP position of the object is motivated by placement of adverbials and negation in the overt forms. The usual properties of expletive constructions hold: [Spec, t_T], the associate of the expletive in [Spec, Agr_S], is nonspecific and determines the number of the verb in the Agr_S position. All three predicted positions are occupied in the overt form.[117]

Case and agreement are checked for the object overtly in [Spec, Agr_O], and for the subject after covert raising of its formal features to Agr_S.

In a TEC, Agr$_S$ and T each have overt specifiers. Hence, each has a strong feature—in effect, a generalization of the EPP to Agr and T independently. In introducing the EPP (section 4.2.1, below (1)), I noted a certain ambiguity about the strong feature that expresses it: it could be (1) a D-feature, (2) an N-feature, or (3) a general nominal feature, either D or N. So far I have been using the terminology (1), but neutrally among the three choices. At this point the choices begin to make a difference, so more care is needed.

The specifier of Agr$_S$ is the expletive, so the strong feature of Agr$_S$ at least allows and may require the categorial feature [D]. The specifier of T is nominal, but there are theory-internal reasons, to which we will turn in section 4.10, suggesting that it might be NP rather than DP. If correct, that could be a factor in accounting for the definiteness effect: the fact that the associate in an expletive construction, whether in [Spec, T] or lower in the clause, is nonspecific, NP rather than DP (D assumed to be the locus of specificity). Furthermore, since Agr$_S$ and Agr$_O$ are the same element appearing in two different positions, if Agr$_S$ has a strong D-feature, then Agr$_O$ should as well. We thus expect overt object raising to favor definite-specific nominals, whereas nonspecific NPs remain in situ (by Procrastinate). That seems the general tendency.

The analysis of the I structures is the same whether the object is raised or not, or even in passive and raising expletives with subject in [Spec, T], as in (162) (translation of Icelandic examples from Jonas 1994).

(162) a. there have [$_{TP}$ some cakes [$_{VP}$ been baked t for the party]]
      b. there seems [$_{TP}$ [$_{Subj}$ someone] [$_{IP}$ t to be in the room]]

Let us refer to all of these as *multiple-subject constructions* (MSCs), whether transitive (TEC) or not.

MSCs fall within the range of options already available, using more fully the available strength features of functional categories. These constructions also provide additional support for the conclusion that the expletives in expletive-associate constructions lack Case or ϕ-features, by simple extension of reasoning already given. MSCs thus offer further evidence that the expletive is pure, as we would expect on general grounds.

In a close analysis of Icelandic, several Faroese dialects, and Mainland Scandinavian, Jonas (1994) found MSCs to be contingent on overt V-raising. We know from languages without overt V-raising, like English, that at least one functional category, T or Agr, can take an overt specifier if it "stands alone," not supported by overt V-raising. Assuming this category to be T, Jonas's generalization states that Agr cannot have a specifier unless supported by V.[118]

MSCs such as (160) raise two basic questions.

(163) a. Why do languages differ with regard to MSCs, some allowing them, others not?

b. How are such structures permitted by economy principles?

These questions presuppose some analysis of simple expletive constructions such as (164a–b).

(164) a. there arrived a man

b. there is a book missing from the shelf

We have found considerable evidence that in such constructions the formal features of the associate raise covertly to matrix I, checking Case and φ-features and functioning as if they were in subject rather than object position with regard to binding and control.[119] I will continue to assume that account to be correct in its essentials.

Returning to question (163a), why do only certain languages permit MSCs? Jonas's generalization is relevant here: overt MSCs require overt V-raising. Could there be MSCs with only covert raising? Example (161) suggests that the possibility should not be immediately discounted. As noted, the sentence is unacceptable (as is (164a), to some degree) though intelligible, and with other lexical choices the construction ranges in acceptability, as Kayne has observed.

(165) a. there entered the room a man from England

b. there hit the stands a new journal

c. there visited us last night a large group of people who traveled all the way from India

Such constructions have been thought to result from an extraposition operation depending in part on considerations of "heaviness," but in our restricted terms, there is no obvious source for such constructions apart from MSCs. A possibility that might be explored is that they are in fact MSCs, with the subject category appearing overtly at the right boundary, perhaps the result of a process in the phonological component that could be motivated by properties of theme-rheme structures, which typically involve "surface" forms in some manner. Prominence of the theme might require that it be at a boundary: to the right, since the leftmost position is occupied by the expletive subject. Icelandic might escape this condition as a reflex of its internal-V-second property, which requires a method for interpreting internal themes. The lexical restrictions in English may reflect the semilocative character of the expletive. If speculations along these lines prove tenable, question (163a) may take a somewhat more complex form; the MSC option may be more general, but with different manifestations depending on other properties of the language.[120]

Question (163b) leads into a thicket of complex and only partly explored issues. The fact that MSCs alternate with nonexpletive constructions is unproblematic; the alternatives arise from different numerations, hence are not comparable in terms of economy.[121] But there are questions about some of the instantiations of the postulated structures (166).

(166) Exp Agr [Subj [T XP]]

Suppose we have the overt form (167). We would expect this to be the manifestation of the two distinct MSCs (168a) and (168b).

(167) there seems someone to be in the room

(168) a. there seems [$_{TP}$ someone [$_{IP}$ t to be in the room]]
       b. there seems [$_{IP}$ t [$_{TP}$ someone to be in the room]]

In (168a) the matrix clause is an MSC with the subject *someone* occupying matrix [Spec, T]. In (168b) the embedded clause is an MSC with *someone* occupying embedded [Spec, T] and the trace of *there* occupying the higher Spec of the MSC. Both possibilities appear to be legitimate (Jonas 1994); (168a) is (162b)).[122] But we have to explain why both (168a) and (168b) are legitimate outcomes of the same numeration, and why (169) is barred in English.

(169) *there seems (to me, often) [$_{IP}$ someone to be in the room]

We do not have a direct contradiction. Principles of UG might bar (169) generally while permitting (168). Tentatively assuming that possibility to point to the resolution of the problem, we then ask why the structures illustrated in (168) are permitted while the one in (169) is barred. We cannot appeal to the numeration in this case, because it is the same in all examples.

We also have to explain why (170) is permitted, with *there* raising from the position of t, where it satisfies the EPP in the embedded clause.

(170) there seems [t to be [someone in the room]]

The problem becomes harder still when we add ECM constructions. In these, the embedded subject *does* raise overtly to a position analogous to *t* in (170), where it is barred (see (169)); and it cannot remain in situ as it does in (170).

(171) a. I expected [someone to be [*t* in the room]] (. . . to have been killed *t'*)
       b. *I expected [*t* to be [someone in the room]] (. . . to have been killed John)

We thus have an intricate network of properties that are near-contradictory. Within the minimalist framework, we expect the escape route to be provided by invariant UG principles of economy.

The questions have to do with overt movement; hence, one relevant principle should be Procrastinate, which favors covert movement. Procrastinate selects among convergent derivations: overt movement is permitted (and forced) to guarantee convergence. Beyond that, the questions bear directly on basic assumptions of the theories of movement and economy.

Let us begin by considering the ECM cases, which contrast with control cases as in (172), *t* the trace of the embedded subject.

(172) a. I expected [PRO to [*t* leave early]]
       b. I expected [someone to [*t* leave early]]

In present terms, these differ in properties of the head H of the embedded phrase. In both structures, the EPP holds, so the nominal feature of H is strong. In the control structure (172a), H assigns null Case to the subject, which must therefore be PRO. In the ECM structure (172b), H assigns no Case, so *John* raises to the checking domain of Agr_O in the matrix clause; more precisely, its formal features raise covertly to this position, we assume.

There are three basic problems about (172b): (1) Why doesn't *someone* raise overtly all the way to the matrix position in which it receives Case? (2) Why is *someone* permitted to raise overtly to embedded subject position? (3) Why must *someone* raise overtly from the trace position (also PRO in (171a))?

Problem (1) is overcome by Procrastinate, which requires that the second step in raising to the Case-checking position be covert, assuming that Agr_O is weak. Question (2) has already been answered: *someone* has accessible features, and one of them, its categorial feature, checks the strong nominal feature of the embedded I (EPP). Problem (3) now disappears: if *someone* does not raise overtly from the trace position, the derivation crashes.[123]

Let us now turn to the contrasting cases (169) and (171). In each case the reference set determined by the initial numeration includes a second derivation: in the case of (169), the one that yields (170); in the case of (171a), the analogous one that yields (171b) with α the trace of raised *I*. Our goal is to show that in the case of (169)–(170), economy considerations compel raising of *there* from the embedded clause, while in the case of (171), the same considerations block raising of *I* from the embedded clause, requiring raising of *someone* to embedded subject position to satisfy the EPP. The properties of the constructions suggest that the answer lies in θ-theory.

Consider first (169) and (170), specifically, the structure that is common to the two derivations. In each, at some stage we construct $\gamma =$ (173), with the small clause β.

(173) $[_\gamma$ to be $[_\beta$ someone in the room]]

The next step must fill the specifier position of γ to satisfy the EPP. Given the initial numeration, there are two possibilities: we can raise *someone* to [Spec, γ] or we can insert *there* in this position.[124] The former choice violates Procrastinate; the latter does not. We therefore choose the second option, forming (174).

(174) $[_\gamma$ there to be β]

At a later stage in the derivation we reach the structure (175).

(175) $[_\delta$ seems $[_\gamma$ there to be β]]

Convergence requires that [Spec, δ] be filled. Only one legitimate option exists: to raise *there*, forming (170). We therefore select this option.

The argument is based on the assumption that at a particular stage Σ of a derivation from numeration N, we consider the reference set R(N, Σ) from a highly "local" point of view, selecting the best possible (most economical) move available in R(N, Σ) at stage Σ. This more restrictive approach is preferable on conceptual grounds for the usual reasons of reduction of computational complexity; and once again, conceptual naturalness and empirical demands coincide, as we would hope if we are on the right track.

Why, then, does the same argument not favor (171b) over (171a)? The common part of the derivations is again (173). We have two ways to fill [Spec, γ], raising of *someone* or insertion of *I*, the latter being preferred.

Suppose we insert *I*, then raising it to form (171b), analogous formally to the legitimate outcome (170). But we already know that the argument chain (*I*, *t*) in (171b) lacks a θ-role under this analysis (see section 4.6). If this causes the derivation to crash, then the unwanted outcome is barred and only (171a) is permitted. If this is only a case of convergent gibberish, then it blocks the desired outcome (171a), incorrectly. We therefore conclude that an argument with no θ-role is not a legitimate object, violating FI and causing the derivation to crash, a conclusion that is natural though not previously forced.[125]

In section 4.6 we reached a somewhat weaker conclusion on different grounds. There we found reason to believe that a derivation crashes if θ-roles are not properly assigned, leaving open the question whether the problem is failure to assign a θ-role, or to receive one, or both. We now have a partial answer: failure of argument α to receive a θ-role causes the derivation to crash. The status of failure to assign a θ-role remains open. In earlier work it has been suggested that external θ-role need not be assigned in nominalizations and is in this sense optional; we have not excluded that possibility, or confirmed it, though we have found reason to suppose that in verb-headed constructions, the question of assignment of external θ-role arises only in a somewhat different form. If a configuration [*v*–VP] is formed with [Spec, *v*], that configuration just *is* an external θ-role, and the question is, what happens if a nonargument (an expletive) appears in this position, violating the θ-Criterion? We will return to this question, leaving it without definite answer.

Let us consider how the economy-theoretic account of raising in expletive constructions comports with earlier discussion of *it*-expletives, as in (83), rephrased here as (176).

(176) it seems [that someone was told *t* [that IP]]

At an earlier stage of the derivation of (176), we have (177), analogous to (173).

(177) [$_\gamma$ was told someone [that IP]]

Since the numeration includes expletive *it*, we have the same two options as in the cases just discussed: we can raise *someone* or insert *it*, the latter option being preferred. Suppose we insert *it*, then raising it to form (178), analogous to (170).

(178) it seems [that *t* was told someone [that IP]]

But the derivation crashes for several reasons (the Case-checking feature of matrix T is not erased, the Case of *someone* is not checked). Since economy considerations select among convergent derivations, the preferred option of inserting the expletive in (177) cannot be employed, and we derive (176), as required.[126]

One aspect of question (163b) still remains unanswered: why is the permitted MSC structure (166), repeated here as (179a), not blocked by the alternative (179b), in accord with the reasoning just reviewed?

(179) a. Exp Agr [Subj [T XP]]
       b. Exp Agr [*t* [T [... Subj ...]]]

In other words, why are (168a–b), repeated here, both legitimate?

(180) a. there seems [$_{TP}$ someone [$_{IP}$ *t* to be in the room]]
       b. there seems [$_{IP}$ *t* [$_{TP}$ someone to be in the room]]

By the reasoning just outlined, we would expect (180b) to block (180a), avoiding the violation of Procrastinate by overt raising of *someone*. Let us delay the question until the next section.[127]

It is worth highlighting the basic assumption about reference sets that underlies the preceding discussion: they are determined by the initial numeration, but in a fairly "local" fashion. At a particular stage Σ in the derivation, we consider only the continuations that are permitted from Σ to LF, using what remains of the initial numeration; the most economical of these blocks the others. But we ask even a narrower question: at Σ, which operation that yields a convergent derivation is most economical *at this point*? Thus, we select Merge over Attract/Move if that yields a convergent derivation, irrespective of consequences down the road as long as the derivation converges; but we select Attract/Move even violating Procrastinate if that is necessary for convergence. The problems of computational complexity are thus considerably reduced, though more remains to be done, no doubt. The assumptions throughout are straightforward, but rather delicate. It remains to investigate further cases and consequences.

4.10 Functional Categories and Formal Features

What precedes substantially revises the framework developed in chapters 1–3. But we have not yet subjected functional categories to the same minimalist critique. In the final section I would like to explore this question, a course that leads to another fairly substantial modification. Even more than before, I will speculate rather freely. The issues that arise are fundamental to the nature of C_{HL}, having to do with the formal features that advance the computation (primarily strength, which drives overt operations that are reflected at the A-P interface) and the functional categories that consist primarily (sometimes entirely) of such features.

4.10.1 The Status of Agr

Functional categories have a central place in the conception of language we are investigating, primarily because of their presumed role in feature checking, which is what drives Attract/Move. We have considered four functional categories: T, C, D, and Agr. The first three have Interpretable features, providing "instructions" at either or both interface levels. Agr does not; it consists of −Interpretable formal features only. We therefore have fairly direct evidence from interface relations about T, C, and D, but not Agr. Unlike the other functional categories, Agr is present only for theory-internal reasons. We should therefore look more closely at two questions.

(181) a. Where does Agr appear?
       b. What is the feature constitution of Agr?

In section 4.2.2 we tentatively assumed that Agr lacks φ-features, just as it (fairly clearly) lacks an independent Case-assigning feature, that being provided by the V or T that adjoins to it. If Agr indeed lacks φ-features as well, we would expect that the φ-features of a predicate Pred (verb or adjective) are added to Pred (optionally) as it is selected from the lexicon for the numeration. We had little warrant for the assumption about φ-features, and so far it has had little effect on the analysis. But it becomes relevant as we attempt more careful answers to the questions of (181). I will continue to assume that the original assumption was correct, returning to the question at the end, after having narrowed significantly the range of considerations relevant to it.

We have evidence bearing on question (181a) when Agr is strong, so that the position is phonetically indicated by the overt categories that raise to it: V and T by adjunction, DP by substitution in [Spec, Agr]. The richest example is an MSC with object raising, as in the Icelandic TEC construction (160). Here three pre-VP positions are required within IP for nominal expressions: expletive, subject, and object. One position is provided by T. We therefore have evidence for two noninterpretable functional categories, the ones we have been calling Agr (Agr$_S$ and Agr$_O$). In MSCs, Agr$_S$ is strong, providing a specifier and a position for V-raising above the domain of strong T: in effect, a "double EPP" configuration. Another VP-external position is provided between T and VP by strong Agr$_O$. That is the basic rationale behind the analyses just outlined. It accords with the general minimalist outlook, but the anomalous status of Agr raises questions.

The background issues have to do with the strong features of T and Agr, and what appears in the overt specifier positions they make available. In the I position, preceding all verb phrases (main or auxiliary), we have postulated two functional categories: T and Agr$_S$. In MSCs the specifier position of each is nominal, DP or NP; hence, the strong feature must at least be [nominal-], meaning satisfied by the nominal categorial feature [D] or [N]. At most one nominal can-have its Case and φ-features checked in this position, which suggests that one of the two nominals must be the pure expletive Exp, a DP. Let us assume this to be the case, though it is not as yet established. The observed order is Exp-nominal rather than nominal-Exp, a fact yet to be explained.

The best case is for Agr$_O$ to have the same constitution as Agr$_S$. Since Agr$_S$ allows and perhaps requires a D-feature, the same should be true of Agr$_O$. Hence, both Agrs attract DPs: nominals that are definite or specific. As noted, it follows that expletive-associate constructions observe the definiteness effect and that object raising is restricted to definite (or specific) nominals. This is close enough to accurate to suggest that something of the sort may be happening.

Recall, however, that the definiteness effect for object raising is at best a strong tendency, and that for expletive constructions its status is unclear. It does not rule out any derivations, but rather describes how legitimate outputs are to be interpreted: either as expletive constructions with at most weakly existential implicatures, or as list constructions with strong existential interpretation (see notes 42, 44). We therefore have no strong reason to suppose that the associate *cannot* be a DP—only that if it is, a certain kind of interpretation is expected.

With strong features, Agr provides a position for T- or V-raising (adjunction) and DP-raising (substitution), so there is evidence that it appears in the numeration. If Agr has no strong feature, then PF considerations, at least, give no reason for it to be present at all, and LF considerations do not seem relevant. That suggests an answer to question

(181a): Agr exists only when it has strong features. Agr is nothing more than an indication of a position that must be occupied at once by overt operations.[128] Substitution can be effected by Merge or Move. If by Merge, it is limited to expletives, for reasons already discussed.

Pursuit of question (181b) leads to a similar conclusion. The function of Agr is to provide a structural configuration in which features can be checked: Case and ϕ-features, and categorial features ([V-] and [T-] by adjunction, [D-] by substitution). The Case-assigning feature is intrinsic to the heads (V, T) that raise to Agr for checking of DP in [Spec, Agr], so there is no reason to assign it to Agr as well. With regard to ϕ-features, as already discussed, the matter is much less clear. If Agr has ϕ-features, they are $-$Interpretable, but there might be empirical effects anyway, as noted earlier. Continuing tentatively to assume that ϕ-features are (optionally) assigned to lexical items as they are drawn from the lexicon, we conclude that Agr consists only of the strong features that force raising.

Certain problems that arose in earlier versions now disappear. There is no need to deal with optionally strong Agr, or with the difference in strength of Agr_S and Agr_O. Since Agr is strong, the first problem is just a matter of optional selection of an element ([strength of F]) from the lexicon for the numeration, the irreducible minimum; and difference in strength is inexpressible. There still remains, however, a conflict between the θ-theoretic principle that transitive verbs have a v–VP structure and the assumption that overt object raising is internal to this construction (see note 81 and p. 316).

Let us turn to the properties that remain.

Since Agr consists solely of strong features, it cannot attract covert raising.[129] We have so far assumed that Subj (subject) and Obj (object) raise to the checking domain of Agr, entering into a checking relation with features of T or V adjoined to Agr (technically, adjoined within Agr^{0max}, the X^0 projection headed by Agr). But with weak Agr gone, covert raising must target T and V directly.[130]

There is now no reason to postulate Agr_O unless it induces overt raising of DP to [Spec, Agr_O]. What about Agr_S? It appears in MSCs, but lacks independent motivation elsewhere, as matters now stand. For languages of the French-English type, then, Agr is not in the lexicon (unless MSCs appear marginally, with extraposition). Agr therefore occurs in highly restricted ways.

The next question is to inquire into the justification for Agr with strong features. Let us first look at Agr_O, then turn to Agr_S.

We restrict attention now to transitive verb constructions, which we continue to assume to be of the form (182), ignoring [Spec, V] (the case of a complex internal domain).

(182)
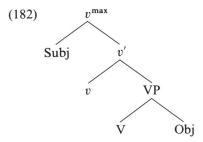

V raises overtly to the light verb v, forming the complex $Vb = [_v V v]$. Assuming unergatives to be concealed accusatives, the only other VP construction is that of unaccusatives lacking the v-shell, not relevant here.

Suppose that a derivation has formed (182) and Agr is merged with it. Agr is a collection of strong features, either [D-] or [V-] or both. As noted, we need not postulate Agr_O except for object raising; it does not consist only of strong [V-]. Holmberg's generalization states, in effect, that it cannot be just strong [D-]. Let us tentatively assume, then, that Agr_O is {strong [D-], strong [V-]}. The effect of adding Agr_O is to compel overt raising of DP to [Spec, Agr] and of Vb to Agr.

Consider the first property. There is a simple way to force overt DP-raising without the functional category Agr: namely, by adding to v itself a strong D-feature (or perhaps, the more neutral strong [nominal-] feature) that requires overt substitution in the "outer Spec" of a multiple-Spec configuration. If Obj raises to this position to form a chain (Obj, t), it will be in the checking domain of V and therefore able to check its Case and (object agreement) ϕ-features. Recall that Subj inserted by Merge in [Spec, v] is not in the checking domain of v, because it does not head a nontrivial chain.[131]

Object raising, then, takes place when the light verb v that heads the transitive verb construction (182) is assigned the strong feature as it is drawn from the lexicon and placed in the numeration; see section 4.2.2. The choice is arbitrary, forced, or unavailable as the language has optional, obligatory, or no overt object raising, respectively. Since Subj is not in the checking domain, as just noted, it does not check this strong feature, so an outer Spec must be constructed for that purpose. One way is raising of Obj; I hope to show that all others are excluded.

Suppose that an adverbial phrase Adv is adjoined to v^{max} and object raising crosses it, yielding the construction $Obj–Adv–v^{max}$. That provides no reason to postulate an Agr position outside of v^{max}: a strong feature need only be satisfied before a *distinct* higher category is created.[132]

Overt object raising therefore seems to provide no compelling reason for assuming the existence of Agr_O. The other property of Agr_O is that it forces overt V-raising—actually to T outside of VP, so the effects are never directly visible. The motivation was theory-internal, but it disappears within the more restricted framework, as we will see. The property was a crucial part of the expression of Holmberg's generalization that object raising is contingent on V-raising, but to introduce that consideration to justify postulation of Agr_O is circular. For VP, at least, it seems that we should dispense with Agr_O.

Consider adjectival constructions such as (55), repeated here.

(183) John is $[_{AgrP} \, t_1 \, Agr \, [_{AP} t_2 \, intelligent]]$

We assumed that *John* is merged in the position of t_2 in AP as [Subj, Adj] (subject of *intelligent*, in this case), raising to [Spec, Agr] for DP-adjective agreement, then on to matrix [Spec, I] for DP-verb agreement.[133] Do we need a strong functional category (Agr) here to head the small clause complement of the copula? Assuming that [Subj, Adj] is analogous to specifier or complement of V—and more generally, that the complementarity of θ-theory and checking theory holds in this case as well as others—then agreement will not be checked in this position of merger. We assumed that the $(-Interpretable)$ ϕ-features of the adjective Adj are checked by overt raising of its subject Subj to [Spec, Agr] and of Adj to Agr—the latter problematic, as mentioned, because Agr is weak in English (see note 51). We can now avoid that problem by eliminating Agr and adopting the analysis just proposed for overt object raising: Adj is assigned the feature strong [nominal-] as it is drawn from the lexicon, and [Subj, Adj] raises to the outer Spec required by the strong feature, entering the checking domain of Adj. In this case the derivation will converge only if the strong feature is selected, so the choice is in effect obligatory. Note that features of Subj cannot adjoin covertly to the Adj, as a review of the possible cases shows (on plausible assumptions).

We therefore eliminate Agr_O in this case too, using simple mechanisms and overcoming an earlier problem about unexpected head raising. The structure of predicate adjectival constructions is not (183) but rather (184).

(184) John is $[_{AP} t_1 [_{A'} t_2$ intelligent$]]$

For small clauses, we have something like the original assumptions of Stowell (1978) on which much of the work on the topic has been based, but consistent with other assumptions that we are now adopting.

If all of this turns out to be correct, we can eliminate Agr_O from the lexical inventory entirely, for any language. Turning to Agr_S, we need to consider only MSCs, which have the surface order [Exp–V–Subj]. Our assumption so far is that the subject Subj is in [Spec, T] and the expletive in [Spec, Agr_S], and that V has raised to Agr_S. Suppose, instead, we follow the line of reasoning suggested for Agr_O, eliminating Agr and adding an optional strong feature that assigns an outer Spec to T. The situation differs from the case of Agr_O. [Spec, v] in (182) is required for independent θ-related reasons, so only one new Spec is required for object raising. In contrast, T requires no Spec, so we have to accommodate two Specs that are induced only by feature strength. Independently, we have to account for the fact that the order is not the expected (185a) but rather (185b), along with other observed properties.

(185) a. Exp [Subj $[T^{0max}$ XP]]
       b. Exp T^{0max} Subj XP

MSCs appear only when the EPP holds. The question of their nature arises, then, only when T already has a strong [nominal-] feature, which is deleted when checked by DP or NP in [Spec, T]. Suppose that the derivation has reached the stage TP with T strong, and the numeration contains an unused expletive Exp. Then Exp can be inserted by Merge to satisfy the EPP, and we have an ordinary expletive-associate construction. The strong feature of T deletes and furthermore erases, since the derivation converges. Hence, overt MSCs exist only if T has a parameterized property of the kind discussed earlier (see below (58)), which allows a −Interpretable feature (in this case, the strong [nominal-] feature) to escape erasure when checked. If the option is selected, then there must be a multiple-Spec construction, with $n + 1$ specifiers if the option is exercised n times. In a language with the EPP but no MSCs, the strong nominal feature of T is introduced into the derivation with

$n = 0$, hence erased when checked. In Icelandic, the descriptive facts indicate that $n = 0$ or $n = 1$; in the latter case, T has two Specs.

Let us see where this course leads, eliminating Agr from UG entirely —and, at least for our purposes here, keeping to functional categories with intrinsic properties that are manifested at the interface levels. The questions that arise are again rather delicate. Let us delay a direct investigation of them until some further groundwork is laid.

4.10.2   Core Concepts Reconsidered
To accommodate the change from an Agr-based to a multiple-Spec theory, we have to simplify the notions of equidistance and closeness that entered into the definition of Attract/Move. These were expressed in the principle (87), repeated here.

(186) β is *closer to* K than α if β c-commands α and is not in the minimal domain of CH, where CH is the chain headed by γ, γ adjoined within the zero-level projection $H(K)^{0max}$.

But this no longer works: with the elimination of intervening heads, minimal domains collapse. We therefore have to exclude nontrivial chains from the account of equidistance, relying instead on the much more differentiated analysis of features now available and the immobility of traces—that is, on the fact that only the head of a chain can be "seen" by K seeking the closest α to attract.

In the earlier formulation, the basic case is (85), repeated here in the more general form (187) to accommodate adjunction of α to X as well as substitution of α in [Spec, X] (where X may already be the head of a complex zero-level projection).

(187)

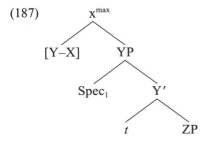

When α raises, targeting x^{max}, it creates a new position $\tau(X)$, which may either be [Spec, X] or adjoined to [Y–X] ($=X^{0\,max}$); call $\tau(X)$ the *target* in either case. The minimal domain of the chain $CH = (Y, t)$ includes

Spec$_1$ and ZP along with $\tau(X)$ formed by raising of α, which is within ZP or is ZP. Crucially, Spec$_1$ is within the "neighborhood of X" that is ignored in determining whether α is close enough to be attracted by X (technically, by its projection). That assumption was necessary in order to allow α to cross Spec$_1$ to reach $\tau(X)$. In a transitive verb construction, for example, it was assumed that X = Agr, Spec$_1$ = Subj, Y is the verbal element that adjoins to Agr, and Obj is within its ZP complement. Obj has to raise to the checking domain of Agr for feature checking either overtly or covertly, requiring that it be "as close" to the target as Spec$_1$.

Most of this is now beside the point. We have eliminated Agr and its projection from the inventory of elements. For the case of overt object raising, the structure formed is no longer (187) with X = Agr and $\tau(X)$ = [Spec, Agr], but (188), with an extra Spec in YP.

(188)

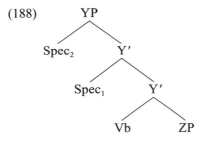

Vb is the verbal element (or its trace, if the complex has raised further to adjoin to T); Y′ and YP are projections of the light verb v to which V has adjoined to form Vb; ZP = [t_V Obj], t_V the trace of V; and Spec$_2$ is the target $\tau(v)$ created by the raising operation. Spec$_1$ is Subj, and it is only necessary that it be no closer to the target Spec$_2$ than α in ZP. For this purpose, it suffices to simplify (186), keeping just to the trivial chain CH = H(K) (the head of K) and its minimal domain. We therefore restate (186) as (189).

(189) γ and β are equidistant from α if γ and β are in the same minimal domain.

Hence, γ = Spec$_2$ and β = Spec$_1$ are equidistant from α = Obj in the illustrative example just discussed.

We now define "close" for Attract/Move in the obvious way: if β c-commands α and τ is the target of raising, then

(190) β is *closer to* K than α unless β is in the same minimal domain as
       (a) τ or (b) α.

We thus have two cases to consider. We ask (case (190a)) whether β and τ are equidistant from α, and (case (190b)) whether β and α are equidistant from τ. If either is true, then β does not bar raising of α to τ. In case (190a), β and τ are in the minimal domain of $H(K)$; and in case (190b), β and α are in the minimal domain of h, for some head h. In case (190a), β is in the "neighborhood" of $H(K)$ that is ignored, in the sense of earlier exposition.

By case (190a), Obj within ZP in (188) is close enough to be attracted by Y' ($= YP$, at this point), since $Spec_1$ is in the minimal domain of $H(Y')$ and is therefore not closer to Y' than Obj; $Spec_1$ and $Spec_2$ ($= \tau$) are equidistant from Obj. Therefore, either Subj in $Spec_1$ or Obj (in ZP) can raise to the new outer Spec, $Spec_2$, required by the strong feature of v. Both Obj and Subj must raise for Case checking, and something must raise to check the Case feature of T (or of some higher category if T is a raising infinitival, as already discussed). By case (190b), overt object raising to $Spec_2$ does not prevent subject raising from $Spec_1$, because $Spec_2$ and $Spec_1$ are equidistant from any higher target; both are in the minimal domain of v. How about direct raising of Obj from within ZP, targeting T, crossing Subj and $Spec_1$? That is barred by the MLC, since Subj and Obj are not equidistant from T, given the v–VP analysis of transitives; they are in different minimal domains. We will return to a closer analysis, reviewing other options skirted here.

Consider the following counterargument. Suppose the language has the EPP and optional object raising: T requires [Spec, T] and v permits an outer Spec, $Spec_2$, beyond Subj in $Spec_1$ (both overt). Suppose that Obj raises to [$Spec_2$, v], then raises again to [Spec, T], satisfying the EPP. That much is permitted. Subj and T have not had Case features checked, but that can be overcome by covert raising of Subj, targeting T, which is also permitted. So the derivation converges, incorrectly. But this derivation is blocked by economy conditions. It involves three raising operations, and two would suffice for convergence: object raising followed by subject raising to [Spec, T] (in both cases, with two violations of Procrastinate, the minimal number with two strong features). So the unwanted series of steps, though permitted, is barred by economy considerations: shorter derivations block longer ones.

The computation is local: after raising the object, we choose the operation that will lead to the shortest convergent derivation: raising of Subj to [Spec, T]. We also have empirical support for the tentative assumption made earlier that shorter derivations, locally determined in this sense, block longer ones (see discussion of (114)).

Note that we have lost Holmberg's generalization and other effects of V-raising on extension of chains; that is a consequence of excluding chains from the definition of "closeness." Such generalizations, if valid, would now have to be stated in terms of a property of Vb in (188): it can have a second outer Spec only if it is a trace. There is no obvious reason why this should be so.

In any event, the earlier, more complex definition of equidistance and closeness is not necessary and in fact not possible. The notion of equidistance may still be needed, as in cases just reviewed and others, but it has narrower scope.

The conclusion that equidistance is still needed relies on a tacit assumption that could be challenged: that the strong feature of v must be satisfied by the outer Spec, $Spec_2$ of (188), not the inner Spec, $Spec_1$. All we know, however, is that *some* Spec of v is motivated by considerations of θ-theory (to host the external argument) and is therefore independent of the strength of v; the other Spec is present only to check the strength feature. But both Specs are within the minimal domain of v, so either is available for θ-marking of the external argument of a transitive verb. Suppose we allow this possibility, so that the outer Spec can host the external argument. In that case we can drop the notion of equidistance entirely, simplifying (190) to the statement that β is *closer* to the target K than α if β c-commands α. It follows, then, that Obj can only raise to the inner Spec, $Spec_1$ of (188), to check the strength feature and undergo overt Case marking. If overt object raising takes place, then Subj will be merged in the outer Spec to receive the external θ-role provided by the configuration. With "closer than" restricted to c-command, only Subj in the outer Spec can be attracted by T (note that Subj always has features that will check sublabels of T). Therefore, Obj is frozen in place after overt object raising, and the conclusions reached above follow directly.[134]

On these assumptions, it follows that Subj always c-commands Obj within IP. In particular, this is true in expletive constructions, whether or not object raising has taken place; that appears to be generally the case, with some unexplained exceptions (see Jonas and Bobaljik 1993). We also have a somewhat more natural account of agreement, with the inner Spec uniformly entering into the relation (the Spec θ-position is not subject to it for reasons already discussed). It also should be the case that only the inner Spec in a multiple-Spec construction can be a binder (assuming that locality enters crucially into binding, in one of several possible ways) though control may be more free, as it often is (see section 1.4.2); that appears to be the case (Hiroyuki Ura, personal communication). Further questions arise when we turn to verbs with complex internal argument structure, which I am ignoring here.

Let us keep available these two options for the notion "closer than," noting however that the one just sketched is simpler, hence to be preferred if tenable (and certainly if empirically supported). I will present the examples below on the assumption that object raising is to the outer Spec to ensure that the required consequences follow even under this more complex alternative; it is easy to check that the arguments run through (more simply, in some cases) if closeness reduces to c-command so that object raising is to the inner Spec and only the outer Spec is attracted by T.

We also have to settle some questions about adjunction that have been left open but become more prominent in this much more restrictive framework, covert adjunction being the most interesting case. Empirical evidence for covert operations and the structures they yield is harder to obtain than for their overt counterparts, but it exists, and conceptual arguments also carry us some distance, at least.

One reasonable guiding idea is that interpretive operations at the interface should be as simple as possible. Barring empirical evidence to the contrary, we assume that the external systems are impoverished—a natural extension of minimalist intuitions to the language faculty more broadly, including the systems (possibly dedicated to language) at the "other side" of the interface. That means that the forms that reach the LF level must be as similar as typological variation permits—unique, if that is possible. These assumptions about the interface impose fairly restrictive conditions on application and ordering of operations, cutting down the variety of computation, always a welcome result for reasons already discussed. At the A-P interface, overt manifestation provides additional evidence. Such evidence is largely unavailable at the C-I interface, but the general conceptual considerations just reviewed carry some weight. We have been implicitly relying on them throughout: for example, to conclude that covert features adjoin to the head of a chain (specifically, a raised verb), not to the trace or optionally to either; see (94) and discussion.

The central problem about covert adjunction concerns the structure of $T^{0\,max}$ at LF. Consider first the richest case: a TEC with object raising (Icelandic). Putting aside the observed position of $T^{0\,max}$, we assume its form at LF to be (185a), repeated here, with YP an instance of (188).

(191) Exp [Subj [$T^{0\,max}$ YP]]

Exp and Subj are specifiers of the T head of $T^{0\,max}$, which is formed by adjunction to T of Vb = [$_v$ V v]. In this case $T^{0\,max}$ is (192) and the complement YP is (193).

(192)

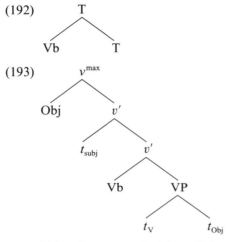

(193)

Here Obj and t_{Subj} are specifiers of the v head of Vb.

Suppose V raises overtly and Obj does not (French, or optionally Icelandic). The complement of T differs from (193) in that it lacks the outer Spec occupied by Obj, which remains in the position t_{Obj}. The formal features FF(Obj) raise to $T^{0\,max}$ for feature checking. Before this covert operation takes place, $T^{0\,max}$ is again (192). To maximize similarity to the LF output (192), FF(Obj) must adjoin to the complex form (192) itself, forming (194), not to the deeply embedded V within Vb, which actually contains the relevant features for checking.

(194)

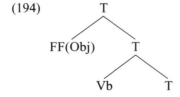

The operation is permitted, since the features of V are sublabels of the target of adjunction; and it satisfies the conditions on "closest target" (t_{Subj} being "invisible," as discussed) and formation of complex X^0s. Assuming this to be the general pattern, we conclude that adjunction is always to the maximal zero-level projection $X^{0\,max}$, never "internally" to one of its constituents—the simplest assumption in any event.

Consider an English-type language with overt raising of Subj but not V or Obj. To achieve maximum impoverishment at the interface, we want $T^{0\,max}$ at LF to be as similar as possible to (194)—in fact, identical except that in place of Vb it has FF(Vb), since V-raising is covert. FF(Obj) therefore cannot raise to V or to the verbal complex Vb before Vb adjoins to T; if it did, the structure formed would be quite different from (194) . After covert V-raising, FF(Obj) adjoins to $T^{0\,max}$, again forming (194) at LF (with FF(Vb) in place of Vb). The ordering is forced by bare output conditions, if the conjecture about poverty of interface interpretation is correct.

Suppose the language lacks overt raising of either Subj or Obj, so that both FF(Subj) and FF(Obj) raise covertly to TP. The poverty-of-interpretation conjecture requires that Vb raise to T before either subject or object raising; we thus have (192) once again, as desired, whether V-raising is overt (as in a VSO language) or not (in which case Vb in (192) is replaced by FF(Vb)). TP now attracts Subj, which is closer than Obj, forming a structure identical to (194), except that the features FF of (188) happen to be FF(Subj) rather than FF(Obj). But it is also necessary for FF(Obj) to raise. That is now possible, since the trace of Subj (unlike Subj itself) is not closer to TP, being inaccessible to Attract/Move. $T^{0\,max}$ therefore ends up as (195).

(195)

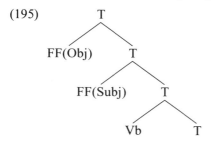

Recall that in a normal expletive construction, the strong D-feature of T is satisfied by an expletive rather than the raised Subj—the case of Merge that was assimilated to Attract/Move (see end of section 4.5). In this case $T^{0\,max}$ is again (195), and [Spec, T] is occupied by the expletive. An expletive construction thus has a certain structural resemblance to a VSO configuration, as has been implicit throughout.

We conclude that adjunction is to the maximal X^0 projection $X^{0\,max}$ and that heads raise before elements of their domains, conditions reminiscent of cyclicity. These are descriptive generalizations that we derive, not principles that we stipulate: they follow from the minimalist principle of poverty of interpretation at the interface. Simple and plausible assumptions suffice to guarantee virtually the same LF form for $T^{0\,max}$, over the typological range we are considering. So far these conclusions are motivated only by the conceptual requirement of maximizing uniformity of LF outputs. They supplement the earlier conclusion that traces of A-movement never enter into Attract/Move, whether overt or covert.

Suppose that output conditions at the LF interface rule out (195) under the rather natural requirement that FF(Subj) must c-command FF(Obj) in $T^{0\,max}$ if both are present. Hence, Obj has to adjoin to $T^{0\,max}$ before Subj does. But that is impossible, since Subj is closer to T than Obj if both remain in situ. It follows, then, that at least one of Subj and Obj must raise overtly if the expression is to converge, a hypothesis that has been advanced several times. The requirement on $T^{0\,max}$ generalizes the conclusion that Subj must c-command Obj overtly, which follows from the simplification of the notion "closer than" to just c-command, as already discussed.

We also have to settle some questions about the positions in which expletives can appear. The problems are not specific to this analysis; they arose before (more broadly, in fact), but were ignored. The basic descriptive fact is (196).

(196) Exp can only be in [Spec, T].

We have to determine why this is the case, a question that has a number of facets.

Suppose that Exp is merged in a θ-position, one of the possible violations of (196). That leads to a violation of the θ-Criterion, hence a deviant expression, a conclusion that suffices to allow us to dismiss the option here. Still, a factual question that has arisen several times before remains: is this a case of convergent gibberish or of a crashed derivation?

Suppose, say, that Exp is merged as subject of a transitive verb construction, yielding the VP (197), an instance of (182).

(197)

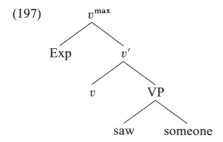

We next merge strong T, which attracts Exp, yielding finally the overt form (198).

(198) there saw someone

Raising of Exp satisfies the strong feature of T (EPP), but not its Case feature. Covertly, FF(Obj) adjoins to T, providing a Case feature. But there are two heads that have to check a Case feature: T (nominative) and *see* (accusative). Hence, the derivation will crash, with one or the other not satisfied. Such a derivation could converge only if the language had a verb SEE, like *see* except that it assigns no Case. Since no issue of blocking convergent derivations seems to arise, we are left without a satisfactory answer to the question of the status of the analogue of (198) with SEE in place of *see*. It could be that the derivation crashes because of a violation of the θ-Criterion, so there can be no such verb as SEE; or it could be that the derivation converges and a language can have such a verb (perhaps English in fact does), though it appears only in deviant expressions violating the θ-Criterion. We have seen that an argument lacking a θ-role is illegitimate, violating FI and causing the derivation to crash; but the question of assignment of θ-role remains open.

Putting the option aside as either nonconvergent or gibberish, we consider only Exp merged in a non-θ-position. We thus keep to the earlier conclusion that the only position that Exp can enter either by Merge or Attract/Move is one induced by a strong [nominal-] feature, hence [Spec, T] or [Spec$_2$, v] (the outer Spec) in (188). We also know that nothing can be raised to a θ-position. Hence, Exp never appears in a θ-position in the course of a derivation.

Can Exp be merged in the outer Spec of v, [Spec$_2$, v] in (188)? There are two cases to consider: Exp remains in this position, or it raises to [Spec, T]. The latter possibility is excluded, because the effect at both PF and LF is the same as merging Exp in [Spec, T] in the first place. Therefore, the economy principle (76) prevents selection of the strong [nominal-] feature of v for the numeration. The only remaining case, then, is merger of Exp in [Spec, v], where it remains at LF.

At LF, Exp is simply the categorial feature [D]. Any phonetic features would have been stripped away at Spell-Out, and we have seen that Exp has no other formal features. Lacking semantic features, Exp has to be eliminated at LF if the derivation is to converge: its D-feature is −Interpretable and must be deleted by some operation. Therefore, [D] must enter into a checking relation with some appropriate feature F. As we have just seen, T does not offer a checking domain to which Exp can raise,[135] so F must raise to the checking domain of Exp, which means that F must adjoin to it. What is F? Independently, there is good reason to believe that the categorial feature [N] adjoins to [D] regularly, namely, in the D–NP construction (Longobardi 1994). The optimal assumption, then, would be that it is adjunction of the feature [N] to Exp that eliminates its (sole remaining) feature. The feature [D] of Exp cannot be erased in this configuration: that would eliminate the category completely, leaving us with an illegitimate syntactic object. Therefore, checking of the categorial feature of Exp (its entire content) deletes it but does not go on to erase it, by the general principles already discussed.

The optimal assumption requires nothing new. Exp has no complement, but in the relevant formal respects, the head-complement relation that allows N-raising to D is the same as the [Spec-α] relation holding between Exp in Spec and the X′ projection of T. In a properly formed expletive construction, the formal features FF(A) of the associate A adjoin to matrix I (which we now take to be $T^{0\,max}$), checking Case and agreement and allowing matrix-type binding and control. The categorial feature [N] of A comes along as a free rider and is therefore in the right position to adjoin to Exp, forming $[_D$ N Exp]. The configuration so formed places [D] in a checking configuration with raised [N], as in the D-complement structure.[136] Like D that takes a complement, expletive D has a strong [nominal-] feature, which attracts [N]—a residue of the earlier adjunction-to-expletive analysis.

Returning to (196), we recall that the sole remaining problem was to show that Exp does not appear at LF in $Spec_2$ of (188)—the object-raising position. We have to show, then, that if Exp is in that position, no [N] can raise to it.[137]

There is only one possibility for N-raising to $Spec_2$: namely, the categorial feature [N] of Subj in $Spec_1$.[138] The operation is permitted, so we have to show that the derivation will crash for other reasons. We already have such reasons. Subj must raise to the checking domain of T, leaving a trace in $Spec_1$. We concluded earlier (see (94)) that traces of A-movement are inaccessible to Attract/Move. Therefore, if raising of FF(Subj) has taken place (either as part of overt substitution in [Spec, T] or as part of covert adjunction), [N] cannot raise from the trace of FF(Subj) to adjoin to $Spec_2$. The only remaining possibility is that Subj remains in situ in $Spec_1$ with Exp in $Spec_2$, and [N] raises from Subj, adjoining to [D] in $Spec_1$, automatically carrying along FF[N]. But FF(Subj) must now raise to $T^{0\,max}$, raising the trace of FF[N], an operation that should also be barred by (94). We see that there is good reason to interpret that constraint (which was purposely left a bit vague) quite strictly. If so, the restriction of Exp to [Spec, T] is explained (with the qualifications of the preceding notes).

These observations suggest that a still stricter interpretation of (94) might be warranted, strengthening the condition on argument chains, repeated as (199), to the provision (200).

(199) Only the head of CH can be attracted by K.

(200) α can be attracted by K only if it contains no trace.

The suggestion would have been unacceptable in earlier versions for a variety of reasons, but the objections largely dissipate if covert movement is only feature raising and some earlier suggestions have merit.[139] One immediate consequence is that overt countercyclic operations of the kind that motivated the extension condition are ruled out (see discussion of (138)). Nevertheless, (200) may be too strong even within the core computational system; we will return to this.

We see, then, that the descriptive observation (196) is well established on reasonable grounds.[140] It is possible that something similar is true of nonpure expletives of the *it*-type, which are associated with CPs with complementizers: *that, for,* or Q (the phenomenon of extraposition, however it is analyzed). They do not appear with control or raising infinitivals.

(201) a. *it is certain [PRO to be intelligent]
     b. *it is certain [John to seem *t* to be intelligent]

Possibly the overt complementizer head of the extraposed associate raises to the expletive, deleting it as in pure expletive constructions and thus satisfying FI. But see note 68.

The analysis of (196) raises in a sharper form an unsettled problem lingering from before. In discussing (168a–b)—essentially (202a–b)—we observed that it is not clear why both are allowed (assuming that they are, when MSCs are permitted).

(202) a. there seems [$_{TP'}$ [someone] t [$_{TP}$ t_{Subj} to be in the room]]
      b. there seems [$_{TP}$ t_{Exp} [$_{TP''}$ someone to be in the room]]

To explain the notations, TP in both cases is the complement of *seem*; t is the trace of *seem*; t_{Subj} is the trace of *someone*; and t_{Exp} is the trace of *there*. Exp occupies the outer Spec of the matrix MSC in (202a), and its trace occupies the outer Spec of the embedded MSC in (202b). The Subj *someone* is in [Spec, T] in both cases, in the matrix clause in (202a) and in the embedded clause in (202b). Thus, the matrix clause is an MSC in (202a) and the embedded clause is an MSC in (202b).

The earlier discussion entailed that (202b) blocks (202a) because at the common stage of the derivation when only the most deeply embedded T projection has been formed, insertion of Exp is more economical than raising of Subj to its Spec. The only permissible alternative to (202b), then, should be (203), with Subj remaining in the unraised associate position.

(203) there seems [$_{IP}$ t to be [someone in the room]]

We now have a further problem. We have just seen that the construction (204), which is rather similar to (202b), is *not* permitted by virtue of the economy principle (76).

(204) Exp T ... [$_{vP}$ t Spec$_2$ [Vb XP']]

Here raising of Exp from the Spec determined by the strong feature of v is barred: the strong feature cannot appear in the numeration because it has no effect on PF or LF output. In (202b), however, raising of Exp from the extra Spec determined by the strong feature of embedded T is permitted, even though it seems to be barred by this condition and, in case (202a), by yet another economy condition: that the most economical step must be taken at each point in the derivation.

The problems unravel in the present framework. By the economy condition (76), a strong feature can enter the numeration if it has an effect on output—in this case, PF output, because only a pure expletive is involved. That suffices to bar (204): adding the strong feature to the v head of Vb has no PF effect. Turning to (202), we see that (202a) derives from adding an extra strong feature to matrix T, and (202b) from adding an extra strong feature to embedded T—two different elements.[141] In each case there is an effect on PF output. Suppose matrix T enters the numeration without a strong feature that allows an extra T. Embedded T is a different element in the numeration: if it lacks the strong feature that allows an extra Spec, then we derive (203); if it has this strong feature, we derive the distinct PF form (202b). Therefore, (76) is inapplicable. The same is true of the economy principle that forced selection of expletive over raising in the earlier theory. That selection is forced only if the derivation converges; and if the embedded T has the strong feature requiring MSC, the derivation will not converge unless raising precedes insertion of Exp, giving (202b).[142]

We have considered various kinds of expletive constructions, including embedding constructions that bar superraising, MSCs of various kinds, and ECM constructions. There is a fairly complex array of options. Within this range of constructions, at least, the options are determined by elementary principles of economy: (1) add optional α to the numeration only if it has an effect at the interface; (2) at each stage of a derivation, apply the most economical operation that leads to convergence. So far, at least, the results look encouraging.

4.10.3.   Empirical Expectations on Minimalist Assumptions
With these clarifications, let us turn to the questions delayed at the end of section 4.10.1. The more restricted framework imposed by strict adherence to minimalist assumptions eliminates mechanisms that previously barred unwanted derivations. We therefore face problems of two kinds: to show that (1) the right derivations are permitted, and (2) the doors have not been opened too wide. The specific line of argument is sometimes fairly intricate, but it's important to bear in mind that at root it is really very simple. The basic guiding idea is itself elementary: that the array of consequences is determined by strict application of minimalist principles (to be sure, construed in only one of the possible ways; see the introduction). To the extent that the conclusions are confirmed, we have evidence for a conception of the nature of language that is rather intriguing.

We may continue to limit attention to simple transitive verb constructions, taken to be of the form (182) before T is added to yield TP. It suffices to consider overt V-raising, which brings up harder problems; the covert-raising alternatives fall out at once if this case is handled.

The first problem that arises is that we are predicting the wrong order of elements for MSCs. As noted, the observed order is (205b) instead of the predicted (205a).

(205) a. Exp [Subj [$T^{0\,max}$ XP]]
       b. Exp $T^{0\,max}$ Subj XP

The best answer would be that the order really is (205a) throughout the $N \rightarrow \lambda$ computation. If the expletive is null, we do not know its position, though (205a) is expected by analogy to the overt case. In section 4.9 we noted the possibility that the expletive in MSCs is overt in order to satisfy the V-second property, which may belong to the phonological component. If that is the case, the observed order is formed by phonologic operations that are extraneous to the $N \rightarrow \lambda$ computation and may observe the usual constraints ($V \rightarrow C$), but need not, as far as we know: $T^{0\,max}$-adjunction to expletive or to TP, for example. Let us assume the best case and see where that leads. We thus take the order to be really (205a), irrespective of what is observed at the PF output.

T and V have intrinsic −Interpretable features that must be checked: for T, [(assign) Case] (nominative or null); and for V, its φ-features and [(assign) accusative Case]. In addition, the nonsubstantive categories T and v may (optionally) have a strong [nominal-] feature, which is also −Interpretable. All have to be erased in a checking relation established by Merge or Move, by substitution or adjunction. Optional features are chosen when needed for convergence, as little as possible, in accordance with the economy condition (76). Features are deleted when checked. They are furthermore erased when this is possible, apart from the parametric variation that permits MSCs; see discussions below (58) and (185). Erasure is possible when no illegitimate object is formed (detectable at once). Checking takes place in the order in which the relations are established. These are the optimal assumptions: we hope to show that they allow exactly the right array of empirical phenomena. We are concerned now only with strong features.

As the derivation proceeds, the first checking relation that can be established is by overt substitution in Spec of v. We have two proposals under consideration: (1) "closer than" is defined in terms of c-command alone and overt object raising can only be to the inner Spec; (2) "closer than" is defined in terms of c-command and equidistance, and the object may (perhaps must) raise to the outer Spec. Again, let us restrict attention to the more complex variant (2); under (1), no problem arises, as can readily be checked.

Suppose, then, that overt substitution is in the outer Spec of v: Spec$_2$ of (188). In this case v has a strong [nominal-] feature. It cannot be checked by merged Subj, as we have seen, so there must be an extra Spec as in (188), more explicitly (206).

(206)

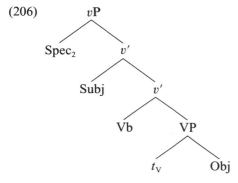

Again, Vb is the complex form $[_v \text{ V } v]$. Subj is in Spec$_1$ for θ-theoretic reasons unrelated to strength.

Spec$_2$ must be filled overtly to remove the strong feature of v before a distinct larger category is formed: in this case, before merger with T. This can be done by Merge or Attract/Move. We have already excluded Merge. An argument inserted in this position does not establish a checking relation (so that the strong feature is not checked) and also lacks a θ-role, violating FI; the derivation crashes. Expletives cannot be merged in this position, as we have seen. The only option, then, is raising of either Obj or Subj. We want to allow only raising of Obj, which, as we have seen, then permits the derivation to converge by raising of Subj to the checking domain of T, and only that way.

We have briefly (and incompletely) considered why raising of Subj to Spec$_2$ of (206) is barred. Let us look at the possibilities more closely, to clarify the issues.

Suppose that Subj is raised to Spec$_2$ in (206). It is in the checking domain of V, and checking relations are established for Case and ϕ-features. If features mismatch, then the derivation is canceled. If they match, then Subj receives accusative Case and object agreement, and the Case and ϕ-features of V erase. The Case of Obj still has to be checked, and that will have to take place in the checking domain of T. But un-raised Obj cannot reach that position, as we have seen, because Subj is closer to T. The trace of Subj in $Spec_1$ is invisible to Attract/Move and therefore does not prevent raising of Obj, but Subj itself does.

The only possibility, then, is that Subj raises further, to the checking domain of T. Now its trace in $Spec_2$ is invisible, and FF(Obj) can raise to T. The trace left in $Spec_2$ deletes, and at LF the result is identical to the result of the derivation in which $Spec_2$ was never constructed. The strong feature of v has no effect on the PF or LF output in this derivation and therefore cannot have been selected for the numeration, by the economy principle (76). This option is therefore excluded. If $Spec_2$ exists at all, it must be formed by overt object raising.

As the derivation proceeds, the next checking relation that can be established is substitution in the first [Spec, T] that is formed (EPP), either by Merge or Attract/Move. For Merge, the only option is an expletive, which (if pure) establishes a checking relation only with the strong [nominal-] feature of T, requiring covert associate raising; raising of an expletive to this position works the same way. The only remaining case is raising of an argument to [Spec, T], necessarily Subj, as we have seen. Then its features enter into checking relations with the "most proximate" sublabels of the target, in the obvious sense: the ϕ-features of V (which are the only ones), and the Case feature of T.[143] Vb cannot have a strong feature at this stage of the derivation, but a checking relation is established with the strong [nominal-] feature of T that forced the overt substitution. The sublabels in checking relations erase if matched by those of Subj; if there is a mismatch, the derivation in canceled.

Suppose either T lacks a strong [nominal-] feature or that feature has already been erased by substitution of Exp in Spec. Then FF(Subj) raises to adjoin to $T^{0\,max}$, forming (194), modified slightly here.

(207)

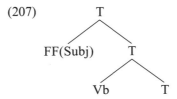

Checking proceeds exactly as in the [Spec, T] case, canceling the derivation if there is a mismatch, erasing −Interpretable features if there is a match. If Obj has raised overtly to [Spec, Vb], its features are checked there and undergo no covert raising. If Obj has not raised overtly, then FF(Obj) raises to $T^{0\,max}$, forming (195), repeated here.

(208)

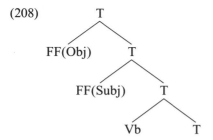

The Case feature of T has already been erased by Subj, so FF(Obj) checks the Case feature of V, canceling the derivation unless its own Case feature is accusative. Nominative Case and subject agreement necessarily coincide.

We rely crucially here on several earlier assumptions, among them that Attract/Move "sees" only the head of an A-chain and that mismatch of features cancels the derivation. In discussing the latter topic, we considered the weaker principle (107) that allows the derivation to proceed after mismatch, possibly converging in some different way. Largely on conceptual grounds, we rejected that option in favor of (108), which cancels the derivation under mismatch: (108) is preferred because it reduces computational complexity. We now see that the decision was necessary on empirical grounds as well: if we were to allow the broader class of derivations, certain choices for the (optional) Case features of DP would have allowed the derivation to converge improperly, with accusative subject and nominative object. Once again, the principles chosen on conceptual grounds are empirically confirmed, as we would expect if the Minimalist Program is capturing something true and important about human language.

This is not an exhaustive review of possibilities, but it includes a range of cases that seem to be central and typical.

The problems that remain have to do primarily with MSCs. We have gone a considerable distance toward the conclusion that the structure (191), repeated here, is the only possible form for MSCs (with or without overt object raising).

(209) Exp [Subj [$T^{0 \, max}$ XP]]

This structure is permitted, and we have seen that a number of unwanted possibilities are excluded. Some remain, however, and there is also a substantial conceptual problem: how do we account for the range of options?

We are concerned with the "double EPP" structure (210).

(210) $[_{TP}$ XP $[_{T'}$ YP T$']]$

We want to restrict the options to (209). Let us break the problem down into several parts.

(211) a. XP and YP cannot both be Exp.
      b. YP cannot be Exp.
      c. XP or YP must be Exp.

If so, we have (209).
The conceptual question is (212).

(212) What optional choices can allow three options: (a) no Spec of T (VSO), (b) one Spec of T (EPP), (c) two Specs of T (MSC)?

Case (212c) is (210), which we hope to restrict to (209). We have to ask how the three options of (212) are specified, along with combinations of them: for example, Icelandic, with options (212b) and (212c).

Let us begin with (211a). The facts are straightforward: there are no structures of the form Exp–Exp, and furthermore, the empirical observation generalizes to a broader class of cases, including the perennial troublemaker (213).

(213) *there$_1$ is believed [there$_2$ to be a man in the room]

These structures are excluded if we take the strong [nominal-] feature of [D] to be [N-], not [nominal-] generally (including [N] and [D]). That is a reasonable move: it limits the possible cases to the ones we find in DPs generally, namely, N → D raising; and it has the consequence (plausible, if not unproblematic) that the associate of an expletive must be nonspecific, whether it is an ordinary expletive construction or an MSC with the associate in [Spec, T] (see pp. 342, 350). Let us adopt this assumption. Then Exp–Exp constructions are straightforwardly barred. Exp is a DP, so the strong feature of the outer Spec will not be checked by raising of the inner one: only DP–NP structures are possible, analogous to ordinary expletive-associate pairs. As for (213), the features of the associate *a man* can raise to embedded T in the normal way, with [N] then raising to *there$_2$* to check its strong feature; but *there$_1$* survives intact to LF, so the derivation crashes (raising of *there$_2$* will not help, because it is a DP).

Since Exp–Exp is barred, to establish (211b) we have to show only that Argument–Exp is impossible in successive Specs. We know that at every point of the derivation, Exp is in the position [Spec, T] and that it must be in the Exp–Subj order of (209) at some stage of the derivation for its D-feature to be deleted by N-raising from Subj. What has to be shown, then, is that once (214a) is formed, Exp cannot raise to become [Spec, H], with a subsequent operation forming (214b) (XP the outer Spec of H).

(214) a. Exp-Subj
      b. [XP [$_{HP}$ Exp H′]]

The problematic derivation is barred straightforwardly. In (214a) the N-feature of Subj adjoins to Exp to delete [D]. But this operation is co-vert feature raising and cannot be followed by overt raising to Spec to form (214b).

It remains to establish (211c) and to answer the questions of (212). Let us begin by assuming (211c) to be true (we will return to this assumption). We now have to address (212); specifically, we have to determine what the choice of options must be. It is easy to make the distinction between no Spec and some Spec; that is a matter of availability of the strong [nominal-] feature for T. The hard problem is to distinguish cases (212b) and (212c), each assuming that T has the strong [nominal-] feature. How can that distinction be expressed, within the limited resources available?

Suppose there is a parameter that allows two choices: one Spec or two Specs. That proposal fails, because the two-Spec option permits Subj and Obj both to raise to [Spec, T], violating (211c): in the current highly restricted framework, nothing prevents raising of both Subj and Obj to the Specs of (210). Suppose we modify this approach, appealing to an economy principle that allows the two-Spec option only if the derivation would not converge without it, a variant of (76). That fails too, because it bars even the desired Exp–Subj structure (209); as we have seen, the derivation converges as an ordinary expletive construction if there is only a single Spec = Exp. A fortiori, the parameter cannot be of the pre-ferred form: n Specs, with $n = 0$ (case (212a)), $n = 1$ (case (212b)), or $n \geq 1$ (with (212c) a special case).

A more promising idea is to attend to the fact that each occurrence of [Spec, T] arises from an operation, either Merge or Move. Merge is cost-less, so it can apply freely. But it can apply only once to form [Spec, T]: only Exp can be inserted in this non-θ-position in a convergent deriva-tion, and as we have just seen, double-Exp constructions are barred.[144] Therefore, Attract/Move must be applied at least n times to form MSCs with $n + 1$ Specs ($n \geq 0$), and $n + 1$ times if no Exp is available for insertion. Each such application violates Procrastinate, which suggests that the parameters involved in (212) should be framed in terms of such violations.

A violation of Procrastinate that is required for convergence is not an economy violation; one that is not required for convergence is an economy violation. To facilitate exposition, let us distinguish terminologically between the two (radically different) kinds of violation of Procrastinate, speaking of *forced violations* (for convergence) and *unforced violations* (true economy violations).

In a VSO structure (type (212a)) with T weak, there are no violations of Procrastinate. In an S–VP structure (type (212b)), there is at most a single forced violation: that is, if no Exp is available for insertion. In an MSC an unforced violation is tolerated: that is, a violation of Procrastinate not required for convergence.

We therefore have two options.

(215) a. T may be strong or not.
     b. T may or may not tolerate an unforced violation of
         Procrastinate.

Option (215a) is taken over from the Agr-T system: T may have the strong feature [nominal-] (EPP), or it may not (VSO). If option (215a) is selected but not (215b), then there is one Spec but there can be no unforced violation of Procrastinate: [Spec, T] is Exp if it is available and a raised argument if it is not. If (215b) is selected as well, there are arbitrarily many Specs; that is still too weak a conclusion, so (215b) must be sharpened.

To clarify the issues, let us compare the Agr-T approach to MSCs with the one we are now exploring. (215b) is the counterpart to the parameter (216) of the analysis reviewed in section 4.9.

(216) T may or may not have Spec.

In the system of sections 4.1–4.9, [Spec, Agr] is always available and (212b) and (212c) (single and double EPP) differ in the value of the parameter (216). The right outcomes are guaranteed by the principle (217).

(217) Only one argument (namely, Subj) can raise from VP to
       [Spec, I].

But as we have seen on the basis of a more careful analysis of properties of features and the empirical phenomena that were to be explained, principle (217) is untenable: Subj, Obj (and other arguments) have Interpretable formal features and thus can be raised even after feature checking if the MLC is satisfied, as it is in the relevant cases once we restrict ourselves to minimalist principles, dispensing with apparatus that is conceptually unnecessary and empirically defective. The apparent generality of the earlier analysis is therefore spurious.

Suppose a language selects (215b) as an option and thus allows a violation of Procrastinate. This yields exactly the right *double*-subject constructions (Icelandic), but it also permits MSCs with more than two Specs. We therefore have to restrict (215b) to the minimal number of violations of Procrastinate—exactly one—revising (215) to (218).

(218) a. T is strong.

   b. T tolerates a single unforced violation of Procrastinate.

A VSO language has a negative setting for (218a) ([negative (218a)]: T is weak. An EPP language lacking MSCs has [positive (218a)] and [negative (218b)]: T is strong but there is no double-Spec. An Icelandic-type language with optional double-subject MSCs has [positive (218a)] and [positive (218b)]. The framework thus covers the typological range we have so far considered.

A prettier picture would include another option, the possibility of more than a single unforced violation of Procrastinate. Suppose, then, we have another parameter that distinguishes two types of language.

(219) T tolerates arbitrarily many unforced violations of Procrastinate.

The languages we have so far considered have the negative value for (219): no more than one unforced violation is tolerated (and no forced violations, if the setting of (218a) disallows strong T). Could there be languages with [positive (219)], allowing arbitrarily many unforced violations of (219), which we may interpret as meaning maximal unforced violations? In such languages all arguments are extracted to a position outside of IP. The candidate that comes to mind is a language in which all arguments do appear outside of IP, their syntactic roles being indicated only by some relation to an element within the remaining complex word: *pro* with matching features, or perhaps trace with arguments appearing in MSCs. If so, then (219) has the flavor of Baker's (1995) polysynthesis parameter.[145]

It seems a possibility worth exploring. If it makes sense, then we would interpret the system of parameters to imply that unforced violations of Procrastinate can be disallowed, minimal (once), or maximal (always). Needless to say, we are now pretty far out on a limb.

Still unsettled is case (211c): the impossibility of a double-EPP construction with no Exp, the two occurrences of [Spec, T] being occupied by Subj and Obj (in either order) (an Icelandic-type language that allowed MSCs with Subj–Obj, for example). The proposed answer to (212) bars this possibility. The language would have to allow strong T and an unforced violation of Procrastinate ([positive (218a–b)]) but only minimally ([negative (219)]). That set of choices (Icelandic) disallows the double-unforced violation required to extract exactly two arguments to [Spec, T] positions.

The options (218b) and (219) can be formulated readily in terms of the mechanisms for multiple-Spec mentioned earlier (below (58)), namely, by allowing a feature to escape erasure after checking. The option in (218b) is rejected if that possibility is disallowed for the strong [nominal-] feature of T, chosen if the possibility is allowed. The option in (219) is rejected if the strong [nominal-] feature can escape erasure once, adopted if it must escape erasure as often as possible.

Consider the unaccusative construction (220), where Nom is the sole argument.

(220)

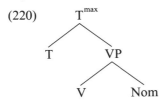

Suppose that T is strong. Then either Nom raises overtly to [Spec, T] or Exp is inserted in that position. Exp cannot raise from a lower clause; that would be barred by the closer Nom. But suppose Exp is merged in [Spec, VP] (a non-θ-position), then raised. The outcome is legitimate, but the derivation is again barred: by the condition that shorter derivations bar longer ones from the same numeration.[146] The conclusion adds further weight to the assumption that this is a true economy condition. Furthermore, we fill the last gap in establishing (196), the basic descriptive observation that restricts expletives to [Spec, T].[147] The observation follows (nonredundantly) from independently motivated economy conditions, as we would hope.

Nothing has been said so far about quantifier raising (QR). The status of this phenomenon has been the topic of much controversy, which I will not attempt to review. Suppose the operation exists. Since it is covert, it must be feature raising: a quantificational feature [quant] raises to adjoin to some $X^{0\,max}$ that is a potential host (presumably T or v, which, we might assume, have optional affix features allowing them to host [quant]). Suppose so. [quant] is Interpretable and therefore need not be checked. The affix feature of the functional categories is optional, therefore chosen if it "makes a difference," assuming that the economy condition (76) holds for this case, which differs from ones we have so far considered.[148] Since there is no PF effect, the result would be to allow QR when it leads to a distinct interpretation, in some sense that must be made precise, an idea proposed by Reinhart (1993) in a broader framework and developed with considerable empirical support by Fox (1994).[149] It falls naturally into the framework already outlined.

If the discussion so far is on the right track, then a variety of apparent reasons for inclusion of Agr in the lexical inventory have been eliminated. The question of its existence is therefore narrowed, though not eliminated. Not all arguments for Agr have been considered.[150] The discussion has been based on the assumption that Agr has no ϕ-features— that these features are assigned to substantive lexical items as they are drawn from the lexicon. If Agr exists as the locus of ϕ-features, it has an even more restricted role and unique status than before, with no apparent impact for the core computational processes; that seems dubious, at least. For the case of subject agreement, these apparent functions of Agr could perhaps be accommodated within the system just outlined by assimilating it with T: by assuming, that is, that as T is drawn from the lexicon for the numeration, it too is optionally assigned ϕ-features (as are nouns; and, I have so far assumed, verbs and adjectives). Note that this carries us back to something like the analysis that was conventional before Pollock's (1989) highly productive split-I theory, though now considerably revised and in quite a different setting. The agreement-based justification for Agr would therefore reduce to adjective and object agreement. To carry the matter further, it is necessary to look into a range of empirical questions that go well beyond the compass of this inquiry.

As matters stand here, it seems reasonable to conjecture that Agr does not exist and that ϕ-features of a predicate P, though −Interpretable, are like the Interpretable ϕ-features of nouns in that they are part of P in the numeration, added optionally as P is selected from the lexicon.

4.11 Summary

Reviewing briefly, it seems that we may be able to eliminate the theory of phrase structure entirely, deriving its properties on principled grounds. Many consequences follow for the theories of movement and economy when these conclusions are combined with other minimalist assumptions. Taking the latter seriously, we are led to a fairly radical reformulation of the theory of the computational system that relates form and meaning, and to a sharpening and improvement of economy and other central notions.

We have been concerned with the computation C_{HL} that maps a numeration N selected from the lexicon to a pair of interface representations (π, λ), at PF and LF, respectively. At an arbitrary point in the $N \to \lambda$ computation, the operation Spell-Out strips away phonological features, which enter the morphological component, are linearly ordered, and then are handed over to the operations that map them to π. The $N \to \lambda$ derivation proceeds in large measure independently of the "extraneous" requirement that language is manifested in sensorimotor systems: the sole effect may be the need to construct derivative chains involving categories to satisfy PF convergence (and, more broadly, the existence of Attract/Move in the first place). Apart from the mapping to PF, C_{HL} satisfies the conditions of uniformity and (virtually) inclusiveness. It consists of two operations, Merge and Attract/Move, which incorporates Merge. Economy conditions that are in large part readily computable select among convergent derivations.

Something like Merge is inescapable in any languagelike system, but the operation Attract/Move reflects peculiarities of human language, among them the morphology-driven "last resort" properties to which we have directed special attention.

Functional categories and their formal features occupy a central position in the workings of C_{HL}. If the general approach of section 4.10 can be sustained, then the only functional categories are those with features that survive through the derivation and appear at the interfaces, where they are interpreted. Of the functional categories we have considered, only T, C, and D remain. Strong features, which play a considerable role in overt manifestation and language variation, are narrowly limited in distribution. We have seen no reason to suppose that N or V, the basic substantive categories, have strong features. The strength property can be restricted, perhaps, to the nonsubstantive elements T and v that head the major projections within the clause, and to complementizers that serve as mood-force indicators (but see note 133).

The various refinements and simplifications along the way sharply reduce the problem of exponential blowup of economy calculations and overcome a variety of conceptual problems concerning Last Resort movement and "shortest move" (MLC). They also appear to be confirmed empirically in an interesting range of cases. Most important, they fall out naturally from minimalist assumptions, which require that we keep strictly to operations on features and local relations among them (categories only derivatively), taking into account the crucial distinction between ± Interpretable features that is determined by bare output conditions. Hence, we have confirmation that the inescapable conditions on language may be satisfied in something like a "best possible" way.

On minimalist assumptions, these seem to be the right kinds of moves, though doubtless not yet the right ones. Like earlier efforts guided by the same goals, they raise many questions and, if plausible, call for a good deal of rethinking of what has been assumed.

More generally, it seems not unreasonable to conjecture that language may approximate a "perfect" system in the sense described in the introduction. If this intuition is accurate, it would make good sense to press it to the limits to see what can be discovered about this curious and increasingly mysterious component of the human mind. To progress further along this road, we will have to find out the answers to a wide range of empirical questions that have come into view and that are sometimes formulable in fairly clear ways. We are left with hard and challenging problems of a new order of depth, and prospects for a theory of language with properties that are quite surprising.

Notes

On the background of this chapter, see the introduction. Thanks to participants in the MIT lecture-seminars of fall 1993 and 1994 for their many suggestions and criticisms in what was (as usual) a cooperative effort, inadequately acknowledged. Thanks particularly to Chris Collins, Sam Epstein, John Frampton, Sam Guttmann, and Howard Lasnik for comments on earlier versions that were the basis for Chomsky 1994a, and to Juan Uriagereka (among others) for improvements on a draft version.

1. The PF level itself is too primitive and unstructured to serve this purpose, but elements formed in the course of the mapping of syntactic objects to a PF representation might qualify.

2. For my own views on some of these issues, see Chomsky 1975b, 1992a,b, 1994b,c, 1995.

3. Recall that the ordering of operations is abstract, expressing postulated properties of the language faculty of the brain, with no temporal interpretation implied. In this respect, the terms *output* and *input* have a metaphorical flavor, though they may reflect substantive properties, if the derivational approach is correct.

4. The work in Optimality Theory mentioned earlier does not address such problems. In Prince and Smolensky 1993 there seems no barrier to the conclusion that all lexical inputs yield a single phonetic output, namely, whatever the optimal syllable might be (perhaps /ba/). That would be ruled out by Prince and McCarthy's (1993) "containment condition" (suggested in passing by Prince and Smolensky (1993, 80) as a "non-obvious assumption" that they have "found essential"). But it is hard to see how this can be sustained in segmental phonology (as in the cases mentioned) without implausible assumptions about parsability, varying widely among languages. It seems likely that these approaches will have to postulate intervening levels within the computation to PF, raising the question of how they differ from rule-based approaches. They may well differ, at least in the domain of prosodic processes (which are hard to separate from segmental ones). At present it seems to me likely that Bromberger and Halle (1989) are correct in holding that phonology, unlike the rest of C_{HL}, is rule-based, perhaps apart from some specific subdomain.

5. In a subsequent paper, referring to the preceding note, McCarthy and Prince (1994) appear to accept the conclusion that in the theory developed in Prince and Smolensky 1993, there is a unique output for all inputs (for each language). Recognition of that conclusion they call "the fallacy of perfection." They allege that comparable problems arise generally in the theory of language. If such problems did arise elsewhere (they surely do not, at least for the cases they mention), that would be a serious matter indeed, and recognition of it, no fallacy. They recognize the need to add input-output relations of some kind ("faithfulness"). Traditional approaches, dating back to Pāṇini and revived in generative phonology from the late 1940s, spell out "faithfulness" in terms of the notion "possible phonological rule" (embodying assumptions about natural processes) and economy considerations on the system of rules (evaluation metrics, markedness considerations, etc.). McCarthy and Prince (1994) propose that "faithfulness" be restricted to input-output conditions, but what they suggest seems to have no relevance to the standard problems (e.g., "identity between input and output," a principle that is virtually never satisfied). The basic problem, long familiar, is the one mentioned earlier: crucial properties appear to hold not of input-output pairs but of intermediate stages, so that no input-output condition is formulable. Pending further clarification, we cannot ask how an approach in terms of Optimality Theory might differ from others, apart from what is suggested by particular cases studied.

6. I put aside further questions relating to interpretation of lexical items at LF (recall that their "descendants" at PF may not be identifiable there, being

absorbed into instructions for the A-P systems that obliterate their identity). Such questions would carry us far afield into issues of language use (including the actual process of referring and the like) that are difficult and poorly understood. See Chomsky 1975b, 1992a,b, 1994b,c, 1995.

7. Note that considerations of this nature can be invoked only within a fairly disciplined minimalist approach. Thus, with sufficiently rich formal devices (say, set theory), counterparts to any object (nodes, bars, indices, etc.) can readily be constructed from features. There is no essential difference, then, between admitting new kinds of objects and allowing richer use of formal devices; we assume that these (basically equivalent) options are permitted only when forced by empirical properties of language.

8. I slightly modify an earlier version of these ideas, in which costlessness was stipulated. The formulation here seems to me to capture the real issues more clearly.

9. For an effort to deal with some such questions, see Epstein, forthcoming.

10. Indications of syllabic and intonational structure are not contained in lexical items. Nor is a good part of the output phonetic matrix: input and output are commonly quite different. Under the Distributed Morphology theory of Halle and Marantz (1993) and Marantz (1994), phonological features do not appear at all in the $N \to \lambda$ computation, words being distinguished (say, *dog* vs. *cat*) only within the phonological computation.

11. One such example, already discussed, is deletion of intermediate traces, which may nevertheless enter into binding relations, it seems; see section 1.3.3, (108). Note that this is consistent with the conclusion that binding is a matter of LF interpretation, if anaphor raising is a syntactic operation; see section 3.5. Implementation of such ideas is fairly straightforward; I will skip technical details, since they do not matter for what follows, except where indicated.

12. Technical questions arise about the identity of α and its trace $t(\alpha)$ after a feature of α has been checked. The simplest assumption is that the features of a chain are considered a unit: if one is affected by an operation, all are. There are other technical questions that can be resolved in one or another way, without obvious consequences.

13. That is part of the motivation for Distributed Morphology; see note 10. Prima facie evidence to the contrary is familiar: for example, Germanic versus Romance properties of English words, the effects of syllable structure in forming comparative constructions and dative shift, and so on. I suspect that these are problems of inadequate idealization, in the sense hinted at in the introduction, note 6. This is not to say that the problems that arise are not real; rather, they arise somewhere else.

14. Thus, even formal features typically have semantic correlates and reflect semantic properties (accusative Case and transitivity, for example).

15. Unless, of course, the system allows the C-I interface to access elements inserted only in the phonology, a significant complication that would have to be

strongly motivated to be considered seriously, going well beyond the possibility discussed earlier that "surface effects" might be accessed at that interface. The counterpart—that the A-P interface might access an item introduced covertly— does not seem to merit attention.

16. These and other notions will be clarified below. The condition will be slightly modified in section 4.10, but its essential content will be left intact. Procrastinate might be violated for reasons apart from feature strength, but I hope to limit such possibilities. We will return to the matter.

17. For an account of cyclicity in terms of economy that will include this as a special case, see Kitahara 1994, 1995. However, this account is based on richer assumptions than those we are considering here. Note that strength must still be removed for convergence, even if not embedded.

18. The term *substitution*, borrowed from earlier theory, is now somewhat misleading because the position of substitution is "created" by the operation, but I continue to use it in the revised sense.

19. English has some constraints relating categorial and other features; in other languages such constraints are far richer, and insofar as they exist, lexical entries abstract from them. Also relevant are the kinds of questions mentioned in section 3.2, in connection with Hale and Keyser's (1993a) θ-theory.

20. See Lasnik 1994, where it is suggested that French and English differ, and that English auxiliaries differ from main verbs.

21. The term is used without any clear relation to reference in a more technical sense. That the latter notion enters into the study of natural language is questionable. See note 2.

22. For example, we still have no good phrase structure theory for such simple matters as attributive adjectives, relative clauses, and adjuncts of many different types.

23. The exact force of this assumption depends on properties of phrases that are still unclear. We return to some of them later.

24. See Fukui 1986, Speas 1986, Oishi 1990, and Freidin 1992, among others. From a representational point of view, there is something odd about a category that is present but invisible; but from a derivational perspective, as Sam Epstein observes, the result is quite natural, these objects being "fossils" that were maximal (hence visible) at an earlier stage of derivation, targeted by the operation that renders them invisible.

25. In present terms, selection of complement CM by head H is a head-head relation between H and the head H_{CM} of CM, or the reflex of adjunction of H_{CM} to H; and chain links are reflexes of movement. Further questions arise about binding theory and other systems. Optimally, these too should reduce to local relations (see Chomsky 1986b, 175f.), a topic of much important work in recent years.

26. Nothing essential changes if a lexical entry is a more complex construction from features; but see note 27.

27. As pointed out by Chris Collins, a technical question arises if heads are understood as sets $\{\alpha_i\}$, where each element is again a set; then the members of α_i will be terms, as the notion is defined—an unwanted result, though it is unclear that it matters. We can leave the issue unresolved, pending some answer to questions left open about the nature of lexical items.

28. Assuming that the HMC is a valid principle, which is not obvious. We will return to this question.

29. Let us put aside the possibility that chains are formed by a Form Chain operation that could be "successive cyclic," as suggested in chapter 3, keeping to the simplest case of two-membered chains. We will return to this issue.

30. Interpreting the informal notation more closely, we might say that *the tree with root* T′ is $\{T, \{T, K\}\}$ (etc.), to overcome the temptation to think of T′ as having some distinct status, as it does in phrase structure grammar (and its X-bar-theoretic variant). I will omit such refinements.

31. Notice that this is a violation of the inclusiveness condition. The alternative is that the specification takes place within the phonological component, requiring a link between some level within that component and LF (see note 15). For more on parallelism and copy intonation, see Tancredi 1992.

32. Not to be confused with the uniformity condition on derivations discussed earlier, or several other notions of "uniformity" discussed in chapters 1–3 and elsewhere. The c-command requirement has been questioned for covert operations, though in a narrow class of cases: where the alleged lowered element either is in or c-commands the position of an overt trace.

33. See Collins 1994b for a similar approach to overt cyclicity.

34. See chapters 1–3 and Chomsky 1986b, 1994a, Lasnik, to appear, Ura 1994, Collins 1994b.

35. A still laxer version would allow the operation if a feature of the ultimate target is checked. I will omit this possibility, later dispensing with (20c) entirely.

36. In earlier work (e.g., section 3.5) I used such examples as **John seems to t that . . .* , **there seem to a lot of people that IP*, for illustration. But these are less interesting for reasons to which we will return, and they may even be irrelevant because of special properties of inherent Case.

37. See Chomsky 1964, and recent work based on much richer typological and morphological evidence (in particular, Tsai 1994 and work summarized there).

38. Note that this modification conforms in part to the theory developed in Lasnik, to appear.

39. This is a marginal phenomenon at best, since Merge does not require establishment of a checking domain. We return to it; any relevant properties are subsumed by the more important case of Move.

40. The tacit assumption here is that overt movement always involves pied-piping of a full category. As noted earlier, that could be too strong. If it is, then *covert* should be dropped in this sentence of the text.

41. An ambiguity might arise if the features F that raise constitute the entire head (so that there is no generalized pied-piping) and the head happens also to be an X^{max}. In that case it would not be clear whether the movement is adjunction to a head or substitution in Spec. I will assume tentatively that this possibility cannot arise; the raised features FF(LI) do not constitute the entire head LI. See section 4.10 for some supporting arguments.

42. Note that we must distinguish *there be NP* constructions with strong existential import from the expletive constructions with small clauses, such as (36), which are much weaker in this respect, differing in other properties as well. For example, (36a) may be true even if there is no book, just a space on the shelf where a book should be, in contrast to *there is a book that is missing from the shelf*, which is true only if the book exists. Similarly, *John has a tooth missing* does not entail the existence of a tooth, now or ever. A fuller analysis of expletive constructions and related ones will also bring in focal stress and other relevant questions that have yet to be examined properly, to my knowledge.

43. As is well known, agreement with the associate is sometimes overridden, as for example in *there's three books on the table, there's a dog and cat in the room* (vs. **a dog and cat is in the room*). The phenomenon, however, seems superficial: thus, it does not carry over to **is there three books . . .*, **there isn't any books . . .*, and so on. The form *there's* simply seems to be a frozen option, not relevant here.

44. One might, however, explore its possible relevance for the definiteness effect, with D taken to be a target for N-features so that it cannot be skipped, and specificity (in the relevant sense) understood as a property of D. On D-N relations, see Longobardi 1994. A perhaps more exotic proposal is that overt $N \rightarrow D$ raising, as in Italian though not English under Longobardi's analysis, obviates the effect, as appears to be true for Italian. See Moro 1994 for extensive discussion, from a different point of view. Note that the status of the definiteness effect is obscure for many reasons, including the fact that it distinguishes interpretations, not well-formedness strictly speaking, and interacts with other properties, such as focus. See note 42.

45. Thanks to Anna Cardinaletti and Michal Starke for the data. They observe that the contrast seems independent of V-movement. Thus, the sentence is bad even if V moves to C in French.

(i) *en   arrivera-t-il un sans casser la porte
    of.them will.arrive   one without breaking the door

They also point out that the French examples, though sharply distinguished from the Italian ones, have a more equivocal status than in the idealization here. On the general phenomenon, see Perlmutter 1983, Aissen 1990.

46. Anna Cardinaletti, personal communication. The same is reported for Icelandic (Dianne Jonas, personal communication) and Mainland Scandinavian (Cardinaletti 1994, citing Tarald Taraldsen).

47. The straightforward way to achieve this is to take α to be narrowly L-related to H if it is *included in* the minimal domain Dom of H, and broadly related to H

if *covered by* (contained but not included in) Dom. If the full checking domain is restricted to minimal domains so construed, as suggested below, the whole picture is simplified, but I will leave the matter here. Recall that the specifier-adjunct distinction does not quite correlate with the A-$\overline{\text{A}}$ distinction. Note that some modification is required for the notion of legitimate LF objects, defined in chapters 1 and 3 with an eye to problems of the ECP and related matters that do not arise (at least, in that form) in this more restricted theory.

48. Given the relation to semantic content, we might expect that a categorial feature associated with no such content, in a pure expletive, should be eliminated at LF. We will return to this matter.

49. Expletives may differ; see preceding note. The analysis comes close to accommodating the layered Case theory of Watanabe (1993a), which requires "validation" of Case assignment by raising of a feature created by the operation. The theory can be simplified by avoiding postulation of a new feature and assuming that the intrinsic Case feature of V and T is not deleted by Case assignment, but must be checked and eliminated for convergence, which requires raising to the checking domain of a functional category. Some additional tinkering is required to ensure that the intrinsic Case of V and T is "validated" only after having checked Case, if nonchecking of these features causes the derivation to crash.

50. We are restricting attention here to the $N \rightarrow \lambda$ computation, putting aside the fact that $-$Interpretable features may have a PF reflex. That raises a problem if the checking relation is overt, in which case $-$Interpretable features erase though their phonetic reflex remains. There are a number of ways to proceed, depending in part on the answers to questions left open about ϕ-features of a predicate; one would be to interpret overt erasure of F as meaning conversion of F to phonological properties, hence stripped away at Spell-Out.

51. A warning flag should go up at this point. This first step of raising is possible only if the adjective raises overtly to Agr, an unexpected feature of English, with weak Agr throughout. We will return to this problem in section 4.10.

52. See Cardinaletti and Guasti 1991 for further evidence for a structure like (55). On the analysis under the earlier theory based on Move α and Greed, see Chomsky 1994a. Note that I am overlooking here potentially important differences between subject-verb and t_1-adjective agreement in (55) (only the former involving person, for example). The ϕ-features of *John* are visible at LF, but not those of *intelligent* and *be*, which are erased after checking.

53. The selectional constraints on raising (essentially, propertyless) infinitivals seem very narrow. Perhaps they suffice to bar such constructions as *John's belief to be intelligent*, *John told Mary [Bill to be likely that t is a successful lawyer]*, and many others that appear problematic.

54. The facts seem not easy to determine, because of many interfering factors. See Grosu and Horvath 1984 for discussion of raising from subjunctive lacking complementizer in Romanian; agreement is manifested in the embedded clause, and if we can assume that nominative Case is associated with presence of the complementizer, the evidence will fall into the same pattern. The latter property

might fall under Watanabe's (1993a) theory of Case validation (see note 49), on the assumption that absence of a visible complementizer in raising-from-subjunctive constructions means that there is no complementizer, as in earlier S'-deletion theories. (Thanks to Alex Grosu for empirical materials and discussion. For analysis along similar lines, as well as empirical evidence that A-movement is indeed involved and an extension to the theory of *pro*, see Ura 1994.)

55. On the latter, see Lasnik 1994b. Being accessible, categorial and φ-features might allow A-movement from an inherent Case position. There may, however, be further reasons why that is barred, perhaps some version of the uniformity condition suggested in Chomsky 1986b, 193–194. In isolation, the noun appears with a language-specific default case, which presumably need not be checked. Recall that Case theory as discussed here is concerned only with structural Case. Inherent Case, which is assigned only in a θ-relation to the Case assigner, is a different phenomenon. It is assigned and also realized, typically within the domain of the θ-marker (the "uniformity condition" of Chomsky 1986b, 192f.), though sometimes in structural Case positions, in various ways. The topic is an interesting one, but has not been shown to have any bearing on (structural) Case theory and its apparently quite strict properties of morphological realization.

56. See Reinhart 1981. On the general topic, see Ura 1994. Also see Miyagawa 1993a,b, Koizumi 1994.

57. The idea of multiple feature checking is generalized to serial verb constructions by Collins (1995).

58. On the infinitival analogue *there seem [a lot of people to be ...], see section 4.9, an analysis that should carry over to it seems [John to be ...] and should also exclude the counterparts even in languages that permit (57).

59. As the concepts are clarified, we should be able to distinguish the possible residual content of such elements as expletive *there* and *it* from true semantic features.

60. See Cardinaletti 1994 for cross-linguistic confirmation and for closer analysis of the feature content of expletives.

61. Perhaps an example of "late insertion" in the sense proposed by Halle and Marantz (1993), Marantz (1994).

62. On this matter, see particularly Cheng 1991.

63. With an exception to which we will return directly; see p. 292.

64. For one, the I → Q option is restricted in English to root clauses and is obligatory there; we will return to a suggestion about why this might be the case. Whatever the reason, it is not the raising of I that satisfies the strong feature of Q; rather, that has some different origin here, possibly within the phonological component.

65. Both Reinhart and Tsai observe that the alleged argument-adjunct distinction is actually an argument-adverb distinction, based, they propose, on the fact that adverbs lack a position for a variable so that the in-situ interpretation is barred. Reinhart suggests a multiple-Spec analysis and Tsai a covert raising analysis.

66. One might expect that some phonological consideration, perhaps roughly analogous to the V-second property, accounts for the well-known facts about obligatory presence of the nonnull variant (see Stowell 1981). Earlier descriptions in terms of government (whatever their plausibility) are not available here.

67. That such comparisons might enter into economy considerations is suggested by Golan (1993), Reinhart (1993), and Fox (1994), in different connections.

68. No link of the *there*-associate type holds between *it* and CP in (80); see McCloskey 1991.

69. See Chomsky 1994a, note 59, Ura 1995, and references cited. For recent discussion of superiority, see several papers in Thráinsson, Epstein, and Kuno 1993. The status of the phenomenon is not entirely clear. Standard examples, such as the contrast between (ia–b) and (ic–d) prove little.

(i) a.   who saw what
    b.   whom did you persuade to do what
    c.   *what did who see
    d.   *what did you persuade whom to do

In the acceptable cases, the *wh*-phrase in situ has focal stress and could be taking clausal scope for this reason alone; the preferred cases degrade when that property is removed. Other properties that have been studied also raise questions. Thus, considerable ingenuity has been expended to explain why in (ii), the embedded *who* takes matrix rather than embedded scope.

(ii) who wonders what who bought

That could be an artifact, however, reflecting a preference for association of likes. Thus, the opposite association holds in (iii).

(iii) what determines to whom who will speak

There are many other problems.

70. See Chomsky 1986a for attempts to deal with this problem, now unnecessary.

71. The derivation of (80) crashes for two reasons: *John* lacks Case, and matrix T fails to assign Case. The latter property suffices, as we see from (57).

72. If the local interpretation of reference sets is abandoned, the same approach to superraising might be feasible on the assumption that a derivation that involves shorter moves blocks one with longer moves, so that (83) blocks the application of superraising in (80). But that raises the problems discussed earlier (p. 268), which do not seem trivial.

73. For some references and discussion, see section 1.4.1. It is possible that the "weak islands" for arguments have to do with the option of multiple Specs, adapting ideas of Reinhart (1981) more generally along lines already indicated.

74. I follow here a suggestion of John Frampton's. See also pp. 135f.

75. Depending on exactly how interface operations are understood, the semantic features of intermediate traces could be accessible to interpretive operations before they become invisible for further interpretation, possibly allowing implementation of ideas about the interpretive role of intermediate traces; see note 11.

A slight variation of this approach would allow an intermediate trace to be assigned a mark (say, *) that is erased at LF in chains that are uniform in the sense of chapters 1 and 2. We then derive properties of the ECP and interpretation of certain problems of anaphora (see section 1.4.1 ((161) and text) and section 2.6.2). Note further that the particular case of chain uniformity discussed there is plainly only one of several. Uniformity in the sense discussed is always "uniformity with respect to P," P some property. The property discussed there was L-relatedness. An equally plausible property is θ-relatedness—that is, the property of being either a θ-assigner or a θ-position. Extension of the analysis to that case allows the incorporation of many familiar cases of "strong island."

76. The conclusion goes beyond what has been shown, which is only that the trace of an argument cannot be raised.

77. The surface order is not a clear criterion because of ordering effects involving "heaviness" and other poorly understood properties. The relation of obligatoriness to specifier-complement choice also leads into mainly uncharted territory. But the conclusions are reasonable and are supported empirically by the fact that α c-commands into Cl, assuming the PP to function as a DP with P adjoined, as a kind of Case marker, so that it does not affect c-command.

78. Even if the light verb v to which *seem* has adjoined raised overtly to adjoin to I, as in French-type languages, that would not affect the matter. The minimal domain of the chain it heads, which determines the "neighborhood of I" relevant for determining closeness, does not contain PP.

79. See preceding note. Thanks to Viviane Déprez for examples and for clarification of the general issue, which, she observes, is considerably more complex than indicated here, with graded judgments and many other factors involved, among them choice of clitic, infinitive versus small clause, ordering of PP and clausal complement, and idiom chunks (which give sharper distinctions) versus other phrases. Esther Torrego (forthcoming, and personal communication) points out that where the clitic is doubled, as in Spanish, the analogue of (99b) is barred, again as expected if (as she assumes) the doubled element is present as *pro*, so that there is no clitic chain but rather a structure analogous to (99a).

80. One possibly related question, discussed in Lasnik, to appear, has to do with the impossibility of such expressions as *there* [$_{VP}$ *someone laughed*], with the intransitive verb *laugh* (which I assume to be a transitive verb with incorporated object, following Hale and Keyser (1993a)). Structures of roughly this form do exist, namely, the transitive expletive constructions of Icelandic and other languages, to which we will return. In this case, as we will see, the subject *someone* must extract to [Spec, T], which is strong. The question still remains for English. There is some reason to believe that a universal principle requires something to extract overtly from VP, but the question remains murky.

81. Unless Agr_O has a strong D-feature, so that overt object raising is obligatory in English. See Koizumi 1993, 1995, for a theory of this general sort. I am assuming the contrary, but the question is not simple. Some considerations that bear on it arise later.

82. A qualification is needed for multiple-Spec constructions, restricting mismatch to the inner Spec.

83. We assume that α is in the checking domain of H(K), in this case. That follows from the definition of Attract/Move, though questions remain about the status of YP-adjunction to XP, to which we will return.

84. Can β raised to target α contribute to θ-role assignment in the configuration headed by α? If so, the situation would be analogous to feature checking by raised β (β = T or V) in a complex $[_\alpha\ \beta\ \alpha]$. The proposal is not in the spirit of the idea that θ-roles are to be identified with structural configurations, and it raises empirical problems, as we see directly.

85. In the earlier theory based on Move α and Greed, the operation would be permissible only if subsequent feature checking is thereby facilitated, not the case here, so that the computations leading to (113) do not qualify as derivations; see Chomsky 1994a. Collins (1994b) notes that such a case might arise under an analysis of adverbs to which we will return. For different approaches to the question, see Brody 1993, Boscović 1993.

86. The discussion of reconstruction as a process driven by FI in chapter 3 might offer a line of argument to support the conclusion that a derivation crashes if it violates FI.

87. An argument to the contrary in chapter 3, which motivated Form Chain, no longer holds under the formulation of Last Resort given here.

88. Checking theory applies in this case if we adopt the second of the two options discussed at the end of section 4.5. If we adopt the first option, the same argument applies, though to a more complex case with raising: for example, the derivation D that yields *John seems* [*t to like Bill*] with *t* the base position of *John*, blocking the correct derivation that assigns *John* a θ-role, if D were to converge.

89. They treat external arguments in a different way, however.

90. One case of Burzio's generalization is therefore immediately accounted for (it follows that in such constructions as *it strikes me that IP*, the object has inherent rather than structural Case). The other case bars a transitive verb (hence one with obligatory external argument) that does not assign accusative Case, as in the hypothetical example (113). The object then has to raise to a higher position to receive Case, crossing the subject, a movement that raises a host of interesting questions (see Ura 1994).

91. Technically, this is not quite correct; see note 1.

92. See Miller and Chomsky 1963 and Chomsky 1965 for review.

93. Not entirely, however. A look at the earliest work from the mid-1950s shows that many phenomena that fell within the rich descriptive apparatus then postulated, often with accounts of no little interest and insight, lack any serious analysis within the much more restrictive theories motivated by the search for explanatory adequacy and remain among the huge mass of constructions for which no principled explanation exists. See note 22.

94. Note that *complement of H* must be understood so that when H is adjoined to X, the complement of X (or the chain it heads) is also the complement of H; thus, in (124) the complement of V after adjunction to v is the complement of v. The definition of *complement* given in chapter 3 left this case open (Toshifusa Oka, personal communication).

95. I evade here a certain ambiguity about adjunction to α that is simultaneously x^{max} and x^{min}. Is it X^0-adjunction? X^{max}-adjunction? Either freely? The unanswered questions carry over to subsequent discussion. Specific answers are readily formulated; the question is which ones are factually correct.

96. See note 75. Recall that the notion of uniformity here is not the notion (17) of uniformity of phrase structure status.

97. Condition (130b) partially generalizes a conclusion in Chomsky 1986a, based on a suggestion by Kyle Johnson, namely, that there be no adjunction to arguments. The motives required that the conclusion be generalized in essentially this way, as has been pointed out a number of times.

98. Branigan 1992. See Friedemann and Siloni 1993 for a reanalysis of the phenomenon with a broader database, within a minimalist framework that distinguishes a participial phrase from Agr_O.

99. The analysis, one way or another, is based on ideas proposed by Martin (1992). See also Thráinsson 1993, Watanabe 1993b.

100. See May 1977. Pica and Snyder (in press) argue on the basis of empirical and theoretical considerations (including experimental study of preference) that the apparent lowering that enters into interaction of quantifier scope is a secondary effect giving nonpreferred readings, even in simple cases such as *someone likes everyone*. For more extensive discussion with somewhat different conclusions, see Hornstein 1994.

101. For general comments on the matter, see pages 233f.

102. Operator phrases formed from adverbials can of course be moved (e.g., *how often*). Here it is the *wh*-feature that raises for checking, carrying the phrase by pied-piping (as, in fact, if *how* raises alone, under the Move F theory).

103. Note that although (140a) is barred, *often* could be adjoined to V', under present assumptions.

104. The adverb will be relevant only if it has features that the [Agr, V] complex can attract, which is plausible though not obvious.

105. The answer could be as indicated in note 75.

106. See Koizumi 1993, 1995, for argument to the contrary, based on an overt object-raising analysis.

107. Fukui 1993; see also Ueda 1990. Note that this proposal requires that ordering be imposed within the N → LF computation.

108. I depart here from Kayne's theory in several respects, among them, by taking linear ordering to be literal precedence, not simply a transitive, asymmetric, total relation among terminals. That is the intended interpretation, but

Kayne's more abstract formulation allows very free temporal ordering under the LCA. Thus, if a class of categories satisfies the LCA, so will any interchange of sisters (as Sam Epstein (personal communication) notes), meaning that consistent with the LCA a language could, for example, have any arrangement of head-complement relations (e.g., *read-books* or *books-read* freely). Kayne considers one case (fully left-to-right or fully right-to-left), but the problem is more general.

109. See Chomsky 1994a for details, along with some discussion of anomalies of the LCA that are removed when we dispense with the X-bar-theoretic notations.

110. L is part of the structure, however; otherwise, we would have a new and inadmissible syntactic object. Thus, the branching structure remains, and m, p do not c-command out of L.

111. Note that V-raising (as in French) does not affect the conclusion that the clitic must raise overtly. If D remains in situ, then whether the trace of V is ignored or deleted by the LCA, D will still be a terminal complement, either to V itself or to some intervening element, and the derivation will crash.

112. Presumably the affixal character of N is a general morphological property, not distinguishing nouns with complements from those without (which must raise).

113. The assumption is not entirely obvious; see Epstein 1989 for a contrary view. Much depends on resolution of questions involving reconstruction after adjunction and word-internal processes at LF.

114. Suppose that, as has been proposed, the upper segment enters into calculating subjacency, scope, or other properties. Then we would hope to show that these effects receive a natural expression in terms of containment and domination, notions still available even if the upper segment is "invisible" for C_{HL} and at the interface.

115. That q c-commands $[m_2, m_1]$ is required in Kayne's theory for reasons that do not hold in the bare theory, where the issue that Kayne is concerned with does not arise.

116. Furthermore, it might be the locus of the optional ϕ-features of verbs and adjectives; see section 4.2.2. I have assumed not, but without consequences, so far. I will use *IP* in the standard sense, but as informal notation only, without any commitment to what the actual structure is.

117. Supporting evidence is provided by Collins and Thráinsson (1994), who argue for a still more proliferated I system on the basis of more complex materials. The analysis here differs somewhat from the ones cited, in the light of the foregoing discussion.

118. Holmberg's generalization follows, as Jonas notes. Her formulation is somewhat different. The argument might be extended to I-to-C raising. If this is a prerequisite for substitution in [Spec, C], we derive a partial account of V-second effects and the oddity in English noted earlier: that both modes of satisfying strength of C are required with *wh*-raising. Other properties of matrix interrogatives remain unexplained.

119. Agreement alone could be expressed in different ways for some constructions. We might reintroduce the otherwise apparently dispensable notion of government or assume that the expletive raises from a position in which agreement with the postverbal NP has already been established: for example, if the structure underlying *there is NP XP* (*there is a man in the room, there is a new proposal under discussion*, etc.) is [I *be* [[$_{sc}$ NP *there*] XP]], with agreement established in the small clause SC to which XP (*in the room, under discussion*) is adjoined. The expletive then raises to subject position. See Moro 1994 for development of such ideas within an illuminating theory of predicate nominal and other copular constructions. The postulated element *there* has different properties from locative *there* (e.g., the expletive interpretation is barred in *over there is a man in the room, where is a new proposal under discussion*, etc.). The proposal does not extend to other properties: the relation of control and binding to agreement, MSCs, expletive constructions with embedded subjunctives.

120. On movement operations within prosodic phrases, see Truckenbrodt 1993, Zubizarreta 1993; such operations would have to follow the LCA, on our current assumptions.

121. I overlook here some subtleties that might prove important. Thus, under the economy condition (76), null expletives are allowed in the numeration only if they have an indirect effect at PF (allowing some structure to appear overtly) or LF (insofar as there are differences of interpretation between overt raising of subject to [Spec, I] and covert raising of its features to I).

122. The range of options appears to be the same in Romanian, which has raising from subjunctive with agreement in place of infinitivals, along with MSCs with null expletive (Alex Grosu, personal communication; see also note 54).

123. In the earlier theory based on Greed and Move α, the account is considerably more intricate; see Chomsky 1994a.

124. There are other possibilities as well, but they will crash or violate general economy and other UG conditions—or so it must be demonstrated; not a trivial problem in general.

125. An alternative analysis suggested in Chomsky 1994a is now excluded: that the contrast between (170) and (171b) rests on the difference between the traces that are "crossed": trace of expletive in one and trace of *someone* in the other. That proposal is untenable in the light of (93) and related discussion.

126. On such structures within the Move α and Greed approach, see Chomsky 1994a.

127. An answer proposed in Chomsky 1994a is no longer tenable, as is easily checked.

128. Partially similar conclusions are reached on different grounds by Iatridou (1990) and Thráinsson (1994). See also Fukui 1992.

129. I put aside the question of covert insertion of strong features at the root discussed in section 4.5.4, which is not pertinent here.

130. Recall Baker's (1988) observation that incorporation is one of the ways of satisfying the Case Filter, here placed in a more general context.

131. See the end of section 4.5. This case provides the basis for the choice between alternative theories of checking with Merge, discussed there.

132. See (3). Note that there are implications with regard to the status of negation and other elements that might appear in this position, which may be significant.

133. Technically, whether [Subj, Adj] is specifier or complement depends on whether the Adj is complex or simple. We have abandoned the wealth of devices that allow us to require that it be a specifier. The conventional result is derived for verbs if intransitives are hidden transitives, but there is no analogous argument for adjectives. I will assume here that the status of [Subj, Adj] does not matter—raising yet another warning flag. Also problematic is that Adj is a substantive category assigned a strong feature, contrary to (3).

134. We need not be concerned that Merge is favored over Move at a given point in a derivation, because the derivation will now crash if the favored option is selected, inserting Subj before raising Obj.

135. It is also necessary to show that there is no other feature that could do so, a question that is not entirely trivial, but that I will ignore.

136. Some interesting questions arise about the category D: if it stands alone, as a pure head, does the derivation crash because the strong [nominal-] feature is not checked? If so, demonstratives and pronouns either would have to involve complements or would have to raise, as in cliticization—a possibility already discussed (see pp. 337f).

137. I am in fact omitting another class of cases: raising of Exp to [Spec, v] *after* [N] has adjoined to it, deleting its sole feature. Checking the possibilities, all seem to be barred.

138. I am again ignoring some possibilities here. Suppose Subj raises to [Spec, T]. Then the only source for [N] raising to Exp in $Spec_2$ would be from DP in the complement of the VP (the internal domain of its head v). Any such DP would have prevented Exp from raising to $Spec_2$ from a lower clause, being closer to the target. That still allows one possibility: covert object adjunction to Exp merged in $Spec_2$, where the object could have its Case feature checked too if it is in the checking domain of $Vb = [V-v]$. We have no really satisfactory way to exclude this yet; the example lies in that zone of ambiguity surrounding the problem of feature adjunction to a Spec that is both maximal and minimal.

139. See section 4.7.3. Condition (200) bars legitimate cases of YP-adjunction to XP (e.g., VP-adjunction), but if these belong to a different module of (I-)language, no conflict arises.

140. I have skipped one case: unaccusatives. I will return to it, showing that (196) is again established on grounds of economy.

141. More precisely, T already has a strong feature for the EPP, and with the mechanism proposed earlier for MSCs, what is added to T is the marked value of the parameter permitting it not to erase when checked by substitution in the inner Spec.

142. We will return to the reasons why this specific order is required.

143. Throughout, I am overlooking the matter of object agreement. That requires some elaboration, pointless to undertake without consideration of a much broader typological range. See section 3.2 for a few comments.

144. Ignored here are possible double-expletive constructions of the *it*-type, with a full complement of formal features. Perhaps these are barred along the lines outlined for (201).

145. The proposal is not only speculative but also too narrow, in that it is restricted to a particular category of multiple-Spec constructions. In others, the situation is different in a number of respects, including the fact that raising to the extra Spec need be neither minimal nor maximal.

146. The earlier argument barring merger of Exp in this position for VP transitive does not hold for unaccusatives; economy condition (76) is not relevant here, because [Spec, V] is not made available by a strong feature, V being a substantive category that cannot have such features.

147. Virtually; see qualifications in notes 135, 137, 138.

148. The affix features are not strong; if they were, the raising would have to be overt. This is a distinction we have not yet made, but it is compatible with the framework so far. Adjunction of [quant] would be to $T^{0\,max}$ or $v^{0\,max}$.

149. Note that the syntactic forms produced differ from standard logical notations, though a simple algorithm Φ will convert them to these notations. To the extent that standard notations serve for semantic interpretation, so do the ones mapped into them by Φ. At the A-P interface enough is known about interpretation of PF to allow some distinctions among interdefinable notations, but at the C-I interface the problem is much more obscure.

150. See, for example, Belletti 1990, where contrasting properties of French and Italian are accounted for in terms of an Agr_s-T distinction. Also see Pollock 1991, on mood and other properties, and many other works, some already mentioned; see notes 20 and 117.

References

Abney, S. 1987. The English noun phrase in its sentential aspect. Doctoral dissertation, MIT.

Aissen, J. L. 1990. Towards a theory of agreement controllers. In P. M. Postal and B. Joseph, eds., *Studies in Relational Grammar* 3. Chicago: University of Chicago Press.

Aoun, J. 1986. *Generalized binding.* Dordrecht: Foris.

Aoun, J., N. Hornstein, D. Lightfoot, and A. Weinberg. 1987. Two types of locality. *Linguistic Inquiry* 18, 537–577.

Aoun, J., N. Hornstein, and D. Sportiche. 1981. Some aspects of wide scope quantification. *Journal of Linguistic Research* 1:3, 69–95.

Aoun, J., and D. Sportiche. 1981. On the formal theory of government. *The Linguistic Review* 2, 211–236.

Baker, M. 1988. *Incorporation.* Chicago: University of Chicago Press.

Baker, M. 1995. *The polysynthesis parameter.* Oxford: Oxford University Press.

Baker, M., K. Johnson, and I. Roberts. 1989. Passive arguments raised. *Linguistic Inquiry* 20, 219–251.

Baltin, M., and A. Kroch, eds. 1989. *Alternative conceptions of phrase structure.* Chicago: University of Chicago Press.

Barbosa, P. 1994. A new look at the null-subject parameter. Ms., MIT. To appear in *Proceedings of Console III.*

Barss, A. 1986. Chains and anaphoric dependence. Doctoral dissertation, MIT.

Belletti, A. 1988. The Case of unaccusatives. *Linguistic Inquiry* 19, 1–34.

Belletti, A. 1990. *Generalized verb movement.* Turin: Rosenberg & Sellier.

Belletti, A., L. Brandi, and L. Rizzi, eds. 1981. *Theory of markedness in generative grammar.* Pisa: Scuola Normale Superiore.

Belletti, A., and L. Rizzi. 1981. The syntax of *ne. The Linguistic Review* 1, 117–154.

Belletti, A., and L. Rizzi. 1988. Psych-verbs and θ-theory. *Natural Language & Linguistic Theory* 6, 291–352.

Benincà, P., ed. 1989. *Dialect variation and the theory of grammar.* Dordrecht: Foris.

Besten, H. den. 1989. *Studies in West Germanic syntax.* Amsterdam: Rodopi.

Bobaljik, J. 1992a. Ergativity, economy, and the Extended Projection Principle. Ms., MIT.

Bobaljik, J. 1992b. Nominally absolutive is not absolutely nominative. In J. Mead, ed., *Proceedings of the Eleventh West Coast Conference on Formal Linguistics.* Stanford, Calif.: CSLI Publications. Distributed by University of Chicago Press.

Bobaljik, J., and A. Carnie. 1992. A minimalist approach to some problems of Irish word order. Ms., MIT. To appear in R. Borsley and I. Roberts, eds., *Celtic and beyond.* Cambridge: Cambridge University Press.

Bobaljik, J., and C. Phillips, eds. 1993. *MIT working papers in linguistics 18: Papers on Case and agreement I.* Department of Linguistics and Philosophy, MIT.

Borer, H. 1984. *Parametric syntax.* Dordrecht: Foris.

Borer, H., and R. Wexler. 1987. The maturation of syntax. In Roeper and Williams 1987.

Boscović, Z. 1993. D-Structure, Theta Criterion, and movement into theta-positions. Ms., University of Connecticut and Haskins Laboratories.

Bouchard, D. 1984. *On the content of empty categories.* Dordrecht: Foris.

Bouchard, D. 1991. From conceptual structure to syntactic structure. Ms., University of Quebec at Montreal (UQAM).

Brame, M. 1981. The general theory of binding and fusion. *Linguistic Analysis* 7, 277–325.

Brame, M. 1982. The head selector theory of lexical specifications and the non-existence of coarse categories. *Linguistic Analysis* 10, 321–325.

Branigan, P. 1992. Subjects and complementizers. Doctoral dissertation, MIT.

Bresnan, J. 1972. Theory of complementation in English syntax. Doctoral dissertation, MIT.

Bresnan, J., ed. 1982. The mental representation of grammatical relations. Cambridge, Mass.: MIT Press.

Brody, M. 1993. θ-theory and arguments. *Linguistic Inquiry* 24, 1–24.

Bromberger, S., and M. Halle. 1989. Why phonology is different. *Linguistic Inquiry* 20, 51–70. Reprinted in Kasher 1991.

Browning, M. A. 1987. Null operator constructions. Doctoral dissertation, MIT. New York: Garland 1991.

Bures, T. 1992. Re-cycling expletive (and other) sentences. Ms., MIT.

Burzio, L. 1986. *Italian syntax*. Dordrecht: Reidel.

Cardinaletti, A. 1994. Agreement and control in expletive constructions. Ms., MIT.

Cardinaletti, A., and M. T. Guasti. 1991. Epistemic small clauses and null subjects. Ms., University of Venice and University of Geneva.

Cheng, L. L.-S. 1991. On the typology of *wh*-questions. Doctoral dissertation, MIT.

Chien, Y.-C., and K. Wexler. 1991. Children's knowledge of locality conditions in binding as evidence for the modularity of syntax and pragmatics. *Language Acquisition* 1, 195–223.

Chomsky, N. 1951. The morphophonemics of Modern Hebrew. Master's thesis, University of Pennsylvania. New York: Garland (1979).

Chomsky, N. 1964. *Current issues in linguistic theory*. The Hague: Mouton.

Chomsky, N. 1965. *Aspects of the theory of syntax*. Cambridge, Mass.: MIT Press.

Chomsky, N. 1972. *Studies on semantics in generative grammar*. The Hague: Mouton.

Chomsky, N. 1975a. *The logical structure of linguistic theory*. New York: Plenum. Excerpted from 1956 revision of 1955 ms., Harvard University and MIT. Chicago: University of Chicago Press 1985.

Chomsky, N. 1975b. *Reflections on language*. New York: Pantheon.

Chomsky, N. 1977. *Essays on form and interpretation*. Amsterdam: Elsevier North-Holland.

Chomsky, N. 1980a. On binding. *Linguistic Inquiry* 11, 1–46.

Chomsky, N. 1980b. *Rules and representations*. New York: Columbia University Press.

Chomsky, N. 1981a. *Lectures on government and binding*. Dordrecht: Foris.

Chomsky, N. 1981b. Response to queries. In Longuet-Higgins, Lyons, and Broadbent 1981.

Chomsky, N. 1982. *Some concepts and consequences of the theory of government and binding*. Cambridge, Mass.: MIT Press.

Chomsky, N. 1986a. *Barriers*. Cambridge, Mass.: MIT Press.

Chomsky, N. 1986b. *Knowledge of language*. New York; Praeger.

Chomsky, N. 1987. Response. *Mind and Language* 2, 193–197.

Chomsky, N. 1988. *Generative grammar, studies in English linguistics and literature*. Kyoto University of Foreign Studies.

Chomsky, N. 1990. On formalization and formal linguistics. *Natural Language & Linguistic Theory* 8, 143–147.

Chomsky, N. 1991a. Prospects for the study of language and mind. In Kasher 1991.

Chomsky, N. 1991b. Linguistics and cognitive science: Problems and mysteries. In Kasher 1991.

Chomsky, N. 1991c. Some notes on economy of derivation and representation. In R. Freidin, ed., *Principles and parameters in comparative grammar*. Cambridge, Mass.: MIT Press.

Chomsky, N. 1992a. Explaining language use. *Philosophical Topics* 20, 205–231.

Chomsky, N. 1992b. Language and interpretation: Philosophical reflections and empirical inquiry. In J. Earman, ed. *Inference, explanation and other philosophical frustrations*. Berkeley: University of California Press.

Chomsky, N. 1993. A minimalist program for linguistic theory. In Hale and Keyser 1993b.

Chomsky, N. 1994a. Bare phrase structure. *MIT occasional papers in linguistics* 5. Department of Linguistics and Philosophy, MIT. To appear in H. Campos and P. Kempchinsky, eds., *Evolution and revolution in linguistic theory: Essays in honor of Carlos Otero*. Washington, D.C.: Georgetown University Press. Also published in G. Webelhuth, ed., *Government and Binding Theory and the Minimalist Program*. Oxford: Blackwell 1995.

Chomsky, N. 1994b. *Language and thought*. Wakefield, R.I., and London: Moyer Bell.

Chomsky, N. 1994c. Naturalism and dualism in the study of language and mind. *International Journal of Philosophical Studies* 2, 181–209.

Chomsky, N. 1995. Language and nature. *Mind* 104, 1–61.

Chomsky, N., and M. Halle. 1968. *The sound pattern of English*. New York: Harper & Row. Reprinted Cambridge, Mass.: MIT Press (1991).

Chomsky, N., and H. Lasnik. 1977. Filters and control. *Linguistic Inquiry* 8, 425–504.

Chomsky, N., and H. Lasnik. 1993. The theory of principles and parameters. In J. Jacobs, A. von Stechow, W. Sternefeld, and T. Vennemann, eds., *Syntax: An international handbook of contemporary research*. Berlin: de Gruyter.

Cinque, G. 1990. *Types of $\bar{A}$-dependencies*. Cambridge, Mass.: MIT Press.

Clements, G. N. 1985. The geometry of phonological features. *Phonology Yearbook* 2, 225–252.

Collins, C. 1993. Topics in Ewe syntax. Doctoral dissertation, MIT.

Collins, C. 1994a. Economy of derivation and the Generalized Proper Binding Condition. *Linguistic Inquiry* 25, 45–61.

Collins, C. 1994b. Merge and Greed. Ms., Cornell University.

Collins, C. 1995. Serial verb constructions and the theory of multiple feature checking. Ms., Cornell University.

Collins, C., and H. Thráinsson. 1994. VP-internal structure and object shift in Icelandic. Ms., Cornell University and Harvard University/University of Iceland.

Crain, S. 1991. Language acquisition in the absence of experience. *Behavioral & Brain Sciences* 14, 597–650.

Curtiss, S. 1981. Dissociations between language and cognition. *Journal of Autism and Developmental Disorders* 11, 15–30.

Dell, F., and M. Elmedlaoui. 1985. Syllabic consonants and syllabification in Imdlawn Tashlhiyt Berber. *Journal of African Languages and Linguistics* 7, 105–130.

Demirdache, H. 1991. Resumptive Chains in restrictive relatives, appositives and dislocation structures. Doctoral dissertation, MIT.

De Rijk, R. 1972. Studies in Basque syntax. Doctoral dissertation, MIT.

Di Sciullo, A. M., and E. Williams. 1988. *On the definition of word.* Cambridge, Mass. MIT Press.

Edelman, G. 1992. *Bright air, brilliant fire.* New York: Basic Books.

Emonds, J. 1976. *A transformational approach to syntax.* New York: Academic Press.

Emonds, J. 1978. The verbal complex V′–V in French. *Linguistic Inquiry* 9, 49–77.

Emonds, J. 1985. *A unified theory of syntactic categories.* Dordrecht: Foris.

Engdahl, E. 1983. Parasitic gaps. *Linguistics and Philosophy* 6, 5–34.

Engdahl, E. 1985. Parasitic gaps, resumptive pronouns, and subject extractions. *Linguistics* 23, 3–44.

Epstein, R. Forthcoming. *Cognition, creativity, and behavior.* New York: Praeger.

Epstein, S. 1984. Quantifier-pro and the LF representation of PRO_{arb}. *Linguistic Inquiry* 15, 499–504.

Epstein, S. 1989. Adjunction and pronominal variable binding. *Linguistic Inquiry* 20, 307–319.

Epstein, S. 1991. *Traces and their antecedents.* Oxford: Oxford University Press.

Epstein, S. 1994. The derivation of syntactic relations. Ms., Harvard University.

Fabb, N. 1984. Syntactic affixation. Doctoral dissertation, MIT.

Fassi Fehri, A. 1980. Some complement phenomena in Arabic, the complementizer phrase hypothesis and the Non-Accessibility Condition. *Analyse/Théorie* 54–114. Université de Paris VIII, Vincennes.

Fiengo, R. 1977. On trace theory. *Linguistic Inquiry* 8, 35–62.

Fiengo, R., C.-T. J. Huang, H. Lasnik, and T. Reinhart. 1988. The syntax of *wh*-in-situ. In H. Borer, ed., *Proceedings of the Seventh West Coast Conference on Formal Linguistics.* Stanford, Calif.: CSLI Publications. Distributed by University of Chicago Press.

Flynn, S. 1987. *A parameter-setting model of L2 acquisition: Experimental studies in anaphora*. Dordrecht: Reidel.

Fong, S. 1991. Computational properties of principle-based grammatical theories. Doctoral dissertation, MIT.

Fox, D. 1994. Economy, scope and semantic interpretation: Evidence from VP ellipsis. Ms., MIT.

Frampton, J. 1992. Relativized Minimality: A review. *The Linguistic Review* 8, 1–46.

Freidin, R. 1986. Fundamental issues in the theory of binding. In B. Lust, ed., *Studies in the acquisition of anaphora*. Dordrecht: Reidel.

Freidin, R. 1992. *Foundations of generative syntax*. Cambridge, Mass.: MIT Press.

Freidin, R. 1994. The principles and parameters framework of generative grammar. In R. E. Asher and J. M. Y. Simpson, eds., *The encyclopedia of language and linguistics*. Oxford: Pergamon Press.

Freidin, R., and L. Babby. 1984. On the interaction of lexical and syntactic properties: Case structure in Russian. In W. Harbert, ed., *Cornell working papers in linguistics VI*. Department of Linguistics, Cornell University.

Freidin, R., and H. Lasnik. 1981. Disjoint reference and *wh*-trace. *Linguistic Inquiry* 12, 39–53.

Friedemann, M., and T. Siloni. 1993. AGR$_{\text{OBJECT}}$ is not AGR$_{\text{PARTICIPLE}}$. Ms., University of Geneva.

Fukui, N. 1986. A theory of category projection and its applications. Doctoral dissertation, MIT. Revised version published as *Theory of projection in syntax*. Stanford, Calif.: CSLI Publications (1995). Distributed by University of Chicago Press.

Fukui, N. 1988. Deriving the differences between English and Japanese: A case study in parametric syntax. *English Linguistics* 5, 249–270.

Fukui, N. 1992. The principles-and-parameters approach: A comparative syntax of English and Japanese. To appear in T. Bynon and M. Shibatani, eds., *Approaches to language typology*. Oxford: Oxford University Press.

Fukui, N. 1993. Parameters and optionality. *Linguistic Inquiry* 24, 399–420.

Gazdar, G. 1981. Unbounded dependencies and coordinate structure. *Linguistic Inquiry* 12, 155–184.

Gleitman, L. 1990. The structural sources of verb meanings. *Language Acquisition* 1, 3–55.

Golan, V. 1993. Node crossing economy, superiority and D-linking. Ms., Tel Aviv University.

Goldsmith, J. 1976. Autosegmental phonology. Doctoral dissertation, MIT.

Grimshaw, J. 1979. Complement selection and the lexicon. *Linguistic Inquiry* 10, 279–326.

Grimshaw, J. 1981. Form, function, and the language acquisition device. In C. L. Baker and J. McCarthy, eds., *The logical problem of language acquisition.* Cambridge, Mass.: MIT Press.

Grimshaw, J. 1990. *Argument structure.* Cambridge, Mass.: MIT Press.

Grosu, A., and J. Horvath. 1984. The GB Theory and raising in Rumanian. *Linguistic Inquiry* 15, 348–353.

Gruber, J. 1965. Studies in lexical relations. Doctoral dissertation, MIT.

Hale, K., and S. J. Keyser. 1986. Some transitivity alternations in English. Center for Cognitive Science, MIT.

Hale, K., and S. J. Keyser. 1991. On the syntax of argument structure. Center for Cognitive Science, MIT.

Hale, K., and S. J. Keyser. 1993a. On argument structure and the lexical expression of syntactic relations. In Hale and Keyser 1993b.

Hale, K., and S. J. Keyser, eds. 1993b. *The view from Building 20.* Cambridge, Mass.: MIT Press.

Halle, M., and A. Marantz. 1993. Distributed Morphology and the pieces of inflection. In Hale and Keyser 1993b.

Halle, M., and J.-R. Vergnaud. 1988. *An essay on stress.* Cambridge, Mass.: MIT Press.

Harman, G. 1963. Generative grammars without transformational rules. *Language* 39, 597–616.

Harris, Z. S. 1951. *Methods in structural linguistics.* Chicago: University of Chicago Press.

Harris, Z. S. 1952. Discourse analysis. *Language* 28, 1–30.

Heim, I., H. Lasnik, and R. May. 1991. Reciprocity and plurality. *Linguistic Inquiry.* 22, 63–101.

Higginbotham, J. 1980. Pronouns and bound variables. *Linguistic Inquiry* 11, 679–708.

Higginbotham, J. 1983. Logical Form, binding, and nominals. *Linguistic Inquiry* 14, 395–420.

Higginbotham, J. 1985. On semantics. *Linguistic Inquiry* 16, 547–593.

Higginbotham, J. 1988. Elucidations of meaning. *Linguistics and Philosophy* 12, 465–517.

Higginbotham, J., and R. May. 1981. Questions, quantifiers, and crossing. *The Linguistic Review* 1, 41–79.

Hornstein, N. 1994. *LF: The grammar of Logical Form from GB to minimalism.* Ms., University of Maryland. [To appear, Oxford: Blackwell.]

Hornstein, N., and A. Weinberg. 1990. The necessity of LF. *The Linguistic Review* 7, 129–167.

Huang, C.-T. J. 1982. Logical relations in Chinese and the theory of grammar. Doctoral dissertation, MIT.

Huang, C.-T. J. 1984. On the distribution and reference of empty pronouns. *Linguistic Inquiry* 15, 531–574.

Huang, C.-T. J. 1990. A note on reconstruction and VP movement. Ms., Cornell University.

Hyams, N. 1986. *Language acquisition and the theory of parameters*. Dordrecht: Reidel.

Iatridou, S. 1990. About Agr(P). *Linguistic Inquiry* 21, 551–577.

Ingria, R. 1981. Sentential complementation in modern Greek. Doctoral dissertation, MIT.

Ishii, Y. 1991. Operators and empty categories in Japanese. Doctoral dissertation, University of Connecticut.

Jackendoff, R. 1972. *Semantic interpretation in generative grammar*. Cambridge, Mass.: MIT Press.

Jackendoff, R. 1977. $\overline{X}$ *syntax*. Cambridge, Mass.: MIT Press.

Jackendoff, R. 1983. *Semantics and cognition*. Cambridge, Mass.: MIT Press.

Jackendoff, R. 1987. The status of thematic relations in linguistic theory. *Linguistic Inquiry* 18, 369–411.

Jackendoff, R. 1990a. On Larson's treatment of the double object construction. *Linguistic Inquiry* 21, 427–456.

Jackendoff, R. 1990b. *Semantic structures*. Cambridge, Mass.: MIT Press.

Jaeggli, O. 1980. On some phonologically-null elements in syntax. Doctoral dissertation, MIT.

Jaeggli, O., and K. Safir, eds. 1989. The null subject parameter. Dordrecht: Kluwer.

Johns, A. 1987. Transitivity and grammatical relations in Inuktitut. Doctoral dissertation, University of Ottawa.

Jonas, D. 1992. Transitive expletive constructions in Icelandic and Middle English. Ms., Harvard University.

Jonas, D. 1994. Clause structure expletives and verb movement. Ms., Harvard University.

Jonas, D. Forthcoming. The TP parameter in Scandinavian syntax. In. C. Hedlund and A. Holmberg, eds., *Göteborg working papers in linguistics*. University of Göteborg.

Jonas, D., and J. Bobaljik. 1993. Specs for subjects: The role of TP in Icelandic. In Bobaljik and Phillips 1993.

Kasher, A., ed. 1991. *The Chomskyan turn*. Oxford: Blackwell.

Kawashima, R., and H. Kitahara. 1994. On the definition of Move: Strict cyclicity revisited. Ms., MIT and Princeton University.

Kayne, R. 1984. *Connectedness and binary branching*. Dordrecht: Foris.

Kayne, R. 1989. Facets of past participle agreement in Romance. In Benincà 1989.

Kayne, R. 1993. The antisymmetry of syntax. Ms., Graduate Center. City University of New York.

Kayne, R. 1994. *The antisymmetry of syntax*. Cambridge, Mass.: MIT Press.

Keyser, S. J. 1975. A partial history of the relative clause in English. In J. Grimshaw, ed., *University of Massachusetts occasional papers in linguistics 1: Papers in the history and structure of English*. GLSA, University of Massachusetts, Amherst.

Kim, S. W. 1990. Scope and multiple quantification. Doctoral dissertation, Brandeis University.

Kitagawa, Y. 1986. Subjects in Japanese and English. Doctoral dissertation, University of Massachusetts, Amherst.

Kitahara, H. 1994. Target α: A unified theory of movement and structure building. Doctoral dissertation, Harvard University.

Kitahara, H. 1995. Target α: Deducing strict cyclicity from derivational economy. *Linguistic Inquiry* 26, 47–77.

Klima, E. 1964. Negation in English. In J. A. Fodor and J. J. Katz, eds., *Readings in the philosophy of language*. Englewood Cliffs, N.J.: Prentice-Hall.

Koizumi, M. 1993. Object agreement phrases and the split VP hypothesis. In Bobaljik and Phillips 1993.

Koizumi, M. 1994. Layered specifiers. In M. Gonzàlez, ed., *Proceedings of NELS 24*. GLSA, University of Massachusetts, Amherst.

Koizumi, M. 1995. Phrase structure in minimalist syntax. Doctoral dissertation, MIT.

Koopman, H. 1984. *The syntax of verbs*. Dordrecht: Foris.

Koopman, H. 1987. On the absence of Case chains in Bambara. Ms., UCLA.

Koopman, H., and D. Sportiche. 1991. The position of subjects. *Lingua* 85, 211–258.

Kornfilt, J. 1985. Case marking, agreement, and empty categories in Turkish. Doctoral dissertation, Harvard University.

Koster, J. 1978. Why subject sentences don't exist. In S. J. Keyser, ed., *Recent transformational studies in European languages*. Cambridge, Mass.: MIT Press.

Kroch, A. 1989. Asymmetries in long distance extraction in a tree adjoining grammar. In Baltin and Kroch 1989.

Kroch, A., and A. Joshi. 1985. *The linguistic relevance of tree adjoining grammar*. Technical report MS-CIS-85-16. Department of Computer and Informational Sciences, University of Pennsylvania.

Kuroda, S.-Y. 1965. Generative grammatical studies in the Japanese language. Doctoral dissertation, MIT.

Kuroda, S.-Y. 1988. Whether we agree or not: A comparative syntax of English and Japanese. In W. Poser, ed., *Papers from the Second International Workshop on Japanese Syntax*. Stanford, Calif.: CSLI Publications. Distributed by Chicago University Press.

Laka, I. 1990. Negation in syntax: On the nature of functional categories and projections. Doctoral dissertation, MIT.

Lakoff, G. 1968. Pronouns and reference. Indiana University Linguistics Club, Bloomington. Reprinted in J. D. McCawley, ed., *Notes from the linguistic underground*. New York: Academic Press (1976).

Lakoff, G. 1970. *Irregularity in syntax*. New York: Holt, Rinehart and Winston.

Lakoff, G. 1971. On Generative Semantics. In D. Steinberg and L. Jakobovits, ed., *Semantics*. Cambridge: Cambridge University Press.

Langacker, R. 1969. On pronominalization and the chain of command. In D. Reibel and S. Schane, eds., *Modern studies in English*. Englewood Cliffs, N.J.: Prentice-Hall.

Langendoen, D. T., and E. Battistella. 1982. The interpretation of predicate reflexive and reciprocal expressions in English. In J. Pustejovsky and P. Sells, eds., *Proceedings of NELS 12*. GLSA, University of Massachusetts, Amherst.

Larson, R. 1988. On the double object construction. *Linguistic Inquiry* 19, 335–391.

Larson, R. 1990. Double objects revisited: Reply to Jackendoff. *Linguistic Inquiry* 21, 589–632.

Lasnik, H. 1972. Analyses of negation in English. Doctoral dissertation, MIT.

Lasnik, H. 1976. Remarks on coreference. *Linguistic Analysis* 2, 1–22. Reprinted in Lasnik 1989.

Lasnik, H. 1981. Restricting the theory of transformations: A case study. In N. Hornstein and D. Lightfoot, eds., *Explanation in linguistics*. London: Longman. Reprinted in Lasnik 1990.

Lasnik, H. 1989. *Essays on anaphora*. Dordrecht: Reidel.

Lasnik, H. 1990. *Essays on restrictiveness and learnability*. Dordrecht: Reidel.

Lasnik, H. 1992. Case and expletives. *Linguistic Inquiry* 23, 381–405.

Lasnik, H. 1994b. Verbal morphology: *Syntactic structures* meets the Minimalist Program. Ms., University of Connecticut.

Lasnik, H. To appear. Case and expletives revisited. *Linguistic Inquiry*.

Lasnik, H., and M. Saito. 1984. On the nature of proper government. *Linguistic Inquiry* 15, 235–289.

Lasnik, H., and M. Saito. 1991. On the subject of infinitives. In L. M. Dobrin, L. Nichols, and R. M. Rodriguez, eds., *CLS 27*. Part 1: *The General Session*. Chicago Linguistic Society, University of Chicago.

Lasnik, H., and M. Saito. 1992. *Move α*. Cambridge, Mass.: MIT Press.

Lasnik, H., and T. Stowell. 1991. Weakest crossover. *Linguistic Inquiry* 22, 687–720.

Lasnik, H., and J. Uriagereka. 1988. *A course in GB syntax*. Cambridge, Mass.: MIT Press.

Lebeaux, D. 1983. A distributional difference between reciprocals and reflexives. *Linguistic Inquiry* 14, 723–730.

Lebeaux, D. 1988. Language acquisition and the form of the grammar. Doctoral dissertation, University of Massachusetts, Amherst.

Lees, R. 1963. *The grammar of English nominalizations*. The Hague: Mouton.

Levin, J., and D. Massam. 1985. Surface ergativity: Case/Theta relations reexamined. In S. Berman, ed., *Proceedings of NELS 15*. GLSA, University of Massachusetts, Amherst.

Lewontin, R. 1990. The evolution of cognition. In D. Osherson and E. Smith, eds., *Thinking: An invitation to cognitive science, vol. 3*, Cambridge, Mass.: MIT Press.

Lightfoot, D. 1991. *How to set parameters: Arguments from language change*. Cambridge, Mass.: MIT Press.

Longobardi, G. 1985. Connectedness, scope, and c-command. *Linguistic Inquiry* 16, 163–192.

Longobardi G. 1994. Reference and proper names: A theory of N-movement in syntax and Logical Form. *Linguistic Inquiry* 25, 609–665.

Longuet-Higgins, H. C., J. Lyons, and D. E. Broadbent, eds. 1981. *The psychological mechanisms of language*. London: Royal Society and British Academy.

Ludlow, P. 1992. Formal rigor and linguistic theory. *Natural Language & Linguistic Theory* 10, 335–344.

Mahajan, A. 1990. The A/A-bar distinction and movement theory. Doctoral dissertation, MIT.

Manzini, M. R. 1983. On control and control theory. *Linguistic Inquiry* 14, 421–446.

Marantz, A. 1984. *On the nature of grammatical relations*. Cambridge, Mass.: MIT Press.

Marantz, A. 1994. A note on late insertion. Ms., MIT.

Martin, R. 1992. On the distribution and Case features of PRO. Ms., University of Connecticut.

Matthews, G. H. 1964. *Hidatsa syntax*. The Hague: Mouton.

May, R. 1977. The grammar of quantification. Doctoral dissertation, MIT.

May, R. 1985. *Logical Form*. Cambridge, Mass.: MIT Press.

McCarthy, J. 1979. Formal problems in Semitic phonology and morphology. Doctoral dissertation, MIT.

McCarthy, J., and A. Prince. 1993. Prosodic morphology I. Ms., University of Massachusetts, Amherst, and Rutgers University.

McCarthy, J., and A. Prince. 1994. The emergence of the unmarked optimality in prosodic morphology. Ms., University of Massachusetts, Amherst, and Rutgers University.

McCawley, J. D. 1988. Review of Chomsky 1986b. *Language* 64, 355–366.

McCloskey, J. 1991. *There, it,* and agreement. *Linguistic Inquiry* 22, 563–567.

McGinnis, M. J. 1995. Fission as feature movement. Ms., MIT.

Miller, G., and N. Chomsky. 1963. Finitary models of language users. In R. D. Luce, R. Bush, and E. Galanter, eds., *Handbook of mathematical psychology II.* New York: Wiley.

Miyagawa, S. 1993a. Case, agreement, and *ga/no* conversion in Japanese. In S. Choi, ed., *Proceedings of Third Southern California Japanese/Korean Linguistics Conference.* Stanford, Calif.: CSLI Publications. Distributed by University of Chicago Press.

Miyagawa, S. 1993b. LF Case-checking and Minimal Link Condition. In C. Phillips, ed., *MIT working papers in linguistics 19: Papers on Case and agreement II.* Department of Linguistics and Philosophy, MIT.

Moro, A. 1994. The raising of predicates. Ms., Dipartimento di Scienze Cognitive, Centro "Fondazione San Raffaele," Milan; and Istituto Universitario Lingue Moderne, Milan.

Murasugi, K. 1991. The role of transitivity in ergative and accusative languages: The cases of Inuktitut and Japanese. Paper presented at the Association of Canadian Universities for Northern Studies.

Murasugi, K. 1992. Crossing and nested paths: NP movement in accusative and ergative languages. Doctoral dissertation, MIT.

Muysken, P. 1982. Parametrizing the notion "Head." *Journal of Linguistic Research* 2, 57–75.

Namiki, T. 1979. Remarks on prenominal adjectives and degree expressions in English. *Studies in English Linguistics* 7, 71–85.

Neidle, C. 1988. *The role of Case in Russian syntax.* Dordrecht: Reidel.

Nishigauchi, T. 1984. Control and the thematic domain. *Language* 60, 215–250.

Nishigauchi, T. 1986. Quantification in syntax. Doctoral dissertation, University of Massachusetts, Amherst.

Oishi, M. 1990. Conceptual problems of upward X-bar theory. Ms., Tohoku Gakuin University.

Oka, T. 1993. Minimalism in syntactic derivation. Doctoral dissertation, MIT.

Perlmutter, D. 1978. Impersonal passives and the unaccusative hypothesis. In *Proceedings of the Fourth Annual Meeting of the Berkeley Linguistics Society.* Berkeley Linguistics Society, University of California, Berkeley.

Perlmutter, D. 1983. Personal vs. impersonal constructions. *Natural Language & Linguistic Theory* 1, 141–200.

Pesetsky, D. 1982. Paths and categories. Doctoral dissertation, MIT.

Pesetsky, D. 1995. *Zero syntax*. Cambridge, Mass.: MIT Press.

Pica, P. 1987. On the nature of the reflexivization cycle. In J. McDonough and B. Plunkett, eds., *Proceedings of NELS 17*. GLSA, University of Massachusetts, Amherst.

Pica, P., and W. Snyder. In press. Weak crossover, scope, and agreement in a minimalist framework. In R. Aranovich, B. Byrne, S. Preuss, and M. Senturia, eds., *Proceedings of the Thirteenth West Coast Conference on Formal Linguistics*. Stanford, Calif.: CSLI Publications.

Pierce, A. 1992. *Language acquisition and syntactic theory: A comparative analysis of French and English child language*. Dordrecht: Kluwer.

Pollock, J.-Y. 1981. On Case and impersonal constructions. In R. May and J. Koster, eds., *Levels of syntactic representation*. Dordrecht: Foris.

Pollock, J.-Y. 1989. Verb movement, Universal Grammar, and the structure of IP. *Linguistic Inquiry* 20, 365–424.

Pollock, J.-Y. 1991. Notes on clause structure. Ms., University of Picardie, Amiens.

Postal, P. M. 1966a. A note on "understood transitively." *International Journal of American Linguistics* 32, 90–93.

Postal, P. M. 1966b. On so-called "pronouns" in English. In F. P. Dineen, ed., *Report of the 17th Annual Round Table Meeting on Linguistics and Language Studies*. Washington, D.C.: Georgetown University Press.

Postal, P. M. 1971. *Cross-over phenomena*. New York: Holt, Rinehart and Winston.

Postal, P. M. 1974. *On raising*. Cambridge, Mass.: MIT Press.

Prince, A., and P. Smolensky. 1993. Optimality Theory. Ms., Rutgers University and University of Colorado.

Pustejovsky, J. 1992. The syntax of event structure. *Cognition* 41, 47–81.

Reinhart, T. 1976. The syntactic domain of anaphora. Doctoral dissertation, MIT.

Reinhart, T. 1981. A second Comp position. In Belletti, Brandi, and Rizzi 1981.

Reinhart, T. 1983. *Anaphora and semantic interpretation*. London: Croom Helm.

Reinhart, T. 1991. Elliptic conjunctions: Non-quantificational LF. In Kasher 1991.

Reinhart, T. 1993. *Wh*-in-situ in the framework of the Minimalist Program. Ms., Tel Aviv University. Lecture at Utrecht Linguistics Colloquium.

Reinhart, T., and E. Reuland. 1993. Reflexivity. *Linguistic Inquiry* 24, 657–720.

Riemsdijk, H. van. 1981. The Case of German adjectives. In J. Pustejovsky and V. Burke, eds., *University of Massachusetts occasional papers in linguistics 6: Markedness and learnability*. GLSA, University of Massachusetts, Amherst.

Riemsdijk, H. van. 1989. Movement and regeneration. In Benincà 1989.

Riemsdijk, H. van, and E. Williams. 1981. NP Structure. *The Linguistic Review* 1, 171–217.

Ristad, E. 1993. *The language complexity game*. Cambridge, Mass.: MIT Press.

Rizzi, L. 1982. *Issues in Italian syntax*. Dordrecht: Foris.

Rizzi, L. 1986a. Null objects in Italian and the theory of *pro*. *Linguistic Inquiry* 17, 501–557.

Rizzi, L. 1986b. On chain formation. In H. Borer, ed., *The grammar of pronominal clitics: Syntax and semantics 19*. New York: Academic Press.

Rizzi, L. 1990. *Relativized Minimality*. Cambridge, Mass.: MIT Press.

Roeper, T., and E. Williams, eds. 1987. *Parameter setting*. Dordrecht: Reidel.

Ross, J. R. 1967. Constraints on variables in syntax. Doctoral dissertation, MIT. Published as *Infinite syntax!* Norwood, N.J.: Ablex (1986).

Rothstein, S. 1983. The syntactic forms of predication. Doctoral dissertation, MIT.

Safir, K. 1985. *Syntactic chains*. Cambridge: Cambridge University Press.

Safir, K. 1987. So *there!* A reply to Williams' analysis of *there*-sentences. In M. A. Browning, E. Czaykowska-Higgins, and E. Ritter, eds., *MIT working papers in linguistics 9: The 25th anniversary of MIT linguistics*. Department of Linguistics and Philosophy, MIT.

Sag, I. 1976. Deletion and Logical Form. Doctoral dissertation, MIT.

Saito, M. 1985. Some asymmetries in Japanese and their theoretical implications. Doctoral dissertation, MIT.

Saito, M. 1989. Scrambling as semantically vacuous A′-movement. In Baltin and Kroch 1989.

Saito, M. 1991. Extraposition and parasitic gaps. In C. Georgopoulos and R. Ishihara, eds., *Interdisciplinary approaches to language: Essays in honor of S.-Y. Kuroda*. Dordrecht: Foris.

Sells, P. 1984. Syntax and semantics of resumptive pronouns. Doctoral dissertation, University of Massachusetts, Amherst.

Shlonsky, U. 1987. Null and displaced subjects. Doctoral dissertation, MIT.

Smith, N., and I. M. Tsimpli. 1991. Linguistic modularity? A case study of a "*savant*" linguist. *Lingua* 84, 315–351.

Speas, M. 1986. Adjunction and projection in syntax. Doctoral dissertation, MIT.

Speas, M. 1990. Generalized transformations and the D-Structure position of adjuncts. Ms., University of Massachusetts, Amherst.

Sportiche, D. 1983. Structural invariance and symmetry. Doctoral dissertation, MIT.

Sportiche, D. 1985. Remarks on crossover. *Linguistic Inquiry* 16, 460–469.

Sportiche, D. 1988. A theory of floating quantifiers and its corollaries for constituent structure. *Linguistic Inquiry* 19, 425–449.

Stowell, T. 1978. What was there before there was there. In D. Farkas, W. M. Jacobsen, and K. W. Todrys, eds., *Papers from the Fourteenth Regional Meeting, Chicago Linguistic Society*. Chicago University Society, University of Chicago.

Stowell, T. 1981. Origins of phrase structure. Doctoral dissertation, MIT.

Stowell, T. 1986. The relation between S-Structure and the mapping from D-Structure to Logical Form. Paper presented at the Princeton Workshop on Comparative Grammar.

Szabolcsi, A. 1987. Functional categories in the noun phrase. In I. Kenesei, ed., *Approaches to Hungarian*, vol. 2. University of Budapest.

Tancredi, C. 1992. Intonation semantics. Doctoral dissertation, MIT.

Taraldsen, K. T. 1981. The theoretical interpretation of a class of marked extractions. In Belletti, Brandi, and Rizzi 1981.

Thráinsson, H. 1993. On the structure of infinitival complements. In Thráinsson, Epstein, and Kuno 1993.

Thráinsson, H. 1994. On the (non-)universality of functional categories. Ms., Harvard University/University of Iceland.

Thráinsson, H., S. Epstein, and S. Kuno, eds. 1993. *Harvard working papers in linguistics 3*. Department of Linguistics, Harvard University.

Torrego, E. 1985. On empty categories in nominals. Ms., University of Massachusetts, Boston.

Torrego, E. Forthcoming. Experiencers and raising verbs. In R. Freidin, ed., *Current issues in comparative grammar*. Dordrecht: Kluwer.

Travis, L. 1984. Parameters and the effects of word order variation. Doctoral dissertation, MIT.

Tremblay, M. 1991. Possession and datives. Doctoral dissertation, McGill University.

Truckenbrodt, H. 1993. Towards a prosodic theory of relative clause extraposition. Ms., MIT.

Tsai, W.-T. D. 1994. On economizing the theory of $\overline{\text{A}}$-dependencies. Doctoral dissertation, MIT.

Ueda, M. 1990. Japanese phrase structure and parameter setting. Doctoral dissertation, University of Massachusetts, Amherst.

Ura, H. 1994. Varieties of raising and the feature-based phrase structure theory. *MIT occasional papers in linguistics* 7. Department of Linguistics and Philosophy, MIT.

Ura, H. 1995. Towards a theory of "strictly derivational" economy condition. To appear in R. Pensalfini and H. Ura, eds., *MIT working papers in linguistics 27*. Department of Linguistics and Philosophy, MIT.

Uriagereka, J. 1988. On government. Doctoral dissertation, University of Connecticut.

Vergnaud, J.-R. 1982. Dépendances et niveaux de représentation en syntaxe. Thèse de doctorat d'état, Université de Paris VII.

Vikner, S. 1990. Verb movement and the licensing of NP-positions in the Germanic languages. Doctoral dissertation, University of Geneva.

Wasow, T. 1972. Anaphoric relations in English. Doctoral dissertation, MIT.

Watanabe, A. 1991. *Wh*-in-situ, Subjacency, and chain formation. Ms., MIT.

Watanabe, A. 1992. Subjacency and S-Structure movement of *wh*-in-situ. *Journal of East Asian Linguistics* 1, 255–291.

Watanabe, A. 1993a. Agr-based Case theory and its interaction with the A-bar system. Doctoral dissertation, MIT.

Watanabe, A. 1993b. The notion of finite clauses in Agr-based case theory. In Bobaljik and Phillips 1993.

Webelhuth, G. 1989. Syntactic saturation phenomena and the modern Germanic languages. Doctoral dissertation, University of Massachusetts, Amherst.

Wilkins, W., ed. 1988. *Thematic relations*. San Diego, Calif.: Academic Press.

Williams, E. 1980. Predication. *Linguistic Inquiry* 11, 203–238.

Williams, E. 1981. Argument structure and morphology. *The Linguistic Review* 1, 81–114.

Williams, E. 1989. The anaphoric nature of θ-roles. *Linguistic Inquiry* 20, 425–456.

Willim, E. 1982. Anaphor binding and pronominal disjoint reference in English and Polish. Master's thesis, University of Connecticut.

Yamada, J. 1990. *Laura*. Cambridge, Mass.: MIT Press.

Yang, D.-W. 1983. The extended binding theory of anaphors. *Language Research* 19, 169–192.

Zubizarreta, M. L. 1993. Some prosodically motivated syntactic operations. Ms., University of Southern California.

Zwart, J. W. 1993. Dutch syntax: A minimalist approach. Doctoral dissertation, University of Groningen.

Index